the CANADIAN JEWISH MOSAIC

the CANADIAN JEWISH MOSAIC

M. Weinfeld
W. Shaffir
I. Cotler

John Wiley & Sons

Toronto   New York   Chichester   Brisbane   Singapore

Published by John Wiley & Sons Canada Limited
22 Worcester Road
Rexdale, Ontario M9W 1L1

Canadian Cataloguing in Publication Data

Main entry under title:
The Canadian Jewish mosaic

Bibliography: p. 485
Includes index.
ISBN 0-471-79929-7

1. Jewish Canadians.   I. Weinfeld, Morton.
II. Cotler, Irwin, 1940-   III. Shaffir, William,
1945-

FC106.J5C36   971'.004924   C81-094418-9
F1035.J5C36

Design: George Guastavino/**Grafika Art Studios**
Composition: **Pickwick Typesetting Limited**
Printed and bound in Canada at
The Hunter Rose Company Limited

10 9 8 7 6 5 4 3 2 1

Dedication

To my parents, Arnold and the late Irene Weinfeld
To my wife, Phyllis
To my daughter, Rebecca

M.W.

To my parents, Mr. and Mrs. M.M. Shaffir, and my
parents-in-law, Mrs. S. Broder and the late Mr. S. Broder

W.S.

To my parents, Fay and the late Nathan Cotler
To my wife, Ariela
To my children, Michal and Gila

I.C.

Contents

Preface

This volume of essays attempts to provide a reasonably comprehensive description and analysis of Canadian Jewry at the beginning of the 1980s. Each paper has been written by an authority on the subject at hand using a style that we hope will be accessible and pleasing to members of the general public, Jew and non-Jew, as well as to specialists in Canadian and modern Jewish studies.

Every book has its own distinctive history from the time someone conceives it to its publication day. In this case, it all began in 1978, when M. Weinfeld suggested to W. Shaffir and then I. Cotler that there was a lack of material accessible to the general Canadian Jewish public about the nature of its community and life within it. After numerous hours of discussion, the three of us became more and more convinced that it would be useful to draw together a single volume that would include a wide range of authoritative analysis and topical information concerning various facets of Jewish life in this country.

Of course, several volumes had already made important contributions to our understanding of the Canadian Jewish community. To name only some of the most outstanding, we have B.G. Sack's *The History of the Jews in Canada*, a pioneering history; Joseph Kage's *With Faith and Thanksgiving* and Simon Belkin's *Through Narrow Gates*, reviews of Jewish immigration to Canada; Stephen Speisman's *The Jews of Toronto*, an authoritative history of that community to the early twentieth century; Evelyn Kallen's *Spanning the Generations*, a sociological study of generational shifts in Jewish identity in Toronto; Louis Rosenberg's *Canada's Jews*, still the basic work of Canadian Jewish social demography, although published in 1939; Arthur Chiel's *The Jews of Manitoba*, a history of one province's Jewish community; William Shaffir's *Life in a Religious Community*, a detailed study of a Chassidic community in Montreal; and a series of studies on the Jewish political organization of ten Canadian cities that have been published as individual reports and form the basis for a forthcoming volume, edited by Harold M. Waller and Daniel Elazar, entitled *The Politics and Organization of Canadian Jewry*. All these works, however, address specific issues and/or audiences and do not attempt to provide an overview of the national Jewish community and all its present characteristics.

Several general works exist: Stuart Rosenberg's *The Jews of Canada*, a useful two-volume introduction to leading personalities in Canadian Jewish history; Abraham Arnold and William Kurelek's *Jewish Life in Canada*, a blend of words and pictures that provides a brief yet insightful summary of basic information; Aron Horowitz's *Striking Roots*, a chronicle of the author's involvement in Jewish educational and cultural activities over five decades; Erna Paris's *Jews: An Account of Their Experience In Canada*, a highly readable account of Canadian Jewish social history, focussing principally on anti-Semitism and fascism in Quebec, Jewish communists in Toronto, and the story of Jewish farm settlements on the prairies.

The book we set out to shape, however, differs from these others in several important respects. First, its focus is primarily modern; although some essays here do contain historical reviews, the emphasis is primarily on consideration of the Canadian Jewish community as it exists in the latter half of the twentieth century. Wherever possible, we asked the authors to rely on the latest available census data (generally that of 1971) or on studies or research of even more recent vintage. Second, we wanted a diversity of perspectives. By seeking out a large number of contributors, we felt we could avoid the subjectivity inherent in the work of any single individual, no matter how competent, and garner the insights of both scholars from a number of disciplines and community activists from across the country.

Third, we attempted to be topical or — to use the current cliché — relevant. Most of the essays here link a discussion of general or theoretical issues to actual concerns facing the Jewish community, to decisions made or yet to be made, to specific problems solved or yet to be solved. We decided not to seek out controversy deliberately — but not to avoid it, either. Our concern in selecting essays and contributors was not with rigid canons of neutrality or impartiality; indeed, many of the writers feel strongly about the issues they discuss, and have been personally involved in some of the events and struggles described. As editors, we tried only to ensure that evaluations or opinions are supported with evidence or persuasive argument.

The choices of content and contributors for the book were a collective effort. As we debated them, we realized that, in many ways, the book we were shaping reflected both our personal histories and our current values. All three of us are fortunate enough to have been spared the ambiguities of a dual Jewish-Canadian heritage that have troubled others of our generation. Each of us received a thoroughly Jewish upbringing, is well grounded in Jewish history and traditions, and is fluent in Hebrew. Most important, each of us has integrated his adult life within the Jewish community, participating in it both publicly and privately.

Yet at the same time, each of us feels himself deeply attached to Canada and dedicated to its cultural and social vitality. Raised in the bilingual milieu of Montreal, we speak both of Canada's official languages and rejoice in the cultural diversity of its many peoples. As children or grandchildren of immigrants who fled anti-Semitic persecution, we appreciate more than most Canadians the breadth of freedom and opportunity that Canada provides and is striving to expand for her citizens in the 1980s and beyond. We hope, therefore, that the information and analysis in this volume will contribute to an understanding of our community in both its dimensions — the Jewish and the Canadian.

For these reasons, we are pleased that most of the essays in this volume are written with an eye resolutely fixed on the future, rather than on a sentimental past, though some do look back in order to provide a framework in which to examine the present. Although they offer more than a little criticism of Jewish life and institutions, at root they reflect an affirmative outlook on modern Jewish life in Canada.

The opening paper discusses Canadian Jewry generally, comparing and contrasting it to other groups in the Canadian mosaic and to the Jewish community of the United States. Of the following five sections, the first is also historical, dealing with both Jewish immigration to Canada in general and the most explosive and controversial issue in the history of Jewish immigration — the Canadian response (or lack thereof) to the plight of the German Jewish refugees in the late 1930s. The second section examines the present state of the four major institutions that sustain and define the Jewish community in Canada: the family, religion, Jewish education, and voluntary organizations.

The third section is devoted to those subgroups of the Jewish community that, voluntarily or involuntarily, have been excluded from the sources of power or the prevailing middle-class, East European lifestyle and culture. This includes, of course, the aged and the poor. We also placed here an essay on Jewish women, who have only recently begun to assert themselves as equal partners with men, and one on the Francophone immigrants who are adapting but preserving their Sephardic, North African identity within Montreal's predominantly Anglophone, Ashkenazic Jewish community. In this section, too, are papers on the Jews of Atlantic and of Western Canada, for the concentration of Jewish power and population in Montreal and Toronto has produced alienation and practical problems in outlying communities, and on Chassidic Jews, who prefer a form of self-segregation.

The fourth section deals with culture and ideology. Of the many possible topics under this heading, we chose three: Yiddish and its role in shaping the identity of Canadian Jewry; the reciprocal relationship of Canadian Jewish culture and the surrounding

Canadian culture; and Zionism, in its classical, organized form and as generalized support for the state of Israel.

The concluding section looks at several present and future problems that flow from the Canadian environment. One essay analyzes intermarriage as a threat to Canadian Jewry coming from within the community and from a surrounding society that is increasingly open to Jews. Another reviews the character of Canadian anti-Semitism. A third looks at a case study of Jewish political advocacy directed at the Canadian government. The final essay examines Jewish reactions to, and the possible consequences of, the independence movement in Quebec.

Obviously, these papers do not cover all the features of the diverse Canadian Jewish community. Jewish youth, Jews and the Canadian left, Jewish intellectuals in Canada, and the impact of the Holocaust are only a few of the other topics that might have been included if limitations of space, time, and energy had not precluded a more encyclopedic effort. Nevertheless, we believe that the essays we did include can give the reader a feel for the pulse of the Jewish community of present-day Canada.

No book is created alone. In addition to our patient contributors, we would like to thank the Canadian Secretary of State's Multiculturalism Directorate, the Jewish Community Foundation of Montreal, and the Ministry of Education of the Province of Quebec for their financial assistance, and McGill and McMaster Universities for their support. Francine Geraci, production coordinator, was extremely helpful in organizing and scheduling production. Lenore d'Anjou did a superb job of editing the manuscript, creating a uniformity and accessibility of style out of many varying manuscripts. Johan Larin typed the manuscript efficiently and accurately. The research and other preparatory tasks were speeded by the assistance of several of our students: Mark Aizenberg, Judith Katz, Jonathan Levy, Michael Lipkin, Jeffrey Regenstreif, Leah Rosenfield, Barbara Solomon, Leora Swartzman, Aviva Tencer, Paula Trossman, and Seth Vogelman. We hope they will share in the pride of the final product.

M.W.
W.S.
I.C.

Canada and the Jews: An Introduction

by William Shaffir and Morton Weinfeld

Are Canadian Jews unique? Can Canadian Jewry truly be distinguished from the much larger, apparently similar Jewish community of the United States? Are the approximately 300,000 Jews of Canada a group that differs from the country's other ethnic groups in kind or simply in details? These themes are reflected in nearly every essay in this volume on the Jews of modern Canada.

The questions are deceptively simple. Absolute answers, applicable to all times, places, and situations, are probably impossible. Nevertheless, we propose that in many ways Canadian Jewry *is* distinct from its American counterpart and unlike the other groups that form the Canadian mosaic.

Early Encounters

Neither Canadian Jewry nor Canada itself can be understood in any way without a knowledge of the immigration process underlying both. At its most significant level, Canada's immigration history is the history of the millions of diverse people who have come, alone or in groups, to the country and contributed to its cultural and ethnic diversity, its institutional arrangements, and its political, economic, and social character.

Over Canada's 114 years of existence as an entity, sentiment has usually favoured population growth, but no tightly organized, coordinated policy has ever reflected a grand vision or purpose for immigration. In retrospect at least, the policies over the years can best be understood as a series of pragmatic adjustments to short-term interests and pressures, successive attempts to sustain a balance among forces tugging in different directions.

The Royal Commission on Bilingualism and Biculturalism grouped into four phases the immigration to Canada of people from a wide variety of ethnic origins. From Confederation to 1895, the prevailing assumption was that the natural forces of supply and demand for population would produce an equilibrium. A second phase of Canada's immigration history is identified with Clifford Sifton's philosophy as minister of the interior. Convinced of the need for more people, especially more farmers to settle the West, Sifton promoted immigration so vigorously that, from 1896 to the outbreak of the First World War, Canada witnessed its greatest influx of immigrants ever. A third phase began in the 1920s and was halted by the time of the Depression, while the fourth phase began after the Second World War and continues to this day.[1]

This capsule account of the country's waves of immigration is quite accurate, but it fails to identify a frequent and prominent feature of official attitudes towards immigration — selection. At Confederation, the country was almost entirely populated by natives and persons of British (English, Scottish, Irish) background or French descent; members of other ethnic groups were isolated exceptions. Generally, governments did not want to change this situation radically, so a basic principle of almost all of Canada's immigration policies became the selection of desirable immigrants. Persons from Northern Europe and the United States were preferred to those from Eastern Europe; Southern Europeans and Orientals were considered undesirable. Only during Sifton's most intensive efforts to attract immigrants to settle the West was selective immigration temporarily suspended and those from non-preferred countries welcomed. As early as 1900, however, the government began arming itself with orders-in-council to enable it to reduce or bar the admission of would-be immigrants who were classified as nonpreferred or undesirable.

The official language eventually softened, but until 1962 the Canadian Immigration Act discriminated in some ways against non-European and especially nonwhite immigration through practices that were shaped by racist views that judged the superiority of one people compared with another. For example, certain ethnic groups were said to possess biological qualities that suited them to particular tasks; assertions of "climatic unsuitability" were used to justify exclusion of the "biologically inferior" people who came from hot, southern lands. The prejudice against Orientals was so great that, during the nineteenth century and the first half of the twentieth, special regulations were framed to restrict the entry of Chinese and Japanese. Between 1933 and 1939, the Canadian government's unwillingness to give entrance to desperate Jewish refugees provided yet another indication that humanitarian considerations did not and have not shaped its immigration policies and practices. Rather, they have reflected the Canadian people's sentiments and prejudices for and against various groups.

The immigration of Jews to Canada must be considered against the backdrops of these policies and of the often intolerable economic, social, and political conditions that prompted the migrants to leave their countries of origin. The first handfuls of Jewish immigrants to settle permanently in what would become Canada were, however, exceptions. Most were educated businessmen who had already met success or were on their way to it and sought to expand their opportunities. Almost all immigrated to Canada from England, either directly or via the United States. Those who came directly from England included some Eastern or Central European Jews whose families had resided there for some time; those from the United States included descendants of Sephardic families. The first Jewish congregation in Canada, founded in Montreal in 1768, was the Spanish and Portuguese Shearith Israel Congregation, which followed the Sephardic prayer ritual. Not until 1846 did the city see the establishment of the Shaar Hashomayim Congregation, which offered a place of worship after the manner of English, Polish, and German Jews.

The first official census to include the number of Jews in Upper Canada was taken in 1831; it showed 107 Jewish residents, a number that had increased only to 154 in 1841. Other colonies — the Maritimes in the late eighteenth and early nineteenth centuries, British Columbia and then Manitoba later in the nineteenth century — also recorded the presence of a few Jews early in their respective histories but the numbers were very small. The federal census of 1881 revealed only 2,445 Jewish residents: 1,245 in Ontario, 989 in Quebec, 104 in British Columbia, 55 in New Brunswick, 32 in Nova Scotia, and 31 in Manitoba. Even then, however, what would be the two great centres of Canadian Jewry were clear: of the total, Montreal had 811 and Toronto 500. The Jewish community in Winnipeg comprised eight families.

The volume of Jewish immigration began to increase in the 1880s and 1890s. During the first two decades of the twentieth century, persecutions and pogroms swept the Russian Empire. A large number of Jews escaped to Canada. It was the arrival of these masses of Eastern Europeans that shaped the character of the Canadian Jewish community as it completed its formative stages. By the time of the 1921 census, the country had 126,201 Jews, with roughly 48,000 each in Quebec and Ontario and nearly 17,000 in Manitoba.

For the vast majority of the Eastern European Jews, their immigration to Canada was encouraged by the wonderful tales about North America that had reached even the most remote towns and villages. These impoverished, tormented people saw the new world as the "Golden Land", a place where freedom and equality reigned and they could fulfill their dreams of finding a peaceful haven for themselves and their families. It took little time for them to discover that no luxuries awaited them, that life in the new country involved a constant struggle for necessities. Moreover, they found that the transition from the lifestyle of the *shtetl* (the Jewish village in Eastern Europe) to that of the new urban environment was difficult. As is typical of immigrants who move to a new culture, their old way of life deteriorated in a series of transitions that often made them feel lonely and helpless. Oscar Handlin has captured this aspect of the immigrant experience:

All relationships became less binding, all behavior more dependent on personal whim. The result was a marked personal decline and a noticeable wavering of standards. . . . Under the disorganizing pressure of the present environment, men found it difficult, on the basis of past habits, to determine what their own roles should be.[2]

The severity of the problems of immigrant adjustment was reflected in the diverse social and economic measures organized by the host Jewish communities for the newcomers' arrival. Yet even this far-reaching relief was not always sufficient to help the newcomers cope with the mental transformation life in the new country demanded. The range of challenges, frustrations, and joys they experienced is expressed most dramatically perhaps in *A Bintel Brief*, a cross section of letters written to the *Forward*, a Yiddish newspaper, beginning in 1906.[3] Although a *A Bintel Brief* is distinctively American, a similar account could be culled from contemporary Canadian Yiddish newspapers.

Although the community and mutual-aid groups could provide the newcomers with a certain amount of financial relief and protection from prejudice, they could do little about the most difficult problem: the conflict between the generations. Families had to marshal their own resources to bridge the gap between immigrant parents and their offspring. The young realized that their ethnicity was economically as well as socially retarding; most were eager to discard the elements of a culture and religion that they perceived as unnecessary or burdensome and to assume the lifestyle offered by the larger society. The result was inevitably a clash, and succeeding generations became increasingly integrated and assimilated into the larger Canadian society.

Since the Second World War, many of the most intense conflicts of the immigrant years have abated, although several waves of new arrivals — from post-Holocaust Europe, from North Africa, from Israel, and from the USSR — mean that thousands of families are still facing problems of acculturation. For the Jews already established in Canada, however, the seeds of the life planted by their parents and grandparents have borne fruit.

Today, the Jews of Canada constitute both an important minority group in the Canadian mosaic and an important element of the international Jewish Diaspora. At the time of the 1971 census, they were the third largest religious group and the eighth largest ethnic group in Canada, and there is little reason to think the 1981 figures will show much relative change. On a global scale, the Canadian Jewish community ranks sixth in size among the world's Jewish communities excluding Israel (behind the much more populous United States, Soviet Union, France, Great Britain, and Argentina). Most Jews thrive in Canada, as individuals and in groups. Communal organizations have reached a sophisticated complexity in the country's huge Jewish centres of Montreal and Toronto. A number of smaller cities — Halifax, Ottawa, Hamilton, Winnipeg, Edmonton, Calgary, Vancouver — also have stable or growing Jewish communities, and others boast at least a synagogue as an institutional core.

Many of the old problems have been replaced by new challenges and tensions rooted in the realities of ever-changing modern life, but it would be difficult to argue with the proposition that the Jewish community in Canada has contributed both to Canada and to world Jewry far in excess of its numbers.

The Distinctiveness of Canadian Jews

It is against this background that we can return to one of our original questions: does Canadian Jewry differ significantly from the much larger and better-known Jewish community of the United States? Clearly any comparative analysis depends on the perspective of the observer. A Martian might well conclude that there are no significant differences between the two communities and that any description of the American scene would do as well for the Canadian Jewish community.[4] Yet in the context of the Diaspora in the modern Western democracies, one can see several important distinguishing features of Canadian Jewry.

First, Canadian Jews are more geographically concentrated than their American counterparts; over two-thirds of the Canadian group live in Montreal or Toronto, and to date, there has been comparatively little diffusion to the West. In the United States, by contrast, the geographic shift from the Northeast to the Sun Belt is well underway; the fastest growing Jewish community is in Florida, while Los Angeles, another growth area, has more Jews than all of Canada.

Second, Canadian Jews, to put it most simply, are more "Jewish" than American Jews. They speak more Yiddish, provide their children with more intensive Jewish education, make higher per-capita contributions and relatively more visits to Israel, are more likely to be Orthodox and less likely to be Reform, and have lower rates of intermarriage. On the other hand, Canadian Jews have only recently begun to attempt to emulate the political sophistication of their American counterparts, who have had much experience (and considerable success) in defending Jewish interests within the domestic political arena. These differences and others will emerge often in the pages of this volume.

That differences exist is clear. What is less clear is the reason for this pattern. Is the basic cause the difference in the immigration patterns of the two communities? Canadian Jews are roughly one generation closer to the Old World than are American Jews. As we have seen, Canadian Jewry really originated with the mass movements at the turn of the century. The Eastern Europeans came then to both North American countries, but in Canada they were free to develop their own institutions and character, without the fundamental influence of a prior German-Jewish migration that existed in the United States. To put it another way, the foundations of the Canadian community were cast more than fifty years after those of the United States.

Moreover, a much higher proportion of Canadian Jews are themselves immigrants. In the 1970s, at least 40 per cent of Jewish household heads in Montreal and Toronto were foreign born. Immigration to Canada continued steadily throughout most of the 1920s, whereas American Jewish immigration more or less dried up by 1924. Perhaps even more important, Canadian Jewry has benefited from a proportionally larger influx of immigrants since World War Two. First came a large number of survivors of the Holocaust, during the immediate postwar period and from Hungary in 1956. Many of these immigrants were experienced in Jewish tradition (though not all practised), knew Yiddish, and had participated in the various Jewish ideological and political debates of the Old World. Their experience infused the Canadian Jewish community with new life, reinforcing its ties to the past.

A second movement to mark modern Canadian Jewry, especially its second largest community, Montreal, is the French-speaking North African group that arrived after 1957. These Sephardic immigrants brought with them and are determined to keep a distinctive form of Jewish identity forged in a crucible of tangible anti-Semitism and stamped with the dual cultural influences of France and the world of Islam. More recently, large numbers of Jews from the Soviet Union and other East Bloc countries, as well as from Israel, have added to the high proportion of foreign-born individuals among Canadian Jews.

Each new group has had an impact on Canadian Jewry. However, if it is the differences in the timing and patterns of immigration that are the chief cause of differences between the Canadian and the American Jewish communities, then reason dictates that these differences will prove ephemeral. As immigration to Canada slows down and as the generations pass, Canadian Jews will become increasingly assimilated into the general North American culture, and eventually any differences will disappear.

Another explanation for these differences suggests that the passage of time may not erase them. It focusses not on the characteristics of the immigrants, but on the nature of the receiving society. If Canadian Jews are different from American Jews, according to this theory, it is because Canada differs from the United States. Social scientists and other commentators have labelled Canada an ethnic mosaic, in contrast to the American melting pot. The United States, they say, urges immigrants to exchange their old identities for a new — American — persona awarded all citizens. Canada, on the other hand, encourages ethnic groups to retain at least part of their ancestral identity and heritage. If this is the true context of Canadian Jewry, it augurs well for the perpetuation of the Jewish community.

What is the reality? The answer is extremely difficult because each of the two contrasting concepts — the mosaic and the melting pot — applies at both the level of ideology and the level of social reality. The former certainly offers ample evidence to support the idea that Canada has generally been encouraging of ethnic diversity. The British North America Act did not declare the absolute equality of all citizens. Rather, by recognizing certain rights for religious groups (Catholics and Protestants) and linguistic groups (Anglophones and Francophones), it has legitimated a collectivistic approach to the notion of rights, in contrast to the American emphasis on individual liberties. The binational origin of the Canadian state paved the way for full acceptance of the plural nature of Canadian society and acknowledgement of the contributions, value, and rights of all Canadian minority groups. And with the passage of the Multicultural Act of 1971, the country adopted an official designation as a nation that is "multicultural in a bilingual framework". Public pronouncements by government leaders, from Prime Minister Laurier to Prime Minister Trudeau, have periodically reinforced the image of a multicultural nation whose whole is defined as the sum of its parts. Words are backed with money in that substantial government grants are now available to assist organizations that work to perpetuate ethnic cultures.

This Canadian concern with ethnicity is undoubtedly the result of the dilemma of trying to forge national unity from an originally binational society. Even religious diversity in Canada has been historically associated with and in recent times submerged by French-English dualism. Thus, ethnicity, language, and national origin have long been the natural dividing lines of Canadian pluralism, while in the United States, they have been race and religion (the latter perhaps because dissenters played such a large role in founding the country). The French concern for *la survivance* — survival in the midst of an Anglophone continent — has brought concerns of language and culture to the national consciousness and led to a strengthening of the ethnic or cultural dimension of modern Jewish identity. In the United States, however, Judaism is always defined as part of the American triumvirate of religions.[5] The vibrancy of Canadian Jewish life reflects the fact that Canadian Jews know that they are more than "Canadians of the Jewish faith".

Canada's commitment to pluralism is exemplified in the Canadian census, which has included questions on religion, ethnic origin, and language since its inception. (In the United States, the constitutional separation of church and state has prevented census questions on religion and limited queries to information on race, not ethnic origin.) In the Canadian census, ethnicity is defined by paternal ancestry and cannot be given as "Canadian" or "American" except by the native peoples. Thus, according to the Canadian census, all nonnative Canadians are of English, French, Italian, Greek, or some other origin, even if their ancestors have lived in Canada for four or five generations.

The census defines Jews as both an ethnic and a religious group, a procedure that can lead to confusion for anyone trying to derive an accurate estimate of the Jewish population.[6] The category of Jews-by-ethnicity includes many persons of Jewish paternal descent who have since converted out of the faith. For example, the 1971 census enumerated 276,000 Jews-by-religion but 296,000 Jews-by-ethnic-origin; many of the extra 20,000 in the latter group in fact claimed various Christian denominations as their religions. These confusions are, however, of concern mostly to statisticians and scholars. The fact is that the census' use of both ethnicity and religion to classify Jews does reflect the realities of Canadian Jewishness and of Canada's ideological approach towards its ethnic groups, an approach that is quite different from that of the United States.

When it comes to the realities of life for ethnic groups, however, some analysts have argued that the two countries are rather similar.[7] For example, the majority society in both countries has often displayed racist attitudes and practices towards nonwhite minority groups, as well as towards Jews. The European and North American public often associates racism more with the United States because of its history of slavery and because the inequalities of its large Black population, segregated in inner city ghettos, are so visible. But for other minorities, little distinguishes

Canada from the United States. Neither country has better than a dismal record on native rights. Both shut their doors firmly on Jewish refugees during the late 1930s. Both discriminated against persons of Japanese descent, even their own native-born citizens, during the Second World War. And so on, through a long, sad history.[8] As Canada's proportion of nonwhite immigrants has increased since 1945, the incidence of overt racism towards them has also increased, as demonstrated in acts of racially motivated violence as well as in public opinion polls that reveal significantly high levels of negative attitudes towards immigrants.

If racism is one dimension of real life in which Canadian and American societies may be rather similar, another may be the rate of assimilation — defined as the loss of ethnic culture in *daily* life. If we isolated comparable groups of second- or third-generation Jews in Canada and the United States, would the Canadians be less assimilated than the Americans? No studies have been reported using this sort of detailed comparison; however, looking at Canada alone, we do know that later generations of Jews demonstrate lower levels of Jewish identification than do foreign-born Jews (though the gap is not as large as for other ethnic groups). Certainly, too, the lay and spiritual leaders of Canadian Jewry have expressed as much concern over the dangers of assimilation and intermarriage as have their American counterparts.

The Uniqueness of the Jewish Minority

Another intriguing question is the degree of difference or similarity between Jews and other Canadian minority groups. Several characteristics of the Jews do seem to make them unique in Canada.

First, as already mentioned, Jews are both an ethnic and a religious group. In some ways, Jews behave as do Catholics and Protestants; in others, they approximate the behaviour of immigrant-ethnic groups, such as the Ukrainians, Italians, or Greeks. Apart from the religious elements of Judaism — the Law, religious ritual, and philosophy — Jews have in their cultural portfolio a host of traditions and as many as three Jewish languages

(Yiddish, Hebrew, and Ladino — a Spanish-derived tongue spoken by European Sephardic Jews). The fact of being both a people and a faith means that identity as a Jew may offer more options of belief and behaviour than those available to other minority groups.

A second characteristic that marks Canadian Jews, like those in most other Western societies, is their relative affluence. They are a predominantly middle- and upper-middle-class group in terms of education, occupation, and income. Many critical observers regard this affluence of North American Jews negatively. They view modern Jewish life as spiritually sterile and overly materialistic in comparison to the glorious traditions of struggling immigrants, leftist workers, and truly pious Jews. Of course, nothing in present-day Jewish life can equal the often exaggerated romance of this Jewish past. For such observers, Jews among them, modern Judaism consists of nostalgia for the historic, often exotic episodes of Jewish life. From such a perspective, it is easy to deride the largely conventional, middle-class, suburban lifestyle of so many present-day Canadian Jews.

Yet this affluent socio-economic position is particularly important not only for its own sake but also as it relates to the dual traditions of Jewish philanthropy and the development of a vast array of Jewish voluntary organizations. Jewish communities have always nourished a sense of collective responsibility for welfare. Today's Canadian Jews have both the desire and the resources to sustain a myriad of communal organizations with educational, fraternal, cultural, political, social, welfare, recreational, and, of course, religious goals. This high degree of "institutional completeness" sets the Jews apart from other groups.[9]

A third difference between Jews and other Canadian ethnic groups lies in the nature of the Jewish tie to Israel. Of course, other immigrant groups have strong ties to a homeland, and members often exhibit them in visits to it and in political concern for political events that concern it. But the Jewish tie to Israel goes much further. One reason is the centrality of Israel to the Jewish liturgy, in the setting of much of the bible — in short, to Jewish peoplehood. Perhaps more important sociologically is the continuing drama of Middle East politics, specifically the Arab-Israeli confrontation in its numerous manifestations, which the media frequently headline in their coverage of international events. Radio, television, and the newspapers provide Jews with daily reminders of Israel's problems and of their own stake in their resolution. A recent survey of Jewish householders in Montreal found that 47 per cent listed "news of the Middle East" as the current events in which they are most interested (followed by 26 per cent who were most interested in "Quebec news" and 20 per cent in "Canadian national news").[10]

Finally, the Holocaust has played an enormous role in differentiating Jewry from other Canadian ethnic groups, particularly in the Jews' own minds. It is difficult to overestimate the degree to which this tragedy has affected Jewish life, both at the communal and individual levels. It has reminded Jews, consciously and subconsciously, of their eternal marginality, inducing a steady state of heightened awareness of the possibility of anti-Semitism, even in contexts where objective observation would suggest little cause for alarm. In other words, Jewish antennae are always tuned to "high". One of the Holocaust's subliminal messages is that Jews must never take anything, including a relatively privileged and secure life, for granted. Another is that after so recent a loss of six million of their fellows, Jews, as a community and as individuals, must redouble their efforts to resist assimilation, so as not to grant Hitler any posthumous victories.

Conclusion

Every minority group with a sense of collective consciousness sees itself as in some ways unique. Certainly, one special characteristic of Jews is their two-thousand-year experience as a minority group in alien environments. Jews are obsessed with survival; in their ongoing insecurity and taking of the collective pulse, they might even be said to resemble Canada. Within the Canada of the late twentieth century, Jews can be considered among the minority groups most committed to collective survival. Yet for each generation, the struggle against assimilation differs. At this stage of the unfolding Jewish drama, the four characteristics described above — the combination of ethnicity and religion, affluence, Israel, and the memory of the Holocaust — will play major roles.

Whether current Canadian-American differences in Jewish life will persist will be revealed with the passage of time. So will the future characteristics, quantitative and qualitative, of Canadian Jewish life itself. We make no predictions. Every Diaspora community begins as an interaction between the immigrant Jews it comprises and the host society, whatever its nature. Yet once launched, a Jewish community may grow into a whole that is greater than the sum of its parts as it evolves its own history, institutional arrangements, mythologies, customs, and peculiarities. As Canada continues her quest for self-discovery, for economic and cultural independence, and for an authentic national character, Canadian Jews cannot help but be affected. Jews are perhaps the most cosmopolitan, the most internationalist, of all Canadian minority groups, as evidenced by their commitment to Israel, by their concerns for Jews in distress in the Soviet Union and elsewhere, by their ties of blood and religion to communities throughout the world. As Canada and Canadian Jews face the twenty-first century, the outcome of the interaction between the Canadian and Jewish agendas will determine the distinct, evolving identity of the Canadian Jewish community.

PART I

Early Encounters

The present situation of Canadian Jewry is best understood in its historical context, of which this section describes several aspects. The first essay is broad in scope, dealing with the very general themes of immigration and occupational adaptation. The next two revolve around case-study analyses of the Canadian response to the plight of European Jewry in the late 1930s. Taken together, the three represent both the zenith and the nadir of the Canadian-Jewish encounter.

The first paper, in other words, speaks to the essential success of the Jews in Canada. By any yardstick, the Jewish immigrants — or more accurately, their descendants — have found in Canada something that long eluded Jews in the Diasporas of the Old World: a combination of material prosperity and political and religious freedom. The struggles of early Jewish immigrants — as factory workers, as small shopkeepers, as tradespeople, as peddlers — have produced native-born generations who enjoy a life that is, in many ways, the envy of Jews all over the world. In his historical overview of Jewish immigration to this country, Joseph Kage describes the patterns of economic adjustment employed by both the immigrants themselves and the Jewish community as a whole to meet the challenges posed by a new environment. As Kage's material suggests, Jewish integration into Canada is an on-going phenomenon and reflects the contemporary Canadian scene as well as the political, economic, and social situations immigrants, especially recent immigrants, experienced before their arrival here.

Yet the celebration of the Canadian Jewish encounter remains less than total. The Canadian host society's acceptance of Jews has had its grave exception. The callous indifference of the Canadian government to the plight of European Jewry in the 1930s — and the impotence of the Canadian Jewish community in the face of this inaction — hangs like a cloud over both the past and the future. The two remaining selections in this section deal with this issue. In an insightful and excellently documented consideration of the official Canadian attitude towards and response to persons fleeing Nazism in 1933 through 1939, Irving Abella and Harold E. Troper convincingly demonstrate that Jewish refugees were simply unwelcome in Canada. The authors, quoting from previously classified government documents, expose the personal and private attitudes of high-ranking bureaucrats towards Jews in general and Jewish refugees in particular, views that included clearly anti-Semitic elements and that shaped this country's official response to the crisis. Abella and Troper also describe the desperate but futile efforts of the organized Jewish community to influence the government's policy towards the refugees.

Complementing this article is Gerald E. Dirks' treatment of the same subject matter from a different vantage point. He discusses attempts during the period to convince the government to change its highly restrictive immigration regulations. Particular detail is given about the efforts of the Canadian National Committee on Refugees and Victims of Persecution, a group made up of a number of liberal, humanitarian Canadians. Unfortunately, its praiseworthy efforts to moderate the restrictiveness of Canadian immigration policy were largely unsuccessful.

Canada's official posture during that early period foreshadowed the recent response to the boat people of Indochina, whose condition failed to arouse the moral conscience of many in this country and whose desperate efforts to find a haven from persecution yielded responses that, although an improvement over those of the 1930s, could have been much greater. Public opinion polls clearly showed many Canadians were reluctant to increase refugee quotas for the Indochinese. Thus, a gnawing, unarticulated fear remains. Have both the Canadian government — indeed the Canadian people — and the Jewish community learned the lessons of the tragic episode of the refugees who were refused entry in the years and months before the Second World War? Are Canadian Jews prepared to rock the boat, to risk their hard-won affluence and sense of acceptance in aggressive defence of Jewish rights? Will Canadian governments place principles and morality above political consideration or perceived economic interest? The evidence is not yet in.

Able and Willing to Work: Jewish Immigration and Occupational Patterns in Canada

by Joseph Kage

Where does an immigrant settle when he or she arrives in a new country? Many personal and social factors determine the answer, among them a desire to settle near friends or relatives. Or, if the immigrant has no close connections in the receiving country, he or she often heads for a community where previous immigrants from the homeland have already settled.

Often, too, the immigrant's destination is determined by his occupation, especially if opportunities for employment of his skills are restricted to or most plentiful in certain areas. If he has no training that is of immediate use in the new country, he is likely to be particularly open to settling near friends or compatriots who can help him. Thus, we see that there are direct, if complex, connections between immigrants' employment in their new homes, their numbers, place, and circumstances of origin, and their numbers, place, and circumstances of resettlement. These connections are likely to be particularly strong if the impetus for emigration came from persecution or other problems that made earning a living difficult or impossible in the old country.

The portions of this paper that deal with immigration before the Second World War draw heavily from my *With Faith and Thanksgiving* (Montreal: Eagle Publishing, 1962).

Jewish immigration to North America is a case in point. Many Jews decided to come to Canada or the United States because prejudice or outright persecution in Europe made earning a livelihood difficult if not impossible. Once on this continent, their patterns of settlement and their occupational profiles were greatly influenced by their desire for employment, the skills they brought with them, their willingness to adapt to available opportunities, and, as the years went on, the existence of Jewish communities ready to help them. The connections are so strong that it is possible to sketch the history of Jewish immigration to Canada in relation to the occupations Jews entered after their arrival.

Jewish Immigration to Canada: An Overview

Jewish immigration to Canada can be seen as a series of waves resulting from circumstances and policies both in the countries of emigration and in Canada (and the colonies that preceded it). Each presented specific sets of socio-economic circumstances — and correspondingly different patterns of settlement and employment.

In this view, the first period may be defined as running from the years of early British colonization until 1841. The individual Jews involved were few in number and came not as penniless refugees but as alert businessmen seeking new economic horizons. Most seem to have come from the United States or Britain.

The period from 1841 through the rest of the nineteenth century was a time of very rapid growth in Canada, with the overall population increasing nearly fivefold. It was also the time of the great outpourings of Jewish immigration from continental Europe to North America. The first of these, from the German states and other Western European nations in the 1840s, barely touched Canada. The second, however, from Central Europe and Russia after about 1880, coincided with the move to fill the vast open land of the young country, and a sizable number of Jews — mostly young, hungry, and eager for any kind of work — were among the many immigrants who were attracted to Canada during the last two decades of the century.

It was the third period of immigration, from the end of the nineteenth century through the 1920s, that brought the tidal wave of Jews to the Dominion. As the situation in Eastern Europe deteriorated, Jews poured into Canada by the thousands. During the period 1900 to 1920, the overall Canadian population increased by about two-thirds, but the Jewish population grew by some 750 per cent. On arrival, the immigrants were often in desperate straits, but many were skilled labourers or artisans and they settled relatively quickly into the growing industrial economy.

Soon after the First World War, however, Canada sought to staunch the flow of newcomers; the eventual result was the restrictive Revised Immigration Act of 1927, which shut the doors on most would-be immigrants. Despite conditions in Europe, few Jews were able to enter the country until late 1946, when the regulations were changed, partly in response to humanitarian pleas but partly in recognition of the fact that many Holocaust survivors had useful job skills. During the last thirty-five years, similar dual considerations seem to have marked the admission of several other significant waves of immigrant Jews, especially those from North Africa, Israel, and the Soviet Union.

Thus, we see that although the first Jews came to Canada around 1760, most of the country's present Jewish population is not descended from these early settlers. Rather, the vast majority are either immigrants themselves or second- or third-generation descendants of persons who migrated to Canada within the last eighty years.

Early Jewish Settlement: 1760–1840

The French colonies of early Canada seem to have had no Jews. Certainly, the charter of the Company of New France, granted in 1627, stipulated that the colony should be populated by Catholics of French stock. This policy applied, of course, to Jews as well as Protestants, so the former were limited to incidental contact with New France and its people.

The early English settlements in Canada do not appear to have included any Jews, either. There is, however, evidence that some Jewish merchants from Newport, Rhode Island settled in Halifax, Nova Scotia soon after its founding in 1749, although the duration of their community is questionable. Reports of occasional — and occasionally prominent — Jewish settlers turn up in the late eighteenth and early nineteenth histories of several other Maritime centres, but they seem to have settled as individuals. There are no records of organized congregations.[1]

Thus, the beginning of permanent Jewish settlement in Canada is usually given as the time New France came under British rule. The Conquest removed the colony's previous bars against non-Catholic settlers, and the first Jews to make their homes there were members of Major-General Lord Jeffrey Amherst's forces, including his commissary officer. This handful of Jewish military men was soon augmented by other Jews from Britain and the thirteen colonies. There were not many of them. The first official census that recorded Jews in Canada was taken in 1831 and showed 107 Jewish residents; a decade later, almost eighty years after the Conquest, the number had only grown to 154.

These first Jewish immigrants were atypical not only in their small number but in their backgrounds and occupational levels. They belonged to the middle class, possessed fine social and educational backgrounds, and were engaged in trade, commerce, and industry, often very successfully. Their adjustment to their new environment apparently did not pose many problems, certainly no more than were faced by British settlers of similar status. A small group, generally well-to-do, and brought up in the prevailing language and culture, they appear to have been well accepted by the middle and upper classes of contemporary Canadian society. In Montreal, which was the centre of the early Jewish community, Jews were among the guests regularly invited to attend the governors' levees. They often participated in the gatherings of such groups as the Saint George's Society, the Saint Andrew's Society, and the Saint Patrick's Society. They were members of the Whist Club and the Hunt Club, and their homes were frequently centres of social gatherings. The governors invited young Jewish men to take up commissions in His Majesty's militia, and many did so. Jews were among the comfortable Montrealers who participated in the colony's various charitable and philanthropic endeavours as well as in its political life.

Aaron Hart is a good example of the heights to which some of these early Jewish settlers rose. Born in England in 1724, he came to Lower Canada as commissary officer to Amherst's troops and remained to become prominent in the fur trade and other enterprises. It has been suggested that he, more than any other individual, was responsible for the growth of Trois Rivières as a vital trading centre. When he died in 1800, contemporary English newspapers spoke of him as one of the wealthiest British subjects living outside the British Isles.

Henry Joseph, born in England in 1775, came to Canada at the close of the eighteenth century. After serving with the military commissariat, he became engaged in business and initiated considerable freight traffic over the inland waterways. Eventually, with his brother-in-law, Jacob Franks, and his father-in-law, Levy Solomons, he established one of the largest chains of trading posts in Canada through the then wild and thinly populated Northwest. He also owned and chartered so many ocean-going ships for freight traffic between England and Canada that some feel he virtually founded the Canadian merchant marine.

Joseph's son, Jesse, established the first direct steamship line between Canada and Belgium, served for many years as Belgian consul-general in Canada, was one of the founders of the Montreal Gas Company, the City Passenger Railway of Montreal, and the Montreal Telegraph Company, and served as a director and officer of a number of other commercial enterprises.

Many additional examples could be cited of Jews who played prominent roles in crucial areas of early Canadian life. Though few in number, they contributed substantially to the colonies' expanding economic growth, and their success provided a base for future Jewish immigrants.

Land, People, and Immigration: 1840–1900

The 1840s marked the beginning of the decades of intensive Jewish immigration to North America. Indeed, the phenomenon was not peculiar to Jews but coincided with and was very much related to a large influx of immigrants into the Americas generally. Europe was crowded and torn by war, revolution, and prejudice; the New World was underpopulated and needed newcomers to underwrite its expansion with their labour.

For Jews, the move across the Atlantic began in continental Western Europe and resulted in thousands upon thousands of German Jews pouring into the United States. Because of various factors, however, proportionally few of these migrants came to Canada, and many of those who did come arrived only after a stay south of the border. A few decades later came a tidal wave of immigration to North America from Russia, Poland, Latvia, Lithuania, Rumania, and parts of Austria and Hungary. This movement had considerably more effect in Canada, although the great period of Jewish immigration to the country was yet to come.

The European migrations of the late nineteenth century coincided with a period of very rapid development in Canada. Its total population grew from 3.7 million in 1871 to 5.4 million in 1901. Much of this growth was the result of immigration, which the government was fostering as a means of filling the country, particularly the sparsely settled West.[2] How many of the immigrants who reached Canada were Jewish? It is estimated that the total was about 15,000 between 1840 and 1900. Certainly the census figures on Jews for this period show considerable growth over the tiny numbers of previous years, a growth that increased towards the end of the century.

The same records show how the growing Jewish population began to spread out across the country, penetrating into newly developing areas. In 1851, Jews resided in nine urban centres (the word is a census term for all nonrural areas and is used for villages and small towns as well as cities). Twenty years later, it was twenty-nine, all but two in Quebec and Ontario. But by 1901 the number of Canadian communities with Jewish residents was 113, and they were found in every province. This widespread distribution of Jewish settlers from coast to coast points up the fact that the Jewish immigrants, although mostly from urban backgrounds, participated in opening up the country and accelerating its development. Their pioneering spirit, when unhampered by the shackles of residential and social restrictions, is further suggested by the fact that of the over one hundred communities in which Jews lived in 1901, the vast majority — eighty-eight — had a Jewish population of less than thirty-five individuals.

The Immigrants' Occupations

Immigrant groups generally experience a fairly high degree of occupational change after resettlement. Some are not trained for specific kinds of employment because of personal circumstances, lack of opportunity, or economic conditions in the old country. Many others have skills but they are not transferable — the immigrants are not able to use them in the new country because its prevailing methods of work are different, because there is an initial handicap of not knowing the dominant language, or because there are few markets for these skills. Social and personal reasons may also prompt a change of occupation.

What was the occupational profile of the Eastern European Jewish immigrant? Again, the question is somewhat difficult to answer because Canadian authorities kept no records of the ethnic origin of the gainfully employed until 1931. United States immigration authorities did, however, make some efforts at recording the occupational classifications of the Jewish immigrants they processed. Because the sources of Jewish immigration to the two countries were the same, we may assume that the American information is valid for Canada. It shows that Jewish immigrants from Eastern Europe between 1870 and 1900 were mostly artisans, unskilled labourers, small merchants, and clerical workers; a considerable proportion had no specific occupation.

This information is confirmed by what we know about the occupational profile of Jews in contemporary Eastern Europe. In the middle of the nineteenth century, about 40 per cent of the Jews in the Russian Empire were engaged in manufacturing and mechanical pursuits, about 32 per cent in commerce, and about 3 per cent in farming. The clothing industry employed about one-third of the Jewish population. Jews played an equally important part in the preparation of food products, in the building trades, and in the metal, wood, and tobacco industries. The Jews of Rumania, Austria-Hungary, and Poland were, in their occupational profile, very much like those of Russia. For example, a substantial proportion of Rumania's glass, clothing, furniture, and textile industries was managed and worked by Jews.

In brief, Central European Jews were engaged as middlemen, businessmen, industrialists, and entrepreneurs. They also made up a large percentage of watchmakers, tinsmiths, tailors, glaziers, painters, bookbinders, shoemakers, joiners, carpenters, bakers, and other artisans and skilled labourers. During the last quarter of the nineteenth century though, Russian Jewry experienced a mass transition from middlemen occupations to labour, especially to handicrafts. This was particularly evident among the members of the younger generation, the primary prospects for emigration.

Because of the lack of records, our best clues to the occupational adaptation of the Jewish immigrants to Canada can be obtained from contemporary sources such as newspaper chronicles and various types of social reports. For example, the Winnipeg *Free Press* recorded the following in 1882. The account is revealing in its detailing of the new arrivals' skills and in its emphasis on their willingness to work.

Jewish refugees from Russian persecution, who were stated in a late number of the Free Press to be on the way to this province, arrived yesterday. The party consists of fifteen men and the wives of four of the number, making in all nineteen; besides four in charge of baggage have not yet arrived. Accommodation was provided for them at the Government Immigration buildings on Fonseca Street, West. There is among the men three carpenters, one blacksmith, one cabinet maker, one painter and one dryer, the remainder of the number being farmers. They are all young, none of them being over 30 years of age, and they are stalwart looking and evidently intelligent. They are able and willing to work and ready to avail themselves of any opportunity that may be afforded them of earning an honest livelihood. The members of the Jewish community here are doing all in their power to provide for the immediate wants of the people, as they are entirely without means; but, as the community is small, embracing only eight families, they would be glad of the assistance of any who may be able to help, especially in finding immediate employment for the strangers.[3]

Another group of Jewish immigrants arrived in Winnipeg a few days later, and according to the next morning's newspaper:

Supper was furnished by the Jewish residents of the city, and it was clear to the spectators who happened to be present that the kindness was well-timed. The travellers ate as if famished, and their evidently destitute condition touched the sympathies of those who saw them. Scarcely had they finished eating when the men were informed that if they liked to go to work immediately and work all night, they might all do so, and that their wages would be paid at the rate of 25 cents per hour. This noble offer was made to them by the firm of Jarvis and Berridge, and the work with which the immigrants began their experience in Manitoba consisted in unloading two rafts of lumber which had just been brought down from Emerson by the SS Ogema. It is said that the people almost wept when the offer was interpreted to them. With the promptness of a company of soldiers, they fell into line and marched to the bank of the Red River, a little south of Broadway Bridge, where they soon were at work. At a late hour, thirty-seven of them were labouring industriously and showing that they were neither averse nor unaccustomed to work. They impressed their employers and others who saw them, very favourably, were regarded as intelligent looking and of good, strong physical constitutions, and were thought to give promise of making hard-working and valuable settlers of this new country.[4]

The Flood of Immigration: 1900–1927

The second and much more intensive phase of Eastern European Jewish immigration to Canada came at the beginning of this century and continued through the mid-1920s. In many ways, it was a continuation of the previous wave, but its numbers were much larger. During these two decades, the general population of Canada grew from 5.4 million to 8.8 million, but the country's Jews increased from under 17,000 to roughly 125,000.

In 1921, according to the census, the now sizable Jewish population was spread out in 573 urban communities. Of these, 533 had fewer than 100 Jewish residents, suggesting that the pioneering spirit continued. But the familiar urban patterns were clear. Two cities (Montreal and Toronto) had 15,000 or more Jewish residents, and eight (three in Ontario, two in Quebec, and one each in Manitoba, Alberta, and British Columbia) had between 1,000 and 15,000. The two provinces with the largest Jewish populations in 1921 were Quebec (47,977) and Ontario (47,798); they were followed by Manitoba (16,699), Saskatchewan (5,380), and Alberta (3,242). The distribution of Canadian Jews at this time indicates that although most lived in the larger cities, especially Montreal and Toronto, small groups were scattered widely throughout the country. The Jewish immigrants chose their places of residence in accordance with their urban and occupational backgrounds and the concentration of their kinship group.

The Immigrants Find Work

In some ways, the Jewish immigrants of the early twentieth century were in an excellent position. Although they were fleeing difficult situations — and often outright persecution — many had already developed occupational skills. U. S. immigration records, which, as we have seen, can be presumed to reflect the contemporary situation in Canada, show a definite change in the background of Jewish immigrants from Eastern Europe as of about 1900. In the preceding decades, many of the wage earners among them had been young unskilled or semiskilled labourers. During the first quarter of the twentieth century, however, about 70 per cent of Jewish immigrant wage earners were skilled workers and artisans, in contrast to about 20 per cent of all immigrants.

This high incidence of occupational skills among Jewish immigrants was an important factor in their occupational adjustment. Two other characteristics that considerably affected their occupational enhancement and stability were the permanence of their migration and the presence of strong family ties. The Jewish immigrants came to stay; in comparison with members of other ethnic groups, very few returned to the Old World. Further, the Jewish family, if at all possible, immigrated together. Coming to a new land with a family posed certain obstacles to mobility, but, on the other hand, the need to provide for dependents greatly contributed to occupational regularity, the desire to learn or adapt skills, and ambition for advancement.

As these relatively skilled Jewish immigrants came to Canada, they found a country whose secondary industry, manufacturing, and service sectors were expanding rapidly. Only ever-growing specialization and vastly increased production could satisfy the needs of Canada in its transition from a basically agrarian to an industrial economy. Immigrant labour filled this need, and Jewish workers were able to assume a specific position in the process. Those who had transferable skills moved into available job openings as carpenters, mechanics, locksmiths, bakers, painters, metal workers, machinists, and bricklayers. Those who had no occupational skills or whose skills were not transferable to the new milieu took any manual job available but usually attempted to acquire a specific skill (and hence more lucrative work) at the first opportunity. The demand for labour was high, and many companies, such as the Canadian Pacific Railway, Vickers, and other expanding firms, often employed Jewish workers. So did many stores, transport enterprises, and small manufacturing enterprises — upholstering, furniture-making, jewellery, tinsmithing, shoemaking, and so on.

It was in clothing manufacture, however, that the Jewish immigrant workers came to predominate. There were several reasons for this development. First, the garment trade of the day was a rapidly expanding industry that demanded a large supply of low-paid workers. Moreover, its extensive division of labour for production made it possible for a novice to acquire a fair degree of skill within a relatively short time. Therefore, many immigrants who had nontransferable or no previous occupational skills tended to gravitate to "the needle trades".

A second factor of considerable importance was the garment industry's concentration in the larger cities, where the Jewish immigrants tended to settle. The work was there, and they tended to accept the first available jobs because they had to support themselves practically from the first day they came to the new country. (It is estimated that the amount of money the average immigrant brought was only about ten dollars.)

A third aspect, also important, was the fact that some established Canadian Jews were already active in the garment industry, some of them as manufacturers, and were able to select or suggest new employees. The numbers of Jews in the trade grew quickly as friends and relatives introduced newcomers to the same occupation. A fourth factor was the illusion of independence that the garment trade gave its workers. It offered possibilities of obtaining piece work to be done at home; thus a man's wife and children could contribute to a family's meagre income and an Orthodox Jew could observe the Sabbath.

Much of the information we have about the employment of early twentieth-century immigrants, in the garment industry and elsewhere, comes from verbal accounts and memoirs by persons who experienced some of these situations. For example, I. Medres described life and work in Montreal's Jewish community in the early years of this century.

The main problem of the newly arrived immigrant was how to get a job which would provide a livelihood and in time an opportunity for advancement. If the immigrant came to a relative who was already settled, then the matter was not too difficult. The immigrant secured the assistance of the relative in finding work. There were, however, many immigrants who had no relatives or whose relatives were not in a position to help. Then help was sought from 'landsleit' — people who came from the same community as the immigrant. Various kinds of advice were given, such as suggestions to learn some phase of the needle trade and work in a factory, becoming a customer peddler or assistant peddler (klapper), or general work. . . . At that time many Jews were employed at the C.P.R. as locksmiths, carpenters, tinsmiths, etc. . . .

Many immigrant Jews sought jobs at the Montreal port. There were Jewish longshoremen and Jews were also employed in various other jobs. . . .

Most of the Jewish immigrant workers were in the needle trade. There were also many without specific occupations who worked as day labourers. Many Jews worked at construction either as skilled tradesmen or as labourers. The earnings were small, and many worker families were in poverty, especially families with children. Because of poverty and need, children would go to work at 13–14 years of age.[5]

As the immigrants to the cities adapted their occupations to the requirements of their new country, the relative few who had resisted the pull of compatriots and urban life to the major centres often found that their skills also suited them for a particular role in the opening West. They became middlemen and country storekeepers. According to one account:

The Jewish country storekeeper who conducted the general stores in many of the hamlets and villages of Manitoba, Saskatchewan and Alberta in the period from 1901 to 1939 played an important and practically indispensable role in the development of the country north of the C.P.R.'s main line.

The population which streamed in to clear and cultivate the land in that area were mainly from the peasant stocks of Eastern and Central Europe. Few of them knew any English, and many could not understand the language of their neighbours of different ethnic origin. Merchants of Anglo-Celts origin from Eastern Canada, the U.S.A. or Great Britain who understood English only, could not have served the needs of the immigrant settlers who differed so widely in ethnic origin, language and folk ways, even if they had been willing to make their homes amongst them.

The Jewish merchant conducting the general store in the hamlet or village had himself come from Czarist Russia, Poland, Austria or Rumania, and was no stranger to the needs, language and customs of the settlers who, like him, had come to make their new home in Canada. He soon acquired a knowledge of English and could often make himself understood in German, Russian, Ukrainian, Polish, Rumanian and Hungarian. If he did not know these languages upon arrival, he made it his business to pick up a speaking knowledge of them, and if there was an Indian Reservation in the neighbourhood he soon acquired a smattering of one or two Indian dialects for good measure.

He often opened a store before the railway actually reached the community and freighted his supplies by wagon team from the railhead. His store was usually the community meeting place in the early days of settlement. He sold groceries, shoes, clothing, yard goods, fur coats, household remedies, harness and hardware. He bought butter and eggs, hides and raw furs from farmers, and knew the name of each article in several languages. He was not only the merchant, but also letter writer, translator, advisor and friend to his customers.[6]

Meanwhile, the concentration of so many new Jewish immigrants in a few cities began to revolutionize the Jewish community of Canada. The Jews from Eastern Europe had brought with them a rich tradition and cultural background, both secular and religious. In the new, friendlier environment of Canada, Jewish communal life began to assume a different shape, partly because of the immigrants' increased social and occupational mobility. Patterns of social and cultural status changed, an active social and intellectual life sprang up, the old forms of communal organization and social intercourse were adapted or entirely replaced to meet the needs of the new environment.

One important such aspect of this era was the rise of the Jewish labour movement. Conditions in the needle trades and other predominantly Jewish industries were poor at the beginning of the twentieth century, with frequent seasonal unemployment, low wages, poor working conditions, and the sweat shop system. This situation, however, radically improved during the first two decades of the century. The clothing industry became the centre of the growing move to unionization and the mainstay of the Jewish labour movement. The latter developed with the dual aims of protecting the Jewish worker and raising the cultural level of the Jewish working people. The impact of this development spread throughout the community in diverse spheres.[7]

Immigration since the 1920s.

The flood tide of immigration to Canada was cut off in the late 1920s when new government regulations virtually prohibited the admission of most would-be new Canadians. The restrictions particularly affected immigration from Eastern Europe, an area of extensive Jewish dislocation after the war and an area of growing anti-Semitism. Thus, at a time when the need for emigration and resettlement was most urgent, immigration opportunities decreased. To Jews already in Canada, the issue of immigration assumed an additional dimension — it became a task of rescue. They needed an instrument to influence Canada's immigration policy, as well as an organization to help Jews who managed to gain entrance. The Jewish Immigrant Aid Services of Canada (JIAS) was created as such an instrument.

Even today, immigrants to Canada can be divided into two categories: those admitted under normal immigration procedures and those admitted as a result of specific projects created through special legislation or orders-in-council. The Jewish condition has often demanded the latter either for individual cases or for groups, and successful requests for such intervention have created a series of minor immigrant waves from various countries.

Unfortunately none of them occurred until after the Second World War left Europe in ruins and Jewish life devastated. The European Jewish population of about 9.5 million at the outbreak of the war was reduced to some 2.8 million in 1950; most of those who had perished died in the ghettos, the concentration camps, and the gas chambers. Those who survived the Holocaust were left uprooted physically, socially, and psychologically. German and Austrian Jews, for example, were actually refugees in their home countries. Many survivors from Eastern European nations could not return to their countries of origin for fear of oppression for religious, ethnic, social, or political reasons. This mass displacement was so great that it has been described as having "eclipsed all previous human floods created by War".[8]

The survivors became known as Displaced Persons or DPs, and the task of resettling them was urgent. The three Rs of Jewish immigration work during the postwar period were rescue, resettlement, and rehabilitation. When the state of Israel was established in 1948, it became the most significant country of Jewish immigration and received more postwar refugees than any other. In Canada, many Jewish immigration efforts were launched as soon as the war was over, but though action was needed immediately, the Dominion was ready to open its gates only after a waiting period.

The horizon became brighter towards the end of 1946, when federal government authorities agreed to introduce emergency measures to admit a certain number of refugees and DPs from European camps. In 1947, additional measures provided for the admission of immigrants under the Group Movement Plan. This device meant that immigrants, rather than waiting to be nominated individually by Canadian citizens, could be selected by labour teams in Europe; the criteria were chiefly based on the needs of Canadian industry. (Permission was, however, also given for the admission of over 1,000 Jewish orphans.) Subsequently, the provisions were extended to include projects for milliners, dressmakers, and domestics and to increase the number of skilled workers allowed to come to Canada. Between April 1947 and March 1950, the country granted admission to 98,057 DPs. Almost half were admitted under the various group movements; the rest were close relatives of people already residing in Canada. Jews ranked third in the number of admissions, exceeded only by Poles and Ukrainians.

During the 1960s and 1970s, the trends in Jewish immigration to Canada have usually followed the general pattern of the country's admission policy. Although immigration regulations have undergone a number of changes, mirroring what has been called a "swinging door" approach to admission controls, their general pattern has been predicated on several factors — population growth, needs of the labour market, reunion of relatives, and humanitarianism — with the relative weight given to each varying with the contingencies of the time. The most recent changes were in 1978; Jewish immigrants, like all immigrants to Canada, can be admitted either as part of the family class (parents, spouse, or minor children) or as independents by virtue of their qualifications as immigrants under selective criteria.

Under general or special rules, Jewish immigrants came to Canada between 1960 and 1980 from some twenty countries, including Latin American nations and the United States. Specific movements have included: a continuation of the immigration that started in the mid-1950s from the lands of North Africa, especially Morocco; immigration from Eastern Europe (Rumania, Czechoslovakia, Poland, and so on); admission of a number of Jewish immigrants from Israel, India, and Lebanon and Iraq, and the arrival of Jews from the Soviet Union. Each of these groups has required special efforts and consideration in terms of both admission and integration. Numerically, the most significant movements have been those from Morocco, Israel, and the Soviet Union. Each had special connotations that makes it worth describing more fully.

The Jews of North Africa

The movement of Jews from the lands of North Africa began after the Second World War, as it became clear that various French colonies there would become independent. Most of the Algerian Jews were able to move to France, where they were received as French nationals. Most of those from Tunisia also gravitated to France, but some went to Israel and other countries, including Canada. The Moroccan Jews, whose civil emancipation was relatively new and who had no history of previous migration in recent centuries, were suddenly placed in the position of seeking compatible new homes. The vast majority went to Israel. The next largest group came to Canada.[9]

The admission to Canada of Jewish immigrants from Morocco (and some from Tunisia) was a pioneering effort in that it was the result of the Canadian Jewish community's expressed readiness to accept them. Moreover, prevailing conditions in Morocco required extensive cooperation among the community, the government, and the individual immigrant during the immigration process. Since complete individual interviewing of the potential immigrants was not always possible, much had to be done by correspondence or through various cooperative sources. Only after a certain number of documented cases had accumulated would a Canadian immigration mission visit Morocco to interview the applicants. The process also necessitated intensive cooperation among various voluntary and government agencies in order to provide the immigrants with transportation, reception, housing, and help in integration.

Even today there is considerable confusion regarding the size of the North African immigrant group, confusion accentuated by many people referring to it as the "Sephardim" or the "French-speaking Jews". Although the majority of the Jews from North Africa are French-speaking, not all French-speaking Jewish immigrants are from North Africa (they may be from France, Belgium, Rumania, and so on). Moreover, some Jews who were born in North Africa immigrated to Canada from France or Israel and were recorded as citizens of those countries. Finally, the group's Canadian-born children may properly be designated as Moroccan (or Sephardic or French-speaking), but they are certainly not immigrants. One set of statistical data, that of JIAS, shows that some 10,000 North African immigrants (mostly from Morocco) came to Canada between 1957 and 1980. Conceivably, there may have been others who did not register with JIAS, but their number is undoubtedly very small. About 75 per cent of the immigrants from Morocco were sent to Montreal, most of the rest to Toronto. (Generally, unilingual Francophones and large families were assigned to Montreal, partly because of their language, partly because that city had the most comprehensive JIAS reception, social services, and integration facilities.)

The Moroccan immigrants generally brought with them experience in various office, business, sales, and teaching situations or in occupations such as barbering, hairdressing, mechanics, and jewellery manufacture. Many of the women were trained as couturiers, hairdressers, steno-typists, and so on. Nevertheless, in order to make their skills marketable, the majority required some retraining to teach them North American methods and terminology. The JIAS Vocational Bursary Fund arranged courses at such institutions as Ecoles des Hautes Etudes Commerciales; most were scheduled in the evening so the immigrants could hold jobs during the day. The effort seems to have paid off since members of the community have since exhibited substantial economic mobility.

Immigrants from Israel

An estimated 22,000 immigrants from Israel live in Canada today, most in Montreal and Toronto but some in communities such as Winnipeg, Calgary, Edmonton, and Vancouver. The majority of them were not born in Israel. Many who came during the 1950s and 1960s are of European origin; some are of North African descent as already discussed. Israeli-born immigrants have recently become more numerous, primarily as a result of 1978 changes to Canada's immigration regulations.

Most of the immigrants from Israel arrived as part of the reunification of families. Others first came to the country on temporary visas and later applied for admission as permanent residents because they had found mates, employment, or other congenial personal circumstances here. The process of integration has generally been eased by the fact that such a large percentage of immigrants from Israel came to join relatives or had already made local connections. Moreover, many of them, because of their origin, arrived with a knowledge of French, English, or Yiddish, in addition to Hebrew. Today, they are represented in many fields of economic endeavour — as entrepreneurs, as teachers in Jewish schools, and so on.

The arrival of immigrants from Israel has created a certain anxiety within some segments of the Jewish community. On one hand, the Canadian Jewish community is committed to Israel's cause, and some of the immigrants themselves have guilt feelings about having left Israel. On the other hand is the deep-seated tradition of helping fellow Jews in need. Although ambivalent attitudes are inevitable and likely to continue, it has been agreed that the community should not be asked to use a double standard — a declared one for Jews who are not from Israel and another for immigrants from the Jewish homeland. Thus, when individual immigrants from Israel seek community aid for integration into the Canadian situation, they receive it. Moreover, it has been aptly observed that the presence of immigrants from Israel with their knowledge of Hebrew, Jewish history, Middle Eastern politics, and so on may prove to be an important asset to the Canadian Jewish community.

Jews from the USSR

Postwar Jewish immigration from the Soviet Union to Canada is a relatively recent phenomenon. The first substantial number of these immigrants came in 1973, but the movement has continued at a sustained pace. It is estimated that some 8,000 Jewish immigrants arrived from the USSR during the 1970s, the peak years being 1975, when 1,149 registered with JIAS, and 1979, when the number was almost identical.

The Soviet Jewish immigrants have several specific characteristics. One is their diverse destination-patterns in Canada. In 1979, for example, some twenty-five Jewish communities received immigrants from the Soviet Union. Another is their high level of educational and vocational qualifications; many are technically trained in various occupations. A third is their having grown up with almost no knowledge of Judaism as a religious or ethnic heritage and with no experience of Jewish communal structures. In a number of larger communities, they have now formed their own associations, but these may be of a transitory character since there is a definite trend of Soviet immigrants entering the mainstream of Jewish community life. This process will no doubt accelerate as the newcomers learn the country's languages, integrate socially, and gain a better understanding of the nature and functions of the existing communal institutions and services.

The Emerging Pattern

Despite the fact that Israel has become the major destination for Jewish immigrants today, Canada continues to play a vital role in receiving them. As long as they continue to arrive, the established Jewish community must provide programs to meet both the needs of immigrants in normal times and the contingencies of any crises that arise. That it will do so seems likely, if only because most Canadian Jews are not far removed from the immigrant generations.

The success of those generations is reflected in the success of Canadian Jews in the past quarter century. As individuals, Jews have entered the mainstream of Canada's growth and become integrated into its economy. Yet a closer analysis indicates that in some respects the Jewish economic structure is characterized by an unusually high degree of upward occupational mobility. This fact showed clearly at least twenty-five years ago. One study based on the 1951 census ranked 343 occupations into seven classes. The highest class comprised only 0.9 per cent of the labour force, but 2.9 per cent of the Jewish ethnic group were in it, followed by 1.3 per cent of persons of British origin. Classes one and two combined (11.6 per cent of the labour force) included 38.6 per cent of Jews and 13.1 per cent of the British group.[10]

During the modern period, the bulk of the Jewish working population has concentrated in industry, commerce, the professions, and clerical services. In trade, Jews are engaged as small businessmen, retailers, and sometimes as wholesale merchants or owners of larger businesses. In such professions as medicine, law, dentistry, pharmacy, social work, and clerical employment, they are represented well out of proportion to the general population. To some degree, these trends reflect Jews' eagerness to better themselves economically — and to provide educational opportunities for their children. However, avoidance of employment discrimination also partially explains Jewish occupational patterns.

In brief, the economic structure of Canadian Jews is a product of political and economic conditions in this country and the Old World over the last 150 years. The Jews came to North America in great numbers at the time when certain areas of economic activity began to expand at a faster rate than others. In the future, as in the past, economic success for Canadian Jews will depend directly on the economic opportunities the country has to offer and on the effectiveness with which access to the job market is kept free from religious or ethnic discrimination.

"The Line Must Be Drawn Somewhere": Canada and Jewish Refugees, 1933–39

by Irving Abella and Harold E. Troper

On 15 May 1939, 907 desperate German Jews set sail from Hamburg on the luxury liner *St. Louis*. Like many who had sailed on this ship before, these passengers were — or at least had been — the cream of German society: distinguished, well-off, educated, cultured. Most had contributed much to their native land. All were now penniless. They had been stripped of their possessions, hounded out of their homes and businesses and now their country. Their most prized possession was the entrance visa to Cuba each carried on board.

For the Jews of Germany life had become impossible. The Nazis were anxious to empty Germany of its Jews — but where could they go? The nations of the world were clanging shut their

This paper is excerpted from a longer article of the same title that appeared in the *Canadian Historical Review* (June 1979). It is reprinted here with the permission of the University of Toronto Press. Complete documentation may be found in the original. The authors are indebted to Robert F. Harney of the Multicultural Historical Society of Ontario, David Rome of the Canadian Jewish Archives, Laurence Tapper of the Canadian Ethnic Archives, the Social Sciences and Humanities Research Council, and the Guggenheim Memorial Foundation for their encouragement and assistance.

gates before these helpless men, women, and children. Germany was determined to throw their Jews out; everyone else seemed just as determined not to let them in.

A poignant joke of the time says it all. A Jew wishing to travel goes to a Berlin travel agent who places a globe in front of him, whirls it, and says, "Choose". After studying the globe for a short time, the Jew looks up with pained expression and asks, "Do you have anything else?"

When the *St. Louis* reached Havana on 30 May, the Cuban government refused to recognize the entrance visas. The search for a haven now began in earnest. Argentina, Uruguay, Paraguay, and Panama were approached, in vain, by various Jewish organizations. Within two days all the countries of Latin America had rejected entreaties to allow these Jews to land. On 2 June the *St. Louis* was forced to leave Havana harbour. The last hope seemed to be either Canada or the United States.

The latter did not even bother sending a reply. Instead it sent a gunboat to shadow the *St. Louis* as it made its way north. The American coast guard had been ordered to make certain that the *St. Louis* stayed far enough offshore so that it could not be run aground nor could any of its frantic passengers attempt to swim ashore. Now only Canada remained uncommitted.

The plight of the *St. Louis* had touched some influential Canadians. On 7 June several of these sent a telegram to Prime Minister Mackenzie King begging that he show "true Christian charity" and offer the homeless exiles sanctuary in Canada.[1]

Jewish refugees were far from the prime minister's mind at this time. He was in Washington accompanying the royal family on the final leg of its triumphant tour of North America. The *St. Louis*, he felt, was not a Canadian problem. Nonetheless, he asked O.D. Skelton, the undersecretary of state for external affairs, to consult the acting prime minister, Ernest Lapointe, and the director of immigration, F.C. Blair, for their advice.[2]

Both these men were known for their staunch opposition to Jewish immigration to Canada. They did not disappoint King.

Lapointe stated that he was "emphatically opposed" to the admission of the *St. Louis* passengers, while Blair, the bureaucrat, claimed that these refugees did not qualify under immigration laws for admission and that, in any case, Canada had already done too much for the Jews.[3] Why should Canada "go out of her way", he asked Skelton, to allow in people who would likely "smuggle themselves" across the border to the United States? Blair's great fear, however, was that if these Jews were to find a home they would "likely be followed by other shiploads". No country, he added, could "open its doors wide enough to take in the hundreds of thousands of Jewish people who want to leave Europe: *the line must be drawn somewhere*".[4]

Canadian Immigration Policy in the 1930s

In 1936 Chaim Weizman wrote: "The world seems to be divided into two parts — those places where the Jew cannot live, and those where they cannot enter." Canada fell into the latter category. Of the more than 800,000 Jews seeking refuge from the Third Reich in the years from 1933 to 1939, Canada found room within her borders for approximately 4,000. In a world that was decidedly inhospitable to refugees, Canada was no exception. Yet even by the standard of the time, Canada stood virtually alone in the niggardliness of her contribution. Argentina, for example, admitted 22,000; Australia 10,000 and was preparing to receive 15,000 more when war broke out; Brazil 20,000; China 15,000; Great Britain 85,000; Palestine 100,000; the United States 140,000; even penurious Mexico and Colombia had each accepted about 20,000.

That Jews were not welcome in Canada during the 1930s is not surprising; no one else was either. With a third of its people out of work, Canada was understandably not receptive to the notion of accepting more job-hungry immigrants. That the economic consequences of the Depression throttled immigration cannot be denied. What should be stressed, however, is that the Depression also afforded the dramatic opportunity for Canadian officials to complete a process of restriction begun in the boom years of the 1920s.

Canadian immigration policy had always been as ethnically selective as it was economically self-serving. When economic necessity dictated the admission of non-British and non-American immigrants, it was always in descending order of ethnic preference. Following British and American immigrants, preference was given Northern Europeans and then Central Europeans. At the bottom were the Jews, Orientals, and Blacks.[5] Those "non-preferred immigrants" were acceptable as long as they were out of sight, risking life and limb in the mines and smelters of the West and North, holed up in lumber camps deep in the forests, or farming the more marginal areas of the western wheat frontier. Those who escaped this life for perhaps the even worse one in Canada's urban centres to compete for jobs with native or British-born artisans were less acceptable. And to immigration officials, the worst culprits were the Jews. Jews, according to Blair, were "city people". To almost every request to admit Jewish farmers or agricultural workers, Blair had the same response: it was impossible to keep them on the farm or in the bush. Every attempt to do so had failed. Jewish workers, he claimed, could not "eat Gentile food" and so took the "earliest opportunity" to leave for the city "which is about the only place [they] can find [their] fellow countrymen".[6]

The onset of the Depression gave the government the opportunity to complete drawing the restrictionist circle around Canada. In 1930, an order-in-council (PC 1957) was introduced allowing in only those immigrants with enough capital to establish and maintain themselves on farms. In the following year, another order-in-council (PC 659) effectively banned all nonagricultural immigrants who were of non-British or non-American stock. For all intents and purposes, just at the time when she was most needed, Canada shut herself off from the rest of the world. For the remainder of the decade — and indeed beyond — a determined Canadian government fought every attempt by the wretched European refugees to breach this protective wall of orders-in-council.

The person entrusted with the task of ensuring that there was no breach was Frederick Charles Blair. As director of the Immigration Branch of the Department of Mines and Resources during these years, Blair made almost all of the decisions — no matter how small — concerning who got into Canada. And from the point of view of European Jewry, this was most unfortunate. Just when they most needed a friend at the gate, they had an enemy; instead of the philo-Semite they required, they had an anti-Semite; instead of the humanitarian, they got a narrow-minded bureaucrat. According to those who knew him, Blair was a tough administrator who stuck to the rules — which is not so surprising since he drafted most of them himself. Blair was, as James Gibson, a Department of External Affairs official, recalled, "the single most difficult individual I had to deal with the whole time I was a public servant. He was a holy terror!"[7] Perhaps this was why he stayed in his job for so long; he was precisely the man the King government wanted in this position. His inflexibility, fetish for regulations, and unchallenged control over immigration matters were a convenience to an administration that had no intention of allowing in Jewish refugees but wished to avoid the stigma of not doing so. Though Thomas Crerar was ostensibly the minister responsible for immigration, in fact Blair made policy and implemented it. Crerar knew little of the workings of the Immigration Branch and cared even less. He relied almost totally on its director for advice.[8]

To Blair, the term "refugee" was a code word for Jews. Unless "safeguards" were adopted, he warned Crerar, Canada was in danger of being "flooded with Jewish people".[9] His task, as he saw it, was to make sure that the "safeguards" did not fail. Indeed, he was inordinately proud of his success in keeping out Jews. As he put it:

> Pressure on the part of Jewish people to get into Canada has never been greater than it is now and I am glad to be able to add, after 35 years experience here, that it was never so well controlled.[10]

Blair expressed a strong personal distaste for Jews and especially for "certain of their habits". He saw them as unassimilable, as people apart "who can organize [their] affairs better than other people" and therefore accomplish more.[11] He complained bitterly that Jews were "utterly selfish in their attempts to force through a permit for the admission of relatives or friends. They do not believe," he added, "that 'No' means more than 'Perhaps'." Furthermore, Jews, he lamented, "make any kind of promise to get the door open but . . . never cease their agitation until they get in the whole lot".[12]

Behind these Jewish attempts to get their coreligionists into the country somehow, Blair saw a conspiracy "to bring immigration regulations into disrepute and create an atmosphere favourable to those who cannot comply with the law". As he commiserated with the traffic manager of the Canadian Pacific Railway, "If there is any surer way to close the door in their own face, I do not know of it."[13]

It seems that Blair's contempt for the Jews was boundless. Only a short time after the outbreak of hostilities in Europe in 1939, Blair confided to his immigration commissioner in London, "Someone has facetiously said that numbers of our Jewish refugees lustfully sing 'Onward Christian Soldiers' but are very content to stay here and grab up all opportunities."[14] In a revealing letter to a strong opponent of Jewish immigration Blair wrote:

> I suggested recently to three Jewish gentlemen with whom I am well acquainted, that it might be a very good thing if they would call a conference and have a day of humiliation and prayer which might profitably be extended for a week or more where they would honestly try to answer the question of why they are so unpopular almost everywhere. . . . I often think that instead of persecution it would be far better if we more often told them frankly why many of them are unpopular. If they would divest themselves of certain of their habits I am sure they could be just as popular in Canada as our Scandinavians.[15]

Though it was Blair who gave the final interpretation of government regulations and who acted as the de facto judge and jury on individual requests for admission, to blame him alone for Canada's response to the refugee crisis would be both overly simplistic and incorrect; after all, he was only a civil servant, albeit a powerful one. As a functionary he simply reflected the wishes of his superiors; it was they who were ultimately responsible for government policy. Not to accept refugees was a political decision, not a bureaucratic one. It was Mackenzie King and his cabinet who, in the final analysis, must shoulder the responsibility.

Early Jewish Attempts to Aid the Refugees

Once Canadian Jews realized that attempting to deal with immigration officials was hopeless, they began flexing their political muscle. Only when it was too late did they discover how flabby it was. Taking charge of the pressure campaign was the organization that was generally recognized as the representative voice of the community on social and political matters, the Canadian Jewish Congress (CJC). Founded in 1919, by the mid-1930s the Congress was a weak and disorganized body. Only in the latter part of 1938, when the wealthy industrialist Samuel Bronfman became active — he was elected its president in January 1939 — did the Congress become a credible and weighty vehicle for Jewish interests. Indeed, until then it was the Jewish Immigrant Aid Society (JIAS), an organization founded by Congress in June 1920, that served as the voice of the community on matters affecting immigration and that did much to help individual immigrants.[16]

By default, therefore, the task of putting forth the Jewish position fell on the shoulders of Jewish members of Parliament. In the Liberal sweep of the 1935 election, three Jews had won seats: two Liberals, Sam Jacobs from Montreal, the CJC president, and Sam Factor from Toronto, and one representative of the Co-operative Commonwealth Federation (CCF), A.A. Heaps from Winnipeg. The Jewish community saw the 1935 Liberal victory as a harbinger of better things. After all, it was the Bennett government that had introduced the restrictive orders-in-council and snubbed various Jewish delegations attempting to have these orders moderated.

These hopes, however, were dashed almost immediately following the elections. In a meeting with Crerar, Jacobs and Benjamin Robinson, president of JIAS, were told that there would be no exception made for German Jews. Unless applicants met the requirements for immigration — that is, unless they had sufficient capital to establish a successful farm — they would not be allowed in under any circumstances.[17]

Crerar kept his promise. For the next two years almost no Jewish refugees arrived in Canada. And those few who did manage to come entered under specific orders-in-council exempting them from the usual immigration requirements. Most of these were relatives of Canadian Jews. Some orders-in-council, however, were granted as favours to prominent government supporters — including Sam Jacobs — to distribute to a fortunate few in the Jewish community.[18] It was a cynical activity, but it worked. For the most part Canadian Jews, though restive, remained loyal to the Liberal government. They had little choice. Making up just over 1 per cent of the population, Canadian Jews knew they did not have the power to change government policy. And until they did, they would accept what crumbs were thrown their way. After all, saving a few lives was better than saving none.

The CJC did establish a refugee committee in 1937, but its main function was to work with railway colonization officials to help in the settlement of the handful of Jewish farmers able to break through into Canada. However, even this activity was shortlived for in April 1938, at the behest of Blair who did not believe that Jews could be farmers, railway colonization agents in Europe were told to allow in as few Jewish "agriculturalists" as possible.[19] Thus, when a German Jew, Hans Heinemann, applied to enter Canada as a farmer, he was told by an overenthusiastic agent of the Canadian Pacific Railway in Hamburg that Jews were no longer being allowed into Canada.[20]

The Calling of the Evian Conference

In March 1938, just when Canada was further restricting Jewish immigration, Hitler marched into Austria and several hundred thousand more Jews became refugees, some — those who had escaped from Germany — for the second time. To quiet the storm of protest raised by more liberal elements in the United States, President Franklin Roosevelt took the bold step of issuing an invitation to most of the nations of the world to meet together to discuss possible solutions to the refugee problem. When the formal invitation to attend this conference arrived in Ottawa in late March, Canadian officials were decidedly uncomfortable. Even though the Americans had assured Canada that no country would be expected to "receive a greater number of emigrants than is permitted by its existing legislation" and that private organizations would be expected to fund this emigration,[21] the Canadians felt Roosevelt was baiting a trap. Once committed to attending the conference, the government would be expected to do something to alleviate the refugee problem. And this, King dreaded, meant "admitting numbers of Jews".[22] His fears were reinforced by Skelton, who warned that the publicity generated by the conference would likely result in strong "domestic pressure" in Canada to do something for the Jews.[23]

The prime minister of Canada was obsessed with the notion that the admission of Jewish refugees might destroy his country. As he confided to his diary, "We must . . . seek to keep this part of the Continent free from unrest and from too great an intermixture of foreign strains of blood." Nothing was to be gained, he believed, "by creating an internal problem in an effort to meet an international one". Allowing Jewish refugees into Canada, he had told his cabinet, might cause riots and would surely exacerbate relations between the federal government and the provinces. In effect, any action permitting an appreciable number of Jews to settle in Canada would, in King's mind, undermine the unity of the nation. This was no time for Canada to act on "humanitarian grounds". Rather, said the prime minister, Canada must be guided by "realities" and political considerations.[24]

The realities King had in mind were the attitudes towards refugees in general and Jews in particular within Quebec. He was absolutely convinced that that province would react violently to the admission of Jewish refugees.

He had reason for his belief. Almost every French-language newspaper had warned the government against opening Canada's doors to European Jews. As *Le Devoir* put it, "Why allow in Jewish refugees? . . . The Jewish shopkeeper on St. Lawrence Boulevard does nothing to increase our natural resources."[25] And this statement was mild compared with vicious anti-Semitic utterances appearing regularly in such papers as *La Nation, L'Action Catholique,* and *L'Action Nationnale*. As well, many French-Canadian politicians spoke out — both within and without the confines of Parliament — against Jewish immigration.[26]

The prime minister and more especially his Quebec lieutenant, Ernest Lapointe, were also aware of the grievous situation in which the province's Liberal party found itself. Thrown out of office in 1936 by the Union Nationale under Maurice Duplessis, the Quebec Liberal party was badly split and in a state of disarray. Anything that might further weaken it, King and Lapointe felt, would have to be avoided — no matter the cost. Allowing in Jewish refugees would, at least to Lapointe's mind, play into the hands of Duplessis' nationalist forces and further weaken Liberalism in Quebec. And King believed that "if the Liberal party was to remain a national party", he had no alternative but to accept the views of Lapointe and his French-Canadian colleagues in the House.[27] The prime minister sincerely believed that illiberal policies were acceptable so long as the basic Liberal objective — national unity — was maintained.[28]

Largely because of this hostility in Quebec, King was reluctant to attend the conference on refugees. No one in Canadian government circles was enthusiastic about attending, least of all the prime minister. Who knew what evil would emanate from this conference? A country — and a prime minister — wedded to the doctrine of no commitments could hardly relish the thought of a conference in which some sort of Canadian commitment would be expected.

As King and his cabinet dallied, Blair was increasingly active. At the behest of Skelton, he drafted a response rejecting the invitation. Attending this meeting, Blair said, might involve "the admission to Canada of many who by training and manner of life are not fitted for the development of any of our primary industries, but would add to the congestion and competition of our cities".[29] More to the point, it was not "feasible", he said, "to encourage the influx of immigrants of one race and not of others". He privately told Skelton that it was unfair "to let down the immigration barriers for the benefit of any particular race or class".[30] Personally, Blair did not feel that the problem was all that serious. As he put it, "No problem exists except for the Jewish people," and the refugee situation, he added, was much worse immediately following the First World War. He warned that the government's first priority must now be to decide "whether Canada can afford to open the door to more Jewish people than we are now receiving" since "there is going to be a general Jewish drive for admissions to other countries".[31]

What apparently most disturbed Blair was the possibility of a successful conference:

> If the nations now asked to cooperate to save the Jews of Germany and Austria, manage by sacrifice to accomplish this purpose it will please the Germans who want to get rid of this group . . . and it will encourage other nations to do likewise and this is probably the greatest danger. Can immigration countries afford to encourage such an eventuality? It is akin in a sense to the paying of ransom to Chinese bandits.[32]

Clearly the real threat to Blair was that the Eastern European countries, such as Poland, Hungary, and Rumania, would learn from the German precedent and attempt to deport their unwanted Jews.

It was not until the latter part of April that King finally made his decision. In fact, Canada probably had no choice. As Skelton warned the prime minister, "It would not look too well to be the only country, except Fascist Italy, declining even to sit on a Committee."[33] On 26 April the Canadian government officially announced that it would attend the conference, which was to be held in the small French resort town of Evian on the Swiss border. (Switzerland had already rejected the honour of holding the meeting on her territory.) At the same time King informed the Americans that he thought it wrong to encourage countries such as Germany that were trying "to throw upon other countries the task of solving their internal difficulties".[34]

The news of the Evian Conference activated the leaders of Canadian Jewry. They felt the time was opportune for some serious, though necessarily secret, lobbying. The Jewish community was in an apprehensive mood. Yet the Congress executive felt that discussions with government officials were "a matter of extreme delicacy". As one CJC leader warned his officers in western Canada, "I have in mind that we refrain from mass meetings, publicity and noise, because such methods would nullify what we have in mind."[35] What Congress officials feared most of all was that the demonstrations might both alienate the government and create an anti-Semitic backlash throughout the country. As the CJC put it:

> Experience concerning the refugee situation has convinced us that too much publicity has always proven detrimental to any request for the widening of the doors for the entry of our co-religionists to Canada. . . . In Quebec any public agitation for the entry of Jews would bring with it . . . a flood of counter agitation.[36]

The Congress role was not to mobilize Jewish opinion but to monitor it — to guard against any outburst, spontaneous or otherwise, that might rebound against the community at large.

Again it was the Jewish MPs who were the most active. They had lobbied unceasingly to get the government to go to Evian. They had met with Crerar in a vain attempt to have the immigration regulations modified. Finally, with their colleagues J.S. Woodsworth and Colonel A. Vien, they met with King and argued vigorously for a more sympathetic approach to the refugee question.[37]

King offered his sympathy but little else. He agreed, however, to set up a special committee of cabinet to look at the problem. This proved to be a hollow gesture since of the five ministers appointed, two, Lapointe and Fernand Rinfret, were openly hostile to Jewish immigration. Indeed, when this committee met with the Jewish MPs, Lapointe pointedly refused to attend.[38] Jacobs, Factor, and Heaps met privately with the two French-Canadian cabinet ministers and vainly pleaded with them to be less inflexible. Even promises by the Jewish MPs that no Jewish refugees would be permitted to settle in Quebec failed to budge them. Rinfret and more significantly Lapointe were unyielding in their determination not to allow Jewish refugees into Canada.[39] The cabinet committee met several more times, achieved nothing, and disbanded.

Meanwhile, without much enthusiasm, the Canadian government began preparing for the Evian Conference. As Canada's representatives, King appointed the Canadian delegate to the League of Nations, Hume Wrong, and the commissioner of immigration in London, William R. Little. Wrong's instructions were succinct: listen, make notes, say as little as possible, and under no circumstances make any promises or commitments.[40]

Similarly, in his instructions to Little, Blair suggested that he go on the offensive and point out to the other delegates that Canada had done much more than was required to help solve the Jewish refugee problem. In an attempt to halt the Jewish exodus from Germany in its entirety, Blair suggested that since Jews were being robbed of both their assets and their citizenship, "the two essentials of immigration", Little should approach the other delegates to persuade their governments to take a united stand against accepting the immigrants "without either capital or recognized citizenship". And in case Little missed the point, in a personal letter two days later, Blair emphasized that there was "not much enthusiasm in many quarters here for any increase in our Jewish immigration".[41]

To make certain that whatever concession that might be forced on Canada at Evian was kept a minimum, Blair found a method that was simple and clever. He delayed the admission of the handful of Jewish refugees with substantial amounts of capital whose applications had already been approved by his department but whose names had not yet been forwarded to cabinet for the necessary order-in-council. If Canada were forced to make a gesture, only then would the names be sent forward. Until then, however, these helpless Jews would have to wait.[42]

As delegates to the conference began arriving, Wrong smelled a rat. The meeting, he predicted, was "going to be a most unpleasant affair" and his participation in it was "an unwelcome duty". The proceedings, he feared, looked "very amateurish", and the entire concept clearly was "not the product of any well thought-out scheme" but simply "one of Mr. Roosevelt's sudden generous impulses". If the Americans were seriously concerned with helping refugees, he wondered, why would they send as their delegates Myron Taylor, "a steel tycoon", and two minor foreign service officers, one of whom was "a capable authority on the administration of the quota law"? Though he realized that there was not much support for the admission of refugees into Canada, he begged the prime minister not to make his instructions "entirely negative".[43]

King ignored Wrong's plea. Rather, in a strongly worded letter he reminded the Canadian delegate that Canada was at Evian only to "exchange information". Furthermore, Wrong was put on notice that if the Americans made concrete proposals to solve the refugee problem, he should oppose them while trying neither to "lead in this opposition" nor to be "obstructionist".[44]

To forestall any American action, King forcefully informed Washington that Canada would neither support nor be a member of any committee that would formulate and carry out a long-range program to solve the refugee crisis. Canada, he reminded the Americans, could make no commitments to accept any refugees as this would "raise real difficulties from the point of view of the Canadian Immigration Service".[45] Though King was concerned with the plight of German Jewry, he seemed even more concerned over the administrative problems of Canadian immigration officers.

The prime minister had already been informed by Blair that, from the point of view of the Immigration Branch, accepting German Jews would only exacerbate the situation. As Blair told Skelton, "The Jews of Canada will not be satisfied unless the door is kept open in some way to all the Jews from other countries." Canadian Jews, he added, were largely from Eastern Europe and would apply unremitting pressure to admit fellow Jews from this area. "We will not", he warned, "satisfy Canadian Jewry by a special effort limited to the Jews of Germany and Austria."[46]

As soon as the conference began, Wrong realized that Canadian worries had been groundless. The American delegate, Myron Taylor, was the first speaker. Instead of the magnanimous gesture all the representatives expected — and feared — the contribution of the United States government to solving the refugee crisis, Taylor announced, would be to fill its entire German-Austrian quota of 27,730. The delegates sat stunned following Taylor's speech. The nations of the world had been mobilized for this? The collective sigh of relief from the assembled representatives was almost audible as Taylor sat down. For the Jews of Europe, Taylor's speech was a cruel letdown; for everyone else at Evian it was a godsend. It was clear that the Americans saw Evian as an exercise in public relations; they had no concrete proposals to solve — or even alleviate — the crisis. If the Americans were going to do nothing, it was hardly likely that anyone else would do anything either.

Sure enough, for the next few days delegate after delegate arose and announced that his nation was doing all it could to solve the crisis and that stringent immigration laws prohibited it from doing more. In a short speech, Wrong echoed these sentiments, announcing that Canada had much sympathy for the impossible situation in which the refugees found themselves but that it could do no more than it was already doing — which was a great deal. "Certain classes of agriculturalists", he said, were welcome; everyone else was out of luck.[47]

The tragic failure of Evian exposed the impotence of world Jewry in general and Canadian Jewry in particular. Not only did the latter have no input to its own government's policy: it was not even told what this policy was. Indeed, only days before the conference began, a JIAS official in Montreal had complained to his colleagues in Paris, "It is quite possible that more will be found about the intentions of our Government in France than we learn on this side."[48]

Canadian Jews had not expected much from their government, but even they were disappointed in how little they received. As the president of JIAS lamented, "It is quite obvious that the most that can be expected of Canada is to be more lenient in its application of the present regulations."[49] But even this was a false hope.

Just one month after Evian, on 26 August, Crerar met with Blair and other ranking immigration authorities to review the government's position on refugees. Clearly Crerar had been moved by the tales of horror emanating from Germany and was anxious to do something to aid the refugees. The minister told his officials that, while he thought "great care should be taken, we probably should admit more of these unfortunate people on humanitarian grounds".[50] The well-meaning but naive Crerar was no match for Blair and his experts. By the time the meeting was over the thoroughly confused Crerar had agreed, in fact, to tighten the restrictions even further.

What is perhaps most appalling about Blair's machinations is his admission to an Anglican clergyman not long afterwards that for some time he had been convinced that the destruction of European Jewry was at hand. In an all-too-prophetic letter to Canon W.W. Judd of Toronto, Blair stated that he feared that Jews were facing virtual "extinction" in Europe. Allowing more of them into Canada, he informed Judd, would not solve the problem.[51]

For A.A. Heaps, who had for some time counselled Canadian Jewry to remain silent and to trust its leaders, the government's response to Evian was the last straw. Screwing up his courage, he wrote a passionate, bitter letter to his friend Mackenzie King, stating that he had been betrayed by a duplicitous government whose "oft-repeated promise" of allowing a reasonable number of refugees to come to Canada had proved to be a hoax. Though Evian had been traumatic for Heaps, he felt that one last desperate appeal to King might shame the prime minister into some action. As he put it:

> The existing regulations are probably the most stringent to be found anywhere in the whole world. If refugees have no money they are barred because they are poor, if they have fairly substantial sums, they are often refused admittance on the most flimsy pretext. All I say of existing regulations is that they are inhuman and anti-Christian. . . . Practically every nation in the world is allowing a limited number to enter their countries. . . . The lack of action by the Canadian government is leaving an unfortunate impression. . . . I regret to state that the sentiment is gaining ground that anti-Semitic influences are responsible for the government's refusal to allow refugees to come to Canada.[52]

King shunted the letter off to Crerar and Blair for their consideration. Heaps did not get a reply.[53] His was the last serious attempt by a Jewish MP to influence the government. Seriously weakened by the death of Sam Jacobs in late September, the contingent of Jewish MPs was no longer a factor in the battle for the admission of refugees.

The Reaction to "Kristallnacht"

Within a few weeks it hardly seemed to matter. Time had run out for German Jewry. On 9 and 10 November occurred the worst pogrom in modern world history to that time. *Kristallnacht* was incited by the government to terrorize the Jews. Countless synagogues, Jewish stores and homes were plundered and razed. Men, women, and children were wrenched from their homes, beaten, shot, or dragged off to concentration camps. Scores were killed, hundreds injured, thousands arrested.

These tragic events finally touched the prime minister of Canada. "The sorrows which the Jews have had to bear at this time," he wrote in his diary, "are almost beyond comprehension.

Something," he added, "will have to be done by our country."[54] Coincidentally, on the following day, he personally shared in Jewish grief as he attended the funeral of Mrs. Heaps. Again, he was overwhelmed by the breadth of the tragedy that was about to envelop the Jews. Writing in his diary that night, he noted that it would be "difficult politically", and his cabinet might oppose him, but he was going to "fight" for the admission of some Jewish refugees since it was "right and just, and Christian".[55]

The following week, while King was in Washington for talks with Roosevelt concerning the upcoming visit of the royal family, the conversation turned to the ghastly lot of Jewish refugees. While the president, Myron Taylor, and Cordell Hull discussed what could be done, King remained silent. In his own words, he "just listened". Yet during the conversation, he told his diary, he "felt more than ever" that since countries with "more crowded areas", such as Great Britain and the United States, were accepting refugees, Canada must open her doors. On his return to Ottawa he wrote that he had told the governor general, Lord Tweedsmuir, that on humanitarian grounds alone Canada should allow in some refugees and warned that "if we tried to keep our country to ourselves, we would lose it altogether some day". It seemed at long last that Canada was prepared to do something for the desperate Jews of Germany.[56]

It was precisely at this time that the Jews of Canada mobilized for one last dramatic effort to help save Germany Jewry. The reports of *Kristallnacht* had driven the community into a state of frenzied activity. On 14 November, at a special emergency meeting, the executive council of the CJC decided to proclaim Sunday, 20 November, "a day of mourning" at which memorial meetings would be held across the country. It instructed its local organizations to ensure that these meetings were "non-sectarian", that non-Jewish community leaders played a "prominent role", and that most of the speakers were Gentile. These meetings were to "capitalize on the sympathy" felt towards the helpless victims of Nazi brutality and to "impress" the government with the fact that public opinion was in favour of admitting some of them to Canada. In addition, each community was sent a draft of a protest resolution that should be adopted at its meeting and forwarded to Ottawa.[57]

Surprisingly, with only five days to organize, the Congress achieved dramatic results. Across Canada, from Glace Bay, Nova Scotia, to Victoria, British Columbia, mass meetings were held and resolutions passed pleading with the government to open its heart and, more especially, its gates. And at almost every one of these meetings the featured speaker was a non-Jew. Mayors, judges, MPs, and businessmen took their places on the platforms in support of the refugees. Some 20,000 persons participated in Toronto, 4,000 in Winnipeg, 600 in Quebec City, 200 in Vegreville, Alberta, 800 in Niagara Falls, 1,200 in Kingston, 300 in Humboldt, Saskatchewan. Telegrams, resolutions, petitions, and letters poured into the offices of the prime minister and various members of Parliament. The demonstrations were, in the words of the Toronto *Globe and Mail*, an example of the "brotherhood of man asserting itself". Scores of newspapers across the nation, with the single exception of the French press in Quebec, called for a more generous policy towards refugees.[58]

To capitalize on this vast outpouring of public support, a high-powered delegation of Canadian Jews arrived in Ottawa on 22 November to meet with the prime minister to plead the case for Jewish refugees. Unfortunately, it seemed they had come too late, for on the day they arrived in Ottawa, the cabinet took up the refugee question. Despite King's urging to make some "provision" for refugees, the Quebec ministers, led by Lapointe, were solidly opposed to change. Rather than press the issue and risk alienating Quebec, King announced to the press that the whole question needed further study.[59] This decision prompted the first serious signs of dissension within the Jewish community. The *Hebrew Journal* of Toronto castigated the Congress leadership for being too timid for too long. It called for more militant action against a government that had humiliated the Jewish community by "shamelessly" making decisions concerning refugees the day before a delegation of Jewish leaders was to meet with the prime minister to make its representation.[60]

It was a shaken group of Jews who were ushered into King's office on 23 November. It included both Jewish MPs and the leaders of all the important community organizations, including the CJC, the JIAS, and the Zionist Organization of Canada. They pleaded with King and Crerar to open up Canada's doors by a crack and to admit 10,000 refugees whom the community would guarantee would not become public charges. They were politely rebuffed. King pointed out that unemployment in Canada was still high and that his first duty was "the avoidance of strife . . . maintaining the unity of the country", and fighting "the forces of separatism". He sympathized with the refugees, he said, but he had "to consider the constituencies and the views of those supporting the Government". Crerar added that there were great administrative problems involved and in any case Canada had already accepted three hundred refugees over the past year. With that the delegation was excused.[61]

On the following day King again met his cabinet and, as he recorded in his diary, he once more asked them to adopt a "liberal attitude", to act as the "conscience of the nation" even though it might not be "politically most expedient", and to offer some aid to Jewish refugees. There was no response to his appeal. The cabinet, according to the prime minister, feared "the political consequences of any help to the Jews". What it was prepared to do, after some discussion, was to help find a home for these Jews "in some [other] land". King then dropped the issue as he "did not wish to press the matter any further".[62]

For Canadian Jews, the cabinet decision was a shock; for their leaders, it was devastating. Following a week of mass organization, demonstration, and protest, a week in which almost every English-language newspaper in the nation had condemned the government for its timidity, a week in which thousands had signed petitions demanding a more generous policy towards the refugees, it had generally been assumed that the cabinet response would be positive. Especially mortified were Jewish leaders who had come to the prime minister with what they considered a minimal package that would cost the government nothing: allowing in a mere 10,000 refugees over a five-year period with the

Jewish community guaranteeing that they would never become "burdens on Canadian society". The prime minister had rejected every proposal.

On 1 December, it seemed as if the Jewish community had won over its most important convert. On that day during a cabinet meeting, Thomas Crerar, obviously troubled by his government's behaviour, announced to his stunned colleagues that he was prepared to recommend the admission of 10,000 refugees. The cabinet would not budge. Disassociating himself from the hapless immigration minister, whose proposal he thought was made "without consideration" of the problems involved, King found a convenient solution. He suggested to his colleagues that they use the British North America Act to justify their inaction. He would publicly announce that nothing could be done for German Jews until the provinces were consulted, since immigration legislation was concurrent. At the same time, he chided Crerar, telling him to do his homework and to prepare a statement that the cabinet would discuss.[63]

On 13 December, the cabinet took up the refugee issue once again. Aware that he had no support either from his cabinet colleagues or his departmental officials, Crerar read a statement, drafted by Blair, that said nothing about the admission of 10,000 refugees but simply recommended the easing, ever so slightly, of the present immigration regulations.[64] After straying somewhat, Crerar had again been brought back into line. A relieved cabinet accepted the new position: not to change the regulations but to interpret them "as liberally as possible". What this meant in practice, according to the prime minister, was that Jews already landed in Canada as tourists would be allowed to remain. However, no more Jewish refugees would be admitted to Canada "lest it might foment an anti-Semitic problem . . . and [create] a new problem".[65] Thus, after months of wrestling with the question of Jewish refugees, the cabinet had at long last found an answer: keep them out.

Ironically, at the same meeting at which it decided not to allow Jews in, the cabinet agreed to permit the entry of Czechs and Sudeten Germans since they were underwritten by a

$500,000 gift from the British, French, and Czechoslovakian governments and since, in King's words, they "had been sacrificed for the sake of the world's peace of which [Canadians] were beneficiaries".[66]

Meanwhile, the Canadian high commissioner in London was using what influence he had to make sure that restrictions on Jews entering Canada remained. For Jewish refugees anxious to come to Canada, it was unfortunate that the Canadian representative in London was, to say the least, no partisan of Jewish immigration. Vincent Massey, the prominent scion of the wealthy Massey family, had, in fact, become a fringe member of the aristocratic, largely pro-German and anti-Semitic Cliveden set centred around Lord and Lady Astor.[67] Though he was much too Anglophilic to have the confidence or even the trust of Mackenzie King — indeed, the prime minister had once told Massey to his face that he was "quite wrong on his views of most things" — his recommendations still had weight with the government, especially when they were in line with policies being considered by cabinet.[68] And on the question of Jewish refugees, the positions coincided.

Massey was enthusiastic about the anti-Nazi Sudetens, most of whom were Social Democrats or Catholics. Many of them, he told the prime minister, were skilled craftsmen, professionals, and farmers — exactly the type of settlers Canada craved. And perhaps even better, only a small percentage of them were Jews. He immediately saw an opportunity to score some public relations points for Canada at minimal cost. Would it not be a wonderful tactic, he suggested to King, to accept "as many as possible Aryan Sudeten Germans". These, he stated, were surely "more desirable" than other refugees. But more to the point: "If we could take a substantial number of them it would put us in a much stronger position in relation to later appeals from and on behalf of non-Aryans." He also pleaded that the government consider Sudeten Germans "quite separately from other refugees . . . as they include . . . many persons who would be much more desirable as Canadian settlers and much more likely to succeed in our country than certain other types of refugees".[69] And in case the prime minister missed the point, Massey emphasized that "these refugees are of a superior type to certain other categories of refugees who are engaging our attention".[70]

The Months before the War

By the onset of 1939 an unofficial unholy triumvirate had been forged in the Immigration Service, the cabinet, and, to a much lesser degree, the Department of External Affairs against refugees in general and Jewish refugees in particular. In Immigration, the intransigent and morally obtuse Blair gave vent to his anti-Semitism by placing every possible bureaucratic encumbrance in the path of refugees. In cabinet, Ernest Lapointe scuttled any cabinet backsliding — including that of the prime minister — on the refugee issue. In External Affairs, Vincent Massey flirted with the aristocratic crowd in London while doing what he could to keep Jews out of Canada. Individually, each had significant power; collectively, they seemed beyond challenge. Each had his own sphere of influence, but on the refugee issue these spheres overlapped. Though there is no evidence that they consulted on this issue — and they likely did not — what united them was a common conviction: Canada did not need more Jews.

Though the prime minister was not a prisoner of this anti-Jewish coterie, he could not help but be influenced by it. When the foremost immigration authority in Canada, the leading French-Canadian politician in the country, and the nation's senior foreign diplomat spoke, he listened, especially since they were all saying the same thing. King himself vacillated. At times his humanitarian and religious instincts led him to argue the refugee case; yet always his political instincts overcame these arguments. His sympathy for the refugees was genuine. He sincerely wanted to find them a home — anywhere but in Canada.

Above all else, King was committed to keeping Canada united. Allowing in Jews, he feared, would disrupt that unity, and not only in Quebec.[71] Anti-Semitism, though perhaps most overt in that province, was prevalent throughout English-speaking Canada as well. Jewish quotas existed in various professions, universities, medical schools, and industries. Jews were restricted from buying property in some areas, from holidaying at some resorts, from joining many private clubs or using their recreational facilities, and even from sitting on the boards of various charitable, educational, financial, and business organizations.[72] Anti-Jewish sentiments were being voiced regularly, and with impunity, throughout these years by many respectable newspapers, politicians, businessmen, and churchmen and by leading officials of such groups as the Canadian Corps Association, the Orange Order, the Knights of Columbus, and prominent farm and business organizations. There had even been some violence as Jew and anti-Semite confronted one another on the streets of Toronto, Winnipeg, and other Canadian cities.

If it is possible to overemphasize the extent of anti-Semitism in Canada at this time, it is not possible to ignore it. It existed, and King was well aware that it did. Any move to admit Jewish refugees, he feared, might cost him political support. Although some organizations and some high-placed members of some religious groups, such as the Anglican and United churches, actively campaigned on behalf of Jewish refugees, most Canadians seemed indifferent to the suffering of German Jews and hostile to admitting some of them to Canada.

Nevertheless, despite all the obstacles, Jewish leaders persevered; they had no choice. In December 1938, all the disparate refugee activities of the Jewish community were united into a single organization, the Canadian Committee for Jewish Refugees (CCJR) headed by the Congress president, Samuel Bronfman.

Buoyed by numerous supporting editorials, the new refugee committee met with government officials in late February. Convinced that there was now a ground swell of popular support in English Canada, the CCJR fully expected "a definite and favourable decision". Though polite and sympathetic, the government was unyielding. Indeed, a disingenuous Blair told the delegates that with respect to the Sudeten refugees, there would be no discrimination against Jews, "a number of whom would be included in the allotment".[73] Two weeks later Crerar announced in Parliament that after a careful study of every family, he could assure the House that "probably 95 percent of these people are Roman Catholics".[74] Quebec could hardly complain, nor could Vincent Massey.

The meeting with Crerar and Blair finally disabused Jewish leaders of any notion they still cherished that the government would change its policy. King saw no need for any shift. He felt that whatever popular support there was for refugees in English Canada was ephemeral. As well, with an election in the offing, could he dare alienate his base in Quebec? As he explained to a refugee sympathizer, the issue was "the most baffling of our international problems". He promised to make a "contribution to its solution" but feared that by doing so he might create a "condition which it may be more difficult to meet than the one it is intended to cure". Allowing in Jewish refugees, he dreaded, would undermine the Canadian unity he had fought so hard to maintain.[75]

It was now almost too much for Canadian Jews to bear. There was no longer any hope of convincing the King administration to change its mind. Yet with newspapers full of horror stories of German Jews being whipped through the streets, thrown off roofs, and dehumanized in every possible way, Canadian Jewry could not possibly admit defeat. Failure was unthinkable even as the unthinkable was beginning to happen in Europe. Thus a newly revamped Jewish refugee committee was formed in March 1939 under the leadership of an energetic young Montreal lawyer, Saul Hayes.[76]

The creation of yet another committee was too much for one prominent Jew. Mirroring the rancour that was now pervading the community, S.M. Shapiro, the publisher of the *Hebrew Journal*, complained bitterly:

The policy of secret diplomacy pursued until now has not brought results. The public was duly impressed by the arguments advanced that any undue publicity was likely to do harm to the cause. . . . For two years the leaders of the Congress sought to assuage any misgivings on the part of the

Jewish public by assuring it that they were negotiating with the authorities in Ottawa. The impression was conveyed that they were given some secret commitment by the government. Yet . . . it is becoming apparent that the secret negotiations accomplished nothing and that our leaders had no more promises from the Ottawa government than if they had done nothing at all in the matter.[77]

Though his judgment was harsh, Shapiro was undoubtedly correct. Jewish leadership had been led down a garden path by the King administration. And yet they were still anxious to have another go at the government, this time with the revitalized refugee committee.

That Hayes and his committee would have succeeded where others had failed is doubtful. They did not even get the chance; events in Europe were moving too quickly. As the committee was making preparations to go to Ottawa, Hitler was making preparations to go to Warsaw.

Hitler struck first. On 1 September Germany marched into Poland. The fate of European Jewry was sealed. Blair, Lapointe, Massey, and King had stood fast just long enough. The Canadian Jewish community would soon turn its attention to saving the remnants of Auschwitz.

The Canadian government's success in withstanding pressure from pro-refugee groups, both Jewish and non-Jewish, was virtually complete. The Depression, the general apathy in English Canada, the outright hostility of French Canada, the unyielding opposition of certain key officials, the prime minister's concern for votes, and the overlay of anti-Semitism that dominated official Ottawa thinking on the question combined to ensure that no more than a mere handful of Jewish refugees would find a haven in Canada.

Even the outbreak of hostilities held its own irony for the refugees. Ever watchful lest Jews might slip past him, Blair did not see the beginning of the war as an excuse to let down his guard. With thousands of Jewish refugees desperately scrambling to escape still unoccupied Europe, Blair confidently advised Skelton that there was no need to worry. The Jews would not get into Canada. After all, most of these refugees were German nationals and, therefore, enemy aliens. Enemy aliens were expressly forbidden admission into Canada.[78] The line had been drawn. It was not about to move.

The Canadian Rescue Effort: The Few Who Cared

by Gerald E. Dirks

During the late 1930s, the Canadian government's restrictive policy towards immigrants and refugees motivated some Canadians to seek to have the regulations modified so that a portion of Europe's oppressed, including Jews, could enter the country. Although these humanitarian activists were never numerous and their efforts bore little fruit until after the Second World War, they were notable for their dedication and persistence and for the support they drew from the political, religious, and intellectual sectors of Canadian society.

In Parliament, pressure to liberalize immigration regulations so as to assist refugees appeared most regularly in the public statements and speeches delivered by members of the Co-operative Commonwealth Federation (CCF), whose two most eloquent spokesmen were A.A. Heaps, a Winnipeg member of Parliament, and J.S. Woodsworth, the party leader. Other parliamentarians concerned over the plight of refugees included three Liberals: Sam Jacobs and Sam Factor, MPs from Montreal and Toronto respectively, and Senator Cairine Wilson.

During the spring of 1938, Heaps wrote Prime Minister Mackenzie King requesting a meeting with the cabinet or a committee of cabinet to discuss the enormous world refugee problem. As a result of this request, a cabinet committee of five — Ernest Lapointe, Fernand Rinfret, Thomas A. Crerar, Ian Mackenzie and

James Ilsley — met with Factor, Jacobs, Woodsworth, and Heaps. During this and succeeding meetings, the concerned MPs attempted to gain some assurance from the cabinet representatives that the government would show generosity to Europeans fleeing political and religious persecution. In a letter to the prime minister, Heaps observed:

> Immigration regulations in Canada are the most stringent in the world. They are inhuman and unChristian. . . . We think it is not in keeping with good liberal doctrine to refuse the right of asylum to a limited number of political and religious refugees.[1]

Hoping to encourage prompt action on the part of the government, Heaps told King he would ensure that "a non-sectarian national committee is formed to care for these refugees in Canada".[2] Although the parliamentarians maintained this sort of pressure on the government, they never obtained the modifications in policy they had set out to accomplish.

Outside Parliament, a small but like-minded group of Canadians was becoming increasingly anxious over the mounting plight of European refugees and the alarming absence of any Canadian plan to assist in alleviating tragedy. They appreciated the need for quick action to rescue tens of thousands of refugees from steadily worsening political and social conditions.

To be fair, these concerned Canadians were generally much better informed about the true state of affairs in Europe than were most of their fellow citizens. Many had connections with international voluntary organizations or the League of Nations. A number belonged to the League of Nations Society in Canada, an organization established to inform and educate Canadians about the League and about world affairs generally. Its members had a particular awareness of the European situation because of their contacts with international public servants (some of whom were Canadians). Moreover, the society's membership included many genuine believers in international cooperation. To such people,

Canada, as a member of the civilized world community, had a moral obligation to assist in the resolution of the European refugee problem.

The CNCR

The Birth of the CNCR

The concern of these internationally minded Canadians was transformed into action within weeks of the Munich settlement, which alone caused 80,000 anti-Nazi Europeans to flee the Sudetenland and become refugees. According to Senator Wilson, "It was realised that many living in Czechoslovakia would be driven from their homes or else subjected to persecution as opponents of Nazism."[3]

At a regular meeting of the League of Nations Society's executive committee, held in Montreal on 15 October 1938, the anxiety of the alarmed members manifested itself in the birth of the Canadian National Committee on Refugees and Victims of Persecution (CNCR). The organization's purposes were to coordinate all efforts in Canada on behalf of refugees, to promote public education and discussion of the refugee problem, and to maintain contact with the Canadian government and voluntary agencies within and beyond the country.

The initial establishment of the CNCR as a committee under the direction of the League of Nations Society was an interim arrangement pending a formal founding meeting for an independent new group. The two organizations, however, had considerable overlap in personnel. Senator Wilson, who had been serving as Society president, resigned her position to become chairman of the new refugee committee, a post she held for the next decade. And she received much assistance, especially during the early weeks of the committee's existence, from other Society officers, one of whom, Constance Hayward, was to become CNCR executive secretary.

The first general meeting of the CNCR, held at Ottawa's Chateau Laurier on 6 December 1938, drew approximately fifty individuals representing more than twenty associations from across Canada. They heard addresses by such respected, influential Canadians as Dr. H.H. Clark, bishop of the Diocese of Ottawa, and R.C. Wallace, principal of Queen's University, who spoke on the responsibilities of Canada and Canadians towards the human problems of Europe. Principal Wallace stated:

> I am strongly of the opinion that Canada should now open her doors to Czechoslovakians and Jews from the oppressed areas of Europe. . . . Protesting about inhuman treatment to these people means nothing if we are not prepared to share in our part of the burden. There are difficulties that there will be a significant amount of opposition but a liberty loving country cannot afford to close the doors when persecuted people are looking for a hospitable home.[4]

Wallace caught the sense of meeting. Although the delegates may have differed with respect to the tactics the new organization should adopt, they all shared a desire to act quickly so as to lessen, if possible, the hardships being faced by the tens of thousands of persecuted Europeans. One of the many resolutions they passed at the opening meeting called on the Canadian government to admit "selected numbers of individuals or groups of refugees whose presence would prove of inestimable value to our national economy by introducing skills and new arts and crafts and industries".[5] The resolution concluded with a plea that the immigration regulations be modified to permit the entry of child refugees, whose care and maintenance, it said, would meet the standards of the various provincial child care and welfare authorities.

During the two-day session, the delegates debated various courses of action open to the new organization and mapped out a detailed plan for attracting governmental and private participation in their activities. They agreed the CNCR should establish local and regional branches, inform parliamentarians and the public of the urgency and intensity of the European refugee problem, and warn all of the growing circulation of anti-Semitic, pro-Nazi publications in Canada.

CNCR Activities: 1938–39

Following the organization's first general meeting, a CNCR delegation requested and received a meeting with Thomas Crerar, the minister responsible for immigration matters. In his statement to these representatives, Crerar said the government was concerned about moving too quickly because the public, influenced by high unemployment and xenophobic attitudes, generally opposed any modification to the existing immigration regulations. He admitted that the recent Nazi actions had started a ground swell of sympathy for the refugees but warned that "this sentiment might at any time be followed by a strong reaction and severe criticism of any governmental refugee admissions".[6] He stressed that the government could only act when public opinion was demonstrably with it.

The CNCR executive took Crerar's statement as a guide and placed a high priority on publicity and public education as well as on organizing local branches across the country. It raised funds through the sale of individual and group memberships; this money, augmented by the League of Nations Society, was used to print and distribute a variety of pamphlets and newsletters that described the group's objectives and urged the public to press the government for a more liberal refugee-admissions policy. For example, a pamphlet titled *Should Canada Admit Refugees?* said that the refugee problem could be eased by opening Canada's doors to selected refugees and by having effective intergovernmental machinery established to resettle refugees in underpopulated countries. As the pamphlet explained:

> If inter-governmental cooperation could solve the refugee problems of the magnitude of the post-war movements, it would seem fairly certain that the tragic plight of the refugees from Germany and what were formerly Austria and Czechoslovakia, could be solved if there were a genuine desire on the part of governments to do so.[7]

The press run for this pamphlet was over 9,000 copies. Along with other printed matter, they were distributed throughout Canada by the CNCR's member associations, such as churches, chapters of the Business and Professional Women's Association, and the Young Men's Christian Association.

The CNCR branches often worked with other pro-refugee-admission groups, such as the Canadian Jewish Congress, to organize public meetings that featured prominent speakers. Typical of the resolutions passed at many of these gatherings was one adopted in Vancouver during the winter of 1938/39:

> The Canadian government is urged to put forth its greatest efforts to secure homes for refugees in all parts of the world, and that the doors of this freedom-loving country, which in the past has received exiles, from other lands, be again opened to an appreciable number of refugees.[8]

The CNCR's executive committee meeting of 7 February 1939 noted the importance of gaining the support of the provincial governments, which would have the constitutional responsibility for the welfare and education of any refugees who managed to enter Canada. Accordingly, all members of the nine provincial legislatures were placed on the committee's mailing list and sent the increasing flow of its pamphlets and newsletters.

The same meeting decided to send another delegation to the federal government to report on the committee's work, to identify the problems the committee had encountered, to press for modification in prevailing immigration policy, and to seek advice as to how the committee might best proceed to achieve its purposes. In taking this action, the CNCR was clearly following its philosophy of working with the government to alter the restrictive immigration policy. The committee wished to acquire the confidence of the government rather than to act as a narrow, partisan interest group. It hoped to use its influential members to negotiate with the government and to modify the attitudes of politicians and officials in relevant departments. This course of action was strongly supported by Senator Wilson and by C.E. Burton, one of her chief associates and president of the Robert Simpson Company.[9]

The CNCR's attempt to bring a sizeable portion of Europe's refugees into Canada took on an air of greater urgency with the extension of German "protection" over the rest of Czechoslovakia in March 1939. During its second general meeting, in Toronto on 20 March 1939, it formulated additional, detailed plans, including provision for a nationwide refugee fund to be used both to aid victims of persecution abroad and to serve as the financial basis for assuring the Canadian government that any refugees entering this country would not become public charges.

Delegates to this general meeting also proposed a refugee bureau that would include representatives of those government departments concerned with the development of new arts and crafts as well as individuals from the private sector willing to assist in the resettlement of refugees who had these particular skills and talents. The representatives believed the way to circumvent the government's fear that admitting refugees would aggravate unemployment was to propose bringing in persons with talents and technical skills unavailable in Canada. Trade unions, it was hoped, would acquiesce if the newcomers were not in overcrowded occupations. The proposed refugee bureau would, therefore, investigate areas of need in commercial and industrial sectors and inform the Immigration Branch of its findings.[10] The plan never came to anything, however, because of the government's lack of interest in it.

During the months that preceded the outbreak of war that fall, the CNCR devoted itself to informing the public, working for the liberalization of prevailing immigration regulations, and gaining the support of groups and associations of every type. It received the endorsement and considerable assistance from a number of religious and ethnic associations, among them the Canadian Jewish Congress (CJC) and its Committee for Jewish Refugees. This support was of particular importance to the CNCR because it was through these organizations that the Jewish community in Canada offered to care for many of the European refugees if they should eventually be admitted into the country.

The CNCR, however, did not publicize any financial assistance it received from the CJC. Both groups feared that anti-Semitic emotions were so widespread in contemporary Canadian society as to lead the public to believe that any Jewish funding meant Jewish control. Such a perception, it was thought, would endanger the CNCR's attempt to carry on its broadly based non-sectarian programs. (These anxieties may have been caused by the fact that U. S. agencies formed to assist refugees newly arrived in the New York area had found that anti-Semitism made it necessary to play down Jewish participation in the movement.)

Other Work for Refugees

The CNCR, energetic as it was, remained small. The limited success it achieved with the government must be attributed to the stature of its members, individuals and associations. It was probably individuals' actions that saved most of the few refugees who were allowed to enter Canada during the two or three years before the Second World War. Members of the CNCR, such as Senator Wilson and Constance Hayward and other prominent individuals, spent hours upon hours defending refugee applications before Immigration Branch officials. Generally, this proved a slow, discouraging process. Each refugee seeking to enter Canada was processed individually. If an applicant could not fulfill even one of the prerequisites, department officials rejected his or her case quickly. In their eagerness to qualify for admission, some applicants did stretch the truth, especially about their agricultural experience. Thus Immigration Branch Director F.C. Blair wrote:

> There are some Jewish farmers in Europe and some are coming to Canada but curiously enough, we rarely find that one of these families is related to Canadian Jews. . . . We find it necessary to inquire closely into the applications in order to prevent the farming proposal from being used, as it so often has been, merely as a means for getting into the country.[11]

Immigration Branch officials also frequently grew impatient and annoyed over the numerous requests from Canadians to bring unqualified friends or distant relatives to this country. According to the officials, the majority of such requests originated within the Jewish community. This situation prompted Blair to comment:

> It is a curious fact that so many of our Jewish applicants are utterly selfish in their attempts to force through a permit for the admission of relatives or friends. They do not believe that "No" means more than "Perhaps", and they keep on appealing and appealing in the hope that the merit of the case lies in the circumstances, rather than in the applicant.[12]

Despite the cynicism of the Immigration Branch, refugees — Jewish and Gentile — kept on applying for admission, and individual Canadians — prominent in the CNCR or not — kept on defending them, case by case.

Meanwhile, many associations affiliated with the CNCR initiated independent actions to secure the admission of refugees and modifications in the immigration regulations. The churches were in the forefront of this drive. Many clergymen used their pulpits to appeal to their congregations and the government. One young minister, E.M. Howse, who would later become moderator of the United Church of Canada, declared in one of his sermons:

> Let the Dominion government make an emergency quota of refugees to facilitate the entry of those who can come under no present scheme. Let the quota equal what is deemed to be a reasonable share for Canada in the present world sorrow and let it give particular care to refugee children who may or may not be orphans, and on whom we have at present shut our doors.[13]

During the spring and summer of 1939 the Canadian press began to raise its voice in support of assisting refugees. Sporadic newspaper editorials urged changes in the regulations. For example, the Toronto *Globe and Mail* stated:

Canada, too, needs the industries that refugees are bringing to the United States. There is a need for the talents and crafts that our xenophobia has so far restricted.[14]

Among Canadian periodicals, *Saturday Night*, under the editorship of B.K. Sandwell, had already published numerous articles and editorials advocating the liberalization of the immigration regulations. Sandwell, who later became a dominant figure in the CNCR, indicated in his writings a sincere feeling for the oppressed peoples of Europe. On occasion, his magazine printed human-interest stories describing the plight of families who were endeavouring to acquire a safe haven beyond the troubled European continent.

Opposition and Indifference

Thus, the year prior to the outbreak of war saw the CNCR, its member associations, and others telling the story of Jewish refugee horrors and the way a liberalized Canadian immigration policy could diminish some of the anguish being encountered by the persecuted victims of intolerant regimes. The results of the committee's endeavours were disappointing, to say the least. The wall of public indifference remained largely unbreached.

Moreover, the CNCR found itself being opposed by such strident organizations as the Native Sons of Canada, the Canadian Corps, and the Leadership League. Illustrative of much of the public mood was a letter addressed to R.J. Manion, leader of the federal Conservative party, that read in part:

Please voice our protests re the refugees who are likely to arrive in our country. . . . We all feel sorry for these unfortunate people but at the same time, we have nearly one million unemployed looking for work, and quite a considerable number of farm help. If Hitler is driving these people from their native land, he should pay the shot. We must always remember that these people are Germans first and Canadians last.[15]

In the face of such a public mood, the CNCR had to content itself with gaining admission for a few individual refugees and countering some of the more irrational claims of the restrictionists. "We are making some efforts in the refugee matters," wrote Senator Wilson, "and I think eventually Canada may make a real contribution but it has been unexpectedly difficult to arouse public sympathy into meaningful action."[16]

The trickle of immigrants to Canada was all but cut off at the outbreak of war by the closing of most overseas immigration processing offices. Only a few European refugees — fewer than a thousand families — managed to enter Canada during the war years. Their admission reflected not moderation of Canadian immigration policy but the constant pressuring of government officials by organizations such as the CNCR and the CJC. Perhaps even more important were British and American suggestions to Ottawa; the Canadian government would make minor concessions when its larger allies requested it to do so. Throughout the war and even beyond, immigration regulations remained unchanged, mirroring the somewhat rigid, illiberal attitudes of many senior officials employed in the Immigration Branch.[17]

Postscript: 1945

As the war drew to a close, a few Canadians began to believe that a new wave of immigration should result from the increased responsibilities the country had undertaken, the prosperity the wartime economy had produced, and the enormous dislocation of peoples the global conflict had caused. Indeed, subsequent years would see great modifications in the policies and regulations governing the admission of immigrants and refugees. The process, however, was frustratingly slow for those people who had been urging such changes throughout the previous decade.

Writing in early 1945, a senior official of the Department of External Affairs asserted that no noticeable change in immigration policy would occur for a considerable time. He believed that in a time of severe shortages of acceptable ocean transport the need to repatriate Canadian servicemen with their dependents would provide the government with reasons for refusing to adopt a revised immigration policy quickly.[18] His prediction proved accurate.

Meanwhile, an unprecedented number of persons who had been displaced by the war and its aftermath sought permanent residence in states other than those from which they had initially fled or been deported. (In the cases of many from Eastern Europe, their desire for resettlement could be attributed to the installation of pro-Soviet regimes in their homelands.) During the postwar months, Canadians who had relatives among the displaced persons of Europe grew impatient with the repeated official response that no immigration could take place until servicemen and their dependents had been brought home and more adequate shipping became available. Furthermore, said the government spokesmen, there were no plans to reopen immigration-processing offices on the European continent until the war-devastated communications systems and economies had been at least partially reconstructed.

Within Canada, however, a momentum for change was growing. During 1946, interdepartmental and Parliamentary committees began dialogues on the prospects for a new era of immigration. So did the press. Members of the business community, ethnic associations, and academia appeared before Parliamentary committees, wrote articles for periodicals, and spoke at public meetings to point out the benefits that would accrue to Canada from a significant population increase. Yet it would be more than a year before the government would adopt the liberalized policy that would bring more than one million Europeans, including many Jewish refugees, to Canada during the next decade.

Many factors contributed to the eventual modifications in the immigration regulations; four were particularly significant. First, a large bloc of ethnic and religious organizations pressed for the admission of relatives and coreligionists. Second, the business community argued persuasively that the economy required thousands of new labourers to fill skilled and unskilled jobs. Third, the press editorialized relentlessly for the opening of large-scale immigration. Finally, the governments of the United States and Western Europe urged countries such as Canada to assist postwar reconstruction efforts by relieving the overcrowding that was hindering the reestablishment of political stability and impeding economic regrowth in Europe.

Meanwhile, Canadian society had undergone a complete reversal of the harsh, xenophobic attitudes of the depressed 1930s. Jobs were available, industry was expanding, the economy growing. Canadians had regained confidence in themselves and their country and no longer perceived newcomers as an immediate threat to economic security. This new mood was, however, of little consolation to those Jews and others who had pleaded for entry into this liberal democracy less than a decade earlier.

PART II

Social and Political Institutions

No society or subsociety can function without a set of institutions that meet important needs of the group as a whole and of the individual members. A social institution can be defined simply as an accepted way in which a society orders the roles and activities of its members to meet recognized needs. Some of these arrangements are as tacit as the conventions that govern informal, social get-togethers; others may be as planned as a school system, with written purposes and rules.

The Canadian Jewish community is no exception in its need for institutions. Indeed, the struggle for Jewish survival in the Diaspora is partly the story of the success — or failure — of Jewish social and political institutions in linking Jews to their community, helping them adapt to their surrounding environment, and sheltering them from both assimilation and hostile threats in their host societies.

Of the many institutions Canadian Jews have developed, we have chosen four for discussion: the family, education, religion, and the formal organizations that mark North American Jewry. Other choices would have been possible, but these four are perhaps the central institutions supporting Jewish communal life.

The family is the most basic institution of any human community. Modern societies, having barely learned to cope with the shift from the extended to the nuclear family, now find the nuclear model being challenged by new lifestyles and the values associated with feminism, individualism, sexual liberation, and the like. These changes may affect — among other things — socializing of the young, one of the central functions of any family

These changes are particularly challenging for Jews, for whom the family has long been the basic unit of Jewish experience and the setting for many rituals and holidays. In the first paper in this section, Leo Davids describes the functions of the traditional Jewish family and the inroads that modern, secular alternatives have made on Jewish family life. One of his suggestions is particularly challenging: the fact that so much of modern Jewish life is child-centred — that parental involvement in things Jewish is so often for "the sake of the children" — may mean that smaller families with a diminished role will lead to new forms of Jewish expression.

Concomitant with the modern decrease in the socializing role played by the family has been the increased responsibility placed on other socializing institutions, notably the school. The same shift from the family to the school is taking place within Canadian Jewry. Are its Jewish schools up to the task? Historically, the function of Jewish education was simply to impart knowledge, not to create a Jewish identity.

Yaakov Glickman addresses the many problems that the Canadian Jewish educational system faces today in attempting both to strengthen Jewish identification and to transmit relevant information to students from a wide range of Jewish family environments. Although day school enrolments are rising and organized Jewish communities have established education as a major spending priority, he calls attention to many unresolved problems, ranging from the inadequate salaries and prestige awarded to Jewish teachers to the appropriate curricula and objectives for various types of Jewish schools.

A religion is a social institution best studied as two interrelated phenomena. First, it is a body of ethical principles, laws, and rituals. Second, it is an organization, staffed by religious professionals and others, that structures the religious life of members of the faith and channels their participation in it. Judaism in Canada plays both roles for many Jews. It operates in the former manner to the extent that its beliefs and values give meaning to individuals' lives. Its rituals, particularly those associated with the life cycle, loom large in the experience of most Canadian Jews. Though only a minority are consistently observant in the Orthodox sense, many tend to celebrate most, if not all, of the major Jewish holidays, with varying degrees of observance and intensity.

Judaism as a formal organization is far from monolithic. Affiliated Jews belong to one of the major branches of Judaism, each of which is an organization unto itself, as is each synagogue. These organizations are involved in an ongoing struggle to make Judaism relevant in a society that is increasingly secular. Stuart Schoenfeld perceptively examines Canadian Jewish religious life at both the personal and public levels, with particular reference to the impact of secularism and assimilationism on the characteristics of modern Canadian Judaism.

One way to think of the modern Jewish community is as a polity, a politically organized society with a series of decision-making bodies. The organized Jewish community of Canada has two kinds of dominant bodies: the Canadian Jewish Congress, which has been called the "parliament of Canadian Jewry", and the welfare federations that combine fund-raising, setting communal budgetary priorities, and administering a network of welfare, cultural, and recreational agencies.

Thinking of the Jewish community as a voluntary political system inevitably raises the questions of power: its source and its exercise. Harold M. Waller dissects the sources of Jewish power, at the local and national levels, ranging from the wealthy elites of big givers to the professionals who actually administer the federations and Jewish agencies. The controversies associated with equal access to power and decision-making are as relevant to the Jewish case as they are in a discussion of Canada itself. Indeed, Waller's discussion of the Jewish elite meshes well with the long-established tradition of Canadian elite studies, reflected in the works of John Porter and Wallace Clement.

One question that remains unanswered is the function that participation in the myriad Jewish organizations fills for their individual members. Many analysts argue that it is as joiners and as financial contributors that modern Jews are most likely to exhibit their Jewish ties and commitments. Yet even here there is no consensus. Some see activity in communal organizations as a substitute for more traditional forms of Jewishness; others feel they are interrelated, so that those individuals who are closest to authentic Jewish culture and religion are also the ones most likely to participate in Jewish communal organizations.

Another question is whether Jews participate in these organizations primarily out of a sense of Jewish commitment or in order to fulfill other personal and social needs. Given the role of Jewish organizations in modern Jewish life, answers to these questions are likely to assume more importance in the years to come.

The Family: Challenges for Survival

by Leo Davids

The family is the arena in which perpetuation of any cultural tradition either succeeds or fails. Understandably, persons concerned with Jewish survival and the continuation of the Jewish heritage are concerned about the Jewish family today. The Canadian family, Jewish or otherwise, is no longer the traditional extended family of three or more generations — grandparents, parents, and several children — living in emotional and physical proximity to each other, often in the same home. At most, it is now the nuclear family of husband, wife, and one or two children; childless couples and single-parent families are increasingly common.[1]

The reasons for these changes are well known. Increases in urbanization and mobility encourage individuals to feel less tied to their families or their places of origin, especially if economic opportunities beckon elsewhere. General North American attitudes towards many family-related issues have shifted, sometimes to the point of reversal. For example, divorce no longer entails social stigma, and sexual mores are much less restrictive. During the last two decades, popular emphasis on the value of individual fulfillment has made links between individuals and families — even between families and communities — seem too confining. These changes are affecting almost all groups in North America, but they have a particular relevance to Jews, who, for millenia, have placed special emphasis on the family as a means of transmitting values, attitudes, sensitivities, and skills to successive generations.

Moreover, in the face of the difficulties of maintaining cultural and religious identity in a multiethnic setting, modern Jewish life has emerged as increasingly child-centred. The identity of the adult North American Jew is often reinforced through activities related to children and the life cycle: births, bar-mitzvahs, weddings, and so on. Synagogue memberships correlate with the proximity of children to the age of bar- or bat-mitzvahs, and many families become synagogue dropouts as soon as these festivities are behind them. The child-centred holidays and rituals, such as Chanukah and the seder, are the ones most likely to be observed. An institution such as a Jewish school, camp, or youth group very often serves as a surrogate for parents in the provision of a meaningful Jewish life. At the communal level, an increasing portion of Jewish organizational life and funding is geared to the socialization of Jewish children.

Since this great emphasis on children has been added to the family's traditional role in maintaining Jewish identity, it is clear that disruptive pressures on the Jewish family threaten the very existence of Canadian Jewry in the future. For this reason, it is worth examining these pressures in some depth, noting the extent to which they exist in reality as well as in myth and attempting to suggest the lines along which Canadian Jewry may successfully adapt to them.

An important point should be noted here. Although this paper refers constantly to the Canadian Jewish family in general terms, one must remember that there are many kinds of Jews in Canada, and so there are many kinds of Jewish families. Chassidic families differ from the large majority, which are not so intimately committed to religious observance. The Sephardic Francophone Jews and the post-Holocaust immigrants differ in some important ways from those Canadian Jews whose ancestors came from Eastern Europe in the great wave of arrivals before the First World War. Except where otherwise stated, this paper deals with Ashkenazic families that are descended from the mainstream. However, many of the observations here may also apply to post-1945 immigrants and to Sephardic families.

Another important point to remember is location. The bulk of Canadian Jewry lives in Toronto and Montreal, which have large and well-organized Jewish communities, where Jewish education and other facilities are readily available to those families that wish to take advantage of them. Canadian Jews outside the great centres lack some or all of these cultural resources and must depend much more on individual family initiatives. The differences between the two major communities and all other places where Canadian Jews live have important effects on intermarriage, Jewish-education levels, and other matters that depend on population density and the size of the "market" for religio-cultural products and services.

Matching and Marrying

The majority of Jewish parents would like to see their children find Jewish mates (preferably of the same level of religiosity as the parents and equal or better social class), enjoy large weddings, "settle down" in comfortable homes, and then "give them grandchildren". For many reasons, this does not always happen.

In some situations, the availability of potential Jewish mates is simply so limited that marriage with another Jew becomes quite difficult. When sociologists study the ease or difficulty of finding marriage partners, one of their primary tools is census information on the sex ratio, the number of men compared to the number of women. Generally speaking, the sex ratio for Jews in Canada is favourable to marriage. In 1971, males and females of Jewish ethnic origin were fairly close in number: 149,240 males and 147,700 females. A one-to-one sorting process would seem to have a good chance of success. The overall figures, however, do not reveal the many problems that become evident when they are broken down in more detail. Complications appear if one looks at the numbers of male and female Jews in the marrying years (ages twenty to thirty-four). This age group had a large surplus of unmarried Jewish men compared to the available Jewish women. The scarcity of Jewish mates must force some of these young Jewish men to remain single, to emigrate, or to take non-Jewish wives. This may help explain why statistics reveal considerably more out-marriages by Jewish men than by Jewish women.

Another problem becomes evident when one considers the total number of Jews in the marrying years who live in communities other than Montreal and Toronto. Even a balanced sex-ratio cannot compensate for a very small pool of marriageable Jewish youth. In Calgary, for instance, the 1971 census reported 190 men ages twenty to twenty-four but only 140 women of the same age group and 220 men ages twenty-five to thirty-four as opposed to 200 women. In sum, the chances of a Jewish male finding a Jewish wife in Canada are limited outside Montreal and Toronto. The unbalanced sex-ratio and small actual numbers may lead to intermarriage.

The same demographic facts present yet another problem to the smaller communities. Parents who fear out-marriage often encourage their children to move to Toronto, Montreal, or even New York when they enter the marrying years. This has, in the long run, harmful effects on community size, since the majority of those who leave to seek a mate do not come back. Nevertheless, traditionalist parents are likely to aid such a move in order to diminish the likelihood of intermarriage.

A new and different kind of marriage-related problem faces parts of the urban Jewish community. Some professionally oriented young Jews (along with their Gentile peers) are deciding either to postpone marriage until they are well past the traditional age for it or to remain single permanently. So far at least, the numbers choosing this course are small; they may not have had any significant effect on Jewish population. But these young adults do present an immediate challenge to the community. Since the family is the normative unit of participation in the Jewish community, we have little experience in accommodating young people who are single by choice.

The Young Couple

Even when a young Jew does decide to marry and finds a Jewish mate, there is no assurance that the newly wed couple will form a stable family within the Jewish community — or even outside it. The divorce rate is rising among Jews as it is among the general population. Obviously, many of the pressures on young married Jews are the same as those encountered in the larger society. Certain tensions, however, arise from the Jewish situation. In contrast to the unquestioned routines set by the community in the past, today's reality is that couples (except for those from very traditional or Chassidic families) have to design and live their own lifestyles, with little guidance from anywhere. Where, for example, should they live? If his or her career presents a valuable opportunity that involves residential relocation, should they make the move? Location has particular significance for many Jews in terms of being part of a Jewish neighbourhood, which means proximity to a synagogue and to facilities such as kosher stores.

Again, each young Jewish couple must work out how it will relate to the Jewish community. This decision often counters the desires and expectations of parents or in-laws and sometimes results in great friction. The elders take it upon themselves to represent the interests of the Jewish community, suggesting or even demanding that the young people do things for the sake of their ethnic and/or religious heritage. In fact, the parents' advice about where the young couple should live and so on may have less to do with concern about the cultural environment of the young marrieds than with anxiety about the kind of setting and experiences that the grandchildren will have while they are young.

The young man and woman facing this sort of tension are already attempting to establish their own secure independence, to adjust to one another after having lived in separate, perhaps quite different, homes for many years, and usually to reexamine traditional male and female roles. With so many challenges, surviving the early months and years of marriage seems to require a great effort on the part of young people, as well as a considerable amount of good luck.

In the major centres of Jewry, growing recognition of the difficulties that young couples face has led to a strong movement in the schools and among many religious groups towards systematic family-life education. In Montreal, an Orthodox Institute for Jewish Brides and Grooms offers classes to engaged couples twice a year. In Toronto, the Jewish Family and Child Service and the Jewish Community Centre run family-life education programs, and small voluntary groups also offer marriage preparation classes. In the smaller centres, however, the situation is sink or swim, since such services are not available locally.

Procreation and Family Size

A major issue in any discussion of Jewish families today is their small size. The birth rate among Jews is actually below the replacement level, a fact that poses as dangerous a threat to future Jewish existence in North America as do intermarriage and other challenges.[2] This very low birth rate is statistically the feature that most distinguishes Jews from other Canadians. Although Judaism, like almost every religion, strongly urges all couples to procreate, many now choose not to. Jews in Canada, as in many other countries, practise birth control so consistently and successfully as to have a lower birth rate than any other major ethnic or religious component of Canadian society.

A popular belief is that birth control and small families among Jews are phenomena of quite recent vintage. This is not so. Some sort of contraception or fertility avoidance has been common among the majority of Canadian Jews for the past fifty years.[3] Indeed, Jewish fertility has been below that of other groups since early in the present century, and below replacement level for many years. Social scientists and historians have attributed this small-family tendency to immigrant Jews' social and economic aspirations, which led them to use what money they had to provide the best possible education for a few children, rather than "squandering" their resources to feed and clothe many little ones.[4]

Over time, the birth rate affects not only a group's total numbers but also the distribution of its population among various age brackets. The median age, for example, is a direct reflection of the relative proportion of younger and older people in the total group. Given Canadian Jews' consistently low birth rate, it is not surprising to find that in 1971 the median age among all Canadians was 26.28 while Canadian Jews had a median age of 33.26, the highest for any major ethnic group in the country.[5] In other words, the Jewish population is highly aged relative to other groups.

New Lifestyles

Many people still believe that North America's common family-related and sexual concerns — marriage breakdown, extramarital sex, homosexuality, single-parent families, and so on — hardly ever occur among Jews. Perhaps one of the best ways to demonstrate that indeed Jewish families are forced to deal with all of these issues is to quote the annual report of Toronto's Jewish Family and Child Service for 1978/79:

> In 1978 we have been facing an unprecedented change in the quality of family life in the Jewish community. Our statistics now confirm the shift from traditional Jewish values in family life to ones that approximate the styles and patterns of North America. We are now dealing with a minimum of 850 open, active cases per month. . . . It is a case load heavily beset by separation, divorce, inter-marriage; single-parent households, mainly mother-led; an increasing number of battered wives, severely beaten children — an increasing number of these adolescent; a sharp increase of Jewish youth in courts, an epidemic of school drop-outs. . . . Plainly speaking, Jewish family life in Toronto has lost its feeling of safety. No single agency could be expected to deal alone with such sweeping social change.[6]

Some, though by no means all, of these social changes are related to the changing sexual attitudes and mores that have significantly influenced Jews along with most other North American groups. The traditional Jewish view limited sexual activity to the married couple (though I.B. Singer and other writers suggest that Orthodox rules of sexual behaviour were not always observed even in the highly isolated ghettos of the Old World). Today, Canadian and American Jews often engage in sexual practices that would have horrified their ancestors. Perceptive writers have noted the threat that these phenomena of new morality pose to Jewish continuity.[7]

With regard to premarital sex, there is some evidence that Jews (particularly males) are less likely to be virgins by the end of their college years than comparable non-Jews. While Jewish premarital pregnancy does not seem to be rising, it is known that Jews have always been efficient at contraception, and the Kinsey report (1948) found that discussions about sex were more open in Jewish than in non-Jewish families.

Ironically, in the face of growing intermarriage, one of the folk beliefs of a previous era — that "Jewish girls don't" so Jewish boys would seek out Gentile girls for illicit sexual pleasures — seems no longer true, although it may have been so formerly.[8] Today, premarital sex appears to be the norm in most of Canada, yet it does not seem to preclude nor weaken the chances of eventual marriage. Rather than seeing sex or cohabitation as a final option, some young Jewish couples now regard it as a required prelude, an experimental step designed to assess compatibility. Nevertheless, premarital sex often does heighten the tensions between the generations and may lead to guilt feelings even among those individuals who consider themselves "liberated".

Extramarital sex, whether in the form of clandestine affairs or mutually agreed-upon sexual exchanges, may impose great strains on a marriage. It is not clear how frequently married Jews are involved in this sort of activity. Open marriages and casual sexual liaisons are clearly incompatible with traditional Jewish life; Jews engaging in them are probably relatively assimilated.

Similarly, it is not clear whether Jews' sexual practices within marriage differ from those of non-Jews. (One must except Orthodox Jews, since they presumably abide by the traditional limits on the timing of intercourse and the nature of sexual activity).[9] Public opinion polls in the United States have generally found Jews more supportive of sex education and liberal abortion laws and more opposed to the censorship of pornography than non-Jews; such attitudes suggest that they may indulge in "liberal" sexual practices themselves. It seems certain that increased sexual expectations (and frustrations) play some role, though by no means the major one, in the rising divorce rate.

Homosexuality is one mode of sexual behaviour that the Jewish community, like most religious communities in North America today, is unhappy about but must face. There are no accurate estimates as to whether homosexuality is more or less prevalent among Jews than among the general population. Jewish homosexual organizations do exist; Montreal has a group called Naches, and Toronto a gay synagogue. The status of homosexuals as members of the Jewish community is still not clear, but the Jewish family is obviously not equipped to accommodate them, both because of religious law — the obligations to be fruitful and multiply, to take a wife and build her a home, to instruct one's children in religious practices, and so on — and because of deep-rooted folk mores and traditions. Still, homosexual families, in which a homosexual couple raise their natural children from other relationships, do occur nowadays. If the gay rights movement continues to grow, Jewish homosexuals may well demand collective representation and acceptance in the community, as well as an unstigmatized status as individuals.[10]

Divorce and Remarriage

Any consideration of Canadian Jewish families must take into account the modern reality of divorce and all that goes with it. The weakening of traditional norms in North America and Europe has played havoc with the idea of the permanency of marriage. In Canada, the general divorce rate rose almost 73 per cent between 1971 and 1977, going from 137.6 per 100,000 (in 1971) to 237.7 (in 1977),[11] and it continues to rise for Jews and non-Jews alike. Social scientists believe the reasons for this massive increase include such factors as the liberalizing of legal grounds for divorce, changes in the economic status of women, and so on.[12]

The social consequences of this large a shift are considerable. From the religious viewpoint, of course, divorce has always been legitimate among Jews, in contrast with Catholicism's total rejection of it. The Jewish stance is based on the passage dealing with divorce in Deuteronomy (24:1–4), which takes it for granted that such things occur and that there is a normal procedure for dissolving a marriage. Nevertheless, divorce was uncommon in the past among North American Jews. Although there may well have been large numbers of unhappy spouses in Jewish communities, couples usually stayed together, for economic reasons, out of shame, or in an attempt to "save the children" from unpleasantness. In the present generation, however, this reluctance to proceed to divorce seems to have given way among the majority of Jews, and even in the most traditional sectors, *gittin* (religious divorces granted by a rabbinic court) have become fairly common.

Divorce in J. families more common

One major indicator of divorce trends in Canada is the marital-status distribution included in the census figures. In 1971, 0.86 per cent of all Canadians were divorced (and not remarried), but for Jews the percentage was 1.38. Interpretation of the higher Jewish figure must, however, be balanced by the fact that the low Jewish birth rate means there are more Jews in the higher age brackets (which are at risk for divorce). In other words, the overall Canadian percentage is kept down by so many Canadians being too young even to have been married, much less divorced. Thus, the relatively high Jewish figure does not necessarily indicate that the probability of a divorce for the individual Jew is much greater than for a Gentile. In fact, the probability may be equal or just slightly higher for a Jew.

Clearly, though, Jews do get divorced. One can estimate that today over 1,000 Jewish couples are divorced in Canada every year, and a decreasing stigma is attached to their action. Some Jews even look upon divorce quite positively as an opportunity for a fresh start, but some of the long-term consequences may be overlooked at the outset.[13] Divorce has powerful effects on the lives of the adults and children involved. The former are likely to remarry eventually, but the children still have to cope with loss, emotional stress, and reorientation.

Children who suffer from J divorce

Another major consequence of the great rise in divorce is the increasing number of single-parent families in Canada, among Jews as well as Gentiles. Although some people are prepared to accept single-parenthood as just another new lifestyle, neither better nor worse than the conventional family, it clearly entails some

Divorce → Single parent families

important risks and hardships. The single parent, most often the mother, is forced to do everything — parenting, housekeeping, breadwinning, plus developing personal interests and commitments — on her (or his) own. Depending on the number and ages of the children involved and the availability of emotional and financial support from others in place of the former partner, the task may be fairly simple or nearly impossible. Poverty, for example, is far more prevalent among female-headed families.[14]

Single-parent families challenge Canadian society at large. Their increasing prevalence also places growing demands on Jewish family and child welfare agencies and poses major policy questions for the entire organized Jewish community. Such families have a greater tendency to withdraw from synagogues and other Jewish institutions and, therefore, leave their children less connected with the Jewish community than the children of two-parent families. These and other related problems are serious enough to have prompted several Jewish organizations in the United States to study carefully the long-term implications of the rising divorce rate and its results, so as to consider the necessary community responses to them.[15]

Not every divorce, of course, results in the permanent establishment of a single-parent family. Remarriage is common, among Jews as among the general population. Jewish law has always permitted remarriage, just as it has considered divorce legitimate. Today, although the Orthodox may be somewhat wary of marrying a divorced person because of the possibility that a *get* (religious divorce) was not obtained or was improper, Jews in general seem to accept remarriage as a normal and desirable thing for both divorced and widowed persons.

Statistical evidence on Jewish remarriage is readily available and plainly shows it is increasing. Indirectly, this information confirms the existence of a large number of divorced Jews, though there is no way to specify to what extent the increasing remarriage of divorced Jews reflects their rising prevalence in the population or a rising acceptability of them as marriage partners. Undoubtedly, the two trends reinforce each other.

Remarriage is increasing and is slightly more common among Jews than among the general population. In 1971, about one out of ten Jewish brides and grooms in that year had previously been divorced (the total Canadian average was then 8 per cent). By 1977, the figure had increased considerably to about one out of six.[16] In brief, divorced Jews are indeed managing to find new marriage partners and thus to resume family life. Remarriage also seems eminently desirable from the Jewish community's point of view.

Parents and Children

The foregoing should have made it clear that the profile of the Jewish family has changed greatly in recent years. No longer do all young Jews marry other Jews and establish stable, conventional families disrupted only by death. In a direct reflection of modern society's acceptance of alternate lifestyles, Jews are trying other arrangements. Some, such as voluntary childlessness and homosexual unions, are relatively rare at present, while others, such as campus-dorm intimacy and single parenthood, are increasingly common. Although these variants represent a previously unknown degree of individual freedom for Jews, they also entail at least some limitations to child-rearing and thus threaten Jewish continuity. The price of freedom may be high indeed.

Frequent relocation and the existence of high-quality residential institutions for the elderly also threaten continuity by reducing opportunities for interaction between older Jews and the nuclear families that include their grandchildren. Modern values have stood traditional Jewish perspectives on their head; where the former exalt youth, the latter revered age as associated with wisdom. Today, more and more elderly Jews, some voluntarily and some with no choice, live alone or in homes for the aged, and they have little ongoing contact with their children or grandchildren. The impact on the Jewish community is serious. Historically, when the Jewish family transmitted continuity, it was particularly the accessibility of grandparents that provided young children with living lessons in Jewish history, practice, ties to the old country, and different forms of Judaic experience. Their absence makes even more difficult the inculcation of Jewish identity among young children.

The relationship between what goes on at home and the cultural vitality of the Jewish subsociety must be considered. The survival of Canadian Jewry as a distinct community knowing and living its own heritage depends on socialization, to some extent by Jewish schools, but most centrally within the family. The new generations are further and further removed from the sights, sounds, and smells of the Old-World Jewish communities.[17] Jewish identity and knowledge have become problematic. Jewish schools may not be capable of meeting this challenge and ensuring a "survivalist" socialization for the majority of Jewish children; many get a very meagre religious or cultural Jewish education as Jews — or none at all. There is now much anxiety about the survival of the particular outlook, behaviour patterns, and culture that constitute Jewishness.[18]

The generation gap so much described and deplored in all of today's developed societies presents further problems. Research among British Jews suggests that Jewish parents and their adolescent children get along to about the same extent as do other families of the same education and economic situation.[19] In the absence of first-hand research in this country, one can assume these findings are truc for the majority of Canadian Jewish families. Many Jewish community leaders and scholars express grave concerns in this area. Parents share the concerns — and have to cope with the consequences in everyday life. For example, one common dilemma is establishing the boundary between permissible and forbidden social interaction with non-Jews. Jews are liberal and try to fight prejudice anywhere, certainly in their own child-rearing. This is especially a problem for non-Orthodox parents, whose children are likely to mix more freely and frequently with non-Jews than do the children of very traditionalist families. As the rising rates of intermarriage suggest, it is increasingly difficult for parents to establish and enforce workable rules concerning social activities; they may, for example, include an acceptance of dating non-Jews yet a prohibition of intermarriage. And, of course, children do leave home as unmarried young adults, either for university or work, whereupon enforcement of such parent-set norms becomes impossible. Only internal controls and self-enforcement then remain — and these operate only if the young person is already predisposed to follow the norms from his or her earliest family training.

With so many pressures on the family, it is little wonder that maintaining cultural identity and continuity remains a central issue of concern among Jewish leadership in North America today, and is often a major focus of research on Jews.[20]

The Future

Predicting the future is always risky, but certain patterns and challenges seem clear. The trends towards the small Jewish family, remaining single, voluntary childlessness, divorce, and so on all have an important consequence for strategies designed to strengthen modern Jewish identity, both at the individual and the communal level: these choices tend to undercut or detract from what has already been described as the child-centredness of modern Jewish life. For some time now, the North American Diaspora has accented — perhaps overaccented — its emphasis on children. As assimilation has made inroads on the Jewish content and meaning of the adult lives of so many Jews, Jewish behaviour "for the sake of the children" has often become more important than Jewish behaviour for its own sake. If social and demographic trends soon make it impossible for many Jews to focus their Judaic commitment so exclusively on the child, the Jewish community and even the Jewish family may be forced to rediscover currently neglected aspects of Jewish life, notably those that can give meaning to an individual's own life and promote adult spiritual quests. It remains to be seen whether such a relevance-restoring individualization of modern Judaism will be possible or successful in perpetuating Jewish life. Certainly the challenge may sorely test the adaptive flexibility of the Jewish family and change its relationship to the organized Jewish community.

On the positive side are various social and cultural forces promoting continuity for Canadian Jewry today. One is the concentration of the Jewish population in two great centres, Toronto and Montreal; three out of four Canadian Jews live in these institution-rich Jewish communities, which offer every facility for the maintenance of both ethnic and religious Jewishness. Another is the sharp increase of enrolments in Hebrew day schools, which continue to produce strong Jewish youth who can be counted on to become the committed future leaders of Canadian Jewry.[21] Other promising developments include the emergence of a well-organized, professional communal structure in the Canadian Jewish Congress and its affiliated organizations and the apparent success of various Chassidic groups in recreating their traditional way of life.

These survivalist forces constantly work against assimilative trends; the result is the emergence of several subcommunities of differing size and inclination among Canadian Jews. On the one hand, a majority continue the long-term drift away from the classic Jewish heritage, becoming more and more integrated with the general Canadian culture and society. On the other hand, a committed and identified Jewish subcommunity continues to involve itself with synagogues, organizations, and philanthropy. By and large, the families who are strongly connected to synagogues and Jewish organizations maintain Jewish practices vigorously at home, have some meaningful knowledge of Yiddish or Hebrew, contribute financially to Jewish causes, and rear their children in the same patterns. Within this category are numerous Orthodox and Chassidic families, who continue to have many children and thus somewhat counteract the general decrease in numbers among Jews on this continent.

The Jewish future in Canada, for at least the next generation or so, is secure because of this minority of families who are active and vigorous in things Jewish. Collectively, their members are building this Jewish future by taking Jewish mates, producing a goodly number of children, and successfully teaching them the necessary concerns, aspirations, and beliefs. On the other hand, we will also continue to see many other families who have little connection with the institutions and organizations of Jewish life, have a very low birth rate but a high intermarriage rate, and provide their children with very little Jewish training in the home or at school.

Jewish Education:
Success or Failure?

by Yaacov Glickman

Transplanted and dislocated over geography and history, Jews have maintained a remarkable solidarity while successfully adapting to their host cultures. The North American version of this adaptation is marked by an increasingly universalistic religious view, maintenance of an identity as a people, and occupational and economic success. The role of Jewish education is to reconcile such varied traits, thereby emphasizing the historically tight relationship between the religious and national components of Jewish ethnic identification.

Like many other groups in North America, the Jewish community has made its education a subsystem of its religious institutions. The importance of this point may elude modern readers until they consider the qualitative differences between the content and purposes of general education in the traditional Jewish ghettos and small towns of Eastern Europe and in the modern Jewish communities of North America. In the former, virtually enclosed and religiously homogeneous, education was an end in itself, an integral part of a sacred way of life. The religious content of general education was so high as to cast doubt upon the very Jewishness of an ignorant man. In the latter, education is a primary means for improving one's position, an avenue to economic success. In other words, Eastern European Jewish culture separated economic life from the fused institutions of religion and education. Educated men were both religious (or at least religiously knowledgeable) and highly identifiable Jews. In North America, on the other hand, economic goals and education became fused, with religion kept apart.

The immigrant Jews brought with them their passion for education and instilled it in their children and subsequent generations. But the education they sought with such enthusiasm here was largely, often exclusively, secular in content and purpose. One result was the creation (for the first time in history) of large numbers of educated but not necessarily religious or identified Jews. Another was the necessity of Jewish parents and religious institutions accepting the responsibility for the religious instruction of children and young people.

As the Canadian system of Jewish education evolved, it did so in a pluralistic fashion. From its early years, its religious content varied from school to school. Some were strictly Orthodox, while others were largely secular; many fell between these two extremes. Today, diversity is a central characteristic of Canadian Jewish education. The orientation and the amount (or lack) of religious study differs in different schools. Some are synagogue-sponsored; others are independent. The language of instruction may be Hebrew, Yiddish, English, or French (or all four). Institutions also vary in structure; they include day schools that integrate Jewish and secular studies, replacing public schooling, as well as afternoon or Sunday schools that supplement public instruction.

A Brief History

Jewish schools have evolved in all Canadian cities with sizable Jewish populations. However, local variations have depended on the particular Jewish community's size, makeup, and economic well-being, on the ideological bents of the founders, and on the activities of the city's other Jewish organizations.

In Toronto, the largest centre of Canadian Jewry, Jewish education has developed from early twentieth-century roots, keeping pace with successive mass immigrations from Eastern

Europe and with the growth of the Jewish community's organizational infrastructure. Today, the schools are an extremely elaborate network with programs, ideologies, and organizational affiliations as diverse as the community from whose cradle they emerged. One of the best known is the multibranch Associated Hebrew Schools, which grew out of Toronto's first Talmud Torah, founded in 1907. Today, though Associated Hebrew Schools maintains its original Orthodox orientation, its general stress on Hebrew culture and use of Hebrew as the language of instruction draws pupils from a larger (albeit mostly traditional) segment of the community. Thus, for Toronto and indeed all Canada, the school is a communal institution rather than a strictly denominational one.

Another well-known and influential Toronto school is the Eitz-Chaim, established in 1915 by a group of Polish immigrants who considered the Associated Hebrew Schools deviant from strict Jewish Orthodoxy. While not manifestly opposed to the teaching of the Hebrew language, they viewed its use — instead of Yiddish — as the language of instruction as smacking of "Hebraist secularism" not befitting "God-fearing" men. Today it is by far less militantly anti-Hebraist and anti-Zionist than in its early years, but nonetheless it retains its strict Orthodox posture.

Jewish education in the Montreal area has developed under the shadow of Quebec's successive and confusing battles over the language of instruction and the confessional nature of the public schools. The most relevant point is that the province maintains two separate school systems: Catholic (mostly French-language) and Protestant (almost entirely English-language); the educational rights of other religions have been ignored. Until recently, Montreal Jews almost all entered the Anglophone sector, so their children had to attend Protestant schools; in 1903, they were, in fact, legally classified as Protestants for educational purposes.[1]

On the other hand, since 1968, the province has given most Jewish day schools, along with many other private schools, per-capita grants for their secular programs. The catch to this largesse has been, since 1973, the necessity of operating the schools "in the public interest", a phrase that is increasingly used as a euphemism for conforming to measures designed to restrict access to instruction in any language except French.[2]

Despite (or perhaps because of) the difficult situation of Montreal's Jews *vis-à-vis* tax-supported education, they began to develop private schools in earnest before the turn of the century. The year 1896 witnessed the establishment of Canada's first Talmud Torahs; a decade later they absorbed the day-school classes of the Baron de Hirsch Institute's Free School for the Poor Children of the Jewish Faith, which had been founded in 1890. In 1917, the five separate Talmud Torahs were amalgamated into the United Talmud Torahs of Montreal, and during the First World War, the Yiddish Peretz School and the Hebrew-and-Yiddish Jewish People's School were established. This kaleidoscope of Jewish educational institutions continued to expand; by 1946 it included day schools at the elementary and secondary levels, congregational afternoon and Sunday schools, a rabbinical college, and two teacher-training seminaries amalgamated in 1949 to form the Canadian Jewish Teachers' Seminary. Today, as in Toronto, Montreal's Jewish schools extend from ultra-Orthodox to Conservative and from left-wing Yiddishist to Zionist-Hebraist.

Meanwhile, similar yet distinctive patterns were evolving in the smaller cities. Late-nineteenth and early-twentieth century efforts led to the establishment of Talmud Torahs; subsequent expansions and ideological changes often created other schools. In Winnipeg, the Hebrew Free School, housed by 1913 in a well-equipped new building, soon became the cultural and religious centre of the Jewish community, whose well-known vitality is still reflected in the school's program. That community has also long been known for its strong left-wing, Yiddish-oriented faction. Ideological division and reunification of its various schools has resulted in a multidimensional system remarkable for a Jewish community of only a little over 18,000 persons.

Talmud Torahs formed the backbone of Jewish education and Jewish community activities in both Edmonton and Vancouver. The Talmud Torah of Edmonton was the first Hebrew day school founded in Canada, no small feat for a community then numbering less than 1,000 individuals. The same is true in Ottawa and Calgary, although here, as in Winnipeg, less traditional but often equally vibrant dissenting schools have constantly challenged the traditionally oriented and Orthodox-controlled Talmud Torahs.

Education and Jewish Community Structure

Education, particularly Jewish education, does not take place only in the schools. Many Jewish organizations transmit both the ideas and the practices of Jewish life. They range from the smallest and most informal ad-hoc gatherings of individuals all the way up to citywide school boards and umbrella organizations, such as the Toronto Jewish Congress and the Allied Jewish Community Services of Montreal, national groups, such as the Canadian Jewish Congress, and even international agencies, such as the World Union of Jewish Students.

The most cursory look at this network, which is quite elaborate, especially in the larger cities, reveals the tight links between the various levels of organized Jewish life and a marked degree of duplication and overlap in the functions of education and in the structures designed to handle them. Jewish institutions offer an enormous range of educational and youth programs, Hebrew-language and other cultural activities, summer camps, and so on; the national organizations have a full array of committees to initiate and oversee programs run by their subsidiaries.[3] Such a high degree of organization blurs the boundaries between the school and the community and between formal and informal Jewish education. It also suggests that Jewish "education" may exert greater influence than Jewish "schooling".

Because the organizations handling education are so interlocked, questions of organization and governance of education seem to inspire conflict. In Vancouver and in Edmonton, for example, the rather sectarian status of the Talmud Torah in relation to the community at large and to its major religious denominations has been an ongoing source of controversy. And when sixty key figures in Toronto were asked to list that community's major disputes of recent years, the largest number of responses were related to education.[4]

The interrelation of issues and organizations was especially clear in this Toronto survey. The controversial issue of government aid to Jewish schools, for example, touches upon both the educational concerns of the community and its relationships with the government and with other non-Jewish organizations. Differing opinions on the relative importance of day schools and supplementary schools relate not only to different educational philosophies but, among other matters, to the question of who controls the community treasury and how much influence each of the major Jewish organizations have on the younger generation. Other disputes that seem to be about education are really issues of rabbinical authority or the distribution of power within large synagogues or other organizations.

Educational controversies tend to be fanned by the interlocking institutional structure so characteristic of virtually all major Canadian Jewish centres. At first glance, each community seems to have evolved its own version of organization and governance, in education as in other matters. These differences, however, are primarily matters of magnitude and style, not organizational principle. For example, within Metropolitan Toronto, the Board of Jewish Education is responsible for the execution of the Toronto Jewish Congress' educational policies, while in Montreal, the Jewish Education Council, supported by the Allied Jewish Community Services, performs similar functions. In most other large Canadian cities, Jewish schools fall under the jurisdiction of Canadian Jewish community organizations.

The similarity of the principles governing these organizations' approach to education is effectively maintained through an elaborate system of fund-raising and fund allocation. In the large centres, this function nominally goes to the United Jewish Appeal, but in reality, a complex and fluid system of interlocking directorships among the boards of the UJA and other Jewish (and occasionally non-Jewish) organizations broadens the decision-making base beyond specific group interests. Democratic considerations aside, this system has proved very effective in maintaining and controlling the treasuries of Jewish communities.

The funding system is of central importance, given the costs of education and the voluntary nature of Jewish organizations. Consider, for example, the following figures: for the academic year 1973/74 in Toronto, the costs incurred by all the schools and educational support-services were approximately $5.3 million, of which the community contributed $1.4 million or 26.6 per cent. (Tuition fees met an additional $2.9 million of this cost, leaving a shortfall of almost $1 million.)

Funding for education in other cities is comparable with their size. Of all the money allocated for local expenditures in 1971, the Edmonton United Jewish Appeal earmarked 25 per cent for schools; in Vancouver it was 33 per cent. (The proportions would be higher if support for other educational activities were included in the statistics.) Only Montreal seems to run low, with 9.5 per cent of 1973's local allocation going to education and culture, but this anomaly is probably a result of the large per-capita grants the city's day schools receive from the Quebec government.

In sum, education lies at the very core of a rather elaborate network of community organizations crisscrossing the various layers of organized Jewish life in Canada. It is characterized by a remarkably efficient fund-raising effort as well as by duplication and overlap in programs and institutions.

Attitudes towards Jewish Education

The worth of Jewish education cannot, however, be measured entirely — perhaps not even primarily — by statistics on funding. What counts in the long run are its effects on individuals and on the community, as seen in the attitudes of those who have come into contact with various educational programs. Although attitudes are at best only a crude measure of actual behaviour, they nevertheless reflect the unifying themes around which a community's belief system revolves. A considerable body of recent information on attitudes exists in a study conducted by the

Toronto Board of Jewish Education.[5] There is no reason to think its findings do not apply to the entire Canadian Jewish scene.

In one question, the researchers asked parents and students to respond to the statement "Jewish children *must* have some Jewish education." Table 1 confirms the overwhelming importance the respondents gave to education. Fully 97 per cent of the parents had a positive attitude towards it ("strongly agree" or "somewhat agree"). Even among the children, presumably the group least likely to share in the basic premises prescribed by the community, positive support reached 83 per cent. These figures, in and of themselves, show a community highly unified around a theme deemed crucial for its cultural survival.

TABLE 1

Response to Statement: "Jewish Children Must Have Some Jewish Education"

Response	Parents	Children	Combined
Strongly agree	84%	52%	72%
Somewhat agree	13	31	20
Uncertain	1	4	2
Somewhat disagree	2	5	2
Strongly disagree	1	5	2

SOURCE: United Jewish Education Welfare Fund, *Study on Jewish Education* (Toronto, 1975).

This consensus is all the more remarkable when compared with further findings of the study, which showed the relative impact of Jewish schooling on the cultural identity of Jewish youth. Students who had had at least some form of Jewish education were asked the extent to which this schooling influenced various aspects of their Jewish beliefs and practices. The results are shown in Table 2. Jewish educators may find these responses instructive. On no issue is the impact of the school very high, and on all aspects combined, it is very small indeed ("negatively" and

TABLE 2

Perceived Influence
of Jewish Schooling on
Students' Beliefs and Practices

Aspect Influenced	Negative Effect*	No Effect	Positive Effect†
Regard for Israel	3%	41%	56%
Philanthropy	5	42	53
Adjustments as a Jew in the community	6	47	48
Tolerance of religious differences among Jews	10	48	42
Participation in Jewish communal life	9	50	41
Jewish education and culture	9	53	40
Avoidance of intermarriage	8	59	33
Religiosity	13	60	28
Choice of educational institution	9	69	22
Subscription to Jewish publications	10	80	10
Mean score	9	69	22

SOURCE: See Table 1.
NOTES: *Includes "very negative" and "negative" responses.
　　　†Includes "very positive" and "positive" responses.

"no effect" answers combine for a mean score of 78 per cent, compared to only 22 per cent for "positive effect").

This finding must be compared with the fact that so many of the student respondents viewed a commitment to Jewish education in either imperative or desirable terms (see Table 1). Evidently, the highly favourable attitude of Jewish students towards exposure to Jewish education is largely unrelated to its influence upon them. The finding also supports the claim of many educational theorists that, compared to the impact of the total culture and especially early childhood education and the family (and later the peer group), the school is bound to lag as an agency of socialization and indoctrination of social value and behavioural patterns. When students were asked to state the reasons for their attending, or having attended, a Jewish school, 95 per cent reported at least some parental influence; grandparents, friends, and the location of the school had much less effect. The most important finding, however, was that the children's own preference was also instrumental, with half indicating that attending a Jewish school was their own choice.

In general, then, attitudes towards Jewish education are rather ambivalent. An extremely high recognition of the need for Jewish education is coupled with a realistic, perhaps even disenchanted view of the limitations of Jewish schooling and of its relatively low contribution to the formation of Jewish identity.

Jewish Education for Whom?

Since Jewish education receives such great support, philosophically and financially, from the Canadian Jewish community, it seems logical to ask if it returns equal benefits. Part of the answer can be obtained by asking three further questions: 1) What proportion of Jewish children receive some form of Jewish education? 2) What proportion receive *intensive* Jewish education? 3) What is the availability of qualified professional teachers?

The best available data on these points come from the two largest centres of Jewish population, Toronto and Montreal. The *Encyclopedia Judaica* has claimed that 48 to 60 per cent of Jewish children (ages five to fourteen) receive an organized Jewish education in the larger Canadian cities and up to 90 per cent in the smaller communities.[6] Recent and more intensive studies conducted in Toronto during 1973/74 by the Toronto Board of Jewish Education estimated that five out of six families — 83 per cent — have had at least one child attend some sort of organized Jewish educational program. But since the study used the *family*, rather than the *child*, as the unit of analysis, the figures seem to present too optimistic a profile. The authors concede this, noting that a family may send only one child to a Jewish school and possibly for only a very short time.[7]

The overstatement of these figures seems borne out by a study conducted in Montreal in 1970 and 1971; it showed 38 per cent of the city's Jewish children (kindergarten to grade 11) had attended a Jewish day school.[8] Many people would regard this less-than-50-per-cent exposure as cause for concern. Further problems lie in the decline, in absolute numbers, of supplementary-school enrolments. The Toronto Board of Jewish Education study indicated a continuous drop across most of the community's rather elaborate supplementary-school system. Enrolment figures for the Conservative congregational schools went down 18 per cent over a four-year period (from 2,435 students in 1970/71 to 1,999 in 1973/74). Only the Reform congregational schools maintained a constant level of enrolment, in both their Hebrew and religious programs. Montreal has experienced similar declines. (Such declining enrolments are of course not unique to the Jewish school system.)

There is much more cheer in the statistics on children who participate in a more intensive Jewish program, normally in a day-school. Even in a time when the overall number of children of elementary-school age is dropping, some of these schools are growing in absolute numbers. In terms of the relative proportions of day-school and supplementary-school students, the shift is radical. The 1971 edition of the *Encyclopedia Judaica* reported that of some 25,000 Jewish children (ages five to thirteen) who live in communities with twenty-five or more Jewish families and attend any kind of Jewish school, 8,300 (30 per cent) are attending day schools (compared to 2.0 per cent in 1933).[9] More instructive are the breakdowns for the larger cities. In Toronto, of 9,650 students receiving any type of Jewish education in 1968/69, supplementary schools enrolled 64 per cent, day schools 36 per cent. The Board of Jewish Education study showed that this ratio was all but reversed by 1973/74, with 57 per cent of 10,204 students attending day schools compared to only 43 per cent attending supplementary schools. The study from Montreal, which has the distinction of having more children attending Jewish day schools on a per-capita basis than any other community in North America, indicated similar trends. Indeed, the day-school movement is firmly situated, in both the United States and Canada, at the forefront of Jewish education and is regarded, by professional educators, community leaders, and many ordinary people, as the new frontier of Jewish identification.[10]

On the other hand, all the studies showed very few older students (ages thirteen to seventeen) in senior day high schools. Indeed, the percentage of young people in this age group who continued Jewish studies in any form was very low (an average of 10 to 14 per cent across the country), and in most cases they stayed in the programs for only one to three years.

No matter what the level of enrolment, education depends largely on those who provide it. Qualified teachers must be both available and attracted to the positions. Yet the Toronto study noted a disturbing paradox: although the community values Jewish education and is prepared to support it financially, it assigns a low status to Hebrew teaching as a profession. The Montreal study echoed a similar feeling, calling education and recruitment of teachers the most acute problem of Jewish education.

Some of the major problems associated with the training and recruitment of Hebrew teachers are suggested by statistics that were quite similar in the Toronto and Montreal studies (and there is no reason to expect the smaller centres have better situations). The shortage of adequately trained teachers is chronic. In Toronto, 29 per cent of all teachers of Jewish subjects (37 per cent in the supplementary schools) were noncertified and only 44 per cent possessed a university degree (including rabbinic ordination). In Montreal, 39 per cent were noncertified, and only 59 per cent of those who were certified possessed a permanent licence. Although many had or were taking educational courses at the college level, a mere 27 per cent of those certified had a degree.

The increasing lack of male teachers of Jewish studies has created an imbalanced set of role models for the children. The Toronto ratio of women to men was two to one; Montreal's was only slightly less. The Toronto study also noted the predominance of women in the general studies departments of the day schools, a trend parallelled in the public school system.

The predominance of part-time positions results in split commitments and consequent erosion in the quality of teaching. Almost half the Toronto positions provided no more than eight hours of work per week, and less than 22 per cent offered more than fifteen. Not surprisingly, over half the teachers either taught in more than one school or had an additional occupation.

Both generation and culture gaps loom between teachers and pupils. Teachers in both cities were, more likely than not, foreign-born and educated (many were born and educated in Israel), low in experience and job attachment, and over thirty years old.

Salaries are very low and benefits insufficient. Only a meagre 10.5 per cent of the Toronto teachers surveyed earned over $10,000 per year; about half made $3,000 or less. (The more specialized all-day Hebrew-school teachers fared better, although their salaries undoubtedly cannot ensure an acceptable standard of living or a reasonably high commitment; fewer than one in five made over $10,000 per year, and more than one in ten earned $3,000 or less.) The figures for Montreal were dismally comparable; almost one teacher in five earned under $2,000 per year. Both studies also showed inadequate fringe benefits; over half of the Montreal teachers reported receiving none whatsoever, and most of the rest indicated only "some". In the language of the frustrated Toronto teachers, the situation amounts to the "subsidization of Jewish education by the Jewish school teachers".

In sum, the profile of Jewish schooling in Canada shows a trend towards the all-day Jewish school, as well as a gradual decline in overall enrolment; the latter is attributable in part to the persistent decline in the birth rates of Jewish families. Although the degree of exposure to Jewish education appears to be moderately high, in reality, the quantity and quality vary widely. A continuously growing constituency of day-school students follow programs, both Jewish and secular, of the highest quality, while the supplementary schools offer the rest of the student population Jewish programs that are much briefer and often of lower quality. Perhaps most importantly, the profile points to an educational system hampered by a shortage of adequately trained and qualified personnel, an imbalanced sex ratio among teachers, too large a generation and culture gap between teachers and students, and low incomes and poor working conditions for staff. These problems reinforce each other in a vicious circle, lowering the status of the profession, reducing the quality of education, and chipping away part of an educational edifice otherwise characterized by longstanding tradition and substantive achievements.

Conclusion

The varied and often contradictory facts about Jewish education need reconciliation. On the one hand, Jews seem overwhelmingly committed to the *idea* of Jewish education. On the other hand, the multiple and often duplicated Jewish educational programs seem to have produced only meagre results relative to the great efforts and resources poured into them. Clearly, this contradiction weakens the popular belief that a person with more and better Jewish education is always more likely to become a more identified or committed Jew.

How is this contradiction to be explained? What are its implications for the cultural survival of the Canadian Jewish community? The answers rest, in part, in cumulative evidence of the weakness of most minority educational systems as sources of community identification. Despite forecasts to the contrary, the North American *family* seems to have retained its role as the major agent of socialization and community identification. The extent of an individual's identification with Jewish tradition and institutions is likely to be formed during the early stages of childhood in a way that mirrors the principles to which his or her family adheres. The Jewish school merely intervenes at a later stage to reinforce something predetermined long before. At best, it changes little or nothing; at worst, it can even reinforce negative feelings towards things Jewish.

In other words, attending a Jewish school is likely to be the effect rather than the cause of Jewish identification: in combination with the family, it is vulnerable to powerful assimilatory forces over which it can exert only a limited degree of control. It is important, wrote Walter Ackerman, to "draw a distinction between the 'educated Jew' and the 'identified Jew' and perhaps even . . . acknowledge that where identity is the goal, formal education may not be the most effective means". To assume, he continued, "that formal education or any kind of educational programme . . . is an adequate substitute for the impact of a total culture is to stretch the parameters of identity formation beyond reasonable limits".[11] The Montreal study echoed this contention:

> The inadequacies of Jewish education today are only, in part, reflective of the inefficiencies of the educational establishments: they also are intimately related to the ambivalence of contemporary North-American Jewry vis-a-vis its own Jewishness. Educational systems, after all, are creations of societies and communities, reflecting to a large extent the ethos and values of their creators. The ills of Canadian and American Jewish education, then, reflect the ills of North American Jewishness. . . . While the North American Jewish community has established the apparatus of an educational system, it has not really come to grips with the contents or purposes of such a system.[12]

Jewish education, however, is certainly not in its death throes nor is it a failure. On the credit side is a rather impressive edifice of educational institutions that are embedded at the very core of organized Jewish life and supported through a highly efficient fund-raising apparatus. Also important is the growth of the day-school movement, supported by an increasing number of Jews in its attempts to maintain the continuity of Jewish culture while reconciling this culture to modern Canadian life.

At present, it seems to be the Jewish community, especially the organized community, that maintains its own cultural survival; the community itself, beginning with the family, provides a series of broadly educational experiences and institutions. The success or failure of Jewish schooling can, therefore, be appraised only within the larger orbit of organized Jewish life, to which it is making an important contribution.

Canadian Judaism Today

by *Stuart Schoenfeld*

The proper role of religion in modern society has been the subject of a continuous debate, a debate that has gone on in Canada and among Jews, as well as in other settings. Within this debate are sharply contrasting conservative and liberal positions. In this essay, these contrasting positions are first used to provide a perspective on different approaches to the role of religion in Canada and then as a guide to the varying views of Canadian Jews about the kind of religious institutions they have been creating and the significance of religious identification to their lifestyles.[1]

RELIGION IN CANADIAN SOCIETY

From the conservative perspective, the state is an expression of the national culture of its people. Religion is seen as one aspect, sometimes a central one, of that national culture. This view of religion in society leads to a legally established church that is publicly subsidized, whose teachings are considered part of the national culture, and that is organized in a centralized structure roughly parallel to the government bureaucracy.

From the liberal perspective, however, the state is a voluntary association of free and equal individuals. Religion is a private matter for each individual. The individual is free to practise his religion as he sees fit and is free from the obligation to support, through legal privileges or taxes, any religious organization. This view of the role of religion in society leads to the strict separation of church and state and to religious groups that rely less on centralized authority and church bureaucracy and more on the commitment of the faithful to the maintenance of the congregations of their choice. Both approaches to the role of religion in society are found in Canada.

A conservative understanding of the role of religion in society is most plausible where almost all the people are of one religion. Although the religious traditions of the overwhelming majority of Canadians are Christian, Canadian Christianity is pluralistic. Nevertheless, there are a few large denominations that have laid claim, in one way or another, to speak for a national community. In the 1971 census, 46 per cent of the population identified themselves as Roman Catholic. The Catholic population is a large majority in Quebec, and the historical association of French Canadian nationalism and Catholicism is strong. There are also large Catholic minorities in other provinces. The next largest denomination listed in the census was the United Church of Canada, with which 17 per cent of the population identified. The movement that produced the United Church was understood in part as a movement towards a national Protestant church for English Canada. The third large Canadian denomination was the Anglican Church, accounting for 14 per cent of Canadians. Membership in the Anglican Church relates the communicant not only to God but also to the Crown.

Although the pluralism of Canadian Christianity has precluded a single national church, a conservative understanding of religion has been expressed in the legal recognition the country has given to it, notably in the field of education. In Quebec prior to the Quiet Revolution of the 1960s, French-language public education was conducted through Catholic school boards that worked closely with the Roman Catholic Church; public education for the English-speaking minority was organized through Protestant school boards. Other provinces still maintain tax-supported parallel confessional school systems. And although religious teaching is more overt in Catholic schools, Canada's public school systems also contain a residual Protestantism.

It is, however, the liberal understanding of the role of religion in society that has become more common in Canada. The reasons for its ascendance are complex — the decreasing salience of religion in the personal lives of Canadians, the growing importance of individual autonomy as a cultural value, the influence of American liberalism, and the pressure of smaller religious groups for complete equality are all involved — but the direction of movement is clear. Only residual, nondenominational traces of Christianity remain in the public schools. The ecumenical movement within Canadian Protestantism has faltered. In Quebec, current conceptions of the national community emphasize a common culture based on language and history rather than one based on religion. The view that religion is essentially a private matter is legally established in legislation that makes discrimination on religious grounds a criminal offense.

The contrast between the conservative and liberal approaches to the role of religion in Canadian society can be used to pose two questions about Canadian Judaism. First, to what extent have the creation, maintenance, and strengthening of religious life been the responsibility of the Jewish community as a whole or of individual Jews joining together to meet personal religious needs? Second, what is the significance of religious identification to the lives of Canadian Jews? The balance of this essay is devoted to these issues.

CONGREGATION AND COMMUNITY

The early Jewish immigrants to Canada came from a tradition in which the conservative understanding of the role of Judaism in the Jewish community was predominant. Judaism and Jewish community life were traditionally inseparable. The synagogue, the Hebrew school, and the rabbi were supported by the community. Rabbinic courts under the authority of a chief rabbi of the community played an important role in local life. In Canada, however, Jews adopted the congregation, a form of religious organization more consistent with the liberal understanding of the role of religion in society. The congregation is a voluntary association that owns its synagogue as private property, chooses its rabbi, and governs its own affairs. (Canadian Judaism hardly pioneered congregational organization; in its movement towards this form, it was following the lead of American Judaism and of many Protestant denominations.)

At first, when local Jewish populations were small, the distinction between communal and congregational Judaism was not clear; the congregation was the community. This is still the case where the Jewish population remains small enough to support only one congregation, especially if it is the only Jewish organization in the locality. But where the Jewish population is larger, the congregation has become one kind of Jewish organization among others in the community; specifically, it is the one that provides for the religious needs of its members.

Jewish Congregations in Canada

About half of the Jewish households in Canada belong to a congregation, or, to use the common term, are synagogue affiliated. Considered as a group, the close to 230 congregations are the largest Jewish organizations in the country. They own a considerable amount of real estate, employ hundreds of religious professionals, receive and disburse large amounts of money, and sponsor a wide range of Jewish activities.

Early History

The census of 1881 reported only 2,393 Jews in all of Canada. Congregations had been organized in Montreal, Toronto, Victoria, and Hamilton; only Montreal, with a Jewish population of 811, had more than one — Shearith Israel, which followed the Sephardic ritual from its founding in 1768, had been joined in 1846 by Shaar Hashomayim, which followed the Ashkenazic ritual.

Many new congregations were founded between 1880 and 1920. Jewish immigration vastly increased the Jewish populations of Montreal and Toronto, established a major new centre in Winnipeg, and settled Jews in cities, towns, and farms across Canada. Where their numbers were small, Judaism was centralized in one congregation. In the larger centres, it was common for congregations to be founded by persons from the same part of Europe. *Landsmanschaften*, groups that drew their membership from the same European city or village, were often combined mutual-aid societies and religious congregations.

The continuation of autonomous congregations became inevitable with the emergence of distinct branches of Judaism. Reform Judaism intentionally changed and modernized many of the practices and concepts of traditional Judaism. Traditional Judaism itself divided into two camps: those congregations that wanted a flexible accommodation of tradition to modern conditions affiliated with the Conservative movement, and those less willing to be influenced by modern culture identified themselves with Orthodox Judaism. With congregations insisting on their right to follow one of several alternative interpretations of Judaism, there could be no central religious authority. On the other hand, the federations that were established to sponsor joint projects for congregations identifying with similar interpretations of Judaism brought some order into what was, and remains, an essentially voluntary, decentralized style of religious organization.

Reform Judaism

The Union of American Hebrew Congregations (UAHC), the Reform federation, was founded in 1873 to support the establishment of the Hebrew Union College in Cincinnati, Ohio. Reform Judaism, which developed among the numerous German Jewish immigrants to the United States in the mid-nineteenth century, was the most prominent branch of Judaism in the States until the 1880s. Only a backwash of the German Jewish wave of migration reached Canada, however, and the spread of Reform in the Dominion was limited. Anshe Sholom Congregation in Hamilton, Ontario introduced many reforms in the 1880s; Temple Emanu-El in Montreal was founded in 1882 by a Reform-oriented group. Both congregations affiliated with the UAHC before the turn of the century. Holy Blossom Temple in Toronto did not affiliate with the Reform movement until 1920, but long before that it was known as the most liberal of the city's synagogues. In Vancouver and Winnipeg, groups favourable to Reform withdrew from larger congregations to form their own, but compromise on both sides led to reunion. Additional Reform congregations were not founded until the suburban relocation of the 1950s. In 1956, the Canadian Council of Liberal Congregations was organized as a separate regional unit of the UAHC.

By the late 1970s, Canada had fifteen Reform congregations, with about six thousand member families. Despite a recent growth of Reform Judaism in Canada, it is still less common than in the United States. Roughly 15 per cent of the synagogue-affiliated Jews in Canada belong to Reform congregations, compared to roughly 30 per cent in the United States.[2]

Conservative Judaism

Conservative Judaism developed around New York's Jewish Theological Seminary, founded in 1886 and reorganized in 1901, and the United Synagogue of America, the federation of congregations organized in 1913. In the United States and Canada, the movement appealed to the same group: the upwardly mobile children of Eastern European immigrants. Conservative Judaism has been well established in Canada since early in the century, when several of the oldest and largest congregations became affiliated with the United Synagogue. By 1936, nine Canadian congregations had affiliated with the Conservative movement.[3] Others changed from Orthodox to Conservative and new Conservative congregations were formed during the suburban migration.

By the late 1970s, twenty-seven Canadian congregations had affiliated with the United Synagogue. Other congregations, not formally affiliated, also considered themselves Conservative.[4] The United Synagogue and the Rabbinical Assembly — the association of Conservative rabbis — have regional branches in Canada. The Canadian Council for Conservative Judaism was created in 1978 to act as the movement's national organization. Approximately 45 per cent of synagogue-affiliated Jews in Canada belong to Conservative congregations, compared to 50 per cent in the United States.

The Synagogue-Centre

The congregational emphasis of Conservative and Reform Judaism is expressed in the importance these groups attach to the synagogue-centre. A synagogue-centre is more than a place of worship; it is a multifunctional building whose staff provide programs for a wide range of age and interest groups. Beth Tzedec in Toronto — one of the largest congregations in the world with some eight thousand men, women, and children — provides an illustration of a fully developed synagogue-centre. The building houses a large sanctuary, two chapels, two reception halls, extensive kitchen facilities, numerous classrooms, a school assembly hall that doubles as a gym, a dozen meeting rooms, a library, administrative offices, the Canadian branch of the Jewish Theological Seminary museum, and a small Judaica shop run by the sisterhood. In addition to serving as a place of worship, the building is used for education, weddings, funerals, community rallies and meetings, and recreational clubs that appeal to a variety of age and interest groups. The educational activities held there include a congregational school, a day school affiliated with the Conservative movement, a nursery school, and adult education classes. To provide these activities and maintain its building, the congregation employs a combined staff of more than one hundred people, including two rabbis, two cantors, an executive director, a congregational school principal, teachers, a choir, youth workers, secretaries, and janitors. Most other Conservative and Reform congregations in Canada have developed synagogue-centres, although facilities and activities vary.[5]

Orthodox Judaism

Orthodox congregations in Canada have evolved along somewhat different lines from those of Reform and Conservative Jews. The many Orthodox congregations founded around the turn of the century offered only the basic facilities of a place of worship and a burial society. Some were organized by followers of particular rabbis, but most were led by laymen. As late as 1931, all Canada had only thirty-three rabbis; about a dozen of them were employed by Conservative and Reform congregations, leaving some twenty rabbis to serve the approximately 140 Orthodox congregations. Forty-three of these congregations were in places where there was no rabbi at all.[6]

Some congregations founded as Orthodox have now merged, become Conservative, or disbanded, but these losses have been balanced by the formation of new Orthodox congregations. The Chassidim who immigrated after the Second World War have established their own congregations, as have the Orthodox Sephardim who came to Canada from North Africa in the late 1950s. New Orthodox congregations have also been organized in the suburbs. As of the late 1970s, there were about 175 Orthodox congregations in Canada. Orthodox Judaism remains more common in Canada than in the United States. About 40 per cent of the synagogue-affiliated Jews in Canada belong to Orthodox congregations, compared to 20 percent in the United States. Orthodox affiliation is especially high in Montreal.

Most Orthodox congregations now have rabbis, but few are synagogue-centres. Orthodox Judaism, more than Conservative and Reform Judaism, relies on other community facilities to supplement those of the individual congregation. Also, Orthodox Judaism is very diverse; various cultural groups or movements have their own organizations. Four congregations in Montreal and one in Ottawa are affiliated with Young Israel. There are branches of the historically more stringent Agudat Israel in Montreal and Toronto. Chassidic congregations are found in Montreal, Toronto, Winnipeg, and Vancouver. Affiliation of Canadian Orthodox congregations with the Union of Orthodox Congregations, the broad federation, is common but far from universal.

Newer Branches of Judaism

The two newer branches of Judaism are also present in Canada. Reconstructionist Judaism, which has gradually emerged from Conservative Judaism into a separate branch, has affiliated congregations in Montreal, Toronto, and Victoria. A Humanist congregation meets in Toronto.

Communal Judaism in Canada

Throughout the Jewish experience in Canada, as a counterpoint to congregational Judaism, there has been a contrasting strategy of communal sponsorship for religious institutions, activities, and authority. Many of the congregations founded around the turn of the century had quite limited resources. A Jewish community with centralized authority and facilities was a living memory to many immigrants, who recognized both the advantages to be gained from cooperative action and the costs of fragmentation. Consequently, in the populous Jewish environments of the larger cities, communal groups came to organize and support Jewish schools, rabbinic courts, supervision of *kashrut* (Jewish dietary laws), ritual baths, chapels, and other religious institutions. This conservative style of religious organization echoes the Old World tradition of the ritually separate, sometimes legally autonomous Jewish community, a largely self-contained entity within society.

At the turn of the century, communal Judaism was expressed in the establishment of educational institutions and the appointment of chief rabbis of various local communities. More recently, the institution of the Va'ad Ha'ir (the religious council) and the meeting of religious needs by nonreligious communal organizations have maintained Judaism as part of the common culture of the Jewish community. The defence of Jewish beliefs and practices has also become a communal responsibility, partly because of the need, throughout Canadian history, to address religious issues in the legislatures and courts.

Communal Religious Education

When the Jewish population was small, Jewish education was mainly under congregational sponsorship. As the population grew, schools were organized with dependence on community rather than on congregational support. The first Canadian Talmud Torah (Jewish school) was opened in Montreal in 1896. Over the next generation, Talmud Torahs offering instruction on Sundays and weekdays after school were founded and expanded across the country. The Edmonton Talmud Torah inaugurated the first religious Hebrew day school in Canada in 1927.[7]

Enrolment has gradually but steadily shifted from the after-public-school programs to the all-day programs. Orthodox day schools have been supplemented by Conservative day schools in Montreal, Toronto, and Winnipeg and by a Reform day school in Toronto. By the late 1970s, religious day schools, financed partly by tuition and partly by community subsidies, accounted for about half of the students receiving Jewish education, with the balance split between congregational and secular Jewish schools.

From Chief Rabbi to Va'ad Ha'ir

As congregations increased and rabbis became more numerous, individual rabbis came to be considered "chief rabbis" of various localities. The position depended on the esteem of the individual's colleagues and on his ability to attract a following, mostly from small congregations without rabbis of their own. Because the position was based on voluntary consent, it was often controversial.

One scandal indicates the kind of trouble that could arise. In 1908, Chief Rabbi Joshua Glazer of Montreal appealed to the city council to refuse to grant Jewish butchers permits without his consent. This action was a tactic in a dispute within the community over supervision of *kashrut* (dietary laws). It led to a public furor, Rabbi Glazer's decree of excommunication against *Der kanader adler* (the Montreal Yiddish newspaper), and a civil-court hearing and judgment on the issues involved.[8]

Rabbi Israel I. Kahanovitch, whom the Canadian Jewish historian Benjamin Sack praised as "A man of rare qualities . . . possessing profound wisdom and learning that won for him the love of all who knew him",[9] was more successful in receiving widespread community support as chief rabbi of Winnipeg. Brought from Poland in 1907 as rabbi of Beth Jacob Congregation, Rabbi Kahanovitch played a leading role in creating a central *kashrut* authority, in fostering a unified Talmud Torah, and in other communal issues. His influence extended beyond Winnipeg, and he was regarded by many as chief rabbi of Western Canada until his death in 1945. However, even Rabbi Kahanovitch sometimes faced chief rabbis of dissident factions.

In large communities today, the personal authority of a chief rabbi has been largely replaced by the authority of a Va'ad Ha'ir. A Va'ad Ha'ir (literally "council of the city") is a representative body that normally takes responsibility for *kashrut* supervision and such projects as support for Jewish education, maintenance of a Beth Din (a religious court of Jewish law), and support for needy scholars. Montreal's Va'ad Ha'ir was founded in 1922, Ottawa's in 1933, and Winnipeg's in 1946. In Toronto the move towards a centralized religious council has a complicated history.[10] There, as in other cities, concern over *kashrut* supervision has been the occasion for attempts to centralize religious authority. Various attempts were unsuccessful until the early 1950s, when the Central Region of the Canadian Jewish Congress established an Orthodox Division to supervise *kashrut*.

The tradition of the chief rabbinate survives to a limited extent. The Union of Orthodox Rabbis of the United States and Canada, the oldest association of North American Orthodox rabbis and the most Eastern European in its ways,[11] acknowledges Rabbi Hirshprung of Montreal as chief rabbi of Canada. The Communauté Sépharade du Québec and the Sephardic synagogues of Quebec brought Rabbi Sabbah from Morocco in 1977 to be chief rabbi and president of the Sephardic rabbinate.

Social and Legal Separation

Until the 1950s, the Jewish communities of Canada were to a great extent geographic, social, and cultural enclaves. In densely populated neighbourhoods with high proportions of immigrants, residences mingled with shops, synagogues, and schools; the whole was a distinctively Jewish environment.

The separation of Jews from the broader society was reinforced by the public status of religion. Because Christianity had legal status within Canada, the legal rights of Jews, as individuals and as a group, became public issues in the federal and provincial parliaments and in the courts. This was particularly true in Quebec, where the majority French-Catholic community and the minority English-Protestant community had clear corporate rights. Among the political issues involving Judaism that have appeared at various times in Canadian history are disputes involving the right of a Jew to sit as a member of the legislative assembly in Lower Canada (Quebec); the right of the Jews in Lower Canada to maintain official registers of births, deaths, and marriages parallel to those kept by the Catholics and Protestants; the rights of Jewish taxpayers and school children in the confessional school systems of Quebec; slanders directed at the Talmud and other Jewish teachings; the burdens imposed upon Sabbath-observing Jews by various Sunday-closing acts; the propriety of slaughtering animals according to Jewish law; legal supervision of butchers' claims to *kashrut*; and public subsidies for the secular portion of Jewish day-school studies.

Communal Judaism Today

By the 1950s Canada had a large native-born Jewish population, and the generation raised in the suburbs in the 1960s and 1970s added to its numbers. Jews are now moving to new neighbourhoods, primarily in the suburbs, that are less homogeneously Jewish than the old ones. Canadian society, in turn, has become increasingly secular. A shopping mall in a predominantly Jewish suburb is little different from a shopping mall in a predominantly Gentile one. The synagogue-centres provide locations where religious identification is appropriate. In other places, secular social conventions set common standards for Jews and Gentiles.

Nevertheless, Judaism has not retreated entirely to the privacy of the synagogue-centre. Communal religious schools, particularly day schools, have flourished in the suburbs. Jewish bookstores, butchers, bakeries, and restaurants have also made the transition. Moreover, the organizational structure of the Jewish community does not rigidly separate the religious from the secular. Synagogues and other religious organizations are affiliated with the Canadian Jewish Congress and its local counterparts, and Congress has a National Religious Committee, which discusses religious issues as they affect the community at large. At the local level, communally funded Jewish organizations are sensitive to the fact that most of the Jews they serve have religious needs of one kind or another, and they respond by providing kosher meals-on-wheels, employing rabbis as chaplains to Jews in institutions, making available space for chapels in communally owned buildings, sponsoring celebrations of some Jewish holidays, supporting Jewish public libraries, and providing public forums for the discussion of religious topics.

JUDAISM IN THE LIVES OF CANADIAN JEWS

A story is told about a rabbi being interviewed for a position by the board of directors of a congregation. On Saturday he was to lead services as a guest. "Don't talk about driving on the Sabbath," advised a helpful board member. "If our members didn't drive, we'd have very few here."

"Don't talk about the dietary laws, either," another joined in. "For some people, it's a delicate subject."

"Watch what you say about intermarriage, too," added a third. And, warming to the task, the board members went on and on, indicating all those topics that were likely to offend.

Finally, the rabbi responded with a question, "What *should* I talk about?"

The reply: "Talk about Judaism — it's wonderful!"

The story is a bit extreme, but it raises the proper issue. What relevance does Judaism have for the lifestyles of those Canadian Jews who identify with it? What difference does Canadian Jews' religion make in the kind of persons they are and the way in which they live?

Public and Private Judaism

From the conservative perspective, religion is a public matter. A public religious identity is one in which the individual is always identifiable as a member of a particular religious group, is considered bound by its prescriptions and proscriptions, and maintains a social distance from those of other faiths. Traditionally, the Jews, in their ghettos, *shtetls*, and similar segregated environments, had a public religious identity, signalled to Jews and non-Jews alike by their distinctive dress, speech, and customs. In such traditional societies, public religious identity does not indicate piety; it is taken for granted that individuals are part of the religious community that they are born into, regardless of personal beliefs or observances. In our modern society, however, individuals have a choice of whether or not they wish to be publicly identified as members of a religious group.

A minority of Canadian Jews have chosen this public Jewish lifestyle. The committed Orthodox, as distinguished from those who are simply affiliated with Orthodox synagogues, have made this choice. The men cover their heads not only in Jewish places, but also in secular ones. The women also follow rules of dress that give them an appearance not always consistent with current fashions. Strict adherence to the dietary laws means the committed Orthodox cannot join others at meals in non-Jewish places — or in some Jewish ones as well. They refuse to take jobs that require work on the Sabbath or other Jewish holidays. Wherever they are, whatever the activity, regardless of whom they are with, they are identifiable as Orthodox Jews, and their participation is restricted to what it is proper for an Orthodox Jew to do.

The committed Orthodox are not the only Jews whose religious commitment is manifest to the public at large. Rabbis, of non-Orthodox congregations in particular, are expected to play a public role of ambassador of the Jewish religious perspective to the non-Jewish community. The vast majority of Canadian Jews, however, do not choose a public identity in which their religious commitment is always visible, just as the vast majority of Canadian Christians do not choose to make a public point of their Christianity. Rather, most Jews, like most Christians, choose to make a distinction between public life and private life.

This distinction follows from the liberal perspective on the role of religion in society. In a society in which faith is a private matter, an individual meets in public with others of different faiths, and they act together on the basis of neutral, secular values and conventions they all share. Considering religious commitment a private matter is one way of handling the tensions of a religiously pluralistic, democratic society.

Public and private life, although distinguishable, are nevertheless interrelated — they are two aspects of one person's life and should make sense together. The religious identification found in the private lives of most Canadian Jews is connected to their public roles. How this connection is made while the distinction between public and private is maintained may be seen in how the Canadian Jew deals with ritual observance, morality, and the search for meaning and community.

Religious Rituals

Judaism has traditionally prescribed a way of life in which the sacred canopy extends to mundane activities, sanctifying them through an elaborate system of ritual. Although the non-Orthodox branches of Judaism have considerably simplified this system, they continue to affirm the value of Jewish rituals.

The anthropologist Evelyn Kallen has studied Canadian Jewish identity through successive generations. Her study indicates that more Jewish rituals were observed in Europe than among immigrants to North America, that second-generation Jews observed fewer than their immigrant parents, and that third-generation Jews observe fewer still.[12] There are numerous exceptions to this trend, but they are not prevalent enough to reverse it. Despite the decline, however, religious observance is still common in the lives of Canadian Jews. The life cycle of the Jew is still typically marked by religious occasions — circumcision of the male child eight days after birth, bar-mitzvah or bat-mitzvah or confirmation at adolescence, marriage, and burial. A yearly cycle of observance also remains. Most Jews attend high holiday services and Passover seders. Large numbers celebrate Chanukah and Purim. Synagogue attendance and observance of ritual by parents is most common while their children are in religious school.

This pattern of ritual retention represents an accommodation of two desires: active participation in secular society *and* Jewish continuity. These ritual practices do not interfere with participation in the normal routines of the broader society. They are annual or infrequent; they can be understood in ways compatible with the values of the broader society. They do not require a daily lifestyle that deviates from convention. On the other hand, these practices are part of a strategy of Jewish survival in private life. They provide alternatives to the broader society's celebrations of Christmas and Easter. They are often child centred, and they symbolize to Jews that they belong to a common community.[13]

Judaism as Moral Guidance

Religion is not only symbolic of community identification; it is also a framework for the social affirmation of ethical behaviour. Ethical concerns have been intrinsic to Judaism throughout its history. Surveys from the United States indicate that to "lead an ethical and moral life" is commonly held as most essential to being a good Jew.[14] Joseph Blau has argued that American Jews feel attached to their religion primarily as a source of morality and only secondarily as an organizational framework with which they feel compelled to affiliate.[15] This understanding of Judaism is important in Canada also, but the greater conservatism of Canadian Judaism suggests that the emphasis of ethics over ritual may not be as pronounced in Canada as it is in the United States.[16]

The identification of Judaism with morality is another means of easing minority group adaptation, of harmonizing the public and the private, for, after all, the ethical principles of the broader society have a major source in the moral insights of Judaism.[17] The Jew can participate, as a Jew, in the social consensus on morality and ethics.

Ultimate Questions and Community

Religion may also be seen as a response to the human need to confront ultimate questions of values and purpose in life and to create supportive communities. The public world of liberal society is secular and rationalistic, but in that society's private worlds, religion can provide comforting beliefs that transcend reason. Even individuals, laymen and leaders alike, who are no longer secure in their beliefs can continue to use the religious framework as the setting in which they address the fundamental issues of meaning in life. The religious community, based on shared beliefs and the common search for ultimate values, emphasizes its members' caring for each other and sharing their resources in contrast to the self-interested competition of public life.

The specific content of the various branches of Judaism differs, but each presents a world view that gives meaning to human existence and Jewish particularity, and each teaches the responsibility of each Jew to the community and the reciprocal responsibility of the community to each Jew.

Uncertainties of Religious Identification

As Judaism moves from public to private life, it becomes a less all-embracing aspect of personal identity. Moreover, for many Canadian Jews, even private life is no longer as religious or as Jewish as it once was. Canadian Jews are now less likely to choose their spouses and friends within the community of faith into which they were born. They are more likely to construct their personal private worlds by finding friends and spouses among fellow students at university, among co-workers or others in the same occupation or profession, or among other persons they encounter with whom they share a special interest.

Thus, the division of public and private life itself creates a gap to be bridged; as Canadian Jews share their private lives more and more with others who do not share their religious identity, uncertainty about what that religious identity involves is to be expected. In particular, the construction of private worlds often leads to confusion about religious commitment and ritual observance and about alternative bases of morality and ways of finding meaning and community in life.

Commitment and Ritual Observance

Jewish children are sent to schools that are primarily under religious sponsorship in order to learn about their religious identity. In these schools, Judaism is taught as something important in itself as well as a means through which the survival of a Jewish community is secured. In many cases, then, children are taught beliefs that their parents do not share and practices that their parents do not observe; the children resent elders who force on them what the parents themselves do not accept. This situation naturally leads to considerable frustration on the part of students, parents, and staff members. Either the parents do not explain — perhaps because they can't — their use of religious practices as symbolic of Jewish peoplehood, or the children don't understand their parents' explanations.

What does this common discontinuity between family and school suggest about the attitude that is being fostered towards Judaism? Some students may come to identify with the values and way of life taught in the school, rejecting the nominal Judaism of their parents. Many others are likely to reject Judaism altogether, identifying with those things that their parents, through their deeds, demonstrate as actually important to them. But such polarization is not inevitable. Children and adolescents troubled by the religious "hypocrisy" of their parents may later in life come to share that attitude towards Judaism. They may also come to understand their personal Judaism as a private commitment that relates them to the public world but is not a visible part of their public identity.

Whether young adults identify with Jewish beliefs about which they are uncertain and practices that they do not observe depends on many things — for example, their relationship with their parents, their emotional response to religious events such as the Passover seder, the friends they have made, the neighbourhood in which they reside, their intellectual sophistication, and their moral courage. Each of these things can move an individual either towards identification with Judaism or away from it. And events normally require that a choice be made.

Alternative Bases of Morality

Understanding Judaism as a source of morality is also a source of uncertainty. If Judaism is reduced to ethics, it becomes simply one choice among alternative ethical systems open to all members of Canadian society. If liberal Christianity, humanism, social democracy, or other value systems can provide equivalent ethics without the social costs of being Jewish, what is the incentive to affirm morality by remaining within the Jewish community?

Secular Values in Private Life

Individuals who choose a public Jewish identity indicate that it is central to their lives. Likewise, a commitment to Judaism that is overt in private life and latent in public life can also be central to a person's identity. The separation between public and private life, however, also allows other relationships between the two. It is possible for the secular values of public life to be used as a basis for private life. Identification with Judaism may be seen as supplementary to a world view that is basically secular. This style of religious identification is described in *Crestwood Heights*, a detailed study conducted in the Forest Hills section of Metropolitan Toronto in the 1950s. A team of social scientists found little overt rejection of religion. Rather, Gentile and Jew alike considered religion a useful means to attain the ends of health, happiness, and success. These central goals were held to be principally attained through success in competitive careers.[18]

Career orientations are hardly unique to Crestwood Heights.[19] Careerism is one aspect of a broader orientation to life that the sociologist Thomas Luckmann calls "the invisible religion".[20] Secularization appears to have removed religion from most of our daily life, but the mass media — television, radio, books, newspapers, magazines — supply a marketplace of ideas that implicitly rest on fundamental beliefs about ultimate values. The belief in the ultimate importance of individual autonomy supports this invisible religion's major themes, including a belief in self-realization and self-expression as the goals of life. The successful career is seen an excellent means of achieving these goals; success creates the material conditions for self-gratification, and a career ideally allows for self-realization in work.

Martin Buber, writing of "the eclipse of God", also perceived the opposition of traditional religious concerns and modern self-centredness. "This selfhood that has become omnipotent," he wrote, ". . . can naturally acknowledge neither God nor any genuine absolute which manifests itself to men as of non-human origin. It steps in between and shuts off from us the light of heaven."[21]

The adherence of many Jews (along with many others in the broader society) to the invisible religion and the eclipse of God in the contemplation of Narcissus[22] are further compounded by the confusion between a commitment to Judaism and an emotional identification with the nation of Israel. Deep concern for other Jews and yearning for Zion are important traditional elements of Judaism. If support for Israel is used as a criterion, Canadian Jews can be judged as quite religious. Their per-capita contributions to the United Israel Appeal are among the highest in the world; their rate of *aliyah* (immigration to the Jewish homeland) is not strikingly high in itself, but it is twice that of the Jews of the United States. However, support for a revived Jewish state can be used as a means of identifying with a religious perspective that is otherwise neither well understood nor deeply experienced. Emotional identification with Israel may make some Canadian Jews comfortable in a religious setting, but it is a way of being comfortable with Judaism that limits its relevance.

THE DILEMMAS OF THE DIASPORA

Jewish immigrants brought to Canada a Judaism that was not only a religion in the limited theological sense but was what Mordecai Kaplan has called "a religious civilization". In this civilization, the elements of their culture — songs, stories, traditions, foods, literature, dress, language, and customs — were all intertwined around a religious core; the judges were rabbis, the law books were the Torah and the Talmud, and the head of state was the always present, always invisible God.

Canadian Jews have created institutions — synagogues, schools, community facilities, and organizations — that perpetuate their religious heritage in an increasingly secular, materialistic society. In these institutions and in their homes, Judaism provides occasions for the symbolic celebration of community identification, gives a basis for understanding morality, and offers approaches to the question of meaning and purpose in the universe.

Yet Judaism is a minority religion that is largely confined to the private sphere of Canadian life. Through their participation in the broader society, Canadian Jews belong to other communities, understand their morality in other ways, and use other approaches to the question of meaning and purpose. If the religion dimension of Jewish culture is attentuated by privatization, does there remain a coherent, meaningful culture to pass on, or are fragments of a culture all that is left? Israel Zangwill related religion to the survival of minority cultures this way:

> So long as the Diaspora believes in Judaism, it has no need of a spiritual centre. . . . A spiritual centre in Zion may suffice to hold the first generation of absentee Zionists minus Judaism without either political or religious substance, but it will not avail to keep their children. No minority in history has ever sustained itself in the bosom of a majority unless fortified by a burning faith.[23]

Canadian Jews are not alone in this situation. The survival of all minority communities depends upon their ability to provide to their members, children, and potential members a way of life more satisfying than the way of life into which they are invited to assimilate.

Power
in the Jewish
Community

by Harold M. Waller

The Jewish community is a political system. Of course, there are
obvious differences between it and a nation state or other government units; most important, the latter can compel compliance
from persons within their bounds while the Jewish community is
a voluntary system. Nevertheless, the Jewish community acts as a
government in a limited sphere for persons willing to submit to
the discipline of membership and accept its decisions as binding.

*Jewish
Commun
as
a
political
gov't*

Any examination of the community must deal with the way
in which those decisions are made and with the people who make
them — in short, with power. Social scientists have dozens of
definitions of power; a useful working one is the ability to accomplish goals. Within a given system, who are the people most
capable of achieving their goals? What techniques do they use to
do so? What consequences do the distribution of power and the
methods of decision-making have for the whole society?

*Power →
ability
to
make
decisions
→
Who has
it*

Power cannot be separated from finances for many of the
key decisions in the Jewish community, as in most political
systems, deal with such matters. In fact, it can be argued that tax-
ing and spending are the most important activities of community-
governing bodies because the amounts available and the manner
in which they are allocated largely determine the scope and nature
of the community's activities. And although the Jewish community cannot use legal compulsion to collect money from its
members, it is possible and useful to view its general fund-raising
as a form of taxation.

*Power
&
finances*

The Jewish Political System

Since biblical times, Jews have viewed political systems in terms of groups formed by consensus through compacts or agreements. Within such a group, traditionally, the concept of equality was paramount, but the notion of the divine source of law limited the use of democratic principles and forms. One historian noted that Jewish regimes have had "aristocratic tendencies that often have degenerated into oligarchic patterns of rule", although infrequently into autocracy.[1] In other words, in the traditional view, people were entitled to equal treatment but not equal participation in what is now called the political process.

Another principle guiding Jewish politics historically was a commitment to bargaining as a key method of decision-making. This brought cooperation and consensus, which were deemed preferable to conflict and divisiveness, and gave less value to voting per se. Such an approach was the result of the idea of a society based on a covenantal relationship between man and God, which implied obligations on both sides.

In modern times, these traditional Jewish views of political systems led to the establishment of federal models of organization whereby disparate groups can affirm common interests and goals without relinquishing their own identities. In other words, the "new" communal federation, which has become so important in North America in recent decades, is really a manifestation of consensus and covenant, a form of relationship basic to the political culture of the Jewish people for millenia.[2]

North American Jewry also inherited what one observer has called the "political tradition of aristocratic republicanism"[3] from its forebears in Europe, where leadership was usually based on scholarship, wealth, or social class. The utility of Judaic learning for leaders declined in America, where the authoritative interpretation of religious questions was not as important as in Europe, but the custom of entrusting communal responsibilities to the wealthy and well-born persists, with certain modifications that have enlarged the pool of potential leaders.[4]

Such emphasis on the economic power and social status of leaders can, of course, raise questions about the nature of governance. If the elite confuses its own interests with those of the community at large, power can become significantly concentrated in the hands of an oligarchy. Fortunately, the Jewish community usually balances this tendency with a general distrust of centralized power and fear of abuse of the masses,[5] an attitude that is particularly strong among American Jews. The result is that the political process in the Jewish community of the United States has evolved into a "trusteeship of givers and doers".[6] Wealth and status are not the only means of entering the leadership; some individuals are self-selected on the basis of their ability and their willingness to assume responsibility.

In Canada today, power in the Jewish community may be observed at three levels: the national, the local, and the sublocal. The last refers to individual congregations or to chapters of some national organizations and is not of great interest here. The other two are closely related. Most national organizations are based upon local units; the general route to power at the national level is through a base in a local organization. It is highly unusual for someone to achieve power and importance nationally without a strong local base. Therefore, the best way to study power in the Canadian Jewish community is to look first at the local communities, especially the two large ones, Montreal and Toronto. Afterwards the analysis can be extended to the national process.

One way in which the national Jewish community structures of Canada and the U.S. differ is in the existence of a fair degree of centralization in Canada. The Canadian Jewish Congress (CJC) was established in 1919 to represent all Canadian Jews and their various organizations to governments, foreign Jewish bodies, and the outside world in general. As a result, Canadian Jews are accustomed to the notion of unified representation in a way that American Jews are not. The CJC sometimes finds itself resisting encroachment of other national organizations, such as the Canadian Zionist Federation or B'nai B'rith, but the idea of communal unity is generally respected.

At the local level in recent years the situation has been a bit more complicated because the CJC and the local welfare federations compete for the dominant role in community affairs. Conceptually the two are separate. The local CJC affiliates, working with, through, and from the national organization, represent corporate Canadian Jewry and deal in particular with the outside world and cultural and educational issues. The federations, on the other hand, are a new phenomenon, heavily influenced by the American experience. Developed out of a desire to unify, coordinate, and fund the increasing social services perceived as necessary in modern times, they became important in Canada in the aftermath of the Second World War. As they became more tightly organized and more centralized, they began to widen their areas of activity, expanding from welfare services into the broader realm of general community policy-making. By the 1970s, theoretical niceties notwithstanding, they constituted a serious challenge to the primacy of Congress, especially since they often exhibited more drive, vitality, and relevance than did local CJC affiliates.[7] The result was a reassessment of the roles of the major organizations, at least in the larger cities. The Winnipeg and Toronto communities each decided to merge the local CJC operation with the local federation, preserving at least the appearance of a centralized structure. The Montreal organizations discussed a similar plan at great length during 1978; although it was shelved, it seems likely to reappear within a few years.

Because of the tradition of centralization, political power tends to be concentrated primarily in those organizations that have the broadest scope. Today these are the CJC, its regional groupings, and the federations (merged or not). Other organizations, such as Zionist groups, fraternal bodies, educational and cultural institutions, and synagogues are generally too specialized to provide their activists with access to community-wide power. Individuals who aspire to positions of leadership generally have to become involved in either the local welfare federation or the local CJC affiliate (or even both) at a fairly early stage in their careers. By succeeding at ever-increasing responsibilities, some reach the higher levels of these organizations and begin to get involved in national activities; eventually, they may be recruited to leadership positions at that level, too.

Jews in the Canadian Economy

Although merit is important in achieving power in the Jewish community, it is by no means the only criterion. Socio-economic realities are of enormous importance in the Jewish community, in the larger Canadian community that surrounds it, and in the interplay between the two. Although power, which is essentially a political concept, is not exclusively a function of economic resources, one need not be a Marxist to recognize the importance of economics in most modern societies. Canadian Jews may have brought their own traditions of communal organization with them from their previous homes, usually in Eastern Europe, but they have hardly been insulated from the patterns that exist in Canadian society in general.

One of the most striking aspects of Canadian life is the importance of ethnicity. At Confederation, the country comprised two main groups: those of British extraction and those of French, with the former politically and economically dominant. Subsequently, Canada absorbed many immigrants from other backgrounds, so many that by the 1971 census fully 26.7 per cent of the population had neither British nor French origins. Nevertheless, as has been amply documented, a WASP elite, based on socio-economic status, and to a lesser extent, family relationships, has retained control of the country's major economic institutions, especially its corporations and financial sector.[8]

In general, this elite is closed to persons of non-British origin. At least one researcher noted that Jews were the most likely members of other ethnic groups to be found among the Canadian economic elite in the early 1970s, but they were not an integral part of it. Instead, they "are more correctly understood as an elite of the Jewish community, separate yet interlocking in a peripheral way with the Anglo-dominated elite".[9] The individual Jews who have penetrated the elite have done so outside of the main sectors of economic power, usually in high-risk enterprises, such as retailing or real estate. Another possible access route has been the legal profession, though very few Jews have used it.

The existence of a parallel Jewish elite has important implications for the study of power within the Canadian Jewish community. It can be argued that the Jewish elite models itself, perhaps unconsciously, on the WASP elite. If so, this represents a major development in the life of a people who migrated to Canada primarily during the twentieth century, mainly after the First World War. The immigrants who came from Eastern Europe were mostly poor and almost entirely working class. Consequently, their leaders exhibited working-class values and aspirations. For example, the Jewish labour movement played an integral part in founding the Canadian Jewish Congress in 1919. As a moneyed class began to emerge, especially after the Second World War, class distinctions became more crucial in Jewish life.

By the 1970s the Jewish community's occupational structure reflected a major shift from both the pattern of the immigrant generation and that of the Canadian population in general. The 1971 census showed that Jews were much more heavily represented in occupations of at least potentially high status than were Canadians in general. This was particularly evident in categories such as management and administration, social science and law, and medicine, as shown in Table 1.

Even so, the financial status of Canadian Jews varies widely. Precise figures are not readily available, but a 1978 sample survey of Montreal Jewish households is probably a good indicator. It revealed a median family income of about $20,000, somewhat higher than that of the general population, even though the existence of a substantial proportion of poor Jews in Montreal tended to pull the statistical median down. At the upper end of the scale, however, 13 per cent of the Jewish households surveyed had incomes over $50,000.[10] Thus, although the median Jewish income in Montreal is only somewhat over that of the general population, the proportion of the Jewish population at the upper income level is quite remarkable.

TABLE 1

Occupations of Total Population and Jewish Ethnic Group, 1971

	Males		Females	
	All Canadians	Jews	All Canadians	Jews
Managing, administration	5.5%	14.0%	2.0%	4.1%
Natural science, engineering, math	3.8	3.5	0.6	0.9
Social science, law	0.9	3.6	0.6	2.6
Teaching	2.4	3.5	7.1	8.5
Medicine, health	1.5	5.1	8.2	4.5
Art, literary	1.0	2.2	0.7	1.8
Clerical work	7.6	8.7	31.8	37.6
Sales	10.1	27.3	8.4	17.9
Service occupations	9.2	4.9	15.1	4.9
Processing	4.9	1.8	2.0	.....
Farming, fishing, etc.	9.8	.....	3.6	.....
Machinery, materials, etc.	8.6	.....	2.6	.....
Product fabrication	8.5	7.7	5.1	3.6
Construction	9.9	2.5	0.2	.....
Transport	5.8	2.5	0.3	.....
Other	10.5	12.7	11.7	13.6
Total	100.0	100.0	100.0	100.0
Number in occupations (thousands)	5,666	91	2,961	48

SOURCE: 1971 census data.

In brief, the Canadian Jewish community is a relatively affluent one, though extremes exist. And since well-to-do Jews provide a large proportion of the community's revenue (which must be obtained by fund-raising), they are in an excellent position to influence policies. Affluence is no guarantee of political power, but, as in the general Canadian situation, it does not hurt. It enables an individual to associate with others who are in positions of power and makes him eligible for entry into the elite. Whether he does, in fact, become powerful depends upon his other assets, including ability, talent, dedication, and commitment.

Leaders at the Local Level

Montreal and Toronto, which are home to about three-quarters of Canada's Jews, understandably dominate national Jewish affairs. Their local political systems are elaborate and highly developed, based on an array of organizations and service agencies. Access to true power, however, is generally limited to those with access to the decision-making process in those organizations whose policies and actions determine the most important factors that affect the lives of Jews within their jurisdiction (insofar as these matters are within the control of the Jewish community at all). In effect, this limitation restricts power at the local level in Toronto to those who can influence or control decisions of the Toronto Jewish Congress (the merged entity), and in Montreal to those who can affect the actions of the Allied Jewish Community Services (AJCS, the Montreal welfare federation) or the Quebec Region of the CJC (which essentially serves Montreal).

Although social scientists (or anyone reading lists of board members and officers) can show that an elite runs these groups, they, like all Jewish organizations, are constantly looking for new "leadership material". Generally, potential leaders are brought into an organization by those already involved, although some people may simply volunteer for responsible work in fund-raising or one of the welfare agencies. Jewish organizations rarely hold mass public elections for council members, board members, and officers (although the CJC tries to come close to that ideal).

A recruit who succeeds in his assigned tasks and appears to fit in well with the rest of the group receives increasingly important tasks. The AJCS and Toronto Jewish Congress invite talented newcomers to participate in leadership training programs. Often major fund-raising campaign responsibilities are a prelude to an important decision-making position.

Hard work and dedication are always keys to advancement. Nevertheless, the system gives a definite preference to the affluent. In the first place, the well-to-do simply have time for unremunerated activity. (This phenomenon has been widely observed in the literature on political participation and seems to hold in Jewish life as well.) Moreover, the selection process helps to create and perpetuate an elite because it is so highly dependent upon the personal, professional, and business connections of those already in power. Disproportionate numbers of communal leaders come from certain business fields or the legal profession. In both Montreal and Toronto, many professions, including medicine, dentistry, academia, and the rabbinate, are not well represented.[11] Whole social, economic, and religious groups tend to be neglected, including women and the poor (especially the elderly poor). In Montreal, which has had a significant proportion of Sephardic Jews, mainly from Morocco, since the 1950s, the major leadership positions remain in the hands of Ashkenazic Jews. (The Sephardim have formed their own communal organizations, which have become quite vigorous during recent years.)

The method of recruitment also tilts the power structure towards older rather than younger men, a bias that is reenforced by the controlled process of advancement. Only in unusual cases does a young person skip stages and move up to the top quickly.

Formal positions in the organizations are not, however, the only basis for power in the Jewish community. Individuals with valuable political resources (wealth, prestige, expertise, and so on) are able to influence the political process. Indeed, the nature of the Jewish political process lends itself to decision-making out of the public eye, a fact that works to the advantage of those who do not hold formal positions of power.

Historically, the best Canadian example of behind-the-scenes power was the late Samuel Bronfman, whose support was an essential element for any successful undertaking in the Montreal Jewish community for years. Though he at times held organizational leadership positions, his status was built on a combination of factors: he headed the wealthiest family in the community, and his personality and commitment enabled him to stand head and shoulders above other community leaders. After his death in 1971, no single person was able to assume a dominant position in the Montreal Jewish community, but several individuals, mostly men of means, became key actors independent of the official positions they held. Toronto has never had a leader comparable to Bronfman. As a result, its tradition is one of plural leadership and perhaps a bit more openness than Montreal's. Even so, a few leaders in the city command respect and deference independent of their official positions.

Another group playing a role in the political process are the community professionals, the people who actually run the organizations. As the groups have become increasingly professionalized in recent years, opportunities for careers in the Jewish civil service have multiplied. Jewish federations, in particular, are no longer seat-of-the-pants operations. On the contrary, they require sophisticated managerial tools and administrative techniques.[12] Opportunities thus exist for Jewish civil servants to establish themselves as separate political entities, distinct from both the leaders and the grass roots and to receive prestige and high status in the community. Simply by virtue of intimate everyday involvement in the affairs of an organization, a professional is in a better position to pull the levers of political power than most lay people, to influence policy without making it in a formal sense. The professional with sharp bureaucratic skills may even dominate an organization without the volunteer leaders being aware of the fact. He has an excellent opportunity to structure the policy choices available to the lay leaders and otherwise to run operations as he thinks best for the organization.

Two outstanding models for the new breed of professionals were the late Saul Hayes, who ran the CJC as executive vice-president for years, and Manny Batshaw, who occupied a similar position at AJCS. For years these able and experienced men shaped their respective organizations. Neither group is likely to have a comparable personality at the helm in the short term, which may mean less even direction for the organizations.

The very influence of popular, highly competent professionals can also be a problem if it becomes a source of tension between themselves and lay leaders. As communities become increasingly centralized, the potential power of the professionals grows. The exact balance between them and the lay leaders depends upon such factors as the professionals' expertise, control of information, and, of course, competence, and the lay leaders' assertiveness, knowledge, and political ability, as well as on the personalities involved.

The Exercise of Political Power

Any decision-making process must be viewed in the contexts of the persons who have the power and of the means they use to reach decisions. In the Jewish community, the traditional methods are those that lead to consensus. Accommodation has a much higher value than does winning by a strictly democratic vote. This sort of accommodation begins with the process of choosing the decision-makers. The composition of the formal statutory body affects the outcome of decisions in any organization. Most Jewish organizations are set up so that current leaders, in effect, choose their own successors. Careful selection and controlled advancement of newcomers can ensure that voting does not get out of hand.

Several other factors constitute a check on democratic forms. One is the custom of key members of the elite discussing an issue before the official body debates it. Studies in both Montreal and Toronto show that persons in contact with the decision-making process are well aware of this practice, whether they are part of the elite or not. As one Montreal professional put it, "We do know that many decisions are made at the Montefiore Club [a dining club for affluent Jews]." Obviously, not all decisions are made by a small group over lunch at the Montefiore Club or its Toronto equivalents; the vast majority flow through the regular channels of the CJC or the federations and are often discussed in fairly large meetings. But for crucial decisions, an inner group moves in quietly and assumes responsibility. A discreet meeting at the club or in someone's home allows these men to work out a position that reflects a certain amount of negotiation but can be presented publically with a reasonably united front. The members of the statutory body to which it is brought may or may not realize that they are ratifying a decision made elsewhere.

In Montreal when Sam Bronfman was alive, every major matter was brought to his attention at an early stage. Then he would call in a few other key men to discuss the matter. Once they were behind the project, he would convene about twenty-five or thirty of the leading community contributors; when he had convinced them, the rest followed in due course. Bronfman's method was a very personal one that could not persist after his death, especially since the AJCS made its structure more formal at about the same time. People in the background can still use their influence to affect outcomes, but the process is more subtle than it was under Bronfman.

The situation is much the same in Toronto. Although its decision-making group has always had the reputation of being somewhat more open than Montreal's, the recent merger of the local CJC and the welfare federation, which caused considerable conflict, necessitated a reshuffling of alliances.[13] Moreover, the structure of the CJC is more democratic in principle. Thus, Toronto's key decision-makers probably now have less scope for action than they did formerly, although they can remain in control by deciding crucial issues among themselves before they reach the floor for public debate.

Another factor that affects the distribution of power in the community dovetails with the system's use of accommodation and behind-the-scenes negotiations. This is the community's financial dependence on the relatively few wealthy families who contribute such a large proportion of its funds. Whether or not the representatives of these families hold official positions of responsibility, their desires must be important in any realistic decision-making process. Although fund-raisers can pressure the wealthy to donate large sums, ultimately contributions are voluntary. The community cannot compel contributions in the way a government can levy a tax. The ever-present, if implicit, threat of refusing to contribute in the future gives substantial weight to the preferences of the "big givers".

Despite these behind-the-scenes pressures, studies show that the formal committees or boards are not mere rubber stamps. Although the key men can shape decisions, they cannot afford to push things through against the wishes of public boards, a consideration that results in a type of elite accommodation. This gives the process more openness than might otherwise have been expected. As one researcher has pointed out, the common concerns and interests of the elites give a certain overall predictability to decision-making, but there is also fragmentation and competition that sustains democratic tendencies.[14]

One problem here lies, of course, in the decision-makers' perceptions of community needs. A recent study of AJCS board members compared their priorities with those of other Jewish groups, such as agency managers and people who use the welfare services. The unsurprising conclusion was that great differences exist.[15] Hence, any group that is not adequately represented within the elite must campaign very energetically in order to persuade the decision-makers of the correctness and desirability of a position outside their usual point of view.

It can be done, however, particularly if the campaigners are able to enlist the support of the community-service professionals, who are placed so that they can ease grass-roots participation in community decision-making, if they wish to do so. In Montreal, for example, social workers (with some support from academics and others) stimulated a group of poor and aged Jews to mount a pressure campaign that persuaded the leaders of AJCS to fund Project Genesis, a service for the aged poor. The group did not succeed easily or without rancor and the project has no assurance of continuity, but the funding was forthcoming.

Another grass-roots issue on which the Montreal elite walked a tightrope but finally decided to avoid controversy involved that city's Jewish day schools. Traditionally, they had received no general community funding. During the 1960s, they faced increasing financial difficulties and, like many private schools in the province, managed to obtain per-pupil grants from the Quebec government. (Eventually, the AJCS, through the

Jewish Education Council, provided marginal increments to the government contributions.) During the early 1970s, however, the Liberal provincial government tied continuing provision of money to conversion of the schools' secular programs to a French-language curriculum, even though the bulk of the students spoke English as their mother tongue. When the Parti Québécois took power in 1976, it increased admissions barriers and added so many curriculum constraints that many parents, students, and educators saw compliance as creating schools that no longer met the needs they perceived. Consequently, the day schools turned to the Jewish community, especially the AJCS, for political support and for financial aid.

Neither was forthcoming. The AJCS leaders made it clear they would refuse to take a strong stand against the government, partly because they perceived being in open opposition to government policies as undesirable for the Jewish community and partly because the big contributors to the fund-raising drive were simply not interested in increasing their gifts in order to ameliorate the problems of the day schools. Yet, grass-roots pressure compelled the originally indifferent leaders to take some responsibility for the day schools. Having done that, however, they were able to nudge the schools to an accommodationist posture, despite the serious misgivings of many parents and educators.

All of these considerations show that decision-making — and hence power — in Jewish communal life rests mainly with an elite. These men take their trusteeship seriously, assuming leadership roles out of a sense of responsibility and even obligation. Other groups in the community can reach them, albeit with difficulty. One primary goal of their decision-making process is to avoid open controversy.

During the early 1970s, when social scientists examined the Jewish elites of both Toronto and Montreal, control of each community's affairs rested in the hands of no more than sixteen or twenty men. These were almost all well educated, successful businessmen or professionals, in their sixties or seventies, residents of affluent sections of town, members of select synagogues and private clubs. Some of them were related to each other through marriage. Many were personally wealthy. With them, though not quite of them, stood a very few top Jewish civil servants in each city, men whose jobs and personalities combined to give them enormous influence in community affairs. These people constitute the Jewish establishment.[16] There is constantly talk about broadening the base of communal leadership by bringing new people in, but during the decade of the 1970s, the only noticeable shift in the profile of Jewish leadership was the inclusion of some relatively younger men.

The elite is not really a closed group, but entry is closely controlled, so unless a powerful insurgent group arises, the elite can perpetuate itself. The likelihood of replacing the present elite with another is small, because the group now in control includes most of the wealthy Jews who care about Jewish life. Any change in political control would prove a futile gesture unless the larger contributors to the fund-raising campaigns accepted it.

The Smaller Communities

Of the Canadian Jewish communities outside Toronto and Montreal, only Winnipeg has more than a few thousand members, so Jewish life in them is not nearly as complex and organized as it is in the two large cities. Nevertheless, wherever there are at least several hundred Jews, there is usually an organized Jewish community, usually some sort of council affiliated with the CJC.

Size precludes the possibility of any of the smaller communities offering the wide range of services that Toronto and Montreal provide. Thus the scope of decisions to be made is relatively narrower, and the political stakes in Jewish community life are not as high. Identification with Israel, however, is an effective motivating force among nearly all Canadian Jews, and the raising of substantial amounts for it and whatever local activities exist is ample justification for energetic fund-raising organizations. Moreover, the fairly recent establishment of a National Budgeting Conference, comprising representatives of the federation or community council in each of Canada's eleven largest cities plus the United Israel Appeal, assured the smaller communities of some role in determining national spending priorities. So there are some consequential stakes for the decision-makers in the organizations of the smaller communities.

In general, the exercise of power in the smaller centres follows the patterns already observed in Toronto and Montreal. However, there are some differences. In Ottawa, for example, the key organization is the Va'ad Ha'ir, a council dominated by the synagogues, in sharp distinction to the essentially secular Jewish organizations of Montreal and Toronto. And since it is not a welfare federation, its operating scope is much narrower than that of the central organizations in the two large cities. Nevertheless, a study in the early 1970s suggested the key people in the Ottawa Jewish community had much the same profile as those in Montreal and Toronto. The Va'ad is dominated by a self-perpetuating elite; the "monetary factor still remains preeminent in leadership choice", and family traditions of leadership and service are also important. The formal holding of an office is not essential to the exercise of political power, and the realities of the sources of community funds weigh heavily on the decision-making process.[17]

In other cities, researchers have described Jewish community organization as oligarchy by the well-to-do. In Winnipeg, for example, the voluntary leaders are generally businessmen who have made it financially on their own.[18] A slightly different situation exists in Calgary, which is gradually moving from government by a few successful men to a more representative oligarchy as some less-than-wealthy people move into leadership positions. Nevertheless, large donors to the annual campaign dominate the community council, and six or eight families control the direction of policy, without necessarily holding office.[19]

The National Level

As a highly organized community, Canada's Jews have long emphasized a national presence. The recent trend in communal life, however, has been towards increased power for the welfare funds, which are local organizations, with the resulting anomaly of national organizations being overshadowed politically by local ones. This trend has particularly affected the CJC because it has no independent sources of financing but depends on money raised by the fund-raising arms of the local federations, especially those of Montreal and Toronto. The result has been two major developments: the merger movement in the larger communities and the establishment of the National Budgeting Conference to regularize the allocation of funds to national organizations.

Nevertheless, in an interesting way, money lies at the root of an important difference between politics at the national and the local level. Most of the latter's issues revolve around funding, budgetary allocations, service programs, and the like. At the national level, however, leaders are concerned with issues that often involve ideas rather than money; this makes it possible for different kinds of people to gain power there than would be the case locally. As a result, the national leadership is more heterogeneous and perhaps a bit more representative. Patterns of recruitment and advancement are more varied and perhaps more open. Spirited electoral battles are not unknown in national organizations, whereas they are extremely rare at the local level. In addition, Congress, which is still the most important national organization, has traditionally been more open to lawyers, intellectuals, and professionals than are the business-orientated dominant local bodies. Moreover, although it could once operate on its own, the CJC is now increasingly dependent upon accommodations worked out with other national bodies; these are usually based on some kind of elite agreement, which opens even more opportunities for leaders at the national level.

Clearly, success at the national level depends to a large extent on an individual's effort and effectiveness. He usually builds on the base of a strong local organization, but occasionally personal characteristics are sufficient. Financial status does not seem to be quite as important as at the local level, although one should not minimize its importance.

Another major factor in entering politics at the national level is home town. Toronto and Montreal make up so large a part of the national Jewish community that their people have generally dominated the political process. Periodically, this situation breeds resentment in other regions, but the sheer size of the two cities and the location of key offices in one or both make it difficult for people from elsewhere to function effectively. Montreal has traditionally been the source of most key national leaders, but the current trend is definitely towards Toronto. The several factors causing this shift include the emergence of that city as the national leader in trade and commerce, Jewish migration patterns, and the effect of recent provincial government actions on the vitality of the Montreal community. Moreover, the existence of a unified community structure in Toronto now provides a more solid organizational base than does the dual structure in Montreal.

Insofar as money issues do arise at the national level, the decision-making body is the National Budgeting Conference. Although it works by consensus most of the time, the interests of the Toronto Jewish Congress and Montreal's AJCS carry the most weight, so their representatives on it tend to be the most powerful people there.

Concluding Observations

In perspective, the distribution of power within the Canadian Jewish community reflects a certain tension between traditional oligarchical tendencies and the democratic impulse of the modern era. The fact that community organization and policies are not the most important considerations of most Jews, however, limits pressure for democratization. Most Jews simply do not make the effort to participate politically, although some may complain about political outcomes.

The trend in Canadian Jewish life is towards increasing importance for the welfare federations, although the existence of a national organization such as the CJC provides some balance. The socio-economic elite that dominates the federations and hence Jewish political life does not govern arbitrarily and is conscious of its trusteeship for the interests of the entire Jewish community. But the extent to which it actually responds to grass-roots sentiments varies, depending on the issue and what is at stake.

Not surprisingly, the system is not well equipped to cope with dissent. The leaders prefer consensus politics and are uncomfortable when faced with active opposition. Organized dissent is, in fact, rare, although individual dissenters do emerge from occasionally. They are often co-opted into the system, a practice that can inject new ideas into it without endangering basic values.

Jewish community politics in Canada is hardly a closed system, but it is not entirely open either. It functions quite well most of the time in delivering services and representing the interests of its constituency. It errs most often in favour of efficiency at the expense of formal democracy.

PART III

Beyond the Mainstream

*Jews and Gentiles alike have a stereotyped image
of Canadian Jews as middle class, primarily of German or Eastern
European background, concentrated in Montreal
and Toronto, acculturated into the larger society's lifestyle and
values, and led by males. For the bulk of Canadian Jewry,
this generalization is quite accurate. Yet it must be recognized
as a generalization, which, by definition, excludes
many particulars and many differences.*

*Although the Jewish community is one of the most cohesive
and institutionally complete ethnic and religious groups in
Canada, it is actually, like all such groups, a collection of
subgroups; each is distinctive, but together they make a whole
that surpasses the sum of its parts. Within Canadian Jewry, some
of these subgroups fit or approximate the stereotypes. But the
subgroups examined in this section — the poor, the aged,
women, the Francophone Sephardim, the Jews of the Atlantic
provinces and the West, and the Chassidim — are not part of the
mainstream and hence are often neglected in discussions and
analyses of the Jewish community in Canada.*

*In fact, some of these groups are so far from the stereotype that
they are increasingly coming to our attention. One reason is that
the Jewish community is affected by the same forces that shape
the larger society. As poverty was "discovered" in the 1960s, so*

too was it uncovered in the Jewish community. As women in
the larger society have increasingly questioned their roles and
status, so too have Jewish women expressed concern about their
role in the Jewish community. As Québécois nationalism
intensified in the 1960s and 1970s in an effort to retain and
reinforce a distinctive identity, so too has the Sephardic
community been encouraged to steer a course that will allow its
members to retain their heritage. And so on.

Less obvious reasons are the increasing general acceptance of Jews
and their relative affluence. As the spectres of anti-Semitism and
discrimination have become less threatening, the Jewish
community has been able to direct more of its energies and
resources inward and has thus become more aware that it is
diversified. Simultaneously, its general affluence has led to an
increase in the number of trained professionals and
institutionalized services encouraging the identification of
subgroups. Finally, the allocation of resources to sponsor
academically oriented research has culminated in various reports
and publications that draw attention to the diversity of the
Jewish community in Canada.

Certainly, one theme in the essays in this section is marginality.
Each of the groups discussed is sufficiently different from
the mainstream for its members to be identified as outsiders. This
phenomenon of exclusion is not related to the group's size
but to its lack of influence on the decision-making apparatus that
affects life in the Jewish community. Thus, it pertains
as much to women who, although roughly half the Jewish population, are effectively excluded from power within the
community as it does to the numerically small Chassidic Jews,
who voluntarily exclude themselves from many of the
concerns facing the community. More significantly, perhaps, is
the self-fulfilling prophecy that exclusion sets
into motion: those identified as marginal come to regard
themselves as such. It is because these people
see themselves as different and powerless that we must be
so alert to the challenges they present.

*In the first selection, on the Jewish poor, Jim Torczyner alerts us
to a fact of life of which most of the community is simply
unaware: a frightening number of Canadian Jews live in grinding
poverty. The author examines the quality and the
quantity of services available to the Jewish poor and suggests
an approach to the growing problems that face both
the impoverished and the community's machinery for
helping them. Although he only intimates the stigma
facing persons identified as poor, it is likely that such labelling
prevents many Jews from requesting financial assistance
through formal community channels.*

*In the next essay, Albert Rose explores the status of the elderly,
as well as the community's response to the needs of this
expanding age group. As happens with the poor, a series of myths
current within both the larger society and the Jewish
community creates the impression that the needs of the elderly
are well met within the community. As Rose argues, these
myths contain some elements of truth, but their totality is false.
And as further investigation would reveal, the elderly, like the
poor, have a marginal status within the community as a whole
and within their individual families that often results in self-
perceptions of failure and inadequacy.*

*The Jewish poor and elderly have not yet mounted a bid to alter
their collective status. In contrast, Jewish feminists are
marshalling efforts to change the position of women within
Judaism. Norma Baumel Joseph describes the rise of this
movement in Canada, adding reflections based on her personal
observations, experiences, and feminist concerns that have, at
times, clashed with the conventions of Orthodox Judaism.*

*In the three selections that follow — one by Jean-Claude Lasry
on North African Jews in Quebec, another by Sheva Medjuck
and Morty M. Lazar on the Jews of the Atlantic provinces, and a
third by Abraham Arnold on the Jews of Western Canada — a
common theme centres around alienation or, more accurately, a
feeling of exclusion. In the case of the North African Jews in*

Quebec, exclusion, as Lasry observes, is both in the spheres of social integration and political participation. Sephardic Jews in Montreal regard themselves and are seen by their Ashkenazic counterparts as forming a community within the larger Montreal Jewish community. In the case of the Western Jews, however, the sense of exclusion rests at the national level only; as Arnold points out, Jews of Western Canada have been part of the struggle against domination by the Montreal and Toronto Jewish communities while striving, simultaneously, to play an effective leadership role nationally. Meanwhile, in the Atlantic provinces, as Medjuck and Lazar describe, Jews are wrestling hopefully with small and declining populations, concentrated in relatively small centres. All three authors locate the current organization and concerns of their respective subjects within a historical context, thus enabling the reader to appreciate each as a distinctive contribution to the Canadian Jewish mosaic.

Unlike these groups, Chassidic Jews have, on the whole, chosen their restricted participation in the political and cultural affairs of the Jewish community. As William Shaffir observes, the various Chassidic groups share a recognition that retention of their unique identity must include a disengagement from everyone whose religious convictions differ from theirs. Many Jews regard the Chassidim's lifestyle as an anomaly, yet this segment of Canadian Jewry continues to flourish, reminding many Jews of their not-too-distant past.

In the end, it is internal differentiation that helps mould the general character of a group such as the Canadian Jews — and the way the mainstream responds to the distinctive needs of marginal subgroups will be a powerful force in shaping its future.

To Be Poor and Jewish in Canada

by Jim Torczyner

To be poor in present-day Canada is to be perceived as and often to think of oneself as having failed in a land of great wealth and opportunity. To be poor in Canada is to be marginal to the mainstream of a consumer society, to survive on minimal funds, often those dribbled out by government assistance programs. For an elderly single person, being poor means living on an inadequate government pension. For a family, poverty means having insufficient income to feed, house, and provide other necessities for adults and children; savings or luxuries are out of the question.

To be poor in Canada is to have no control over the basic decisions that affect one's life. The poor do not participate in setting the rates of government pensions or welfare assistance or choose which services are to be provided them, much less their quality or physical location. The poor do not even consult with the politicians, community leaders, and social workers who set forth and implement policies on their behalf. To be poor in Canada is to be powerless, isolated, and barely able to survive.

To be poor and Jewish in Canada is to have these indignities compounded by two myths: that there are very few, if any, Jewish poor, and that the Jewish community takes care of its own. The reality is typified by a man who lives in the central Jewish district of Montreal. Confined to a wheelchair, he has had no visitors for the past year, although he lives within two blocks of a synagogue and within five blocks of the city's major Jewish community institutions. He speaks little English and no French, fears his neighbours, and is harassed by a landlord to whom he pays almost two-thirds of his income in rent. He is left with $105 a month for all other expenses. On holidays, he tries to supplement his meals with kosher food. At other times, he ekes out his diet with canned cat food. The meanness of his life and his lack of contact with the Jewish community are all too characteristic of the Jewish poor — whose existence popular legend denies.

Facts can dispel myths. The more difficult task is to understand why the Jewish community, with its long tradition of charitable endeavours, has neither solved the problem of Jewish poverty nor developed awareness among Jews or non-Jews that the problem even exists. This paper can only begin to remedy the situation by demonstrating poverty among Jews; examining the relationships among the poor, Jewish communal institutions, government policies, and the public at large; and suggesting steps towards a solution.

Poverty among Jews: The Available Data

North American social scientists and writers have given poverty among Jews scarce attention during the past fifty years. The problems of the earlier part of the century are well known. The struggles of the waves of immigrants on the lower east side of New York, on the Main in Montreal, and in countless other cities have become part of our folklore, woven into the fabric of North American Jewish identity. Through perseverance in adversity and hard work, runs the legend, the immigrant storekeeper, the peddler, and the worker prospered, retained their Jewish identity, and made it possible for their sons and daughters to succeed.

Insofar as it goes, the story is true. Many Jews did prosper. As they moved out of the ghettos, however, they gave less and less recognition to those who did not succeed. Only in the early 1970s, as an outgrowth of the United States War on Poverty program, did researchers in centres of American Jewry begin to pay some attention to that country's Jewish poor. *Poor Jews: An American*

Awakening, published in 1974, gave the findings of several major studies, including some startling statistics. For example, it estimated the existence of between 400,000 and one million poor Jews in the United States. And it showed that in New York City, 15.1 per cent of the Jewish population was living below the official poverty line; perhaps two of every three of these poor Jews, it said, were also elderly.[1]

Very little such research has been conducted in Canada. Only Montreal has statistically accurate estimates of the number of its poor Jews, thanks to a McGill University study based on 1971 census data.[2] So, although this volume addresses Canadian Jewry as a whole, the dearth of data makes it impossible to report on Jewish poverty nationally. The major findings of the Montreal study, however, do not substantially differ from those reported in United States studies and may be representative of conditions for Jews in other Canadian cities.

Jewish Poverty in Montreal

The Montreal study used data collected through an analysis of eighty-seven census tracts that included 93 per cent of the total Jewish population of the metropolitan area in 1971.

In 1971, metropolitan Montreal included approximately 102,000 Jews, one-third of the Jewish population of Canada. About 17,000 of them — one in six — were poor according to contemporary government definitions, which set the poverty line at an annual income of $2,310 or less for a single person, $5,400 or less for a family of four.[3] Projections to 1976 suggested that by that year Montreal had at least 20,000 poor Jews and possibly as many as 23,000.[4] The study showed the poor to be isolated by both neighbourhood and living arrangements and to lack education. They were most likely to be elderly and/or female.

Although metropolitan Montreal had eleven major concentrations of Jews, five of them contained 70 per cent of the city's poor Jews. These were all old Jewish neighbourhoods — often ones where the immigrants had first established themselves. Those who succeeded moved out; the poor remained. In the area along Boulevard St-Laurent, the famous neighbourhood along the Main, for example, 58.1 per cent of the total population had been Jewish in 1951.[5] By 1971, it was only 3.9 per cent, but more than two out of five of the Jews living there were poor.

In or out of such neighbourhoods, living arrangements tended to isolate the poor. One in four of the poor Jews lived alone or in a rooming house, compared to one in twenty of those above the poverty line. Education and income are closely related. Jews generally have gained higher levels of education than most Canadians; fewer than one in five in the survey had received no formal education after completing primary school. But one in three of the Jewish poor had less than a grade-seven education.

Poverty affects all age groups but is especially common among the aged, as shown in Table 1. In 1971, elderly persons (ages sixty and over) accounted for 19 per cent of all Montreal Jews but 33 per cent of the Jewish poor. Poverty was much more prevalent among women of all ages than among men. The Jewish community of Montreal had only slightly more women than men in 1971, yet poor females outnumbered poor males by 15 per cent. Half of all households headed by women were poor, as were almost three-quarters of all women living alone.

TABLE 1

Jewish Poor by Age

	% Poor or with Marginal Incomes	% above Poverty		% of Total Jewish Population	% of Total Jewish Poor
Under 15	13.3	86.7	100.0	17.7	16.1
15–29	24.5	75.6	100.0	8.4	12.2
30–44	13.1	86.9	100.0	23.9	16.9
45–59	11.6	88.4	100.0	30.6	21.4
60 and over	28.7	71.3	100.0	19.4	33.4

The study divided the adult poor into the elderly (ages sixty and over) and those of working age (fifteen to fity-nine) and sub-divided the latter group into the working poor and the poor living on relief. Interestingly, this resulted in comparable numerical groups: 4,260 aged, 4,300 working poor, and 4,285 poor on relief. Each of these groups showed marked characteristics that are worth further attention here.

The Elderly

Most of the elderly Jewish poor were segregated, isolated, and sup-ported only by government pensions. Sixty per cent of them lived in the Côte-des-Neiges neighbourhood. Although less than 10 per cent of all Jews lived alone or as boarders, 22 per cent of elderly Jews lived in these isolated conditions, and the majority of them were poor. Sixty per cent of all the poor elderly Jewish also had no source of income other than government assistance, a fact that guaranteed their poverty since the maximum government pension fell below the government-defined poverty lines. Equally startling was the fact that 13 per cent did not receive *any* government assistance, either because they were ineligible or because they had not exercised their rights.

The female elderly were significantly worse off than males. Approximately one Jewish man in five over the age of sixty was poor, but for women of the same age it was one in three. Over 80 per cent of all the poor elderly Jews living alone were women.

The Working Poor and the Poor on Relief

Adults of working age accounted for half of all the Jewish poor; they were almost evenly divided between employed persons and persons existing on some form of relief — welfare, unemployment benefits, disability payments, or assistance from Jewish agencies. The two groups had interesting similarities and differences. One striking difference was sex distribution, as shown in Table 2. Almost two-thirds of the working poor were men, while more than two-thirds of the poor on relief were women. In most em-ployment categories, the working women were significantly less likely than the men to earn enough to live above the poverty line.[6]

TABLE 2

Jewish Working Poor
and Poor on Relief
by Sex

	Males	Females	Total
Working Poor	2710 (68%) (63%)	1590 (35%) (37%)	4300 (100%)
Poor on Relief	1285 (32%) (30%)	3000 (65%) (70%)	4285 (100%)
Total	3995 (100%) (100%)	4590 (100%) (100%)	8585

Contrary to popular belief, the working poor tended to live in smaller families than those with incomes above the poverty line. Almost half of the working poor lived alone or in two-person families, compared to one-third of the more affluent Jewish labour force. Similarly, individuals living in families of five or more persons constituted 20 per cent of the labor force who fell above the poverty line, but only 15.6 per cent of the working poor.

The poor on relief, however, did tend to live in larger-than-average families. Some 75 per cent lived in family units of three or more persons; only 70 per cent of the general Jewish population did so. The majority of these families were headed by women.

Both the working poor and the poor on relief had low levels of education. Some 37 per cent of those employed had not completed grade eleven (the final year of Quebec's secondary schools), compared to 29.5 per cent of the more affluent workers. Almost half the women on relief had not completed secondary school.

In brief, poor working Jews tended to have smaller families and lower levels of education than did more affluent workers. Not many were women, but employed women were more likely to be poor than employed men. Poor Jews on relief were likely to be women, and many of them headed fairly large families. They tended to have even less formal education than poor women who worked. Limited education and few employment opportunities combined with family responsibilities suggest the need for provision of more day-care and more vocational training.

Who Is to Meet the Need — and How?

The extent of poverty among Jews is distressing but not surprising since it does not substantially differ from poverty among non-Jews in Canada. Most researchers estimate that one Canadian in five is poor. Among Jews, at least those living in Montreal in 1971, one in six was poor. There is little reason to think the figures would be very different today in Montreal or in any other urban concentration of Canadian Jewry.

What is surprising is that most middle-class Jews are unaware of the extent of poverty within their own community. Poor Jews, as Ann Wolfe has said, have indeed become the "invisible poor".[7] One obvious cause of this ignorance is the lack of contact between Jews who have money and those who do not. In the old days, Jews lived in concentrated neighbourhoods, and communal activity was focussed at the grass-roots level; as one rabbi has put it, "Everyone knew who was poor, and everyone also knew who was pretending to be rich." But as prospering Jews moved to more desirable neighbourhoods and went off to school or careers in other cities, their contact with the poor and the elderly began to diminish. Finally, as Jews achieved positions of success well beyond their proportion of the general population, non-Jews as well as Jews focussed on those who had succeeded and generalized this perception to the Jewish community at large.

Meanwhile, success and stratification were accompanied by the erosion of grassroots Jewish communal structures. The once-flourishing religious, fraternal, benevolent, labour, social, and recreational societies lost much of their membership. The growth and scattering of the Jewish population made it inconvenient to provide relief for the poor at the neighbourhood level. Benevolent societies amalgamated, confederated, and emerged over time as centralized fund-raising and service organizations.

This inevitable process, which has been repeated in every North American Jewish centre, led to a greater fund-raising capacity, to improved coordination in planning, and to the professional provision of service. Unfortunately, it also led to fewer individuals participating in decision-making and fewer volunteers delivering services. Centralization has progressed so far today that the relationship of most Jews to communal organizations begins and ends with a donation to the local federation. Few come into contact with the poor or feel any obligation to do so; rather, they support their federations, which are mandated to do the job for them. In their eyes, the federations' professional employees, who actually serve the poor, and the decision-making board members, a relatively small group of philanthropists and appointed community leaders, seem to be doing an effective job.

In some ways, this arrangement is indeed an effective modern adaptation of the long Jewish tradition of communal organization for relief. Its success in fund-raising is especially marked. For example, in 1978 the United Way of Canada raised $66 million from the country's general population, while the United Jewish Appeal raised $48 million from 300,000 Jews. In Montreal alone, the Combined Jewish Appeal raised more than $18 million from a community of not more than 110,000 Jews; Centraide, the United Way of Montreal, raised $11.5 million from a general population of a little over 2 million.

A large portion of the money raised by a given Jewish community is not, however, used to provide services for its own poor. The federations send approximately 60 per cent of their funds to Israel and spend an additional 8 per cent on national agencies, including the national budget of the Jewish Immigrant Aid Society (JIAS), a relief-giving organization for new immigrants.

The 32 per cent remaining to be spent locally, however, is a considerable sum. Typically, local federations spend part of it on service to the poor by funding three types of programs:

1. Aid for the poor that is not provided by goverment. JIAS in Montreal, for example, provides food, money, and shelter for new arrivals.

2. Supplements to government-sponsored programs for the poor that are inadequate or lack a Jewish dimension. For example, both the Montreal and Toronto federations offer financial supplements to welfare recipients and fund Jewish vocational services because government services are deemed inadequate in these areas. They also fund meals-on-wheels and certain counselling because they feel both that the government does not provide enough for these services and that only a Jewish organization can properly provide certain elements of them.

3. Services for the entire community that benefit the poor through scholarships made available by the constituent organizations. For example, the federations provide funds for scholarships to Jewish summer camps, Jewish schools, and the YMHAs.

The Montreal federation, Allied Jewish Community Services (AJCS), claims that at least half of its local funds are spent on services to the poor in these kinds of programs. But a close examination of its spending for 1978 reveals that far less than that amount was spent on direct, essential relief (cash allotments, food, shelter, health care, and home care). These items accounted for only $860,000 (18 per cent) of the $4.7 million spent locally. Even taking into account Montreal's contribution to the national JIAS, which does provide direct relief for immigrants, only $1.7 million of the more than $18 million raised went to direct, essential relief. From this perspective, roughly ten cents of every fund-drive dollar went to support the essential needs of the Jewish poor.[8]

These figures raise some important issues. Who decides — and on what basis — priorities that result in the allocation of such a relatively small proportion of funds for the essential needs of the poor? Who decides — and on what basis — to supplement inadequate government programs, rather than to challenge government to raise its level of support? Who decides — and on what basis — which services require a Jewish dimension? Who decides — and on what basis — that money should be spent on scholarships for camps, schools, and the YMHAs rather than on essential relief?

Some New Ideas

Certainly the mandate of federations is to look after the welfare of the whole Jewish community, not only of the poor. However, as Harold Waller has shown, federations do not base decisions and judgments on the opinions of most contributors.[9] Rather, a relatively small number of people who have not been elected or selected by any other democratic means make these important decisions. Consumers of services, especially the poor themselves, do not participate in the decision-making and are not consulted by the decision-makers.

The very lack of research about Jewish poverty suggests that the federations have done insufficient planning for providing service to the poor — or have given it a low priority. Yet relevant data are far easier to obtain in Canada than in the United States because this country's census, unlike that of the Americans, gathers information on religious affiliation, ethnic background, and income. This material could become available to the federations with a minimum of effort and expense.

Moreover, the services the decision-makers do provide, although important and helpful to those they reach, do not touch the lives of the vast majority of the Jewish poor. Of the estimated 20,000 Jewish poor in Montreal, only 450 received financial supplements from the Jewish community in 1978, although many others had overwhelming needs. And not more than 10 per cent of Montreal's poor Jews took advantage of the services the Jewish community provided. The agencies conduct very little outreach, and many who could use their aids, especially the elderly poor, are intimidated by the bureaucratic structures, lavish offices, and professional styles of most social service organizations.

The last problem is not peculiar to Jewish organizations. Over ten years ago Alfred Kahn wrote of North American social service agencies in general:

In the 1950's social workers began to talk about "reaching out" to the most disadvantaged problem families. If such people could not get to services, the services should and could find and engage them.

During the 1960's social workers increasingly faced the need to ask questions about agencies and institutions. Is it the client who is hard to reach or the services? Are the non-participants truly drop-outs or are they "push-outs"? The lesson taught by hard and sad experience is that to assume a priori that the case failure is always an instance of client pathology, incapacity and lack of motivation is to engage in modern day poor law social analysis or in what we think of as "social Darwinism".[10]

Most public agencies in the United States and many in Canada responded to these problems by placing more facilities in the communities where the poor live and by developing outreach and self-help community-organizing programs. Jewish federations in New York, Chicago, and Alameda County, California, introduced similar programs. Canadian Jewish federations lag in this respect. An important ingredient of these new efforts is having the recipients of social services participate in agency decision-making. This enables an agency to be informed of the needs of those who use its services and also affords some measure of accountability.

Because federations develop policies and implement programs without participation by the people who need and use the services, needs that the Jewish poor perceive as important often go unmet. In particular, Canadian Jewish federations have not funded community-organization programs to help the poor to help themselves in such matters as tenant organization, day care, and the like. Indeed, it is difficult to find the Canadian Jewish examples of what Maimonides proposed as the highest level of charity: to help the poor help themselves.

One exception is Project Genesis, funded by Montreal's AJCS since 1977 after two years of independent operation. Run from a storefront in the hub of the city's low-income Jewish community, this program is operated by forty volunteers under the direction of a neighbourhood board, which employs three professional staff members. It conducts extensive door-to-door outreach and community-organization programs. In one year, Project Genesis was able to help 1,000 people in such matters as rental advocacy, government assistance, and home help. No Jewish social agency had known two-thirds of these individuals before, despite their great need and despite the fact that they live within ten blocks of the city's major agencies.[11] One study attributed Genesis' success to its high visibility in the community and its use of neighbourhood volunteers in its service delivery.[12] This project has yet to be duplicated in other centres of Canadian Jewry.

While many Jewish social services are inaccessible to the poor or do not meet their needs, other programs, especially those focussing on the elderly, have long waiting lists. In Montreal, combined funding from the AJCS and the governments has been used for low-cost housing; for every elderly Jew admitted to it, ten other equally eligible applicants are turned away for lack of space. Maimonides, a chronic-care facility, has a waiting period of at least two years for admission.

These waiting lists suggest another basic problem. Although it is clear that certain services provided by the Jewish community must become more accessible and that consumer participation could greatly benefit the decision-making process, it is also clear that federations alone are unable to solve the problem of Jewish poverty. For example, were the Montreal Jewish community to extend its financial supplements program to all of its poor Jews, the cost would be $20 million a year. Such a level of funding would preclude programming in any of the other vital areas of Jewish concern. Moreover, the costs of federation services are likely to increase more quickly than contributions to the Combined Jewish Appeal; professionalization, specialization, inflation, and the increasing number of elderly Jews will spiral service costs upwards over the next decade.

In the 1980s, government legislation and entitlements will be central to the lives of Canada's poor, including the Jewish poor. Pensions, welfare and unemployment benefits, manpower services, and the health and social services are now and will continue to be the primary responsibilities of government. Federal and provincial government policies and services in these areas play a far more critical role in the lives of the Jewish poor than do the Combined Jewish appeals and the Jewish federations of Canada. Since the days of the Depression, private charities have been transformed into public institutions. (Many Jewish hospitals and agencies, in fact, were models for present government institutions.) Consequently, the solution to Jewish poverty cannot rest primarily with federation services. Only governments have the financial capacity to ensure sufficient food and adequate shelter and health care for all people.

Today's government-sponsored programs, however, leave much to be desired. Decision-makers at all levels of government have balanced the needs of the poor against the demands of taxpayers and consistently produced social legislation that provides a minimum of care and support for those who need it most. Yet the Jewish federations seem more willing to spend money on supplementing inadequate government programs than to challenge governments to change their policies.

Steps for the Future

The Jewish community has much to be proud of in its social services. Although one can question some of their content, forms, and priorities, there is no question that the Jewish community has surpassed any other in Canada in terms of what it has done and continues to do for its own. The services it provides are an extension of a fine and long tradition that developed over centuries in Europe and in North Africa and that finds its roots and source in biblical literature and law.

This tradition arose during millenia when Jews could rarely expect governments to enhance their well-being and did not dare use their communal organizations to pressure governments for increased social welfare benefits. Particularly in Europe, persecution made it apparent that all Jews were linked together and that their survival as a people rested on the readiness and ability of the Jewish community to take care of its own. For this reason, the suggestion that Jewish communal organizations should now take social and political action on behalf of the poor meets varied responses. To some it is a welcomed, even long overdue challenge.

To others, it represents political naiveté buttressed by a lack of understanding of Jewish history, past, recent, and perhaps present.

Should Jews raise these issues and press for these reforms — and perhaps enrage a non-Jewish majority? Or should they continue to look after their own and avoid a potential anti-Semitic backlash, even if this approach is unsatisfactory? To restate the problem: should the Jewish community help its poor by fighting for the welfare of all disadvantaged Canadians?

These questions are not to be taken lightly, but it seems to me that they must be answered with an unquestionable fact in mind: over the next decade, the federations will be *less* able to look after the needs of the Jewish poor than they are now. Consequently and in light of the modern North American situation, I believe Jewish communal organizations should now begin to ally themselves with non-Jewish groups and work with them to convince federal and provincial governments to develop more adequate social legislation. The same alliances should attempt to ensure that services are physically and psychologically accessible to all the poor, including the Jewish poor.

Meanwhile, Jewish communal institutions must also work to improve the quality of their own services without necessitating markedly increased costs. For one thing, the federations could add substance to their decision-making and planning bodies by opening them up to representatives of all segments of the Jewish community, including the poor, to discover true communal priorities.

The federations could also promote outreach and advocacy programs in order to assist low-income Jews to make full use of both the public and the private services to which they are entitled. Moreover, by initiating community organization programs, the federations could assist the poor to develop their own self-help potential. Additionally, the federations need to consider carefully which social services require a Jewish dimension that only can be or ought to be provided by Jewish organizations, and then implement these services in ways that will make them most accessible to those who need them. Finally, by initiating a return to a high level of volunteer activity in the areas of social justice and social service, the federations could make certain that our now-invisible Jewish poor do not become forgotten.

The Jewish Elderly: Behind the Myths

by Albert Rose

It is now common knowledge that the number of elderly Canadians is increasing significantly in itself and relative to the rest of the population. The 1971 census revealed 1.7 million Canadians ages sixty-five and over, 8.1 per cent of the total population. The official estimate for the mid-1970s was 8.6 per cent, which does not seem much of an increase but represents an addition of some 300,000 persons for a total of more than 2 million elderly individuals. Projections for the future show a rapid rise: the elderly in Canada will number 3.3 million (10.9 per cent of the population) by the year 2001 and at least 6 million (16.1 per cent) by 2031.[1] Granted, the projected *percentages* are subject to the birth rates of the future — always unknowns — but the *total numbers* themselves are almost unassailable because they represent persons who have already been born. The only possible variables affecting absolute numbers are alterations in immigration patterns and changes from the current life expectancy of over seventy years. If significant changes do occur in either or both these two areas in the near future, they are most likely to increase the numbers of elderly Canadians in decades to come.

For today's Canadian Jewish population, the startling fact is that it already includes the levels of elderly persons projected for twenty or thirty years from now for Canada as a whole. A study in Winnipeg, for example, estimated that 15.1 per cent of the city's Jewish community was elderly in 1971; in Vancouver the figure was 11.1 per cent in 1972. In Metropolitan Toronto, where the Jewish population numbers about 120,000, the heads of various Jewish community services put the number of Jews over age sixty-five at about 14,000 or 11.7 per cent in 1978.[2]

The phenomenon of the elderly being a relatively high proportion of the Jewish population is common to many developed countries, including Canada, the United States, and Australia. It is the result of a series of demographic trends that are rooted in the Jewish experience in the new world. Briefly, waves of Jewish immigrants, settling in industrialized cities, saw the possibility of their children both avoiding discrimination and achieving a standard of living much higher than they had known in the ghettos and segregated villages of Europe. Their high expectations were realistic — if they did not have too many children. Most Jews had no moral objections to birth control, so the immigrants used it.

Many members of the second generation did become successful; their relatively high-income families followed the common pattern of having fewer children than did working-class families. Thus, when almost all birth rates started to fall in the 1960s, the Jewish birth rate started its decline from a point that was already below the norm. Meanwhile, advances in health care had benefited Jews as much or more than the rest of the North American population. The resulting increase in life expectancy, combined with the unusually low birth rate, could have only one outcome: a relatively high proportion of elderly Jews.

This fact has not gone unnoticed, at least during the past twenty-five years, but no one has worried much about it. Jews and non-Jews alike have relied on a series of traditional socio-economic phenomena to take care of the Jewish elderly. These include a conviction that the Jewish extended family can be counted on to take care of "its own", a conviction that most elderly Jews have sufficient income to meet their requirements without community supplementation, and a conviction that, in any event, the network of community resources and services is quite adequate if the first two safeguards do not operate.

An examination of these convictions forms a useful structure for examining the present state of the numerous Jewish elderly. If they are true, there is no reason for worry. If they are not true and have not been replaced by other safeguards, there is much cause for concern. If the community's mechanisms for caring for the elderly do not work now, they must be repaired as soon as possible, before there are even greater numbers entering old age.

Family Responsibility

Extended-family participation in the care and support of its members implies the likelihood of providing a role for the elderly and taking care of them as they age by at least attempting to meet such problems as financial support, housing accommodation, medical care, friendly visiting, and, if necessary, finding and paying for long-term residential care.

Jews are by no means the only group in Canada thought to provide this sort of support — for example, the Italians, the Greeks, and the Chinese retained their family traditions well into the mid-twentieth century — but the public view of Jews' generally providing it was unquestionably true at one time. Jewish religious and social values played a role here, as did the customs of the immigrants. The commandment to honour one's parents and the biblical adage to "stand up before the aged" laid the foundation for this reverence. Most of the rabbis and leaders of Jewish communities in the Old World were elderly; indeed, it was often assumed that wisdom was correlated with having lived a long life.

Nevertheless, it is too easy to assume that these traditions of responsibility for the care of elderly family members have continued in almost all respects into the present day. In fact, the pace and change of modern life have significantly weakened the extended family. Grandparents, parents, children, grandchildren, and great-grandchildren often no longer live within easy access of each other in the same village, town, or city. Mobility is the North American pattern, and Jews have adopted it. Evidence shows that elderly Jews, for example, tend to remain in the city to which they migrated or in which they were born as second-generation Canadians, while their children and grandchildren may move thousands of miles away to other Canadian provinces, to the United States, or to other countries. Many Canadians from the eastern and central provinces are today migrating to Alberta and British Columbia, seeking economic opportunity.

This general mobility means elderly Jewish Canadians can no longer count upon their children or grandchildren to house them or even be present when needed as companions or in arranging health and social services or residential care. This is not to say that the children of the elderly are generally unsympathetic or unwilling to provide financial assistance when necessary. More often they are simply far away and preoccupied with their own concerns on a day-to-day basis. (Given today's life expectancy, one of their preoccupations may well be concern for their own requirements after retirement.)

This distraction may have a greater effect on the elderly than does mobility. Given the concentration of Jewish Canadians in a few population centres, most elderly Jews probably do have some family member — often a child or grandchild — living in the same community. The obvious question is whether these members of the second, third, and fourth generations are as concerned, sympathetic, and ready to help as were members of the extended family twenty-five or fifty years ago. Probably, the younger generations are as concerned and sympathetic but not as ready to help. The fact is that their lives are far more complicated and their personal responsibilities in the society far more extensive than were those of their elders. In short, they may have the income with which to assist, but they are likely to lack the time and perhaps the will to provide the continuity and intensity of care that many elderly persons require.

Another consideration may limit the younger generations' provision of financial aid. Family members are well aware of the existence, since the 1950s, of a continuously expanding health-care and social-welfare system in Canada. No longer are elderly persons likely to be reduced to absolute penury if they become ill, require hospitalization or surgery, or need accommodation in a convalescent facility or nursing home. The Canadian system of medical care and hospitalization has taken over a significant proportion of the responsibilities that family members had to bear a half-century ago. Moreover, the twin programs of Old Age Security and the Guaranteed Income Supplement at least provide an income floor for the basic living requirements of elderly people. The amounts provided may not be sufficient to meet the expectations of some individuals, but they do help in an important way by comparison with the situation thirty or more years ago.

Family members also know that other help exists for the elderly in a number of communities. A network of community organizations, Jewish and general, offers several possible sources of help. Community-wide programs such as meals on wheels and homemaker services, senior citizens' clubs, and ethnic associations offer a full range of services that are aimed at replacing those lost with the disappearance of the extended family.

Self-Suffiency — Financial and Otherwise

Many people are aware that the Jewish extended-family system does not work as well in modern North America as it did in nineteenth-century Europe or even among the immigrants of the earlier twentieth century. The public perception is, however, that almost every older Jewish person is financially well off to the point of being able to meet his or her own needs by purchasing the appropriate services. Complementary beliefs are that all such services are available for purchase and that the elderly who need them know how and where to obtain them.

Some research exists on these interrelated subjects. During the past twenty-five years and particularly the last decade, Jewish community organizations have become highly aware of the growing number of elderly Jews and concerned about their needs. In major centres of Jewry across Canada, they have sought to identify more clearly the numbers of persons over the age of sixty or sixty-five within the community, the needs of such persons for a variety of services that already existed or that agencies thought might be required, and, perhaps of equal importance, the services that elderly Jews said they either required or were interested in receiving, if they should exist. These studies have often combined such research with rudimentary censuses of the Jewish population as a whole, particularly when there have been widespread impressions of shifting neighbourhoods (such as a large-scale movement of Jews to the suburbs) and/or the arrival of a comparatively large number of Jews from other cities or countries.

One of the first such studies was carried out in the Toronto Jewish community in 1956 and 1957. Interviews with 307 persons indicated that many needs among older persons were not being met in full measure; this information helped social workers plan locations for a variety of community services as much of Toronto's Jewish population moved to the city's northern suburban areas during the 1960s.[3]

Perhaps the first study of elderly Jews during the 1970s was in Vancouver in 1972.[4] Its first step was a census that identified an estimated total population of 7,500 Jews, located them geographically in various districts and suburbs of Greater Vancouver, and revealed 11.1 per cent as sixty-five years old or over, with an additional 13.1 per cent in the fifty-five to sixty-four age group. The second phase used interviews of a random sample to evaluate services and project needs for the next decade.

In doing their work, the interviewers learned a great deal about the elderly Jews of Vancouver, and their findings destroyed a number of misconceptions held in that city's Jewish community. In the first place, they found that, on the whole, the elderly were relatively well housed and adequately provided with income from their own employment, investments, or savings. Few were destitute, significantly isolated, or in need of a plethora of services. Moreover, because Vancouver is a favourite place for retirement, it had been thought that many newcomers to its Jewish community were older people. The interviewers, however, found that recent arrivals were more likely to be young families from the prairies or other parts of Canada.[5] Thus, the study showed, there was clearly some need for family services and even financial assistance for Vancouver's elderly Jews, but the problems were by no means of massive proportions.[6]

The Vancouver study touched on the purchasing power, resources, and needs of the elderly but did not centre on them. In Winnipeg, however, studies during the 1970s did focus on them. Many of that city's 3,000 elderly Jews made it clear that, for the most part, they were economically secure in 1978. Nevertheless, about one in seven stated that he or she was in some difficulty, and three in five termed their ability to meet their financial needs as "only adequate". Moreover, almost a quarter of the group anticipated trouble in meeting their future financial needs.[7]

The first study, published in August 1976, was a basic demographic analysis of Winnipeg's elderly Jewish population; it identified income distribution and living arrangements as well as geographic areas of population concentration.[8]

The second study, completed in 1978, may well be the most comprehensive examination of the needs of the Jewish elderly in Canada, although it is not entirely comparable with other work because it defined the elderly as persons over sixty years of age, rather than the more common sixty-five. The Winnipeg researchers delineated nine basic need areas — psycho-social; shelter; food and clothing; ethno-cultural; physical health functioning; mental health functioning; economics; accessibility of resources; and availability of family, friends, and community resources — and measured the respondents' perceptions of their own unmet needs in them in five levels. An important finding was the absence of statements of either minimum or maximum needs in any of the nine basic areas. "This means that most of those who were interviewed are in the middle group, not necessarily getting needs met, but not feeling extreme need."[9]

This study was unique in that the interviewers asked the elderly about their needs in reference to *both* general Winnipeg resources and specifically Jewish ones. The responses showed the accessibility (defined as "the visibility or outreach of services") of general community services was not nearly as great as the perceived needs in any of the categories studied. In other words, elderly persons perceived needs but were not aware of general community resources that could meet them and/or lacked information about the techniques of obtaining such services.

In reference to specifically Jewish resources, the study's most important conclusion was that in six of the defined areas — psycho-social; shelter; food and clothing; physical health functioning; mental health functioning; and accessibility of resources — needs exceeded resources or currently accessible services. Even for those areas where the least need was expressed, it became clear that if only Jewish resources were used, there would not be enough available to meet the needs described.[10]

Within Toronto's huge Jewish population, some 17,000 persons (or 14.8 per cent) are over sixty; nearly half this group are described as "camp suvivors", with a complex of psychological factors complicating the normal emotional and economic aspects of aging. The head of the Jewish Family and Child Service claimed in late 1978 that almost one in every four of the Jewish elderly was "at risk".[11] Not all are totally without assets. Some are still employed but have low earnings; some receive very modest pensions or income from German reparations; some are house-bound invalids supported by their families; some are recent immigrants; some own their own homes and thus possess substantial assets but have very modest incomes.

As a response to the needs of its older members, during the past twenty-five years the Toronto Jewish community has created the Baycrest Geriatric Centre, a set of institutional and community services for almost all the formally conceived requirements of an elderly population. Its high standards of professional service in medicine, nursing, social work, and other disciplines have made it internationally known and respected. Nevertheless, outside this system there is an additional, unmet need for nursing-home beds, places in homes for the aged, and other facilities.

Community Response to Needs

In short, the Jewish elderly do need aid — financial and otherwise — and to some extent the community does provide it. In many ways, this provision is a further extension of the extended family and very much in the tradition of the immigrant experience. During the late nineteenth and early twentieth centuries, Canada's Jewish communities developed within a clear framework of priorities. The first, most important step for the newcomers was to organize a synagogue and perhaps to build a building for it. A closely related priority was locating land for a cemetery, since membership in the religious congregation always included the right of burial within sacred ground.[12] The infant community did not neglect the needs of its two important dependent groups, children and aged persons. Synagogue premises almost always included space for a religious school because the Jewish tradition marked the education of children as a major aspect of survival. A second requirement was ensuring a decent life for the community's elderly, whom tradition accorded reverence and respect.

In many cities and towns, the first manifestation of service took the form of mutual-help organizations of persons from the same community area in Europe. The immigrants, most of whom knew little or nothing of an English-speaking, Protestant-dominated urban society, organized these "sick-benefit societies" to offer friendly visiting to the sick, assistance in burying the dead, financial support during periods of unemployment, and, particularly, help to persons, many of them elderly, who needed to deal with general community organizations, such as hospitals, clinics, and government offices. Such assistance was needed because most Jews, especially the elderly persons, could not communicate in the dominant language. The Volks Farein in Toronto, for example, used volunteer interpreters to assist hospitalized Jews so that they might communicate the nature of their illnesses to physicians, who were almost all Anglo-Saxon Protestants. Moreover, many Jews were frightened of bureaucrats and needed help, at least translation services, to obtain papers, such as those required to obtain hospitalization at public expense.

Considerations of languages and backgrounds different from those of the dominant society thus soon led the immigrant Jews to establish their own embryonic social services. By 1919, federations of Jewish philanthropies existed in both Toronto and Montreal; they brought together volunteers in the interest of meeting the particular needs of Jews, in particular, children and the elderly who required health and welfare services.

In the larger Jewish communities, the traditional requirement of providing a decent existence for the elderly combined
with the perceived need for separate social services and produced
separate Jewish institutions for the aged. These early homes in
Montreal, Toronto, Winnipeg, and Vancouver lacked many present-day amenities but the wider community generally regarded
them as models of high-quality care.

Moreover, they provided care that met the residents' special
needs in language, the dietary laws, and religious habits. Contemporary Jews in the general hospitals of Toronto had to depend on
the Volks Farein not only for translation but for the cooking and
delivery of special meals several times a day throughout Passover.
These problems did not arise in the Jewish homes for the aged
because their kitchens were kosher and enough workers spoke the
languages of the Jews to enable communication. Above all the
atmosphere was such that the elderly residents could feel they
were at home, as far as was possible in an institution.

As the twentieth century progressed, the special health and
social welfare agencies developed by the Jewish community, no
different in spirit from those developed by the Roman Catholic
community, continued to offer services of a family type that
elderly Jews not only desired but required. During the 1930s and
1940s the need actually increased, although the second or even
third generation was reaching adulthood. During the Depression,
the problem of poverty became more desperate. Moreover, many
of the elderly were now widows who were almost completely
dependent upon Jewish communal services. Many of the men
who headed immigrant families had learned the languages of Canada in order to get jobs, but their wives had stayed at home, raising
the children and keeping house. As far as the dominant culture
was concerned, these widows were illiterate, helpless women
because they could not read English or French and had not become acclimated to North American society.

Today, some people suggest that separate facilities, such as
Jewish homes, are anachronisms, and that the Jewish community
would do better to merge its resources with those of the general

population. But Jews have not, in fact, lost their requirements for separate services because the group has been reinforced by survivors of the Holocaust, by a proportion of Hungarians who fled Europe in 1956, and by recent emigrés from the Soviet Union. These recent immigrants mean that well into the twenty-first century there will be Jewish aged who need a set of special services, residential institutions, nursing homes, and chronic-care facilities. The very demand for kosher food makes the provision of these services almost inevitable.

The social quality of care in Jewish institutions also makes one suspect that the demand will continue. Interestingly enough, during the past two decades, a number of ethnic groups within Canadian life have begun to develop separate institutions. Canadians of Italian and of Chinese origin in Toronto have already opened substantial homes for the aged. The basic considerations are similar to those that led to separate Jewish homes — language barriers, the existence of distinctive habits and customs, and, perhaps most important, a desire to come as close as possible to extended-family care. Many Canadian institutions founded under general public auspices seem unfriendly, cold, and rigidly formal in their emphasis upon discipline and regulated behaviour. By contrast, the residents of the Italian Villa Colombo, like those of Maimonides in Montreal, of Baycrest Centre in Toronto, and of the Jewish Home for the Aged in Vancouver, feel relaxed and among "their own". The simple matter of alcohol is a case in point. Within the homes for the aged operated by Metropolitan Toronto, a resident must obtain special permission to imbibe a small quantity from his or her own bottle of liquor, which is kept carefully locked up in the cupboards of the infirmary. But Villa Colombo has a wine cellar, and Baycrest follows the tradition of wine in moderation at the Sabbath dinner.

Conclusion: Myths and Reality

More than two decades ago the President of Central Mortgage and Housing Corporation, Canada's federal housing agency, expressed the firm view that two major groups within the Canadian population were clearly concerned about and invariably took care of their elderly; these, he said, were the French Canadians and the Canadian Jews.[13] Implicit in this statement were three myths: that the extended-family still operates; that most elderly Jews have adequate financial means or access to them; that the community has sufficient resources and services to make up for what any families or individuals lack.

Like all myths, these have some elements of truth, but their totality is false. The extended family is disintegrating quickly under modern lifestyles; a large number of elderly Jews hover on the poverty line or have fallen below it; the Jewish community does not have the assets to meet all its needs. There is, however, some cause for optimism. The Jewish community clearly does care about its elderly, and all its centres display examples of community determination to expand services, to create new services as required, and to ensure assistance to those elderly persons who are indeed deprived so that they can live in decency and dignity within our affluent society.

Personal Reflections on Jewish Feminism

by Norma Baumel Joseph

Over the centuries, Judaism has met many challenges. The 1970s brought a new confrontation in the form of the feminist movement. This essay is an attempt to explain at least part of that challenge, to analyze some of the issues relevant to being female and Jewish today, and to outline some of the Canadian responses. It is by no means a socio-historical treatise, filled with statistics, or an attempt to relate every pertinent incident in every centre of Canadian Jewry. Rather, it is a personal observation based on my own experiences as a woman and teacher of Judaism whose feminist concerns and Jewish lifestyle have often clashed, sometimes merged, and most often required greater scrutiny and critical appraisal. Because I live and work in Montreal, my descriptions of specific incidents and institutions are primarily from that city, though I think parallel examples could be found in Toronto and other Canadian Jewish communities.

The Challenge of Feminism to Judaism

Feminism was not a creation of the 1970s, but as a challenge to modern North American Judaism, it might as well have been. In the 1960s, many women who were Jewish were involved in the feminist movement, but these individuals were not rooted in Judaism, so their concerns never directly confronted the Jewish community. In fact, being Jewish was so peripheral to them that they almost all dismissed Judaism with one word — "patriarchal" — and went about seeking their feminist goals without even trying to reconcile them with their Jewish heritage.

Many people — men and women — have tried to describe these goals. Although the resulting definitions vary in specifics, generally speaking, they centre on the desire and need of women to be equal to men. Equality, however, does not mean sameness, and by and large, feminists do not want to be identical to men. Rather they seek to be on an equal footing, to have the same rights and responsibilities, the same opportunities, the same choices and rewards. Most important, they want to be recognized, appreciated, and treated with respect as individual persons.

It is essential at this point to emphasize that not only do people differ in defining the feminist goals, but a large part of the Jewish community does not even share them. For many men and women — especially those of the Orthodox persuasion — there is no problem, no challenge. For them, the traditional role of women within the Jewish community is completely satisfactory. Feminist concerns do not bother them. They do not ignore woman's place, but value it as is and attach great significance to the role of mother. Women are seen as the essential support system. As wives and mothers, they ensure the continuity and survival of the people, and since there is no greater task, there is no need to seek glory, fulfillment, or meaning in any other context.

However, those feminists of the 1960s who gave a cursory glance to the Jewish community were quite correct in perceiving it as not receptive to their desires. The contemporary Jewish community in North America regarded a woman primarily as a wife and mother. Any other roles she might have had were still defined in terms of that all-important relationship to husband and child. In this view, the woman was the support system, the enabler, ensuring the continuity and survival of the people but with little individual or personal importance. The religious, political, economic, social, and even educational realms of Judaism and Jewish communal life limited or excluded her.

Religious Judaism obligated women unequally with men; the Law exempted them from fourteen *mitzvot* (obligations) including public prayer, the wearing of a prayer shawl and phylacteries, and study of the Torah.[1] They could not lead the congregation in prayer, be the rabbi, or have an *aliyah* (be called to read from the Torah or pronounce certain blessings over it).The great celebrations at birth and puberty were reserved for males. Many synagogues physically segregated women in such a way as to prevent or discourage their participation in prayer.

These exclusions were often blamed on Jewish law as interpreted by the Orthodox, yet it was not necessarily the major barrier. As Paula Hyman would write perceptively in 1972:

> The most formidable barrier to change and to the acceptance of women as authority figures and as the equals of men lies in the psychological rather than the halachic (legal) realm. It can be argued that there are few halachic prohibitions preventing women from taking up on themselves an even greater role in many aspects of Jewish religious life. . . . Yet the psychological effects of tradition and upbringing are difficult for both men and women to overcome.[2]

The proof of this statement is found in the actions of Reform Jews who do not regard *halacha* as binding. The Reform Movement had declared in 1846 that women were equal to men, and by 1922, women were able to enter the rabbinate — in theory. Yet by the end of the 1960s, Hebrew Union College had yet to ordain a single female rabbi.[3]

Politically and economically, one could not readily find women leaders in the Jewish community. Men alone made communal decisions, with seldom a woman present. This sharp division between the public and domestic spheres paralleled the traditional division of labour between men and women. Enablers have no independent achievements; their success is achieved through others. Thus, women belonged in the home, their contribution to society limited to what they could do as wives and mothers.

In education, for centuries only men formally learned the traditions and texts of Judaism. Mothers taught daughters the practical facts, but texts, reasons, debates, analyses, and interpretations were usually withheld from women.[4] This educational exclusion nurtured the erroneous notion that girls were and are not capable of learning. A regrettable cycle developed: since women were not obligated to all the commandments, they were not taught all the texts. Without knowledge, they could not choose to be obligated and could not intelligently understand their Jewish tradition. They did not become knowledgeable enough to lead or to learn; indeed, they did not *need* to learn.

The social corollaries of these religious, economic, and educational exclusions were almost endless. Perhaps the most tragic was in the area of divorce. By law and custom men could give women a divorce, but women did not have the same rights of redress; the resulting inequity often placed them at the mercy of vengeful men. Rabbinic changes to the original, one-sided biblical law gave women some protection but not equal access to the Law and its courts.[5]

Return to Judaic Sources

Jewish women's feelings of exclusion, deprivation, and unworthiness seemed to be summed up and confirmed in the traditional prayer men recited each morning: "Blessed be Thou, O Lord our God, for not making me a woman." Jewish women attracted by feminism in the early 1960s assumed that Judaism had to encompass the entire set of limitations implicit in that prayer. It was not that they saw anything wrong with being a wife or a mother. Any society needs enablers, and Jews are especially aware of this fact because they are so survival oriented. The feminists had learned, however, that to be completely limited to one role was to be excluded from most others. And Jewish society apparently relegated women to the subsidiary enabling role only.

As the 1970s unfolded, however, women who cared about being Jewish began to wonder if they truly had to make a radical choice between their heritage and their individuality. Some turned a questioning eye towards their tradition and community. As one commentator put it, "The point is not that Jewish women want equality with men, but *as Jews with Jews*."[6] Feminism had projected the ideal of women aiming for personal success and achievement, independent of their other roles. Setting aside the views of the extremists who wished to erase the successful role of enabler completely, some women now asked if it was not possible, perhaps necessary, to advocate enabling and personal growth for both men and women *without abandoning the Jewish heritage*.

In this attempt "to justify our personhood in the face of the tradition",[7] to be full participants, to be active and no longer passive, some Jewish women found the key in education. To understand the processes that had led to their exclusion, they began to study Judaism and Jewish history. By returning to the sources, they discovered that they — and most of the Jewish community — were labouring under many misconceptions as to the teachings of the bible, the Law, and history. Their work was, in fact, developing a renewed understanding of ancient truths.

For example — and perhaps most important — they began to see the implications of the notion of human equality that is fundamental to the Jewish faith. The Talmud teaches the absolute equality, value, and uniqueness of every person. "Male and female, He created them" (Gen. 1:27), both in the divine image, equal in character and quality. The Jewish understanding of Genesis is not that a woman's sole *raison d'être* is the bearing and rearing of children. She exists as a separate unique person, created individually by God in the image of God.[8] The bible places the mothers alongside the fathers. Women stood at Sinai, where God directly commanded them. Since that moment, although perhaps differently obligated, they have had the same moral responsibility and goal as men. Part of it is the sacred task of nurturing children, but this was a task given to *both* men and women. (Interestingly, the commandment to "be fruitful and multiply" [Gen 1:28, 9:1] has always been understood as a man's obligation.)

Throughout the biblical narrative, women appear in a variety of roles: political leaders, witches, wise women, dancers, queens, warriors, and prophets. It certainly portrays them as mothers, too, but attempts to claim that motherhood is their only function are no less misinterpretations for being fairly common. Distortions of the roles played by women also appear in many versions of postbiblical Jewish history. No monolithic, uniform Judaism has existed for these two thousand years. Neither has the Jewish community — more properly, Jewish communities — remained static. Over time and in different countries, many variations have developed. In some countries, at some times, Jewish communities did limit women to the domestic scene, but in others, women were active in the public domain as property owners, traders, money lenders, philanthropists, poets, legal experts, teachers, scribes, martyrs, and even ritual meat slaughterers.

The crux of the Jewish feminist argument, nevertheless, lies in the true lessons of history. Jewish law and custom have been responsive to changing social conditions and changing attitudes. When women became economically and socially involved in community affairs, rabbis even adapted some laws to reflect the new reality. On the other hand, when the rabbis recognized that women were in need of protection, they often acted to alleviate dependencies, for example, by reinterpreting the law of inheritance to give a woman a more equal share in her father's estate.[9]

Thus, women were often more than wives and mothers in our history, though they are not usually presented as such in the history books. But with increased awareness and education, researchers are beginning to fill the gaps in our knowledge and correct our understanding of our past.

Further complicating the distortion of history in North America are the popular stereotyped images of modern Jewish women. Too many people have accepted fictional portraits of the Jewish Mother and the Jewish American Princess as sociological truth. Of course, some mothers (Jewish and otherwise) are domineering and stifling, and some girls are spoiled, selfish, shallow, and materialistic. Yet not all Jewish women are so lacking in virtue, despite the popular images. Unfortunately, these symbols can be self-fulfilling prophecies. If Jewish women are told often enough that they are greedy, shallow, and domineering, they are all too likely to accept the mould — or to try to avoid it by rejecting their Jewishness.

In fact, the popular stereotypes combine too often with Jewish ritual and accounts of Jewish history to leave positive female imagery in short supply. Yet popular images, like speech patterns, both indicate and determine perceptions and worldviews.[10] One obvious deficiency is the prayerbook. The great deeds of women are not recounted alongside those of men. Prayers involving our ancestors do not include female ancestors, although they could do so quite properly. The constant reference to God as male is especially problematic. God is neither male nor female. If we relate to God, our father (*Avenu*) then we can also speak to God, the *Shechina* — the feminine aspect of comfort and mercy — as did the Jewish mystics who developed the Kabbalah.

The Response

By the early 1970s, the realization that the Jewish heritage does not preclude feminist goals had challenged a number of women, especially in New York. They began to challenge the community by organizing and asserting themselves. One of the earliest groups, Ezrat Nashim, a woman's religious organization formed in 1971, promoted female separatism not as a goal but as a necessity. In 1972, some women challenged the Rabbinic Assembly of the Conservative Movement to count women in the minyan (the quorum for prayer). A raging debate ended in permission for each Conservative congregation to choose for itself. The minyan controversy (should women be included as part of the quorum of ten Jews needed for communal prayer) established Jewish feminism as an issue in the United States. By 1973, the first National Conference on Jewish Women was held in New York. One year later the Jewish Feminist Organization was formed. Major American Jewish publications began to speak to the issue, and *Lillith*, a periodical addressed specifically to feminist concerns, appeared.

In Canada, the rise of Jewish feminism has been quieter, less explosive, almost an outgrowth of American debates rather than an indigenous concern. There is still no active Jewish feminist organization, no great dialogue with religious leaders concerning women's rights, no major confrontation. As late as 1977, an analyst of North American Jewish feminism could write, "Clearly, the *Minyan* decision' had triggered a movement, which seemed to be lagging only in Queens, N. Y., and in Canada."[11] Nevertheless, the issue has surfaced in many ways in the Canadian Jewish community, and it seems likely to continue, although in a more quiet fashion than south of the border.

Responses in Education

The first and perhaps most striking response has been in the area of adult education, encouraging women to study Judaism not only as teachers of children but also as persons who need the acquired knowledge and the religious experience of learning.

Specifically, the quest for women's rights has been an educative force in two mutually reinforcing ways. First, in order to assert their rights, women had to discover what their rights were and what barriers existed; in the process of doing so, they learned about women's role in Judaism. The second result comes from the first; women are developing a deepened Jewish identity. This has become particularly clear to me while teaching in the informal setting of small study groups. When we begin to talk about women in Judaism, all sorts of questions come up. How can one discuss women as rabbis without investigating the legal, historical, and sociological role of the rabbi? We wander from philosophy and theology, to the history of Passover, to the meaning of the bible for the modern Jew, to the Sabbath, to the differences between Jews from Morocco and Russia, Chassidic and Reform Jews. And during that wandering, we learn. Yet when I ask each group if they would have invited me to speak on Judaism only, invariably the answer is no. They need to learn and want to learn but have not been in the habit of thinking about gaps in their Jewish education. Concern with feminist issues has produced Jewish enrichment; the result can be a greater commitment.

Such study groups are probably the most common format for women's education, but they do not stand alone. Various institutions have begun to offer increasing numbers of courses, seminars and conferences. In Montreal, for example, the Saidye Bronfman Centre (SBC) began with one course in 1974. In 1975, International Woman's Year, the SBC celebrated with the first Canadian Jewish Women's Conference, which centered on the topic, "The Jewish Woman — Who Is She?". The experience itself was valuable for the participants and had many positive side effects. Women started thinking about being Jewish and discovered that perhaps the Jewish community did have room in which they could express themselves. As a direct result of this new interest, the following year the SBC offered many courses for women. Four of them dealt with various aspects of the role of women in Judaism. Significantly, all four were fully enrolled. Furthermore, in 1975, Concordia University began to devote part of its "Women in Religion" course to Judaism.

Some synagogues are supplementing these credit courses and women's study groups by devoting time to consideration of women's role in Judaism. Especially noteworthy have been several efforts addressed to both men and women, using the format of long-weekend study sessions with keynote speakers.[12]

The Jewish day schools seem to have been least affected by modern feminist concerns. Early in this century Jewish education for girls began on a formal and serious level. In 1918, with the blessing of the Belzer Chassidim and the crucial formal approval of the Hafetz Hayim, Sarah Schenirer founded the Bais Yaakov Schools for girls. At that time, the Jewish education for girls was a radical idea.[13] Today, we can point with pride to the many girls who receive a formal Jewish education in a variety of Canadian institutions. However, there are ultraorthodox schools in Montreal today in which girls are not allowed to study the Talmud, in which only boys are encouraged to pray, in which girls are trained to be mothers *only* and boys are pressed into the world of learning and leadership. Many still use old textbooks that reflect sexist stereotypes. On the other hand, some schools have begun to address themselves to the problems of feminism, and have even held special sessions on avoiding sexism in the classroom.

To be sure, all this is only a beginning, but in seeking information, positive role models, and increased commitment to Judaism through education, Jewish women are beginning to challenge and change the Jewish community while acknowledging and attempting to remain within the tradition.

Responses in Religious Ritual

As women have become more knowledgeable about Judaism, they have begun to uncover more areas for religious growth. One of the most important is through participation in religious rituals. Thus, women seeking greater involvement and obligation have begun to wear prayer shawls, say the Friday night *kiddush* (a blessing recited over a cup of wine or over bread), recite the *havdalah* (a ceremony at the outgoing of the Sabbath), recite the *kaddish* prayer during mourning, and generally perform rituals that had been considered the sole prerogative of men. Such actions are not trivial steps, for they break down the rigid barrier between male-female and public-private domains. Moreover, they expose misconceptions, for there are significant legal precedents for women's performing many of these rituals. Their needs for positive symbolic identification can often be met within the tradition. Perhaps what is new and radical is that the permissible is being sought after and granted, at least some of the time in some segments of Canadian Judaism.

An interesting example is women's seeking to have a *hakafah* (a chance on the holiday of Simhat Torah to march around the synagogue holding the Torah scrolls). The action is an expression of the love of Torah, the most sacred object of Judaism, and exclusion from such contact previously caused many women feelings of exclusion, deprivation, and hostility. Consequently, as women began to express their need to be involved in Judaic ritual, they especially requested participation in the *hakafot*. Since 1975, in both Canada and the United States, some synagogues, even Orthodox synagogues, have responded positively. Women are being allowed the joy of carrying a Torah, and in doing so they are correcting a common but serious misconception about our religion: that a woman, because she menstruates, cannot touch a

Torah. This is simply not so; women may touch, carry and kiss a Torah anytime and anyplace.[14]

Given the religious importance of the Torah and the increasing prevalence of *hakafot* for women, one would also hope to find women regularly being given an *aliyah* (the honour of being called up to read from the Torah and pronounce certain blessings over it). In fact, female participation varies greatly from synagogue to synagogue. Reconstructionist and Reform congregations give them this privilege regularly. The Conservative movement allows each congregation to choose its own way; in Montreal, most such synagogues do not give women *aliyot* except on special occasions. No Orthodox synagogue in Canada or in the United States does.

It is very difficult to accept this denial of permission since the Talmud includes women among those allowed *aliyot*.[15] Citing a unique concept of *kvod hatzibur* (honour of the community), it states, however, that although women can have *aliyot*, they do not in fact. In other words, an ancient social attitude was sufficient to direct the practice, if not the law, for centuries, and it is still often used to prevent women from enjoying a privilege that is rightfully theirs. In our world, female participation is generally acceptable in so many walks of life that it need not be dishonourable for women to stand before *their* Torah as Jews.

The point is that even the Talmud reflects the possibility of change from within, without discarding roots that run deep. In seeking to be obligated to the Law, Jewish feminists do not wish to renounce the *halachic* system but rather to strengthen the ties that bind them to the varied Jewish community. And in many cases it is custom, not the Law, that they seek to change.

One such area in which they are realizing a measure of success is that of the rituals of transition at birth and puberty. When a boy is born, the family and community have traditionally welcomed the child in a joyful circumcision ceremony. Are we not as pleased at the birth of a girl? In today's world we are, but tradition offered only a minimal naming ceremony, no great public celebration to welcome her. In answer to modern needs and social attitudes, many communities and congregations now celebrate a *simhat habat* on the birth of a girl. It in no way goes against Jewish law but recalls the European *mazel tov* and the Sephardic *zeved habat* and adds to existing ritual.[16] The ceremony can have many variations — allowing creativity and freedom of individual religious expression — but they all sanctify the moment of admitting a new female child into the community.

The growing popularity of the bat-mitzvah, the female puberty ritual, is even less revolutionary, merely an acknowledgement of an ancient tradition. All that is new is the manner of public celebration. For millenia, when a girl reached twelve and a boy thirteen, each automatically became a bat- or bar-mitzvah, obligated to obey Jewish law from that moment on.[17] For a variety of reasons, a boy's coming of age has in recent times come to be marked by an elaborate celebration, while a girl's reaching majority became an ignored fact.

Historical precedent — as well as current Israeli custom — existed, however, for girls' joyfully marking their acceptance into the community as adults.[18] And today in Montreal, as in other cities, more and more girls do so mark it in celebrations that range from imitation of the bar-mitzvah to new experimental services — individual or group, at home or in the synagogue.[19] All indicate the potential for change within the tradition.

Perhaps nothing on the agenda of the Jewish feminist movement can be considered more important and pressing than the divorce issue. There is too much power in the Jewish divorce process — separate from any civil proceeding — left in the man's control, rendering women unjustifiably vulnerable. According to traditional Jewish law, only a man can give his wife a *get* (a Jewish divorce). If he refuses, disappears, or goes insane, she remains tied to him forever, an *agunah*. While scholars may be trying to find legal solutions, following the tradition of changing the law to protect the individual, some groups have begun to seek community-based solutions. Thus, in the United States, an organization called GET — Getting Equitable Treatment — is promoting ways of aiding helpless women. In 1981, Montreal will hold its first conference on divorce to educate the community and propose strategies and resources to help men and women with Jewish divorce problems. The survival and credibility of the Jewish community is at stake on this issue.

Responses in Social and Economic Affairs

Another area in which Canadian Jewish women are winning a place for themselves is the social and economic arena. Canada is now able to boast of women in lay leadership positions in synagogue organizations, even though the country still has no female rabbis. The first woman president of a Reform congregation in Montreal recently completed her term of office, while a Conservative congregation just installed its first female president. Other congregations, even some Orthodox, have women among their highest officers. Relegation to sisterhood affairs has broken down.

Women are also becoming more visible in the organized Jewish community. Of course, they begin at the bottom of the bureaucratic pyramid for men still hold the majority of lay and professional positions. But women are no longer completely excluded from decision-making committees. Often their presence is a symbol, a mere token, but it is quickly becoming precedent. Here and there, a woman now holds a key position as principal of a school, director of a community agency, chairperson of the city's Combined Jewish Appeal. Each one has set a precedent for female leadership in the future.

The growing number of women in positions of Jewish community leadership is primarily a reflection of the growing importance of women in the work force. Women do work — and have in the past. The view of women's place being only in the home is not only no longer accurate; it does not even correctly portray her role in history. At times, Jewish women have been not only active in but indeed famous for their economic achievements.[20]

Since significant numbers of women work today for economic or personal reasons, society must clearly adjust its attitudes, its social priorities, and the sheer logistics of such things as daycare arrangements and other support systems. Many Jewish communities have begun to concern themselves with working women. For example, Montreal's Allied Jewish Community Services (AJCS) recently held a workshop titled "The Contemporary Jewish Woman's Approach Towards Work and Motherhood".

The second Canadian Jewish Women's Conference also focussed on working women. In addition to providing general enrichment and possibilities for growth for its participants, it had two specific results. The first was to give many people an increased awareness of single women, who had complained they felt left out of the conference and the community in general. (Interestingly, many single women had been involved in planning the conference.) The second was the organization of an AJCS women's business and professional group, paralleling the men's structure. This seems only proper in light of recent statistics that indicate more than 50 per cent of Jewish women work, many at professional jobs.[21]

With so many women entering the work force and taking active leadership roles within the Jewish community, what is happening to the traditional women-only organizations? Who is left to join and run the sisterhood? Moreover, is there a need for a sisterhood? "How can an organization of women have any meaning in a society that increasingly rejects that kind of sexism?" asked one recent article on Hadassah in the United States.[22]

Hadassah and many other similar organizations are clearly alive and well in Canada, although they do face problems of adapting themselves to a changing society. Canadian Hadassah's members have not decreased in numbers, but their average age is higher than in times past. Many of the traditional and previously successful women's voluntary organizations, fearful for their own demise, are desperately trying to develop ways to attract younger women, to find new ways to increase volunteerism, even to involve men. In light of this willingness to change and of their great accomplishments, the volunteer organizations seem likely to survive, though perhaps with new formats and structures. Jewish feminism, after all, poses no threat to their achievement nor to the concept of Jewish community; in fact, it represents the same urge to be active in the community, to build, develop, and enrich Jewish life that led to the founding of the women's organizations in the first place.

Conclusion

The usual question is "What do you women want?". The questioners miss the point; the issue is not just what women want but the survival and welfare of the whole Jewish community. It can no longer afford to exclude half its population from full participation. It needs every member's contribution. If, for example, women are not allowed to become rabbinic scholars, then the rabbinate loses potential leaders and perhaps even great Talmudists.

As Cynthia Ozick has said, after "having lost so much and so many" in the Holocaust, Jews must "share Jewish history to the hilt".[23] As early as 1973, Rabbi Saul Berman understood:

> The creative religious energies of Jewish women remain a major source of untapped strength for the Jewish community as a whole, and those energies must be freed.[24]

Or, in the words of another commentator:

> The disaffection of bright, concerned young people is a reality the Jewish community cannot afford to ignore. Cutting off a potential source of educational and communal leadership simply because of sex has dangerous consequences for a community already beset by the problems of assimilation and alienation.[25]

Much depends on women. They must exercise their rights and push existing boundaries. The process is maddeningly slow. It will take time for women's participation and involvement to become normal and normative, accepted and even expected. Yet for the sake of Jewish survival, women must continue their struggle to be accepted as full citizens, with the same faith, customs, and abilities as men. Women must be counted as Jews. They are bound by the same covenant with God and committed to the survial and enrichment of the same people.

A Francophone Diaspora in Quebec

by Jean-Claude Lasry

dédié à André Chouraqui

The renaissance of Sephardic identity and traditions among North African Jews living in Quebec is the result of a propitious conjunction of time and space. Their immigration started in 1957, in the midst of an irreversible process of assertion of French culture in Quebec. This dynamic evolution pulled along the French-speaking Jews in its wake, reinforcing their pride in their double heritage: Jewish biblical roots and modern French culture.

Not all Quebec's Francophone Jews share the Sephardic, North African tradition. Some originated in Central or Eastern Europe but fled the Nazi genocide to France and Belgium. Their stay there often led to the *francization* of themselves and their children, especially in the case of Jews from Rumania (where French had long been the language of the elite), but also for many from Poland, Czechoslovakia, Hungary, and so on. By the time of immigration to Canada, these European Jews shared French language and culture in addition to having a common denominator in terms of Jewish ritual: they are Ashkenazim, a word that comes from the Hebrew root *ashkenaz* ("Germany").

Most other Francophone Jews who live in Canada today emigrated from Morocco, Algeria, and Tunisia, which together

The author wishes to thank the Department of Manpower and Immigration (PIL No. 211-1573) and the Ministère des Affaires Sociales du Québec (RS-136) for their financial support, which made this study possible.

make up North Africa or the Maghreb (the word is the Arabic for "where the sun sets" or "the Occident") and from Egypt, Lebanon, and Turkey. Their religious practices are slightly different from those of their Ashkenazic brethren; their customs and mores, though, are quite different, because they have been deeply influenced by the Arabic, almost exclusively Moslem, societies in which they lived. They are called Sephardim from the Hebrew root *Sepharad*, "Spain".[1] (In Montreal, one can also find Anglophone Sephardim who came from Middle Eastern countries, such as Syria and Iraq, over which Great Britain held a mandate. Their numbers are small compared to the Francophone Sephardim, and their presence is much less felt, since they have integrated fairly well into the existing Anglophone, Ashkenazic community of Montreal.)

Historical Overview

The settlement of Jews in North Africa dates back to the Diaspora subsequent to the destruction of the First Temple (586 B.C.E.), but their presence became really noticeable around the second and first centuries B.C.E. The edict of Expulsion of 1492 brought to the shores of the Maghreb tens of thousands of Spanish Jews, who were received by the Moslem princes and sultans as additions to their population. The local Jewish communities received them much less warmly. Segregation and feuds, sometimes over minor points of ritual, persisted for many years.[2] Even in Montreal, Moroccan Jews from the Spanish zone have grouped together on the basis of their Spanish language, differentiating themselves from French-speaking Jews, whom they still call *forasteros* ("strangers"), a centuries-old expression.

Life under Islam

The Caliph Omar, successor of the prophet Mohammed, was the first to regulate the status, rights, and obligations of the "peoples of the book" — Jews and Christians — who believed in God but not in the Koran. Al Mawardi, in the eleventh century, codified this Charter of Omar as an ensemble of twelve laws that defined the status of the Jew and the Christian as *dhimmi* ("protected"). They were forbidden to touch the Koran, to speak of the Koran, of the Prophet or of Islam in derogatory terms, or to touch Moslem women. They were also forbidden to build synagogues, churches, or houses higher than mosques, to own a horse, to drink wine in public, and so on. They were compelled to wear distinctive clothes, which varied according to time and place, and to pay special head taxes and property taxes.[3]

The Christian communities disappeared from North Africa in the twelfth century, so the *dhimmi* status really applied only to Jews. Until the French conquest, with a few exceptions, North African Jews lived in conditions of medieval poverty, like their Moslem neighbours. They inhabited a precisely outlined quarter, called the *mellah* in Morocco and the *harah* in Tunisia (in Algeria, the district did not have a specific name). In several ways, life in the *mellah* or the *harah* resembled life in the *shtetl*. Jews barely subsisted as peddlers or craftsmen; they centred their aspirations and daily activities around Jewish festivals and rituals.

The status of *dhimmi* determined second-class citizenship for the Jews, who were subjected to the wills and whims of the local princes and to frequent assaults and insults from the populace. On the other hand, this status protected the Jewish communities. As "people of the book", sharing a common biblical origin with the Moslems, they received a basic respect the Ashkenazim did not encounter in Europe. The few Maghrebian Jews who were merchants and traders became a needed link with Europe and often held important diplomatic positions.

The sultans took seriously the duty of protecting their Jewish citizens, ordering the *mellahs* to be built under the walls of their palaces. There were instances of Jewish quarters being sacked,[4] but they never reached the scope of the pogroms of the Ukraine, Russia, or Germany. In more recent times, during the Second World War, King Mohammed V protected Jews from the Germans in Morocco;[5] the Bey Moncef did the same in Tunisia.[6] Although far from idyllic, the relationship of Jews and Moslems was, nevertheless, based on a commonality of sources, ways of life, and shrunken horizons.

The French Conquest

The French military conquest of Algeria in 1830 was followed by a gradual emancipation of the Algerian Jews. In 1831, they were recognized as a Hebraic nation, with inviolable rights. French Minister of Justice Adolphe Cremieux, himself a Jew, fought from 1848 to 1870 to have the government grant French citizenship, with full rights and privileges, to the Algerian Jews; when the decree was finally enacted, it bore his name.[7]

The consequences of the French conquest of Algeria were more felt in Tunisia than in Morocco. In 1857, Tunisia abolished *dhimmi* status, and Moslems and non-Moslems became equal before the law. Security, property, and dignity were guaranteed without distinction as to race, nationality, or religion. Special articles dealt with the religious freedom of the Jews, respect for their religion, and their participation in criminal courts. The French government established a protectorate over Tunisia in 1881, but it did not interfere in Jewish affairs there as it had in Algeria. Tunisian Jews, nevertheless, continued to beseech the Parliament of Paris to grant them French nationality. It did so in 1923, but only under certain conditions.[8]

The strategic location of Morocco had attracted the European powers since the seventeenth century. France and Spain were granted particular rights there in 1906. In 1911, the sultan called on the French army for assistance against insurgent tribes besieging the royal city of Fes, and Morocco became officially a French Protectorate in 1912. Pockets of rebellion persisted till 1934 when the French army achieved the pacification of Morocco.

Colonization and Independence

The French conquest was a very important factor in the cultural identity of the North African Jews. In each country, the degree of assimilation into French culture and the consequent secularization and lessening of Jewish religious practices were directly related to the duration of French rule: one hundred and twenty-five years for Algeria, seventy-five years for Tunisia, and forty-four years for Morocco. French colonization also changed totally the economic structure of the Maghreb. For their process of industrialization, the French needed middlemen. They recruited those intermediaries from the local Jews, who were a particularly literate group for North Africa. Many had learned French following the establishment of Alliance Israëlite Universelle (AIU) schools. (The AIU was created in 1860 in Paris to safeguard the rights and dignity of Jews and to promote French culture among "Jews of the Orient". It created a network of schools across the Maghreb and Middle East whose curricula combined secular and scientific subjects with Jewish and Hebraic studies.[9])

With the creation of the state of Israel in 1948, Jews started to emigrate *en masse* from North Africa, and in particular from Morocco, to settle in the Holy Land. During the years that led to the independence of their countries in 1956, many Moroccan and Tunisian Jews immigrated to France. After 1957, some also settled in Canada, where lobbying by the Jewish community of Montreal helped open the gates to immigration. The Algerian Jews held French citizenship, and most of them settled in France after 1962, the year Algeria gained independence.

Thus, considerable differences exist today in the relative composition of the North African Jewish communities of Canada, Israel, and France.[10] In France, more than half the immigrants are from Algeria; their French citizenship granted them the same rights and privileges as French natives. Many Moroccan and Tunisian Jews, however, experienced difficulties in obtaining French work or residence permits for France. This problem, coupled with a cold or even hostile reception, explains why Moroccan and Tunisian Jews preferred emigration to Israel around 1948 and later to Canada. In both those countries, the vast majority of the North African immigrants were from Morocco; today, they make up 93 per cent of the North African Jewish community in Canada, 82 per cent of the one in Israel.[11]

The Immigrants' Adaptation to Montreal

By the early 1970s, some 11,000 North African Jews lived in Montreal.[12] A survey of them carried out by the author in 1972 provided an interesting overview of the community, their relations with other Montreal Jews, and their integration into Quebec. A sample of 469 respondents, stratified by year of arrival, was drawn from a master list based on several organizational lists. The length of Quebec residence of the respondents ranged from two to fifteen years, the age from eighteen to sixty-two.[13]

Most immigrants to Canada leave their home countries for economic rather than political motives.[14] Most Jews left North Africa, however, because of the political situation, insecurity, and fear of an all-Moslem government succeeding the French one. Only a few left for economic or professional reasons.[15] Since the mass emigration was essentially political, it was nonselective, and the immigrants represented a broad range of occupations and socio-economic backgrounds. Those who went to Israel did so primarily for ideological — Zionist — reasons. It should be noted, however, that North African Zionism was quite unlike its European counterpart. Whereas European Jews went to Israel to build a secular society, rejecting the religious character of the ghetto, North African Jews made their *aliyah* for religious reasons, to fulfill the millennial messianic prayer, "Next year in Jerusalem".

The first wave of North Africans now living in Montreal arrived between 1957 and 1965; most came directly from the home country. Of those who came in the second period (1966 to 1970), almost half had first tried immigration to another country, most commonly France (40 per cent) and Israel (around 10 per cent). Those who left France reported they did so because of difficult social integration, isolation, and rejection by the native French. The alternative of Canada, particularly Quebec, seems to be gaining a tremendous popularity among the North African Jews living in France. The magnetic power of Quebec can be attributed not only to its French culture but also to its better professional, educational, and social opportunities.

Community Reception and Integration

Quebec has proved a congenial new home for many of the North African Jews who have moved there, although their integration has not been completely trouble free, especially in terms of relations with the preexisting Montreal Jewish community.

In the survey, most of the immigrants reported that case workers of the Jewish Immigrant Aid Services (JIAS) had welcomed them right at their port of entrance and in many cases had located housing for them. Any family in financial need was provided an allowance, clothes, rent, and basic furniture until the household head found a job, which he often did through the Montreal Jewish community's employment agency, the Jewish Vocational Services. The majority of the respondents felt that the existence of the JIAS had positively influenced their decision to immigrate to Canada. They said the information it had given them overseas was fair and its assistance precious at the individual level.

Problems arose at the community level, however. The Groupement Juif Nord-Africain, the first North African Jewish association, organized social events, such as picnics and celebrations, with the help of JIAS. But North African leaders expressed a desire to preserve the group's distinct identity, and organized Montreal Jewry equated that wish with a desire for separation or separatism, an explosive political subject in Quebec.[16] The establishment had looked favourably on the formation of other immigrant associations, and even promoted some, as in the case of those created by Russian Jews, but the grouping of Francophone Jews seemed to carry an underlying threat.

JIAS attempted to set up a countercommittee of more docile North African immigrants.[17] This action led to communal disorganization, which lasted till 1965. New leaders emerged again in 1966 with the creation of L'Association Sépharade Francophone. After ten years of a North African Jewish presence in Canada, the group had finally decided to define its own goals and the means of achieving them, with no outside interference.

Economic Adjustment

Like any immigrant group, the North African Jews were faced with a problem of economic adjustment on their arrival in Montreal. Generally speaking, they have done rather well in this regard, partly because they arrived knowing the majority language of the host society and most had had a fair amount of education.

Almost all the survey respondents had received their elementary education in French, the males mostly in AIU schools. At the secondary level, however, only 25 per cent had attended AIU schools, whereas about 60 per cent had been to French-language public schools that had no Jewish curriculum. (This switch, from a Jewish elementary school to a public high school, seems to have been another example of the assimilation of North African Jewry into French culture and its concomitant secularization.)

Although North African men have traditionally had more education than women,[18] the Montreal sample showed only a minimal difference; 75 per cent of the men had had some secondary education as had 74 per cent of the women. This equality contrasted with the traditional, clearly hierarchical male-female roles prevailing in Arab countries, where North African Jews moulded their cultural personality.[19] The women owe their emancipation mostly to the influence of the AIU schools, which actively spread the ideas of the French Revolution: *liberté, egalité, fraternité.*

The immigrants from North Africa have made full use of the Canadian college and university system. Of the total sample, 23 per cent had gone back to studies. Among those who had had some secondary education in North Africa, more than a quarter had returned to finish high school or even to seek a university degree in Canada. Among those who had had some postsecondary education, the attraction was much higher: two out of three respondents had studied either to further their training or to obtain a university degree. The number of those who had acquired university degrees was triple the number who had obtained one in North Africa.[20] This high use of educational opportunities sets the Jewish North Africans ahead of other immigrant groups in Montreal.[21] The stereotype of a poorly educated North African Jewish community has little basis in fact.

Of the North Africans surveyed in 1972, less than 8 per cent were unemployed, a percentage equivalent to the contemporary Canadian unemployment rate. Among the male respondents in the active labour force, 38 per cent were owners or professionals, compared with 44 per cent of the overall Canadian immigrant sample. Forty per cent of the North African men were working in the clerical or sales category, compared to 14 per cent of all immigrants. In the skilled worker category, however, the figures were 12 per cent and 26 per cent respectively.[22] This over-representation in the clerical and sales category is basically the result of the French conquest of North Africa: Maghrebian Jews had filled the white-collar vacuum between the French industrialists and landowners and the Moslem labourers.

Many studies have shown that immigrants usually suffer a drop in occupational status right after migration.[23] Ours was no exception. Whether we looked at stays of two to six or seven to fifteen years in Canada, the first jobs our respondents had held in this country represented a significant drop in prestige; the jobs they had at time of interviewing were significantly better than the first ones but still lower in prestige than the jobs held abroad. But those immigrants who had resided longer than fifteen years in Canada had attained occupational positions equivalent to those they held abroad. Given sufficient time then, the immigrants from North Africa can climb back up the occupational ladder to the rungs they occupied in their home countries.

The loss in prestige was most severe for those in the highest occupational category: owners and professionals. For white- and blue-collar workers, the difference between their jobs in North Africa and those at the time of the interviews was almost nil. Student status prior to emigration generally led the newcomer to an occupation of much higher prestige than did worker status. Still, more than half the North African Jews in Montreal were stable in their occupational status.

The occupational mobility of the female immigrants was quite similar to the men's. The striking difference was in how many entered the work force at all; 16 per cent had been housewives in North Africa, but the figure more than tripled, to 49 per cent, in Montreal. Thus, settlement in Canada seemed to have been quite economically favourable for the North African family, since many previously working women have been able to stay out of the work force. Ironically, moving from a traditional to an industrial society may have reversed the trend towards the modern role of women working outside the family. More North African women seem to be opting for the traditional role of housewife.

In general, the immigrants from North Africa were fairly satisfied with the jobs they held in Montreal — with their work conditions and earnings. For the men, as occupational level rises with length of stay, so does their income. Median earnings in 1972 increased almost linearly from $7,600 for those men who had resided in Canada two years to $12,600 for those here for fifteen. The incomes of the women did not seem to be influenced by their length of stay, probably because most of them had not begun to work soon after their arrival, but rather at the most propitious time for their family circumstances.

Self-employment increased more than four times over the years. The very high percentage (37 per cent) of employees who became their own bosses (compared to only 5 per cent of the overall immigrant sample) identifies the immigrants from North Africa as a dynamic group that improved its economic situation quite rapidly. This economic achievement may explain why 93 per cent of the eligible male respondents had acquired Canadian citizenship, compared to only 70 per cent in another survey of Montreal immigrants.[24]

Social Patterns

How have the North Africans adapted socially in Montreal with regard to both the Anglophone Jewish community and the French Canadians of Quebec? The 1972 survey revealed clear evidence of a social schism between the Francophone and Anglophone Jewish communities of Montreal, evidenced in both friendship circles and the workplace.

Social Relations

The North African immigrants reported little difficulty in establishing a new network of friends.[25] For the majority, these friends were mainly new acquaintances met in Montreal, and not simply relatives or friends they had known previously in North Africa. They were, however, mostly other North African Jews.

The survey asked the immigrants about their preferences regarding the ethnic background of fellow employees and employers. Here we found striking preferences for French Canadians over Canadian Jews. In our sample, 33 per cent preferred French Canadian colleagues, 19 per cent North Africans, and only 10 per cent Canadian Jews. Living in an occupational world where the majority of their colleagues are French Canadians, the North African Jews enjoy their company. Most would rather have a non-Jewish boss, either French or English Canadian, and one-third would reject a Canadian Jew.

The high rejection rate is related both to community tensions between the Ashkenazim and Sephardim, and also to the fact that many are employed by Canadian Jews who do not treat them differently from non-Jewish employees. For example, some respondents complained they did not want to work on Friday evenings or Saturdays, but their Jewish employers refused to consider this religious observance.[26]

Intermarriage

Patterns of intermarriage are often seen as important indicators of intercommunity tensions. A study of the records of the Civil Office and of two synagogues where Francophone Jews would most likely celebrate marriages revealed interesting trends.[27] Both synagogues are Orthodox and require religious conversion of the non-Jewish marital partner; from 1962 to 1972, they recorded 1,510 marriages. The Civil Office was not established in Quebec until 1969; after that date, it performed mixed marriages without requiring conversion. A search of its records of 4,840 marriages between June 1969 and December 1972 brought to light 157 in which one partner was Jewish.

The average intermarriage rate stood at 50 per cent for the North Africans, 19 per cent for other Sephardim (Egyptians, Syrians, Lebanese, and so on) and 12 per cent for the Ashkenazim.[28] The last indicates that the Ashkenazic community of Montreal is quite similar to other North American Jewish communities in terms of intermarriage.[29]

The high intermarriage rate for the North Africans likely reflects an assimilation process that started in the Maghreb under French rule. AIU schools had been the instruments of a swift change from Judeo-Arabic language and mores to French but the strong socio-ethnic barriers of colonial society acted as an obstacle to intermarriage. The French *colons* kept to themselves, as did the Moslems — and the Jews. In Montreal, however, these obstacles do not exist, since the society is an open one that allows great freedom of social interaction. The quasi-absence of socio-ethnic barriers and the sharing of a common language with the host society brought the latent assimilation to full bloom.

Another contributing factor to the North Africans' high intermarriage rate is the very great cohesion and high in-marriage rate of the Ashkenazim. The latter are much more likely to marry non-Jews than to marry Jews who are not Ashkenazic (12 per cent compared to 3 per cent). Canadian Jews give the North Africans pejorative labels and express condescending attitudes that reflect their rejection of the immigrants. Doubtless this rejection has played a role in the high degree of social interaction the North Africans established with the French Canadian population.

Attitudes

The survey also measured the attitudes of the respondents towards ten ethnic and national groups. It showed that the North African Jews of Montreal prefer first and foremost members of their own ethnic group. This finding of a positive group identity flatly contradicted the self-rejection other studies have reported about North African Jews living in Israel, a phenomenon usually explained as the internalization of a prevailing negative stereotype.[30] Our respondents next preferred "Sephardim" (which, in the minds of Montreal Jews, includes most North Africans) and "Israelis". "French Canadians" followed, preferred over "Canadian Jews". Despite North African Jews' infatuation with French culture, the "French" (from France) ranked very low. This latter resentment may have been caused by the French colonialist attitudes in the Maghreb and, more recently, by a perceived pro-Arab shift in France's Middle Eastern foreign policy.

The "Ashkenazim" were the group least preferred by the North African Jews of Montreal; more than one out of five respondents expressed dislike of them. This rejection is a symptom of intracommunity tensions that could lead to a dangerous schism in Montreal Jewry. But the clear preference for Canadian Jews over Ashkenazim means that the two concepts are well differentiated in the mind of our respondents. And it also means that community relations should improve as Canadian-born Jews take over the controls of community affairs and business.

The picture of grim intracommunity relations was also brightened by the following finding: more than half the North Africans wanted their children to have Canadian Jewish friends; only 15 per cent preferred North African Jewish playmates. The hope for the future of the Montreal Jewish community is expressed in the fact that, although they feel their own battle is lost, North African Jews want their children to succeed where they failed: in making friends with the Canadian Jews.

Intracommunity Tensions

Several factors may be responsible for the tensions between the Sephardim and the Ashkenazim of Montreal. The first is the usual animosity that earlier settlers express towards the later ones. (The history of Jews in the United States, for example, reflects successive waves of immigrants struggling to become accepted by their predecessors, who had become the establishment.)

Another factor, specific to the North African Jews, is the fact that they emigrated from Arabic countries. European Jews tend to feel superior to "those people" whose culture and heroes were unknown in the *shtetl*, and they often refer to the Arabic origins of the Sephardim as an insult. This insult still carries weight among the North Africans, who have yet to accept the fact that part of their personality and cultural heritage is Arabic.

Fortunately, their pride in these Arabic roots is slowly emerging. For example, many of them have learned in Canada to enjoy Arabic music, although they disapproved of it in North Africa. La Semaine Sépharade is the group's annual cultural exhibition, and it stresses the Arabic component of the North African Jewish heritage through art and folklore. The Kinor Choir, whose members are mostly Moroccan Montrealers, sang in French, Hebrew, English, Spanish, Ladino, and Yiddish for ten years; it finally presented two songs in Arabic at its annual gala. In Switzerland, a Sephardic Jew recently made a movie about the plight of the so-called Oriental Jews of Israel and entitled it *Nous, Juifs Arabes*. In Israel, according to Shalom Cohen, a Black Panther leader, the term "Arab" is no longer an insult since Egyptian president Anwar Sadat's visit; on the contrary, "Arab Jew" is taken as an identification to be proud of.[31]

Another important element of the Sephardic-Ashkenazic conflict is language. English-speaking Quebec Jews have tended to perceive French-speaking North Africans as a threat, especially since the Quiet Revolution of the early 1960s and the rise of French Canadian nationalism. As Francophones, North African Jews are a constant reminder to the Jewish community (Anglophone by historical accident) that the government of Quebec is determined to make the province French. For many, especially middle-aged unilingual Anglophones, the French language of the North African Jews associates them with the highly anxiety-provoking nationalistic orientations of Quebec.

The Francophone Sephardim's creation of their own day school, Ecole Maimonide, in 1969 reinforced this threatening association, more so since the Quebec government was simultaneously forcing the English-language Jewish day schools to augment the number of hours they devoted to French.[32] Consequently, Ecole Maimonide was treated as an outcast during its first seven or eight years of existence. It was first excluded from the

Association of Jewish Day Schools (AJDS), then considered not completely Jewish since the AJDS decreed its Jewish curriculum insufficient (as a consequence, it received only part of its allotted subsidy from Jewish community funds). Deliberate attempts were made to exclude it from participating in community activities or celebrations.[33] Even when its full membership in AJDS was finally established, Ecole Maimonide's name never appeared on the organization's letterhead, and it was not represented on its executive while schools a quarter of its size were. Relations improved, however, when the inevitability of Quebec's *francization* became evident to the Jewish day school leaders. Ecole Maimonide's struggle for acceptance within the total Jewish community is representative of the Sephardic–Ashkenazic conflict in Montreal.

Organizational Development

The development of the North African Jewish community can be seen in its organizational structure. Communauté Sépharade du Québec (CSQ) is an umbrella organization that acts as the official representative of the Sephardic community of Montreal. The name of this body, which succeeded the Association Sépharade Francophone (ASF) in 1976, is in itself significant. The adjective *Francophone* was dropped in recognition of the fact that Sephardim may also be Spanish-speaking or English-speaking, and the word *Québec* was added to indicate the group's aim of speaking for Montreal and its suburbs (such as Laval, Ville St-Laurent, Côte St-Luc, and Dollard-des-Ormeaux, where a sizable number of North African Jewish families have settled).

Three constitutent organizations reflect the CSQ's different functions: Ecole Maimonide deals with Jewish education, the Centre Communautaire Juif of the YM-YWHA with social and recreational services, and the rabbinate with religious needs. This last function is never included in the Canadian or American umbrella organizations, which maintain strict separation of "church and state". The CSQ, in contrast, devised the rabbinate structure, helped choose its rabbi, promoted his image, housed his office, and obtained permission for it to keep legal records of births, death, and marriages. This inclusion of religious affairs in a community organization was a deliberate strategy by CSQ leaders to adapt for Montreal a community structure that had worked well in Morocco.[34] The new structure is a hybrid: democracy *à l'américaine* plus an embedded religious dimension. The president and half its board are elected by the community at a general assembly meeting, while the other board members are nominated by the constituent agencies.

In 1976, the CSQ itself became a constituent agency of the Allied Jewish Community Services (AJCS), the umbrella federation of the Jewish community agencies of Montreal. This affiliation was the culmination of a battle that had lasted more than ten years. When the old ASF realized it needed community money to ensure its survival, it presented briefs to successive presidents of AJCS and of the Canadian Jewish Congress, but to no avail. As a result, ASF leaders retaliated, in 1970, by sending letters of resignation to the Jewish community boards of which they were members. This act of open rebellion created a furor, as well as an almost indelible stereotype of North African Jews as separatists plotting to overthrow the Jewish establishment.[35]

During the following years, however, the intense general community involvement of the North African leaders was taken as proof that they did not seek to undermine and destroy the Jewish community. As Anglophone Jewish leaders became aware of the French fact in Quebec, they also came to realize that North African Jews had a right to preserve their specific identity and that this could even benefit the total Jewish community.[36] In 1976, twenty years after their arrival in Canada, Francophone Jews finally became integrated, on a collective basis, into the Jewish community of Montreal, through the official affiliation of CSQ to AJCS. On an individual basis, however, integration has yet to be fully achieved.

The need to have a separate organization dealing with Israel prompted the ASF leaders to establish such a body in 1973. Fédération Séphardie Canadienne is a national group, including representatives from Montreal, Toronto and the rest of Canada. A member of the World Sephardi Federation, it has geared its activities mainly to Jewish education and culture (providing teachers, lectures, tours of Israel, and so on); in Israel, it has tried to understand the situation of the Sephardim and to act as a lever to promote their case.

Leadership

As we have seen, the CSQ is a crossbreed between Maghrebian and North American community structures, combining a religious dimension with a democratic pattern of selecting leaders. In Morocco, the North African Jews' leaders were appointed by the king, upon recommendation of the community. In Montreal, the CSQ, like the ASF before it, follows an election model whereby candidates for the board of directors, as well as the president, are elected by vote at a general assembly of the community. The majority of the candidates have usually been Moroccan-born, but many have come from Tunisia, Algeria, Lebanon, Egypt, and Turkey, reflecting the Sephardic dimension in the CSQ name.

The constraints of office, particularly the need for flexibility of time, have narrowed the top echelons to young men (thirty to fifty years of age) who are university professors, professionals, or occasionally, businessmen. Challenges to the leadership have been rather infrequent. Those confrontations that have occurred came mostly at the general assemblies over elections to the board; the opposition was generally younger persons, often university students, eager for more "democratic" procedures.[37] A current challenge to the CSQ leaders, from the rabbinate, seems more serious than the preceding ones, which never lasted very long. The polarization between lay and religious leaders may well spell the dismemberment of the CSQ.[38]

Most ASF and CSQ leaders have been graduates of AJCS leadership programs, where they have been sensitized to the necessity of leadership training. They have thus organized leadership programs of their own, on occasion jointly with the AJCS. The small number of North African Jewish leaders derives from the age of the community, which is still too young to have many members who can afford the constraints of community leadership. Most are still too busy trying to establish themselves to devote time — and thus money — to community responsibilities. The issue is even more critical for women. Several organizations have tried to woo North African women and to include them on their boards, with mixed success. The attainment of middle-class status should remove the last obstacle to complete community involvement.

Relations with the Provincial Government

The community's relations with the Quebec government have developed fairly smoothly. In 1968, the ASF Education Committee (chaired by the author) presented a brief to the minister of education about the bind the Francophone Jews faced: loss of their religion if they attended the Francophone schools (which were Catholic) or loss of their culture and language if they attended Jewish or Protestant schools (which were Anglophone).

The positive response given to the committee members led to the creation of Ecole Maimonide, the first Jewish day school in Canada in which the language of secular instruction was French.[39] In 1969, a first grade of fourteen pupils was housed within a school of the Montreal Catholic School Commission. Relations with the principal and the other parents became so tense and difficult, however, that two years later, in 1971, the leaders of Ecole Maimonide decided to move the school and become completely independent, like the Anglophone Jewish day schools. Education Minister Dr. F. Cloutier granted the school "public interest" status; Ecole Maimonide was the first elementary school in Quebec to achieve this designation, which has significance for provincial funding.

The school has since attained an enrolment of more than 750 (as of June 1980) at the preschool, elementary, and high school levels. To achieve this, its leaders had to reverse the traditional mentality of immigrants in Montreal — that English was the only key to high status. What appeared to some as a grave mistake in 1968 in fact proved to be an appropriate reading of the Quebec political *devenir*; French would regain its preponderance in Quebec. The increasing dominance of French, which appeared long before the Parti Québécois made it the province's only official language, was responsible for the increase in the school's enrolment.

Relations with other government agencies have been equally positive. For example, the Quebec Ministry of Immigration gave the ASF operational grants as early as 1972, even though its services were then embryonic. Whenever ASF, CSQ, or Ecole Maimonide leaders have needed to meet a minister, whether of education, immigration, cultural affairs, or even the premier of Quebec, the doors have always been open.

The consideration that the Quebec authorities have demonstrated towards the North African Jews has obvious political underpinnings. Indeed, Anglophone Jewish leaders have expressed their fears to the author that the government was trying to divide the Jewish community, pitting Anglophones against Francophones. They cite, as an example, a meeting Education Minister J.Y. Morin held in February 1978 with CSQ leaders just after he met the Anglophone leaders. The minister did not have any grand design, as some had feared, of luring the North African Jewish leaders into a situation of Francophone good guys versus Anglophone bad guys. His openly expressed aim was to reinforce the French orientation of this part of the Jewish community, while letting the Anglophone Jewish community know he was quite aware of the existence of the Francophone segment.[40]

Politically, North African Jews are probably more diversified than many immigrant or ethnic communities, for their French culture helps them empathize with the French Canadian aspirations. Some are staunch federalists, like many middle-aged, middle-class French Canadians. Those who vote for the Parti Québécois are mostly from the younger generation. Although they are troubled by the idea of political independence for Quebec, many share the French Canadian dream of achieving predominance for the French language and culture while remaining within Canada.

Conclusion

The North African Jews of Quebec are privileged when compared to those who settled in France or Israel. Their most visible advantage stems from living in a highly technological and affluent society, which has greater educational, social, occupational and economic opportunities. Another advantage is the structure and organization of the Montreal Jewish community, which, over the years, has developed a comprehensive network of agencies devoted to meeting the needs of newcomers — its very lifeline. However, a more important fact is that the established Jewish community exists in a highly polished form to serve as a model. Emulating it has proved to be a tremendous force for growth for the North African Jews of Montreal.

Another, probably key element for the long-range survival of all Montreal Jews is the social philosophy of Canada towards its two founding nations. Dedicated to the preservation of French and English Canadian identity and culture, Canada has used a mosaic approach, in contrast to the American, French, and Israeli policy of the melting pot. The government has looked benevolently upon immigrant groups' efforts to maintain their own culture and has even created a Ministry of Multiculturalism to help ethnic groups maintain their cultural identity.

Intracommunity tensions still exist within Montreal Jewry, but they are bound to diminish gradually as Canadian-born Jews take over the reins of business and community affairs. The presence of children of North African Jewish parents among the Canadian-born and the efforts of the Anglophone Jews to learn French are two other key factors for the integration — better yet, the fusion — of the two communities.

To transmit to their children their Sephardic and Francophone heritage, North African Jews in Montreal have created their own Jewish schools. This achievement, as well as the growing awareness of their cultural roots at the individual and the organized community level, ensures the perpetuation of a North African Jewish Diaspora in Montreal, as well as its integration within a multifaceted Jewish community.

Existence on the Fringe: The Jews of Atlantic Canada

*by Sheva Medjuck and
Morty M. Lazar*

Although the history of various ethnic groups in North America differs, all have faced substantial pressures of assimilation and a sense of representing some form of "survivals from an earlier age, to be treated variously with annoyance, toleration, or mild celebration".[1] Yet many ethnic and religious collectivities persist, appear to grow, and seem to provide viable forms of social life.

A case in point is the Jews of Atlantic Canada. Even in centres as large as Montreal and Toronto, Jews have had to struggle to remain an identifiable ethnic group in a society that, although dedicated to ethnic pluralism in principle, has been hospitable enough to create problems for group survival. That Jewish communities continue to exist in such places as Yarmouth and Glace Bay is a source of fascination and pride. Small, widely scattered, with a relatively long but uncertain history, their survival as viable communities is on the surface enigmatic.

The Current Situation

Large Jewish communities in North America have relatively extensive institutional arrangements that function, at least in

This paper is an outgrowth of a larger project on Jews in Atlantic Canada. The authors express gratitude to the Secretary of State for Multiculturalism and to the Atlantic Jewish Council for their generous support.

part, as mechanisms of survival. An array of religious, semi-religious, and secular institutions provides various avenues for those who wish to maintain Jewish identity. The existence of a network of Jewish organizations is of major importance for non-religious Jews since it provides a secular alternative for continued Jewish identification.[2] However, for Jews in smaller communities in general and those in Atlantic Canada in particular, secular Jewish organizations and institutions are generally nonexistent. They have no Young Men's/Women's Hebrew Associations, no Jewish community centres that are not synagogue based (although Saint John and Halifax did have such centres in the past), no Jewish welfare agencies, no Jewish day schools. Whatever secular Jewish education — in language, history, customs, art, literature, and so on — exists does so as part of synagogue-based programs. Synagogues scattered throughout the region are the major permanent, publicly identifiable Jewish institutions available.

Lacking secular communal facilities, faced by British uniculturalism, and pulled towards assimilation, the Jews of Atlantic Canada have nevertheless persisted as an identifiable ethnic group in the region for over one hundred years. Their problem is further complicated by the social nature (or rather, the perceived nature) of the Atlantic provinces. Except for the Acadian, Francophone parts of New Brunswick, the region is considered largely British in ethnic identity, and, therefore, very few immigrants choose to settle there. In a circular reaction, these provinces are, therefore, seen as representing British uniculturalism, and it has been suggested that, as a result, it is "highly unlikely that the residents of this region will push for a heterogeneous mosaic".[3] In fact, the thesis may be open to some debate (since ethnic groups of various sizes continue to be found in Atlantic Canada), but the proposition does touch on a regionwide problem that can only compound the difficulties faced by any ethnic group trying to preserve itself there.

Two more, related complications to the problem of maintaining Jewish identity in Atlantic Canada are the relatively open nature of the surrounding host society and the very small size of the Jewish community. Most Jews in the region participate in both the relatively impersonal aspects of the larger society, such as politics and economics, and also in more intimate areas, such as friendship networks and kinship ties through intermarriage. This participation complicates the problem of maintaining ethnic identity in that it promotes assimilation into the host society.

Given the problem of Jewish identity as *the* Jewish problem, the situation would seem to be very serious. The question arises as to what mechanisms, if any, work today to alleviate it. It is possible to identify at least four: the synagogues, the unique Atlantic Jewish Council, various kinds of Zionist activity, and, ironically, the existence of occasional anti-Semitism.

The Synagogue

Given Atlantic Canada's lack of any network of Jewish organizations, the one existing institution — the synagogue — plays a role in preserving Jewish identity that goes beyond its traditional religious one. This development is similar to what has happened in large Canadian centres as Jews have moved out from the central cities. Many suburban synagogues have had to embrace a relatively wide variety of activities beyond religious ones, taking on recreational, educational, and social-service activities that were traditionally the function of Jewish community centres and local Jewish welfare and social service agencies. In the cities, however, the secular organizations have gradually expanded their fields of operations into the suburbs. The Atlantic provinces, however, have few other organizations with which their synagogues have to compete — or with which they can work. Given this absence, the synagogues have become the paramount conservers and preservers of Jewish ethnic identity in Atlantic Canada and are forced to take on some of the functions that secular communal organizations carry out in larger Jewish communities.

The result has been an intense use of both physical and social facilities. And since Atlantic-region synagogues tend to be relatively small in membership and relatively costly to maintain and operate, such heavy use puts considerable strain on the synagogues and on their professional staff and lay volunteers.

Another result is the development of enormously high expectations regarding the role of the synagogue. Because the communities are not very large, the existence of a synagogue provides a focal point for organized Jewish life. When one closes, the Jewish community it served comes to an end for all practical purposes. Without the synagogue, the community's anchor is lost.

The centrality of the synagogue is illustrated by the Jewish community of Yarmouth, Nova Scotia, where one has existed for over seventy years. Although the community numbers fewer than twenty-five families and has been without a full-time rabbi since the mid 1960s (it relies on a "fly-in" rabbi from Boston or, in emergencies, on one from Halifax), it still struggles to maintain an active synagogue. It has gone so far as to advertise in *Shalom*, the publication of the Atlantic Jewish Council, about the attractiveness of Yarmouth as a community, and the existence of the synagogue has played an important role in its advertising.

Related to the importance of the synagogue in Atlantic Canada is the role of the rabbis. In this region so far from centres of Judaism, where a rabbi can expect perhaps only one other colleague within talking distance, they come and go with predictable frequency. (There have been interesting exceptions. The late Rabbi Lippa Medjuck served over thirty years in Moncton; Rabbi David Spiro has been in Fredericton since 1944; Rabbi Israel Kenner served the Sons of Israel Congregation in Sydney, Nova Scotia from 1927 until his retirement in 1972, when it was said that he had had the longest tenure at a single synagogue anywhere in Canada.) The typical pattern has been a short tenure. Even those few rabbis who are native to the region have not returned after leaving for their studies. (One exception, a Halifax native, returned in the late 1970s to serve as rabbi in St. John's, Newfoundland; however, he remained less than two years.)

We can suggest several possibilities for this frequent turnover. One is the increasing perception of the rabbinate as profession, a view that is not unique to the region. For some, a concern for advancing their careers seems to have replaced the sense of mission that may have motivated earlier rabbis to serve in out-of-the-way places. At the same time, Jewish communities' expectations, perceptions of their needs, and their demands regarding what a rabbi *alone* can and should do create a burden that even a *tzadik* (saintly person) would find hard to carry.

Atlantic Jewish Council

Because of its geographic location, Atlantic Jewry has historically been cut off from larger Jewish centres. This means that Jews of Atlantic Canada have to rely largely on their own resources. An outstanding example of their success in this area has been the creation of the Atlantic Jewish Council, which, since 1975, has been an additional support in the struggle to maintain, develop, and improve Jewish life in the region.

Such a council serving small communities is unique in North America. It acts as the region's official representative to such national bodies as the Canadian Jewish Congress, the Canadian Zionist Federation, and the United Jewish Appeal. Its board of directors is composed of representatives of all the region's existing Jewish organizations (synagogues, Zionist organizations, youth groups, and so on), as well as regional representatives. Besides serving as an umbrella organization for these groups, it is also a focus for those Jews who do not belong to any of them (its mailing list includes many otherwise unaffiliated individuals).

Since 1975 the council has supported or sponsored seminars, speakers, movies, publications, radio and television programs, entertainments, celebrations of major Jewish holidays, Holocaust remembrances, the celebration of Israeli independence, Young Judaea, a children's camp, and a various Zionist activities. Its programs are not restricted to the larger Jewish communities of Halifax, Cape Breton, Moncton, and Fredericton but reach out to the smaller, even the unorganized communities. One result has been the development of Jewish education on a regular basis in some very small communities.

In its five years of existence, the council, like the synagogues, has attempted to be many (perhaps all) things to many people. It is still too early to predict whether it will be successful in its objective of ensuring the continued survival of a Jewish presence in Atlantic Canada. The general feeling seems to be, however, that despite its problems and mistakes, its very existence has enhanced the quality and quantity of Jewish life in the region. Moreover, the model of service it provides is the envy of small Jewish communities across North America.

Zionism

Any consideration of modern Jewish identity in Atlantic Canada must recognize the impact of Zionism. Zionist organizations exist in every major community of the region and some of the minor ones. In fact, the typical growth pattern was to establish first a cemetery, then a synagogue, and various Zionist groups soon after.

One of the most significant developments for Jewish identity in the entire region — the creation of a camp for its Jewish children — was an outgrowth of Zionist activities. Camp Kadimah came into existence rather quickly following a suggestion made in Montreal at the beginning of April 1943. Through the efforts of various individuals involved with the young Judaean Council of Halifax and the Halifax Habonim Lodge, it opened for its first season that summer. Since then the camp has at times gone from pillar to post, but it has managed to continue to operate every year. Its importance as a source of Jewish identity is well recognized throughout the region, especially in those communities that lack synagogues. Its effects as a Jewish/Zionist experience are difficult to measure directly. Nevertheless, it is interesting to note that Atlantic Canada has produced a disproportionately large number of both national leaders of Canadian Young Judaea and young people who have studied for various periods in Israel.

The ultimate commitment of Zionism, of course, is *aliyah* (immigration to Israel), and although Atlantic Canada has not known a great outpouring, it has been steady and dates from before Israel's independence; for example, Lionel Druker, one of the few Canadian officers in the Haganah (the forerunner of the Israel Defense Forces) and founder of Israel's Sightseeing Bus Ltd., was a Cape Bretoner. Moreover, *aliyah* picked up during the 1970s. A *shaliah* (Israeli emmissary) suggested in 1979 that if the rest of Canada met the Atlantic region's proportional *aliyah* rate, the Canadian *olim* would number over a thousand annually, rather than a few hundred.

Aliyah as the ultimate expression of Zionist commitment does, however, present a major problem for Atlantic Canada with its relatively small Jewish population. If its most committed young people go up to Israel, then the future of its Jewish community will become more problematic than ever. At present, however, Jews in the region, like most North American Jews, find the major focus for their Zionism in fund-raising for Israel. For Jews in the Atlantic region, this activity also functions to bring communities together in a collective expression of Jewish experience and identity.

Anti-Semitism

Finally and perhaps ironically, no discussion of the mechanisms that help to bind the Jewish communities of Atlantic Canada can avoid dealing with anti-Semitism. The region has little in the way of organized, large-scale anti-Semitic groups (although the Klu Klux Klan is now attempting to organize there), but both concrete and amorphous kinds of anti-Semitism do exist. Fliers prejudicial to both Jews and Blacks have been distributed to apartment mail boxes in the larger centres. Several visible members of the Jewish community have received anti-Semitic (though not threatening) letters. A case in point was a Holocaust survivor who spoke to a group of high school students; soon after this public appearance, he received a letter that stated that the Holocaust never took place, that the whole thing was an invented story. Another Jewish individual had a swastika painted on his driveway.

The tension that these instances of anti-Semitism and earlier ones have created has intensified Jewish activity, both as a concrete response to the episodes *per se* and as a recognition of the need to further strengthen Jewish identity.

In the Beginning

Another aspect crucial to understanding Jewish identity in Atlantic Canada is the historical basis of the Jewish communities in the region. Although most of us pay lip service to the truism that it is important to understand the past to appreciate the present, we usually then cease to give it further reflection. Jews in general certainly do not lack a sense of their collective history, but there has been no major attempt to provide a thorough analysis of the particular history of Jews in Atlantic Canada (unlike the situation regarding Jewish communities in central and western Canada). Yet if we are to understand their present-day problems, it is imperative that we appreciate their historical roots. A brief overview is best presented province by province.

New Brunswick

In 1783, a large number of United Empire Loyalists fled the victorious Thirteen Colonies into what is now Atlantic Canada; the consequences of this mass immigration still reenforce the general feeling of British uniculturalism in the region. The colony of New Brunswick was created for these Anglo-Saxon refugees, and they dominated it even after the Francophone Acadians outnumbered them. This pattern of majority-minority relations is reflected in the history of Jews in New Brunswick.

Jewish settlement in the region can be documented as far back as 1781, when a land grant was given to an A. Shepard.[4] Unfortunately, no further information is available on him, so it is more common to trace the province's Jewish settlement to Solomon Hart, who came to Saint John with his family in 1856. Two years later Hart was joined by his brother-in-law, Nathan Green, and his family. This group of fifteen Jews formed the nucleus of the Saint John community, maintaining a strong identity by looking to Boston as a religious centre.

It took over twenty years for Saint John to recruit further Jewish settlers — Abraham and Israel Isaacs, who arrived in 1878. But in 1879, Saint John became the first Maritime centre to hold Yom Kippur services. The story of this high holiday celebration has become one of the favourite tales of New Brunswick Jews because it provides an indication of the strength of Jewish identity despite the lack of communal supports. At the time, the Saint John community included only eight adult males; for these high holy days, however, they thought they had available the ten men required for a minyan because a Jewish salesman from Montreal was in town and a cantor was scheduled to come in from Boston. Their preparations continued with the importing of a Torah scroll and a shofar from Boston. Then their plans came apart when the salesman suddenly had to return to Montreal before the holidays. Undaunted, Solomon Hart combed the registers of Saint John hotels for Jewish-sounding names. Finally, he found a Jew who was just about to sail to Boston for the high holidays and greeted him with "You are Elijah Havani," referring to the legend that the prophet Elijah once returned to earth to complete a minyan. Thus, this Jew was cajoled into staying in Saint John, and the high holy days were celebrated for the first time in Maritime Canada.[5]

The Saint John Jews were also pioneers in other Jewish matters. In 1880, they erected the Maritimes' first permanent cemetery, which would serve all the New Brunswick communities until the 1930s, and also celebrated the first Jewish marriage in Atlantic Canada. As early as the last decades of the nineteenth century, Saint John was clearly on its way to becoming a centre, albeit in a limited way, of Jewish life in New Brunswick. The Jewish community, however small, seemed willing and able to mobilize. For example, when a bigoted immigration officer turned away Jews and others who were seeking entrance at the port, the community organized the Hebrew Benevolent Society of Saint John to serve all immigrants who appealed for help. One historian has commented, "This was the first organization of its kind in Canada to consider its work more a social duty than a philanthropic enterprise."[6] Again, the organizational drive of Saint John Jews can be seen in their campaign to build a synagogue; calling on their non-Jewish neighbours for help, they succeeded by 1898. Another indication of their strength was their early creation of a Young Men's Hebrew Association. All these activities indicate that although Saint John Jews often looked to Boston and then to Montreal for aid, they clearly recognized the need to establish their own institutions in order to guarantee the survival of their Jewish identity.

The second largest Jewish community in New Brunswick is Moncton, whose history has been documented by Michael M. Baig in a paper titled "The Folklore of Moncton Jewry".[7] Jewish immigration to the city was somewhat atypical in that it began at the turn of the century with the mass settlement of twenty-two families. The men arrived first, from Durbonne, Lithuania, and established themselves, then sent for their wives and children (a fairly common practice among Jews and other immigrant settlers in the region). These Durbonners, as they were called, all settled on the same street and formed the nucleus of a very cohesive community. By 1909, it was large enough to hire its first rabbi. Soon it also felt the need for a synagogue. Here the Moncton Jews had a more difficult time than those of Saint John. Baig wrote:

> Plans were made to build a synagogue. Each member paid 10¢ a week and by 1924, enough money was amassed to purchase land. In that year, Jake Marks and Sam Borenstein bought the land, upon which our present synagogue stands, at an auction sale, for the sum of $650. Steadman Street was then the choicest street in Moncton, and many of the non-Jewish residents strongly objected to building a synagogue on their street. The bidding went as high as $650 because non-Jewish people were bidding on the land in order to prevent Jews from building their synagogue on this site. After the synagogue was built, many put their homes up for sale, and some Jewish people bought them.[8]

These obstacles, however, did not destroy the resolve of the Moncton Jews, and construction of the synagogue began in 1927. Four years later, with only twenty Jewish families in Moncton, the building was completed. At the same time, they bought land for their own cemetery.

The sense of solidarity among the Jews of Moncton was never more evident than during and immediately after the Second

World War, when they readily welcomed Jewish airmen stationed in Moncton. After the war, many Jewish immigrants on their way west passed through the city; members of its Jewish community met their trains, often in the middle of the night, and attended to their immediate needs.

Thus, with only minimal supports, and often under adverse conditions, the Moncton Jewish community survived and grew. Today many of its members, like their counterparts elsewhere in North America, have penetrated the host society's institutions. They have, for example, become lawyers, doctors, and university professors. An incident in the late 1970s, however, suggested that undercurrents of prejudice remain among members of the non-Jewish community. A Moncton school teacher published a book that was blatantly anti-Semitic. Members of the Jewish community were not only unsuccessful in getting local bookstores to remove the volume from their stocks but were also unable to convince the school board to investigate whether or not the author's conduct in the classroom reflected his anti-Semitic attitudes. The reaction of the New Brunswick Human Rights Commission was only somewhat less disappointing; when a complaint was filed with it, it conducted an "investigation" but decided it could do nothing but request that the classroom situation be monitored.[9] In general, there is much truth to Stuart Rosenberg's conclusion that "Although the Jewish community in Moncton is hardly a major one, its presence reflects the growing acceptance of minorities in Canada's mosaic."[10] Unfortunately, incidents such as this serve to qualify this kind of optimism.

The Jewish community in Fredericton began later than that of Moncton or Saint John (its first Jewish family arrived in 1912), but by 1925 it was able to organize the first Atlantic chapter of Young Judaea. The Jews of Fredericton appear to have coexisted in relative harmony with the Gentile community. No written record suggests any problems, and in discussions today, they stress pride in their relationship with their non-Jewish neighbours.

Much smaller Jewish communities developed in Dalhousie and Bathurst. For a time, the Bathurst group was able to support a

Hebrew school teacher, had a Torah scroll, and held services on a periodic basis. Unfortunately, Bathurst Jews then began to move to larger centres, and the community became too small to support even this minimal activity. An indication of its loss of viability was the donation of its Torah scroll to the Moncton community.

Nova Scotia

The Jewish history of Nova Scotia is rather different from that of other parts of the country. The beginning of a Jewish community was laid well over two hundred years ago during the earliest days of Halifax; it survived for several decades, then disappeared, but was finally reestablished in the late nineteenth century.

The first Jewish settlers arrived in Halifax shortly after its establishment in 1749. By 1752 there were approximately thirty of them — 1.5 per cent of the population of the town. Land was even set aside for a Jewish cemetery (near the intersection of what is now Brunswick Street and Spring Garden Road).[11] By 1758, however, the town had decided to use one common cemetery, and the Jewish site was taken over for a workhouse. These early Jewish settlers came, in large part, from New England, particularly Rhode Island, bent on establishing businesses to supply and service the new colony. As early as 1751, Nathan Nathans and Isaac Levy were partners in the firm of Levy and Nathans. Other Jews established businesses in Halifax during the same period and generally seem to have prospered.

The outbreak of the American Revolution had a major effect on the Halifax Jews. A number returned to New England to fight against Britain; others went to Britain. Records pertaining to Jews in Nova Scotia are somewhat scanty for the period after the Revolution, but few Jews seemed to have been in the colony. An exception was Samuel Hart, a notable individual who arrived in the early 1780s to establish a general mercantile, coastal trade, and ships' chandlers firm. In the early 1790s, Hart became active in politics. Since he represented the township of Liverpool in the House of Assembly from 1793 to 1799, he appears to have been the first Jew to serve in a British legislative body; it seems, however, that he took an oath of office that included the phrase "one true faith as a Christian".[12]

No figures are available on the Jewish population of Nova Scotia from 1824 to 1861. In the latter year, however, at least three Jews were living in Halifax, and by the 1880s, a Jewish community had reestablished itself there. The 1901 census reported 449 Jews in the province, a number that increased to 1,360 by 1911 and to 2,161 by 1921. For the next fifty years the Jewish population fluctuated from 1,348 (in 1941) to 2,535 (in 1971).

Generally, Nova Scotian communities developed in a familiar pattern, establishing first a cemetery, then a synagogue. (There were exceptions. The New Glasgow community established a cemetery, which is still in existence, but no synagogue. Springhill had neither, though at the turn of the century it had the largest Jewish population in the province.) Between 1895 and 1915, synagogues were established first in Halifax and then in Glace Bay, New Waterford, Sydney, and Yarmouth. The first Halifax synagogue was ready for Nova Scotia's first Jewish wedding, between Sarah Cohen and Harry Glube on 19 February 1895. With the establishment of synagogues, the developing Jewish communities provided the beginnings of institutional support mechanisms for the maintenance of both religious and ethnic identities — something that had been lacking for those first Jewish settlers in the eighteenth century.

For most of the present century, Halifax has served as the centre of Nova Scotia's Jewry. It has been the province's largest single Jewish community since 1911, and since 1961, more than half Nova Scotia's Jewish population has lived in its metropolitan area. Few Canadians realize how important a role Halifax has played in the lives of many Jewish immigrants. Until the advent of long-range, inexpensive commercial air travel, the port was one of the major debarkation points for European immigrants heading to other parts of Canada, and thus it was their first experience of Canada. (This was the case with one parent of each of the authors.) For most newcomers, it was a case of off the ship and onto the train, with contact in Halifax limited to a quick meeting with a representative of the local Jewish community. For some, however, the experience was different. For example, Rabbi Aron Horowitz recalls arriving in Halifax in 1926, just before the last days of Succot. Since he would not travel to join his family in Winnipeg until after the holiday, arrangements were made for him to spend the holidays of Shmini Atzeret/Simchat Torah in Halifax. His strongest memory of his first experience in a Jewish community in Canada was the brawl, to which the police were summoned, that broke out in the synagogue on Simchat Torah during the *hakafot*.[13]

Many other immigrants, however, had more positive experiences. For example, the first executive director of the Atlantic Jewish Council has recounted arriving in Halifax in 1946 as a very young child, after surviving the Holocaust. The group, which included his parents and brother, was met by members of the Jewish community and provided with food (he particularly recalled oranges) for the trip to Edmonton.

The importance of Halifax as Nova Scotia's centre of Jewish communal affairs was accentuated by events in Nazi Europe. During the late 1930s, a number of Jewish refugees were brought to Halifax; some settled there, others moved on to the larger urban centres of Quebec and Ontario. During this prewar period, attempts were also made to settle a number of refugees as farmers in the province's rural areas, particularly in the Annapolis Valley.

The war years strained the resources of the community because Halifax was a major jumping-off point for Europe, and many Jewish service personnel came through it. Yet with some help from the Canadian Jewish Congress, the community was able to provide for the needs of these transient Jews, partly by establishing the Jewish Servicemen's Centre, which provided kosher food, social events, and other services for Jewish military personnel. After the war, Halifax became the major port of entry for Jewish displaced persons. From late 1945 to 1951, the community, again with some national help, met numerous ships, overcame immigration difficulties, provided temporary housing, and finally put immigrants on west-bound trains.

Today the Jews of Nova Scotia appear to be relatively well integrated into the larger community. Halifax and Dartmouth have had Jewish mayors, as have smaller communities. Jewish judges have sat and still sit in the provincial court system and as members of the Legislative Assembly. Jews have served and still serve on the boards of governors of many of the province's universities. Jews have been and still are prominent physicians, lawyers, engineers, accountants, university professors, and business people.

Yet there has been some evidence of anti-Semitism in Nova Scotia as well as in New Brunswick. During the period between the two wars, the "Protocals of Zion" appeared in the province, and pro-Nazi groups had some support. Until relatively recently, some of the more exclusive clubs excluded Jews. Anti-Semitic literature is still circulated periodically. Although provincial universities have generally been open to Jewish students, certain faculties have not (oddly enough Dalhousie's faculties of medicine and law never seem to have been closed to them). More recently, a professional faculty at a Nova Scotian university was accused of not hiring Jewish faculty members for either full-time or adjunct positions. The case is still being fought out. An interesting aspect of the situation is that the particular faculty apparently does not discriminate against Jewish students.

On the whole, however, Jews are accepted in Nova Scotia. What makes the future of viable Jewish communities seem uncertain is not prejudice but demographics. Jews and Gentiles alike are moving out of the smaller communities in a trend that most likely will not be reversed. Given their tiny numerical bases, the province's smaller Jewish communities seem destined to continue to decline until they eventually disappear. The future of the Jewish communities of Halifax and, to a lesser extent, Sydney, are somewhat less problematic. Both are relatively large, though only that of Halifax is undergoing any visible growth at present.

Prince Edward Island

There is a curious story about a very early Jewish settlement on Prince Edward Island. Colonel David Dunbar, in a report dated 25 August 1732, claimed that Louisburg harboured "six French men-of-war full of Jews to settle the Island of St. John's [Prince Edward Island] in Bay Verte", and that the French settlers there "would supply that new intended settlement with bread, corn and live cattle, if not prevented".[14] Obviously, if this story is true, nothing came of the attempt, as the first recorded Jewish settler on Prince Edward Island arrived at the turn of this century.

Originally, Prince Edward Island was a proprietary colony whose absentee landlords made group settlements the initially dominant pattern of colonization and actively discouraged and prevented settlement by single individuals or families, Jewish or Gentile. Consequently, the province has only a handful of Jewish families, most of whom arrived after the 1920s. There is still no organized Jewish life on the island itself. Those Jewish families that wish to participate in some form of communal organization look to the communities of Moncton, Halifax, or Montreal. They did hold what appears to have been the province's first public Jewish worship during the high holy days of 1975, using a Torah and shofar loaned to the "community" by a synagogue in Halifax, but the services have not been repeated.

In brief, the Jewish community of Prince Edward Island must be labelled the least viable in Atlantic Canada.

Newfoundland

The history of the Jewish community of Newfoundland, like much else about that province, is spoken of in terms of "firsts". It was Joseph de la Penha, a Jewish merchant-adventurer from Holland, who first claimed Labrador for England in 1677. Twenty years later, he rescued King William III from a sinking ship and was granted title to Labrador in gratitude. Although de la Penha never availed himself of the grant, these two incidents may be thought of as the first officially documented Jewish contact or influence in what was to become Canada.[15]

Much of the rest of the early history of the Jews in Newfoundland is open to speculation. It is believed that the first Jewish settler was an Englishman engaged in the fur trade who came to Newfoundland around 1800. It has also been suggested that the colony's first postmaster, appointed in 1809, was a Jew.[16]

The real history of the Newfoundland Jewish community began, however, with the arrival in St. John's of Israel Perlin from the United States. He was instrumental in founding the province's first synagogue, the Hebrew Congregation of Newfoundland, in 1909. The Jewish community of Newfoundland has grown slowly since then. The first census in the colony to include Jews as a separate religious denomination was taken in 1935; it reported 215. The 1971 census reported 360, most in St. John's.

Although most of the province's major towns have a few Jewish residents, St. John's has remained the centre of the Jewish population. The province's only presently existing synagogue, Beth El, is found there, as is the only rabbi. Up to the mid-1960s, however, small Jewish communities in Stephenville and Cornerbrook, on the west coast of the island, attempted to maintain congregations without professional staff. They had undoubtedly been influenced by the existence of nearby American military bases, which had been established in the very early 1940s and had some impact on the Jewish communities of the west coast and, to a lesser extent, of St. John's. The closing of these bases removed an important outside support mechanism and affected the viability of the small, west-coast communities.

Although the Jews of Newfoundland seem to be well integrated into the larger society (they have even produced an MP from Cornerbrook) and there is little evidence of public anti-Semitism, the future viability of the community is uncertain. The young are moving out of the province, and they are not being replaced by Jews.

Postscript

In trying to understand the development and problems of Jewish communities of Atlantic Canada, we encounter a number of difficulties, the greatest of which is the lack of reliable sociological and historical data.

In examining what is available on the history and present-day life of the Jewish communities dispersed throughout the region, the researcher may feel both skeptical and confused. All too often, the material emphasizes only Jewish commitment to things Canadian and Jewish contributions to the public good. Most of the little that exists consists of pious literary monuments erected to the local past and decorated in pleasant reminiscence. They offer sentimentality, but hardly anything else, and they convey no sense of historic tension or modern problems. However pleasing these works are to their authors and sponsors, they can neither arouse more than passing interest nor aid the serious understanding of the Jewish communities in Atlantic Canada. Moreover they increase the tendency towards a romanticization of the past, towards the notion that Jewish life in the past was somehow less problematic than it is today.

Yet it is quite clear that popular mythology can no longer suffice as a guide to social reality.[17] Although today's problems are to some extent different from yesterday's, the Jewish communities of Atlantic Canada have always faced major obstacles to their survival. Each generation, in its turn, feels that the threats to its existence are greater than those faced previously. Nevertheless, each finds ways of dealing with its crises. The modern generation is no different from its predecessors; it is coping, at times in vain, but more often successfully, with the problem of survival.

The Mystique
of Western Jewry

by *Abraham J. Arnold*

In May 1969, two events in Winnipeg epitomized the enthusiasm and mystique that have marked Western Jewry for nearly a century. More than 900 people gathered at a kosher banquet in Winnipeg's Marlborough Hotel — then owned by the Rothstein family whose progenitor, Nathan, homesteaded at Lipton, Saskatchewan in 1904 — to celebrate the fiftieth anniversary of the first Canadian Jewish Congress. It was the only public celebration of that anniversary anywhere in Canada.

Winnipeg Jewry has always considered itself one of the founding communities of the CJC, but the gathering at the Marlborough was more to celebrate the Western Jewish mystique than the national achievement. For the participants, the most important part of the banquet was the honouring of some 300 pioneer Western Jews. The glittering guest list included Maitland Steinkopf, the first Jewish cabinet minister in Manitoba; Saul Cherniack, a former CJC regional chairman and then deputy leader of the provincial New Democratic Party, and Justice Samuel Freedman, soon to become the first Jew named a chief justice in Canada; all three had helped shape the Western Jewish community and had parents among the earliest settlers.[1] Guest speakers included two from Montreal: Louis Rosenberg, who had lived in the West for thirty years, beginning in 1915 as principal-teacher of Tifereth Israel, a prairie school in Lipton, Saskatchewan, and Rabbi Solomon Frank, who had served from 1926 to 1947 as spiritual leader of Winnipeg's Shaarei Zedek synagogue.

While 900 people were publicly celebrating these past Jewish achievements in the West, a private political meeting was taking place in the provincial capitol building; a month later it would result in the famous election that brought the provincial NDP to power with three Jewish cabinet ministers, dramatizing thereby the mystique of Western Jewry.

Less than 15 per cent of Canada's Jews live in the four Western provinces. In absolute terms, the Jews of Western Canada accounted for only about 36,600 of the total of 276,000 Jews-by-religion recorded in the 1971 census. On a statistical basis, it would, therefore, be all too easy to overlook the importance of this part of Canada's Jewish population. Considered from a sociological viewpoint, however, Western Jewry emerges as more important than its numbers relative to the nation's total Jews and as surprisingly influential in the overall history of the West.

It is this influence and the concurrent vibrancy of Jewish life in the West that is sometimes called the mystique of Western Jewry. That mystique is no more unfathomable than the facts of history, geography, and politics that all Westerners have had to grapple with. Jewish experience and tradition found it much easier to assert itself in conditions of pioneer freedom than it did in the contemporary East, and it was, therefore, able to contribute to moving the West forward from its status as "the colony of a colony". That subcolonial status, which held the seeds of Western alienation, applied not only to the general relationships of the Eastern government authorities to the West and its people but also to the dealings of Eastern Jewish leadership with Jewish settlers in the West. Thus, Western Jews have been part of the larger struggle against Eastern domination, while also fighting for an equal place in Canadian Jewish leadership.

A brief history plus a description of the present-day situation seems sufficient to prove the point, which is so rarely appreciated in the East.

Early Beginnings

The Jewish mystique of the West began in Winnipeg in the summer of 1882 with the arrival of Russian Jewish refugees, who first thought they had come to a new *Mitzrayim*, a new land of Egyptian bondage. They had been told that land would be granted to them, houses built, and ploughshares and other supplies provided to enable them to live and work as farmers. Instead, one of the newcomers recorded, "They have sent us to a desolate place to become servants and maids." Some also went to work on the railway, where they were soon attacked, beaten, and robbed in a vicious reminder of the persecution they had fled. But Kiva Barsky, one of the victims, succeeded in pressing charges against his assailant, who was convicted and sent to jail for a month.

By September, many of the immigrants recognized that hard work did not mean slavery, and that they could enjoy religious freedom even if it meant conducting holy day services in a tent near a railway station forty miles from Winnipeg. Their hope for a New Jerusalem began to grow. And after the turn of the century, Winnipeg did indeed begin to acquire a reputation as the *Yerushalayim* of Canada; the development of its synagogues, Jewish schools and other institutions kept pace with and often set precedents for the much larger Jewish communities of Montreal and Toronto. Moreover, as prairie settlement expanded, Jews showed they could cope with the frontier as homesteaders and peddlers, as small-town storekeepers and pioneer entrepreneurs. In the spirit of Judaic traditions, they founded synagogues and Hebrew schools in many small settlements, while adapting to the harsh natural conditions and participating in the life of the ethnically mixed human community that surrounded them.

The Russian immigrants who developed the New Jerusalem and the vibrant Jewish life of the prairies were not, however, the first Jews in the Canadian West. Those arrived on the Pacific coast in 1858 with the opening of the British Columbia territory to general settlement at the time of the Fraser River gold rush, and on the prairies at the beginning of the land rush of the late 1870s.

In both cases, the first comers were immigrants from Eastern Europe. Many of them had first tried their luck in different parts of the United States and gradually moved westward, then north. Some were already living in California when they heard about the gold rush. On the coast, they followed the ocean-shipping route north from San Francisco to Victoria, while on the prairies they came via the inland trade route from St. Paul, Minnesota to Winnipeg. They differed from other contemporary pioneers mostly in their chosen occupations. There was hardly a gold prospector among the early Jews in the Pacific colonies, and there were no would-be farmers before 1882 in Manitoba. Just as the first permanent Jewish settlers in Lower Canada came as suppliers to the British army in the 1760s, so the first Jews in the Pacific territory served as traders and provisioners for the gold-seekers, and the first Jews in Manitoba were suppliers to the homesteaders.

The first Jews on the Pacific coast, therefore, centred in the fledgling town of Victoria, and they did very well in all sorts of business enterprises. They also soon founded the first Jewish institutions west of Toronto: a cemetery in 1859 and a synagogue in 1863 (both are still in use). When the latter opened, it reported some sixty-five members and claimed a Jewish population of 300 or more for Victoria,[2] though the 1881 census was to record only 104 Jews in British Columbia.

The Jews of Victoria also quickly established their political rights. In 1859, Governor James Douglas found that he had to amend a naturalization proclamation that included the words "on the true faith of a Christian" in the oath. The following year Selim Franklin, an English Jew who was BC's first government auctioneer, was elected to the legislature of Vancouver Island. Once again the oath of office became an issue, but the protracted debate had a satisfactory conclusion, unlike Ezekiel Hart's experiences of expulsion from the Lower Canada Assembly in the early nineteenth century.[3]

Lumley Franklin, Selim's brother, served as mayor of Victoria in 1866; although some Jews were signing a petition favouring the annexation of BC to the United States, he supported BC's joining Confederation. And when BC became a Canadian province, one of the first two MPs elected from Victoria was Henry Nathan, another Jew. Jews were also among the founders of the city of Vancouver in 1886. David and Isaac Oppenheimer were elected to its city council in 1887, and a year later David began a four-year term as mayor.[4]

After these early years, no Jew became prominent in BC politics until David Barrett was elected to the legislature in 1960. In 1972 he became the first Jew to serve as a provincial premier and he is now leader of the NDP Opposition.

By comparison with BC, the earliest years of Jewish settlement in Manitoba were undistinguished, although the lowly immigrants to the prairies would eventually have a far greater influence on the course of Canadian Jewish development than did the group that so quickly scaled the political heights on the Pacific coast. Between 1877 and 1881, only thirty-three Jews settled on the prairies, including twenty-one in Winnipeg. They held high holy day services, first in a private home and later in rented halls, but there is no evidence of any other communal activity before 1882. During the next decade, however, the Manitoba Jewish population greatly outstripped that of British Columbia in numbers and organization. By 1891, the Jews of Manitoba had increased to 743, including 645 in Winnipeg, while the BC had only 277, including 148 in Victoria and 85 in Vancouver.[5]

The watershed event was the arrival in Canada in 1882 of some 500 Jews fleeing czarist persecution. Most were channelled westward, and the Jews of Winnipeg, who were not yet sufficiently established to conduct weekly Sabbath services, were immediately drawn into the front line of immigrant aid. Stephen Speisman has described the provision of temporary care for seventy Jewish immigrants in Toronto in June 1882 as "a mammoth task considering that there were only about 500 Jews in the city".[6] How then should one describe the task that faced the twenty-three Jews of Winnipeg who had to cope with the more-than-temporary influx of 350 destitute immigrants in a city with a total population of about 8,000?

The motive for sending so many Jews out West so quickly was mixed. It was suggested that they all wanted to take up land, and it was naively expected that the government would quickly make homesteads available. Complying with the official view that Canada had opportunities only for farm settlers, Jewish leaders in Montreal and Toronto sought to restrict, as far as possible, the numbers of immigrants settling in the cities. Nonetheless, the government's failure, at this point, to assign quarter-section homesteads for the Jews led to the growth of a new urban community in Winnipeg, which quickly became the third largest Jewish centre in the country.[7]

Jewish Agriculture

Of course, some Jews did get involved with the prairie land rush, especially in what is today Saskatchewan. Before the turn of the century, there were Jewish settlement efforts in the southeast, at Moosomin, Wapella, and Hirsch. After 1900, several more notable Jewish farm colonies began at Lipton-Cupar in the Qu'Appelle Valley, at Edenbridge along the Carrot River, and at Sonnenfeld-Hoffer near the U.S. border. Only the colony at Moosomin was a total failure. The others established Saskatchewan as the only Canadian province in which a number of Jews became successful farmers for half a century or longer. (Several Jewish farm settlements were also started in Manitoba and Alberta, but none of these worked as well as those in Saskatchewan.[8])

Some Jewish leaders in the East, however, were unhappy with what they saw as too low a level of achievement in Western agriculture. In the 1890s they had fostered the idea of settling as many as 2,000 Jewish families on homesteads. Some even believed that the Canadian government might grant some kind of autonomy to a major Jewish agricultural community. The government clearly denied this in the early 1900s, but the idea continued to be described as a "missed opportunity" for many years.[9]

Some of those Jews who did go on the land in the West looked to the Jewish Colonization Association (JCA), which was founded in Paris in 1891 by Baron de Hirsch to assist in agricultural settlement efforts. However, the leaders of the JCA maintained a colonialist attitude like that of the federal authorities towards the West as a whole. Moreover, for years, the JCA gave help not in the spirit of assisting people who were struggling to meet the challenge of cultivating unbroken land, but as though it were charity, like that doled out to the Jews of Montreal or Toronto who could not find jobs.[10] The JCA and the government alike showed little recognition of the difficulty of homesteading or of the fact that Mennonites, Ukrainians, Poles, and others might be more persistent and successful at farming because of their peasant background in the old country.

Under such circumstances, it is not surprising that some Jewish homesteaders left the land to follow the familiar pursuit of peddling, though many Gentiles and even some of their fellow-Jews considered such an occupation to be base. (Indeed in April 1895 the "Jew pedlars" of Calgary were the subject of an abusive debate in the House of Commons.) In the pioneer decades of the 1880s and 1890s, the itinerant peddler probably did little better than the homesteader waiting for his crop or the trapper counting on his catch, but at least the hope for improvement was there. And soon the peddler who achieved a degree of success moved up to become a storekeeper. In this way Jews became an important part of the rural population; by the 1920s, they were living in over 200 rural communities in Manitoba, Saskatchewan, and Alberta.[11]

Nevertheless, the Jewish population of the West continued to be largely urban, as it had been from the beginning, concentrated in the major centre of Winnipeg, with outposts in the developing cities of Calgary and Edmonton, Regina and Saskatoon.

The Development of Jewish Organizations

No matter where they lived in the prairie West, Jews found that the vastness of the land and its sparse population made it difficult to develop and maintain community institutions and religious practices, especially in centres outside Winnipeg. The Jews of the West, therefore, had to be hardier, more determined, and more resourceful than their Eastern counterparts, not only to succeed economically but to maintain their rituals and to build synagogues, schools, and other communal institutions.

Organizational growth in Winnipeg, however, was very rapid, though it involved some conflicts. At first, the tension was between the strongly Orthodox, who dominated the community by the end of the 1880s, and a Reform element of the pre-1882 arrivals, who received few reinforcements. By 1893, Winnipeg had two synagogues, both officially Orthodox although one followed the Sephardish Minhag (an East European version of the Sephardic ritual).

The Orthodox population continued to grow as the twentieth century began, but qualitative changes began in 1905. First came immigrants infused with the ideal of Zionism, then several varieties of socialists — Bundists, Labour Zionists, Territorialists, and even anarchists — most of whom had turned their backs on Jewish religious practice and became known collectively as secularist-Yiddish radicals. They were all "alumni" of the 1905 Russian revolution, and those who settled in Winnipeg probably had a greater influence than did their counterparts in Montreal or Toronto. It was the newest of the three major Jewish centres and the one that experienced the largest proportional growth during this decade.[12] Moreover, the radical Jews who came there found it easy to ally themselves with the growing socialist-labour-oriented element in the total population, a group that made the city the Canadian centre of the social dissent that culminated in the Winnipeg General Strike of 1919.

By 1912, all parts of the Winnipeg Jewish community, including the substantial Orthodox groups, the growing number of Zionists, and the secularist-Yiddish groups were actively involved in the development of Jewish institutions. The first Talmud Torah (also known as the Hebrew Free School) had opened in 1901; the Jewish Radical School, which quickly became the Peretz School (emphasizing Yiddish) was started in 1914. Landsmanshaften (societies of Jews who had emigrated from particular geographic areas), a B'nai Brith lodge, various charitable and mutual aid groups, an orphanage, a home for the aged, a YMHA centre, and new synagogues were all organized as the population grew.

Political Development

Jewish participation in the general political life of the prairies did not begin with the arrival of the secularist-Yiddish radicals. In fact, the sparseness of population in the vast Western territories and the Jewish presence during the earliest days of many new cities and towns made it possible for Jews to become involved in public life more quickly than was usually the case in Eastern Canada. Those who became well established economically found it relatively easy to develop business and political relationships with members of the Anglo-Celtic branch plant of the Upper Canada establishment (who had themselves only begun to settle in the West in the 1870s). Max Steinkopf, for example, whose family settled in Winnipeg before 1890, articled with Sir Hugh John MacDonald (Sir John A.'s son), became the first Jewish lawyer in Manitoba, and remained a life-long Conservative, as did other prominent Jews. After the rise of the Liberals under Wilfrid Laurier, however, more Jews began to support that party.

The first Jew on Winnipeg's city council was Moses Finkelstein, a Conservative, who was chosen in 1904. In 1910, S. Hart Green, a Liberal, was elected to the Manitoba legislature, the first Jew to sit in a provincial parliament after Confederation. By 1917, however, a Jewish Conservative, Alter Skaleter, who had been on city council for five years, lost his seat to A.A. Heaps, a labour candidate who later became one of the General Strike leaders and eventually the first Jew elected to the House of Commons from Winnipeg. And after the General Strike, Conservative Max Steinkopf, who had been involved with the anti-strike Committee of 1000, lost his seat on the Winnipeg School Board to Rose Alcin, a labour candidate.[13]

The ideological influences at work in Winnipeg were significant. By the mid-1920s, large numbers of Jews had turned to socialist or labour candidates, breaking with the Eastern Jewry's tendency to support the Liberals, particularly at the federal level. This became clear with the 1926 election of Heaps, who later joined the Co-operative Commonwealth Federation (CCF). Support for labour and socialist candidates became a tradition in Winnipeg, not only among Jews, and helped to build the power base of the NDP.

Anti-Semitism in the West

During the early days of prairie settlement, some immigration agents made anti-Jewish statements, some Canadians signed protest resolutions against reserving land for Jewish homesteaders, and a good many people expressed prejudice against "Jew pedlars". But the Jews learned to fight back, as did Kiva Barsky, who won his court case in 1882 against a non-Jewish assailant.

In the 1920s the Ku Klux Klan had a brief upsurge in Saskatchewan and Manitoba; anti-Semitism was part of its baggage. Anti-Semitic elements were also involved in the coming to power of the Social Credit party in Alberta in the 1930s and even in British Columbia in the 1950s. Moreover, before the Second World War, Winnipeg became a centre for pro-Nazi anti-Semitic activity, which included a publication called *The Nationalist*. But as a result, the Manitoba legislature adopted the first group-anti-defamation legislation in Canada. Passed in 1934, it was an amendment to the provincial libel law and provided for injunctions against the publishers of racially defamatory material. (The bill was introduced by an opposition member, Marcus Hyman, a Jewish MLA who belonged to the Independent Labour Party.)[14] Attempts were made during this period to introduce group libel laws in Quebec and Ontario as well as in Manitoba, but only in the western province was the effort successful. Ten years later a debate in its legislature also led to the end of the quota system that had limited the entry of Jews and members of other minority groups to the Manitoba Medical School.[15]

In reality, of course, the West is no more immune to the virus of anti-Semitism than any other part of the country. The swastika-daubing of synagogues and cemeteries that began in Cologne, Germany in December 1960 reached all the way to Vancouver. And six years later, the synagogues of Winnipeg experienced another outbreak of defacement with swastikas, apparently unrelated to anything that was happening elsewhere at the time. On the whole it must be said, however, that the establishments of Western Canada do not seem to have been influenced by anti-Semitism in the same way as have parts of the Roman Catholic hierarchy in Quebec, the Protestant Orange Order in Ontario, or some of the ruling political groups in Ottawa, especially before the Second World War.[16]

The Present — and the Future

Today the Winnipeg Jewish community is still the largest in the West by far, with more than half the total Jewish population of the four Western provinces. And it continues to be a pace-setter on the national scene, even though its population stood at only 18,300 — about the 1931 level — in the 1971 census (Montreal and Toronto then had over 100,000 Jews each).

The Jews of Winnipeg have long played a significant part in the development of Canadian Jewish life, from providing active support for all branches of the Zionist movement, to helping found the Canadian Jewish Congress in 1919, to promoting the establishment of Canada's first permanent Judaic Studies Department at the University of Manitoba in 1952. Local community organization continues apace. In 1973, Winnipeg established a unified Jewish Community Council structure by merging the Winnipeg Jewish Welfare Fund (which had operated since 1937) and the local branch of the CJC. The Winnipeg Jewish Council has led the way in unified school management by bringing the four local Jewish day schools (three primary schools, one high school) under the aegis of a central board of Jewish education.

Elsewhere in the West, the Jewish population figures for 1961 and 1971 censuses reflected the overall shifts of westward movement and urbanization. The Vancouver community was growing (from 7,300 to 8,900), though in 1971 it still stood at little better than half of Winnipeg. Calgary's was also expanding (from 2,900 to 3,300). Edmonton had held its own at 2,500. Regina and Saskatoon had dropped from 1,600 to 1,300 between them.

Despite their small size, Calgary and Edmonton have Jewish community council structures and are developing Jewish community centre programs. They each have several synagogues, conduct annual campaigns for Israel and local institutions, maintain services for families, children, and the aged, and support university studies and student and other youth activities, as well as Zionist endeavors. As the 1980s begin, the Jewish communities of both cities are in the midst of building sprees, but these are probably more the result of the direct and indirect benefits of the Alberta Heritage Fund than of population growth.

Vancouver is also highly organized, with all the services and facilities of larger Jewish centres. The Jews of Regina and Saskatoon maintain themselves as communities based on a single synagogue apiece. Each of these communities retains its affiliation with the Canadian Jewish Congress.

In the religious sphere, the West has seven Conservative synagogues and at least thirteen Orthodox congregations. Reform congregations are just beginning to get a foothold in Winnipeg and Vancouver. Although the physical partitions between men and women have come down in Conservative synagogues, the men still do most of the top-level community planning and fund-raising, while the women, with some notable exceptions, are still largely involved as grass-roots workers in Hadassah, the National Council of Jewish Women, the Pioneer Women or B'nai B'rith.

The smaller towns have fared less well. On the prairies, many Jews left the small centres in the general population exodus between 1961 and 1971.[17] The result is that, outside the major cities, Jewish life on the prairies has all but disappeared, and virtually every synagogue has been closed. In British Columbia, the small-town Jewish population has grown somewhat, but only in Victoria, with its 117-year-old synagogue, has numerical increase led to renewed community endeavours.

Today, the Jews of the West continue to represent the Western Canada mystique within the national Jewish community and the Canadian community at large. Some of them are active in the struggle for Western ascendancy in Canada, though a Western

Jewish separatist would be a rare bird indeed. Many others have shown the initiative and ability needed to win personal recognition in the East and elsewhere in competitive arenas such as politics, the federal bureaucracy, the arts, and big business.

For example, the Senate now includes three Jews from the West: Sidney Buckwold from Saskatoon, Jack Austin from Vancouver, and Nathan Nurgitz from Winnipeg. Sylvia and Bernard Ostry, among many other Westerners in Ottawa, have become household names. Many Western expatriates, from Winnipeg in particular, have been successful in the world of arts and letters; a partial list must include Norman Mittlemen in opera, David Steinberg and Monty Hall in American TV, John Hirsch in theatre, Paul Kligman in Canadian TV, Miriam Waddington in poetry, and Jack Ludwig and Adele Wiseman in novel writing. And to cite just one example of Western success in the corporate board rooms, Senator Buckwold sits beside Charles Bronfman on the board of the Bank of Montreal. Bronfman is, of course, the scion of the best-known Jewish family to move from the West to the Eastern pinnacle of economic power.

There is really no special secret to the success of Western Jewish expatriates; for most of this century, the able person who wanted to get to the top in a specialized field often had to go East. For several decades, people have been a major export of the Western provinces, a fact that has been much resented.

As the 1980s begin, however, the tide is turning. Alberta has joined BC in gaining rather than losing overall population, and Saskatchewan is catching up. The Canadian Jewish population has known a Western movement for several decades, and it undoubtedly accelerated during the 1970s with increasing numbers of Jews from Montreal and Toronto, as well as Winnipeg, moving to the Alberta oil capitals and to the lotus-land of Vancouver. It remains to be seen, however, whether the growth of these communities will lead to a lessening of Western Jewry's alienation from the East or to a reinforcement of isolation within new city-state structures. To assess these possibilities, one must realize that the Jewish communities farther west may now group Winnipeg with the East from which they feel alienated. This is partly because the Jewish community of Winnipeg, in spite of being much smaller than Montreal and Toronto, has achieved structural equality with the two eastern centres and plays a growing role in national leadership. Moreover, communities farther west, perceive it as part of the national Jewish establishment.

The West has always been noted as an incubator for both rugged individualism and movements for social progress; Jews have been active both as individual shapers of economic opportunity and social reformers. As economic power and opportunity draw more people to the West, more Jews will be there too. It is unlikely, however, that the Jewish population balance between East and West will be greatly affected; in the short term, in fact, the shift from Montreal to Toronto will be more significant than the shift from Eastern to Western centres. The growing economic strength of Calgary and Edmonton will enlarge their Jewish communities but probably not enough to enrich their Jewish life and culture significantly or to bring them to a position of greater influence on the national Jewish scene. They may even end up feeling more isolated. Jewish Winnipeg, on the other hand, can hold its own, even if it remains in a no-growth situation, and the city may long continue to be the only true oasis of Jewish culture between Toronto and Vancouver.

Chassidic Communities in Montreal

by William Shaffir

The Chassidim — bearded men in black suits wearing round black hats over side curls; women in high-necked, loosely fitting dresses of unfashionable length with kerchiefs or traditional wigs covering their hair. A people dedicated to their God, to the strictest observance of the Law, to living lives uncontaminated by contact with modern society except in accord with the demands of the workplace and the state. They do not own television sets or attend movies or the theatre. Although they pursue religious studies zealously, they shun the universities and teach their children secular subjects only as required by the government. In brief, they dress and pray like their forefathers of nearly three centuries ago, and they refuse to make concessions to the enticements of the secular world.

During recent years, other Jews have become aware of the Chassidim as never before. Academics have researched their communities and reported the findings in scholarly books and journals. Martin Buber has written a sensitive interpretation of the movement. Chaim Potok's best-selling novels have presented many details of their lives to a wide audience, as have some of Elie Wiesel's books. Explorations of Eastern religions have led a number of young people to discover Chassidism, and for some it has provided a refreshing alternative to the more traditional forms of Judaism, with which they have become disillusioned.[1]

At the same time, some Chassidic groups have drawn attention to themselves. The Lubavitcher have organized a series of highly visible institutions, events, and activities aimed at intensifying other Jews' identification with and commitment to Orthodox Judaism. Neon billboards in large Jewish centres remind women and girls to observe the lighting of Sabbath candles. Youths hand out circulars announcing that Lubavitch will provide up to 50 per cent of the costs of making a kitchen kosher.

In a somewhat different vein, the Tasher Chassidim, who live in an isolated rural area north of Montreal, have also garnered considerable public attention since 1978 through their efforts to convince the Quebec government to grant their community full municipal status, including the authority to convert their religious rules into municipal by-laws. In mounting their unsuccessful battle, they made considerable and effective use of the mass media, gaining both local and national publicity.[2]

Yet despite this flutter of publicity, the Chassidim remain largely misunderstood, even — or especially — by much of the wider Jewish community. The approximately 3,000 Chassidim in Montreal live almost completely apart from other Jews. This is mainly through their own choice but also partly because they are not truly known. Minimal contact compounds the confusion. Outsiders tend to focus on externals and find the Chassidim's dress and lives, so circumscribed by meticulous observance of the Law, old fashioned and perhaps ridiculous. Even sympathetic outsiders fail to see such things as the rather extensive differences among Chassidic groups or the purpose of many of their distinctive modes of behaviour.

The deliberate aloofness of most Chassidim has only added to the confusion, as has the lack of research on them in Canada.[3] Though not unaware of how they are viewed, they believe they can maintain their chosen lifestyle only by carefully avoiding or offsetting the secular influence of the surrounding society.

Their commitment to their goal is so intense that they are skeptical about outsiders who seek to penetrate the boundaries of their communities. Nonetheless, individuals who want to learn more about the Chassidim can do so. Since 1969, I have spent extensive periods of time talking with them and participating in many of their activities. Within the brief confines of this paper, I hope to share some of the information I have gained about the organization of Chassidic life in Montreal and, using education as an example, to explain the way in which they seek to prevent secular influences from interfering with their distinctive way of life. (Unless otherwise indicated, the data and quotations used here are from my own interviews with Chassidim in the Montreal area.[4])

An Overview of Chassidic Communities

Briefly, the Chassidim are ultrareligious Jews who live within a framework of Jewish law and their own distinctive, centuries-old traditions and customs. They follow the Orthodox practice, but their observance is so meticulous as to be outside the experience of most other Orthodox Jews.

Many people do not realize the experiential basis of the Chassidic movement. It was founded in the early 1700s, in the Carpathian Mountains, by Israel Ben Eliezer (1700–1760) who became known as the Baal Shem Tov (Master of the Good Name) at a time when deplorable social and economic conditions had left the morale of the Polish Jewish masses at its lowest ebb. In contrast to the prevailing mechanical and rigid forms of worship, he preached piety of heart and service of God through the emotions. It is every Jew's duty to serve God, he said; this duty is not confined exclusively to the study of Talmud but embraces every aspect of daily life. As one scholar has explained, "He counselled against asceticism and self-affliction, preaching instead a hallowing of all passions and delight in the service of God."[5]

Although the Baal Shem Tov's ideas were opposed by many scholars, who perceived this new movement as a threat, they strongly appealed to the Jewish masses. Shortly after his death, half the Jews in Eastern Europe had become Chassidim, a name taken from the Hebrew word *chassid* ("pious").

During the mass migrations of Eastern European Jews, from 1881 to 1914 and during the period after the Second World War, Chassidim came to North America and established the movement on this continent, where it has continued to thrive, though without attracting great numbers.

In North America today, what is commonly referred to as the Chassidic community is, in fact, a number of communities. The members of each are devoted to the teachings of a particular *rebbe* or leader and are prepared to organize their lives according to his teaching and advice.[6] Thus, although the Chassidim are united in their very strict interpretation of the Jewish law, they also differ in details of attitudes, customs, and beliefs, which, as Jacques Gutwirth has pointed out,

> may be reflected in personal appearance (such as the wearing of a special type of hat or other clothing). . . . Or again, there may be sharp contrasts in politico-religious attitudes — for instance, . . . anti-Zionist . . . [or] pro-Zionist. . . . There are also differences based on geographic origin, occupations, and social kinship networks.[7]

Though each Chassidic community has its own customs, traditions, and specific teachings, all place a high priority on preventing assimilation by insulating its members from the secular influences of the surrounding culture. The isolation is mainly social, and its goal is to minimize contact with behaviour and ideas contrary to the beliefs of the community.

In North America, of course, the Chassidim are forced to give economic, legal, and political consideration to the dominant society, and nearly all groups do so efficiently while preserving their integrity without much fuss. The groups' relations with the wider Jewish community are more complicated and much influenced by their various views regarding the potential threats posed by such contacts. A member of the Klausenburger community contrasted his group's attitudes towards non-Chassidic Jews with that of the Lubavitch and Satmar communities:

I'll tell you an example. There's a storm at the water, a gale. Anybody who goes near the water drowns. Someone is drowning. Here are the thoughts of three people: One says, "I don't care. I'll jump in even if I drown. I'll give up my whole body." Another says, "I'll run away. Look at the terrible storm. He's lost but I can save myself if I run away." The third person . . . gets himself down to the water and he sets himself strong. He throws a rope and calls out: "Catch it and I'll pull you out."

Lubavitch is like the first. . . . They'll live in the worst community in the world, even though something could go wrong with his children. Satmar is like the second: "If I see a person not religious, not only will I not have anything to do with him, but I'll chase him away." We put down a Yeshiveh, make it as orthodox as we want. If a man who is not religious sends us his son, we take him in. If he wants to grab on to us, we take him in. We don't chase after him.[8]

Although this statement is overgeneralized, it is accurate in pointing out Lubavitchers' willingness to initiate contacts with less observant Jews. In fact, it has carefully organized various activities through which it attempts to attract to Orthodox Judaism all segments of the wider Jewish community.[9]

Such contacts do sometimes incur the displeasure of members of other Chassidic communities. In New York, for example, a recent clash between followers of Satmar and Lubavitch stemmed from the latter's efforts to establish contact with minimally observant Jews. A Satmarer said of the Lubavitcher contact with nonobservant Jews:

I think it's a disgrace to put on *Tefillin* [phylacteries] with someone who two hours later, or even five minutes later, might be eating *traif* [non-kosher food]. That approach reduces the holiness of the *mitzvess* [religious commandments].

A Tasher summed up his community's approach to proselytizing:

> We don't believe that we can be responsible for people's *ruchneeyess* [spiritual well-being], it just isn't possible. Instead we feel we have a responsibility for your physical well-being. If I see you in the street I won't ask you if you put on *Tefillin*, but I will ask if you'd like a cup of coffee. What you do about religion is your business.

Despite these differences in approach, the Chassidim of North America generally believe social contact with members of another Chassidic group is safer than, and thus preferable to, contact with others, Jew or Gentile. Where community size precludes offering a full range of services — ritual baths for men and women, boys' and girls' schools, the provision of kosher food, a burial society, even a synagogue — the various groups in a given area cooperate rather freely.

The Chassidic Communities of Montreal

Nearly all Canada's Chassidim — some 540 families — live in the Montreal area.[10] Today they comprise seven distinct communities whose followers have established yeshivas and/or *shteeblech* (a Chassidic house of prayer used for both religious services and study meetings).[11] The largest communities are those of Belz, Lubavitch, Satmar, and Tash — whose followers are known as Belzer, Lubavitcher, Satmarer, and Tasher respectively; each numbers between one hundred and one hundred and ten families. The Klausenburger Chassidim include approximately sixty families and the Bobover and the Vishnitzer about twenty apiece. Family size is large — an estimated 4.5 children per family — so Montreal's total Chassidic population is probably about 3,000.[12]

Until the early 1940s, Montreal could claim only ten or fifteen Chassidim, followers of several different *rebbeim*. Although they formed no community, they maintained a synagogue for prayer and study meetings, and despite their small numbers, they attracted sympathetic supporters among the city's Orthodox Jews.

In 1941, nine Lubavitcher Chassidim arrived in Montreal. Following the instructions of their *rebbe*, they immediately established a yeshiva that became the centre of the city's first Chassidic community. A school and summer camp followed shortly. The circle expanded significantly in 1943, when some fifteen young Jewish men, released from an interment camp at Ile-aux-Noix, Quebec, affiliated themselves with the community, and again after the war, when a number of Lubavitcher immigrated to Montreal from Europe.

Adherents of other Chassidic groups began to arrive in Montreal as the decade turned. In the spring of 1949 the Klausenburger *rebbe* helped establish a traditional yeshiva called First Mesiphta of Canada; the founding of the Maor Hagolah yeshiva followed a few months later.

The Lubavitcher kept themselves separate from these other Chassidim, who, in the beginning, were too few to separate into distinct communities and, therefore, worshipped and socialized together. The groups' customs and religious philosophies were, however, too different for anything but a merger of convenience, and as numbers increased, they established separate communities. For example, the followers of Satmar separated from the other worshippers at Maor Hagolah to organize their own community; similarly, in 1952, the Belzer Chassidim constituted themselves as the *Hassidei Belz Umahzik Hadath* ("Chassidim of Belz and Upholders of the Faith"). By the summer of 1954, the Montreal Jewish community was sprinkled with yeshivos and *shteeblech* reflecting the divisions of the Chassidim.

None of the distinct, small communities could, however, support enough autonomous institutions to meet its followers' needs. In 1954 they joined together to establish the Community Holy Association of United Jewish Congregations, which now serves the city's Chassidim and some other Orthodox Jews; included among its activities are a program for visiting the sick, a free-loan association, and a burial society with a cemetery in Ste-Sophie, north of Montreal. In 1964 it also founded the United Orthodox Jewish Schools, a body designed to coordinate secular studies in the Chassidic schools.[13]

During the 1940s and early 1950s, almost all Montreal's Chassidim lived in a section of the city that was a contemporary Jewish residential centre.[14] Today the area is populated mainly by Greek immigrants, but perhaps half Montreal's Chassidim — the followers of Belz, Satmar, Bobov and Vishnitz — remain. The followers of Lubavitch, Klausenburg and Tash have relocated their communities in more suburban areas. The Tasher *rebbe*, in fact, led his followers in 1964 to a rural location in Ste-Therese, eighteen miles north of the city.[15]

The Organization of Secular Studies

Although the Tasher are the only Chassidim of Montreal to isolate themselves in a rural setting, all share a common view of modern secular society, which they believe has reached a degenerate state as evidenced by the prevalence of marital separation and divorce, crime, illegal drugs, and lust and greed for material possessions. The misguided course of modern society, they argue, is reflected in many individuals' unhappiness with their lives; in the case of unobservant Jews, such disenchantment stems from their unwillingness to organize their lives around the tenets of Orthodox Judaism. The assimilative features of the larger secular society cause too many Jews to distance themselves from their Torah heritage; therefore, conclude the Chassidim, insulation from these influences is absolutely necessary.

The way Chassidic schools organize their secular curricula exemplifies and deliberately perpetuates such a view of secular society. School administrators and community leaders arrange all secular studies so as to ensure that their content does not conflict with religious studies.[16] To this end, they devote careful attention to both the hiring of teachers and the screening of the curriculum.

The schools must go outside the Chassidic communities to recruit teachers for their secular departments because their own graduates are strenuously discouraged from pursuing secular studies beyond the secondary level.[17] Although the Chassidim recognize the benefits that would come from having their own kind staff the secular departments, the general view is that the risks involved in exposing young people to a university environment would more than offset the advantages it would bring. A Lubavitcher told me:

> You see, I feel that you have no right to expose somebody to danger. You never know what will be the outcome if somebody goes to college. It would be very nice [if secular teachers came from within the community]. But . . . we don't want to expose our girls to the university and that makes it very hard. . . . You can't have teachers if they're not going to go to university. And the university is a dangerous place especially, I think, for our children, who have been so cloistered all their lives. To let them out like that, they have to be very strong minded not to get pushed around and not to be pushed onto the wrong paths.

The view of secular education as having a probable negative influence affects the choice of which outsiders are hired as teachers. Although most school officials claim they pay primary attention to an applicant's educational qualifications, less formal considerations clearly play a large part in hiring decisions. As a Satmarer school official said:

> If you have a B. A. and a teacher's certificate, it's important. But for us there's something even more important — how will you affect the children? That is what we are even more concerned about than if you went to college.

A Tasher yeshiva administrator echoed this view:

> If my choice is to have a qualified teacher who may be dangerous for the kids or someone who isn't so qualified, I'll take the less qualified. We are dealing with children and we can't be too careful.

The ideal secular teacher — a practising Orthodox Jew with a teacher's certificate — is difficult to find. Given a lack of ideal candidates, administrators sometimes hire Gentiles in preference to nonreligious Jews, believing the former less capable of swaying students, intentionally or not, from their religious beliefs.

Such a careful selection process affords the students considerable protection; the schools add to it by expecting teachers of secular material to remain strictly within the limits of their subjects[18] and by screening all teaching methods and materials. A researcher who studied the Satmarer Chassidim in the Williamsburg area of New York City, explained the rationale for exercising this striking degree of control:

> What concerns community leaders most is the possibility that the exposure of the youngsters to strange people and materials may be an avenue for undesirable acculturation, a gap in the isolating wall they try to build around the young until they grow up and are ready to deal with the environment from the more favorable vantage point of adulthood and full-fledged incorporation in the community.[19]

Some Chassidic schools give teachers a handbook informing them of proscribed areas of discussion with students. A teacher at an Orthodox girls' school that includes students from Chassidic families told me:

> At the beginning of the year the rabbi made up a manual for all the teachers. A section of this manual was devoted to explaining to teachers what we must not teach. It said something to the effect of: everything contrary to Jewish religion must not be taught . . . such as evolution. Anything philosophical and contrary to Judaism must not be taught. Sex is absolutely out. If a teacher feels a serious need to communicate these ideas to the students, then she is to consult the rabbi first, but under no circumstances is free discussion to be allowed in the classroom.

In other cases, the principal of the school gives teachers verbal instructions. For example, a university graduate who had taught students from several Chassidic groups reported:

He [the principal] told me a few things that I shouldn't be discussing with the kids. Things that would conflict with their religious beliefs. . . . Don't talk in terms of time, long periods of time, because they just won't believe you. They all just sort of block it out or they'll challenge you . . . because the earth has been in existence for a certain amount of time for them and if you talk in terms of millions of years. . . .

The authorities complement such instruction by inspecting all secular books to ensure that neither written nor pictorial content even suggests anything contrary to community beliefs. This sort of censorship, the Chassidim believe, prevents classroom discussion of certain areas by avoiding all references to them. For example, another teacher, who taught in a boys' school, recalled:

Now, when the *rebbe* wanted them to learn English, even in the highest classes, they had to learn from certain books that were approved by them. For instance, if there was a picture of a woman, even a cartoon picture, anything, it didn't matter whether she had a long skirt on or not, it had to be marked in black. And I told the *rebbe* that if I marked it in black, the boys will be more curious, but this had nothing to do with it. It had to be marked off. All the *rabonim* [rabbis] saw that, even for the youngsters, every single illustration was taken out and all references to women were taken out.

All the Chassidic schools limit the secular educational experience to the classroom or, at most, to assignments to be done at home. They discourage extracurricular activities as offering too many temptations to secular involvement. Another teacher noted:

I wanted to take my kids to the museum . . . and it had to go through the council and it was refused just like that — they just wouldn't allow it. Also I wanted to start a library. It was refused obstensibly . . . on technical grounds that there wasn't enough room in the school. They didn't know which books I would bring in and they thought the threat was too great and it would be too much trouble anyway, so they said forget it. . . . Their list of priorities didn't include their kids reading anything like Hardy Boys mysteries, or anything to get them interested in reading.

The secular programs in Montreal's Lubavitch boys' and girls' schools follow public-school guidelines more closely than do those of other Chassidic schools. Nonetheless, the Lubavitch school administrators screen secular subject matter and stay aware of the kinds of discussions and arguments that teachers enter into with their students. This, claim the administrators, is to avoid bringing into the open ideas contradictory to the students' religious beliefs. As in other Chassidic schools, administrators inspect the books to be issued to students to prevent stories related to other religions or in direct conflict with traditional Jewish beliefs from being studied in class. In this regard, the main difference between the Lubavitch and other Chassidic schools is that the latter usually cross out content perceived as negative, while the Lubavitch schools replace it with substitute materials.

In spite of such careful screening of curricular materials and supervising of secular teachers, the Chassidim are aware of the impossibility of shielding their students from all potentially disruptive secular influences. Leaders and parents view these influences as the inevitable accompaniments of secular education and expect that the schools' religious studies will offset them.

To an outsider, such overriding and meticulous concern about the secular curriculum borders on fanaticism. What right do Chassidic parents have, ask their less religious counterparts, to deprive their children of a well-rounded secular education? The Chassidim, on the other hand, claim that Jewish parents who pay only scant attention to their children's religious upbringing are acting in a scandalous manner that is detrimental to their moral development as Jews. Children, contend the Chassidim, must be raised with a Torah-grounded education, and deflections from this path either eliminated or carefully controlled. The remarks of a Satmarer parent reflected this view:

To me the secular studies are not very important. The religious studies are what count. I can't understand how Jewish parents pay so little attention to their children's religious education. They neglect this education and then have to pay the price when the children take drugs. [Translated from Yiddish.]

In brief, the Chassidim's coordination of secular education helps them uphold community boundaries, screening potentially harmful secular influences and contributing to the maintenance of a particular lifestyle. Many other community institutions perform a similar function. For example, activities within the family unit are organized so as to transmit to the young particular values and ideals that will help ensure their staying on the time-honoured chosen path.

Conclusion

Ever since Chassidic immigrants arrived in North America, people have been wondering whether they would be able to maintain their lifestyle in an urban, secular setting. So far they have done so, but some Jews in the larger community today expect that modern technology and secular influences will inevitably chip away at the Chassidic lifestyle, until the Chassidim cease observing their distinctive way of life and simply blend into the Orthodox Jewish community. These doubters are puzzled by the fact that even today Chassidic Jews continue to dress in distinctive garb and observe the ways of their forebears to the minutest detail; they are even more perplexed as to why so many younger Chassidim have not abandoned the ways of their parents and how the size of the Chassidic population continues increasing.

In fact, the Chassidic communities of Montreal are not only increasing in population. More important, the young in them display as intense a commitment to the Chassidic lifestyle as their parents. Young Lubavitch men and women are an increasingly common sight in Jewish neighbourhoods and shopping centres, but the zeal and fervour of the young of all Chassidic groups is best observed by witnessing their behaviour in such contexts as the school, the synagogue, and the home. Very simply, they follow the ways of earlier generations because they are carefully socialized to recognize and become committed to the patterns of their parents' lifestyle. Furthermore, each community provides the young with a well-organized system of support, which helps ensure their faithfulness to the ancestral ways.

To be sure, Chassidic institutions are only comparatively autonomous, since they are more or less linked to those of the larger Jewish community.[20] For this reason, the future of the Chassidic communities cannot be divorced from the influences shaping and moulding the wider Jewish community. Nevertheless, they seem only mildly affected by the events, conflicts, and strains affecting the latter. For example, Chassidic day schools in Quebec have experienced considerably fewer difficulties than their non-Chassidic counterparts in adapting to the Quebec government's insistence that the number of hours taught in the French language be increased. As one Chassidic school administrator remarked, "It doesn't make any difference to us if we teach in English or French."

The insulating mechanisms adopted by the Chassidim do work, not least because several of them, including the very careful supervision of secular education, are designed not only to transmit a way of life to the children but to avoid or offset the influence of the surrounding society on the young.

PART IV

Culture
and
Ideology

In this section, two essays examine aspects of the culture of the Canadian Jewish community, and a third looks at one of its oldest and most important ideologies — Zionism.

Before suggesting some of the challenges these topics raise, it is necessary to point out that culture exists on two quite different levels. One is what is sometimes called high culture — serious works of art, scholarship, and so on — which is generally produced by a small elite and consumed by a slightly larger one. For a minority group, it reflects the crowning achievements of a given heritage and tradition, and one measure of the group's cultural development may be the degree to which such creations are appreciated by its average members.

The second level of culture is the way ordinary people live their lives. This notion of culture from the ground up, often termed "folk culture" or "popular culture", is tied directly to the anthropological notion of culture as lifestyle replete with patterns of dress, speech, cuisine, and so on and with conventions of social interaction.

At either level, no minority-group culture can resist some influence from the surrounding host society. Clearly, the minority can preserve and develop its distinctive culture best if it is wrapped in the cocoon of a group language different from that of the larger surrounding society. As Eugene Orenstein explains in his essay, the Yiddish language once sheltered and nurtured an authentic Jewish culture with both popular and elitist dimensions. Indeed, one cannot understand the social history of the Jewish immigrants at the turn of this century without a knowledge of "Yiddishkeit", the cultural milieu that used Yiddish as the language of the home, shop, school, synagogue (except for the Hebrew prayers), theatre, library, fraternal organization, labour union, and endless ideological debate. It is not surprising then that Canada has produced an impressive array of Yiddish writers, poets, journalists, and scholars.

Even though Yiddish has declined as a language of daily use, it retains a prominent role in Canadian Jewish life. It is the spoken language of many older Jews and of the ultra-orthodox Chassidic groups. Selected phrases play a symbolic role in the cultural repertoire of most Jews. Few Jewish writers hesitate to use a Yiddish bon mot in their English-language work. Moreover, Yiddish language and literature are still taught on college campuses, in Jewish community institutions, and, perhaps most important, in several Jewish day schools to new generations of Canadians. The writing of a final obituary would be premature.

Yet in Canada today, English and French have become the major languages of cultural expression for Jews. How does modern Jewish culture interact with Canadian society? Four academics — Mervin Butovsky, Howard Roiter, Morton Weinfeld, and Ruth Wisse — address this topic in a four-way discussion. The wide-ranging scope of the conversation clarifies different understandings of the nature of Canadian society and culture and the meaning of Jewishness in the modern period. Is a Jewish cultural creation something that deals with a specifically Jewish theme or simply something produced by a Jew? Has the experience of Canadian Jewish writers been different from that of their U.S. counterparts? Can Jewish culture survive the assimilationist trends in Canada and other modern societies? Whatever answers emerge seem to suggest that the interplay between Canadian and Jewish culture has been both destructive of elements of traditional authentic Judaism and conducive to the creation of new forms.

*Just as forms of cultural expression have changed over the
decades, so have ideologies. The passionate ideological debates
that once characterized the immigrant Jews no longer
move many North Americans. Zionism may be the only
ideological conviction to which most Jews subscribe today.
But as Harold M. Waller describes, most Canadian Jews no longer
espouse the classical Zionist belief that the only solution
to the Jewish problem is for all Diaspora Jews to immigrate to
Israel. The new ideology is a more generalized support
for the state of Israel and an attachment to it strong enough to
play an important role in the consciousness of even
those Jews who are relatively assimilated.*

Yet the relations between Israel and Diaspora communities
like Canada are full of irony. One the one hand, Canadian Jews
are sustained as Jews by the existence of Israel, a state founded by
the Zionist movement, which was historically committed to the
negation of Diaspora Jewish life. On the other hand, Israel itself
remains dependent on Diaspora Jewry for financial and political
support. In other words, the Diaspora and Israel, rather than
competing as mutually exclusive solutions to the Jewish
Question, have evolved a symbiotic, mutually reinforcing
relationship. This new reality seems functional, but it poses
serious and as yet unresolved problems of self-definition for
Zionist organizations in Canada. The problem is particularly
acute because other Jewish groups have assumed so many of the
traditional organizations' functions — fund-raising, lobbying,
cultural, education and the promotion of the homeland.

Another question emerges unanswered from this section.
What in daily life distinguishes a native-born, English-speaking,
nonobservant Jew from any other typical Canadian?
Perceptive Jews and non-Jews argue that cultural peculiarities
persist even among this group. They are reflected in
patterns of speech and body language, in food preferences, in
mannerisms, and so on. Politics, too, are a clue (Jews are
either solid liberals or guilty about not being so).

By many conventional measures of behaviour, the majority
of typical Jews are highly assimilated. Yet many of them claim to

"feel" very Jewish, even though they do not express that feeling in explicitly Jewish acts such as going to the synagogue or observing the dietary laws. What they seem to be describing is a new and secular Jewish cultural style. This can be seen in the American scene, which has given us the stereotyped New York Jew as an example of Jewish behaviour that is not intrinsically Jewish. Examples range from the urban, somewhat neurotic intellectual (distilled for the movie screen by Woody Allen) to the much-satirized ostentatious suburbanite whose actual knowledge of or involvement in Judaism may be slight. Certainly, neither of these types will ever be as authentically Jewish as the immigrant Yiddishist, the Hebrew-speaking committed Zionist, or the traditional Orthodox Jew. But both the Jewish intellectual and the "bagel and lox" Jew do inhabit true, modern, Jewish subcultures. A full understanding of modern Jewish life in Canada may require more serious study of these subgroups on their own terms.

Yiddish Culture in Canada Yesterday and Today

by *Eugene Orenstein*

Yiddish, the mother tongue of some 50,000 Canadian Jews today and a symbol of Jewish identity for many immigrants of earlier generations, has a thousand-year-old tradition. Developed among European Jews as a fusion of components from Middle High German, Hebrew-Aramaic, and the Romance and Slavic languages,[1] it became, from the eleventh century to the end of the eighteenth, the spoken language and often a literary one for the Ashkenazic Jews from Holland to the Ukraine. Eventually, assimilation and emancipation led to its decline in Western Europe, but among the relatively numerous, more segregated and vibrant Jews of Eastern Europe, Yiddish continued to dominate. Indeed, the traditional religious, legal, and socio-cultural self-sufficiency of the Jewish communities within the non-Jewish states of this area encouraged the flourishing of a distinctive Jewish language and culture.

Beginning in the second half of the nineteenth century, a great national and social awakening occurred within Eastern European Jewry. One result was to infuse the language and its culture with new vitality. Yiddish literature flowered, and the language became a political and ideological instrument in many of the diverse Jewish movements of the modern age. Moreover, the great Jewish emigrations of the late nineteenth and early twentieth centuries expanded the Yiddish-speaking community beyond the boundaries of Eastern Europe to many corners of the globe, including North America.

Yiddish Roots in Canada and the U.S.

Many of the Jews who emigrated to North America from Eastern Europe had a deep-rooted tradition of Jewish autonomy and were involved in an intense struggle to continue their separate culture in a modernized form. Yiddish was their language, and they were used to using it for a broad range of media and institutions — from belles-lettres to new political concepts to the language of daily life. In the United States, however, the immigrants found the price of opportunity was acceptance of a new set of political and socio-economic circumstances that offered scant opportunities for communal or even linguistic autonomy. English was the language of work, of education and — within a generation or so — of daily Jewish life. Yiddish creativity thus became limited to literature, the press, and the theatre.

Although the same assimilative process occurred in Canada, its pace and results were somewhat different than in the United States. Here, particularly in Winnipeg and Montreal, assimilation came less completely. Perhaps most important, Yiddish cultural activity did not become a strictly literary movement; to this day it includes a significant involvement in Jewish education. The secular day school with instruction in Yiddish (or Yiddish and Hebrew) and Yiddish culture as a significant component of the curriculum is an institution that never took root in the United States. In Winnipeg, Montreal, Toronto and Calgary, however, it has had considerable success and has influenced both the general development of Jewish education and the formation of a Jewish national identity among second- and third-generation Canadians.[2]

Various sociologists and historians have attempted to explain this Canadian Jewish achievement. One group of scholars stresses the fact that when Eastern European Jews began their mass immigration to the United States in 1881, that country already had a well-established, predominantly German Jewish community numbering approximately a quarter of a million.[3] The prosperous, Americanized men at its helm were well on their way to shaping Jewish life in a liberal, bourgeois, denominational mould that had no place for particularist or national forms of Jewish expression.

The institutional patterns of these assimilationists exerted considerable influence on the life and views of the new immigrants in the United States despite the ensuing conflict between the established community and the newcomers.

On the other hand, the Eastern European Jews who came to Canada in the late nineteenth century found a country that held only 2,393 other Jews. Although many of the latter probably had an ideological affinity with their counterparts in the United States, they were numerically too few to exert as strong an influence. The new arrivals, therefore, were to create institutions in harmony with their own views.

Scholars point out that Canadian and American Jewry also differed in both the timing and the ideological orientation of their most massive waves of Yiddish-speaking immigrants. American Jewry created its new communal structures and cultural institutions from about 1881 to 1900, years during which approximately half a million Eastern European Jews entered the United States. These immigrants included pioneers of the Jewish labour movement, the most significant and dynamic social movement of the Yiddish-speaking masses during the 1880s and 1890s. They were cosmopolitans and assimilationists who believed in an imminent social revolution in which national differences would dissolve, leaving one socialist humanity. Socialism, as they understood it, required the complete negation of the Jews as a people. Indeed, long after their zeal for revolutionary socialism had abated, they remained opposed to any form of organization along the lines of Jewish peoplehood. For them, and hence for the institutions and movements they led, Jewishness was something to be transcended.[4]

Although this wave of immigrants swept over almost all the centres of Jewry in the United States, only about 13,000 came to Canada during the last twenty years of the nineteenth century. In contrast, the first two decades of the new century saw approximately 108,500 Eastern European Jews emigrate to the northern country. And many of these were part of a new generation shaped by a changed emotional and intellectual climate in the Old World, permeated by a flowering of the Jewish national renaissance.

Many of them had been active in the revolutionary Jewish political parties that had appeared in Eastern Europe around the turn of the century or had at least been influenced by their intensely Jewish national and cultural platforms, as well as by their generally socialistic orientation.[5] Many had also developed considerable Jewish nationalism under the impact of heightened anti-Semitism and the wave of pogroms in Russia.

This new generation of Jewish immigrants poured into both the United States and Canada. When the newcomers sought to express their national consciousness in the Yiddish-speaking communities of the United States, they faced an assimilationist leadership that had become entrenched over some twenty years. In the small and not-yet-organized Jewish communities of Canada, however, they found a relatively untouched field for activity. Moreover, adherents of the Poalei Zion (Labour-Zionist Party) and Socialist-Territorialism — the very groups that placed the greatest emphasis on Jewish national identity and culture *as expressed in Yiddish* — assumed much importance in Canada.

Historians have not yet explained how these groups, numerically weak and relatively uninfluential in the United States until well into the First World War, managed to gain a foothold in the Canadian Jewish community during its pioneering days. Perhaps Canada's promise of land for agricultural settlement attracted a larger number of Territorialists to this country than to America. Or perhaps the percentage of these ideologies' adherents was not actually higher among the immigrants to Canada, but the social vacuum in this Jewish community simply encouraged them to form organized groups that could expand and influence others. Another or additional explanation may be the presence of two prestigious intellectual figures in Montreal's Labour-Zionist camp, Dr. Judah Kauffman (Even Shemuel), the scholar and educator, and Reuben Brainin, the renowned writer in Hebrew and Yiddish.

Yiddish Institutions: A Paradox

Whatever the causes, the cultural nationalist spirit of these movements attained a degree of popular acceptance during the critical years (1903 to 1915) of the crystallization of the Canadian Jewish community. The result was a Canadian Jewish culture noticeably more separate than that of the United States and a more pervasive use of Yiddish. The continuation of a separate culture and language was by no means restricted in Canada to the ideologically oriented work of educated leaders. In fact, for several decades it might have seemed that the masses of Eastern European Jews who lived on Montreal's St. Urbain Street, in Toronto's Spadina area, and in Winnipeg's North End were creating self-contained communities in which Yiddish would be maintained forever.

The very customs of the immigrants seemed to encourage the growth of Yiddish-speaking communities. After an immigrant family had settled down, it often brought over a fellow townsman or *landsman*, sometimes even taking him into its home until he could manage on his own. When the newcomer was more or less established, he frequently did the same thing. The result was a pocket of immigrants from the *shtetl* (town). These *landsleyt* often worked in the same trade, perhaps one that had been popular in their old town or one that the first-established immigrant had taught the new arrivals so they could find employment in his shop. Thus, industries such as the needle trades came to have concentrations of workers from the same *shtetl* or province, and Yiddish became the language at work as well as at home.

Many of the earliest community organizations were created — in Yiddish — in the same informal way. Immigrant men who had left their families behind in the old country wrestled with loneliness and tended to gather at the home of a *landsman* and his wife to socialize, exchange letters and news from home, and find relief within an intimate circle from their feelings of alienation and loss. These social gatherings often resulted in the formation of a *landsmanshaft*, a fraternal organization of Eastern European immigrants from the same town or city; it provided them with the base of a religious congregation, with mutual-aid, sick, and death benefits, with social and cultural activities, and with an organized channel for sending relief to the hometown.

The language of these vibrant organizations was (and still is, to the degree that they continue to function) Yiddish. The members most often used Yiddish in their activities, and they recorded their proceedings and wrote their constitutions in it (sometimes accompanied with an English translation). Thus, these true grass-roots organizations, which played a significant role in the lives of many immigrants, helped them to perpetuate tradition, to keep alive the memory of a *shtetl*, and to ensure continuity of language and culture. Yet, in some ways, the *landsmanshaftn* also carried the seeds of assimilation. They were often the first organizations to help immigrants become integrated into their new environment; in the process of doing so, they eventually began to defeat their previous aims of cultural preservation.

One can, however, still see traces of the *landsmanshaft* experience in Canada's major Jewish communities. The Lithuanian and Byelorussian Jews who pioneered the immigrant community in Montreal left their particular stamp on its Jewish institutions. In the same city, one congregation was formed by young Rumanian immigrants who had participated in the *fusgeyer* movement, a march all the way to the ports in 1899/1900 to publicize their flight from anti-Semitic persecution and economic misery. Toronto attracted a large concentration of Jews from Radom and Kielce, two provinces of old Russian Poland; the names of their towns — Apt (Opatw), Staszw, Lagw, Chmielnik, and others — are still associated with many Jewish organizations.

Like the *landsmanshaftn*, the Jewish labour movement both protected and undermined Yiddish language and culture in Canada. Since Yiddish was the language of the working class that was such a visible element of the new Jewish community, the movement used it extensively in its printed material and in its daily activities as it organized sweat-shop labourers in the needle trades and other industries that employed many Jewish workers. But although the labour unions used Yiddish, they simultaneously facilitated the integration of the immigrants and their children into the surrounding English-speaking society.

Thus, even as the number of Yiddish-speakers in Canada reached its height, the process of linguistic assimilation was at work. An excellent example of the strength of the assimilative forces came as early as 1929/30. For various reasons, the Jewish community of Montreal then had an opportunity to renegotiate its status *vis-à-vis* Quebec's educational system and to establish an autonomous Jewish school board. Both the well-to-do Jewish leaders and representatives of Jewish labour rejected the idea. The masses also showed little interest in educational autonomy, which seems to have been their only hope of maintaining the language. Canadian Jews were embracing social integration enthusiastically, and among the prices they were willing to pay was the sacrifice of Yiddish as the predominant vernacular.

The Core Institution: Yiddish Education

On the other hand, a minority segment of Canadian Jewry was very receptive to the protection of Yiddish through secular Jewish education. The movement to create a new kind of Jewish school in the new world was the work of Jewish radicals who were also cultural nationalists. Believing that modernized Jewish education was essential to the continuity of Jewish identity and national creativity, they created the secular Jewish school with Yiddish as a language of instruction. This institution became a hinge on which the issue of Jewishness turned in the Yiddish-speaking community. In 1910, Dr. Chaim Zhitlowsky, the Jewish socialist movement's theoretician of secular Diaspora nationalism, addressed an historic convention of the American and Canadian Poalei Zion in Montreal; the group then adopted a resolution urging the creation of Yiddish-language "national-radical" schools for the education of Jewish children.

Such institutions were soon established as afternoon schools in Montreal, Toronto, and Winnipeg, as well as in a number of cities throughout the United States. The Jews of Canada, however, pursued Zhitlowsky's goal with greater seriousness and devotion than did their brethren in the United States. In 1920, the I.L. Peretz School in Winnipeg became the first Yiddish day school in North America. In Montreal, the Folkshul followed in

1928 and the I.L. Peretz School in 1943. The left-wing Morris Vinchevsky School also became a day school for a short time during the early 1950s.[6]

Attempts to transform the Yiddish afternoon schools into day schools were never successful in the United States.[7] The three major Canadian schools, on the other hand, rooted in a broad segment of this country's Jewish community, were — and still are — both successful and influential. They have now educated three generations of Canadian Jews, attracted the support of intellectual and creative personalities, and contributed to activating and invigorating the Jewish national and cultural life of their respective communities. By helping to make Yiddish culture a part of the daily life of numbers of people, the schools have succeeded in building bridges of cultural understanding between the generations, bridges that are much weaker or nonexistent in Jewish communities in the United States.

Some commentators have suggested that in Montreal at least a contributing factor to the success of the Yiddish-Hebrew day schools has been Quebec's continuing organization of education on a denominational basis. Winnipeg's I.L. Peretz School, however, has flourished in a province where a unilingual public school system has prevailed since 1916. Shlomo Wiseman, principal of the Montreal Folkshul for fifty years and a theoretician of the Yiddish schools, has credited its success to the movement's pedagogical goals and idealism rather than to any advantage offered by the Quebec environment.[8]

The World of Yiddish Letters

The establishment and relative success of the Yiddish day schools distinguish the Canadian Jewish community from its counterpart in the United States. In the field of Yiddish literature, however, the experiences of the two communities are more similar.

Offshoots of Yiddish literature appeared in all the countries to which the Eastern European Jews immigrated. The last two decades of the nineteenth century saw the birth of the Canadian branch of Yiddish literature. By the two decades between the world wars, the United States, Poland, and the Soviet Union were the three main centres of Yiddish literature. Canada, however, also became a visible point on the map of world Yiddish literature at that time, and today it continues to be the home of several important Yiddish writers and scholars, as well as of a long-lived Yiddish-language newspaper and a Yiddish theatre group.

The Yiddish Press

The Yiddish press has played a very special role in North American Jewish life, not only as a disseminator and interpreter of news but also as the chief tribune of Yiddish literature. Given the great numbers of Eastern European Jews who immigrated to the United States' eastern seaboard, it is not surprising that the Yiddish press of New York developed quickly and on a large scale. Even today it attracts the attention and interest of many Canadian Jews. But a Canadian Yiddish press also sprang up to play a role that could not be filled by any other. Yiddish-language newspapers in Montreal, Toronto, and Winnipeg reported international news, both general and Jewish, discussed broad Jewish issues, and featured Yiddish literature; they also informed their readers of local events and activities and raised questions of specific Canadian concern, thus creating a sense of local and Canadian community.

As early as 1887, when the Jewish population of Canada numbered less than 6,000, the Yiddish lexicographer Alexander Harkavy foresaw the need for a Canadian Yiddish press separate from that of the United States. When he was working temporarily in Montreal as a Hebrew teacher at the Shaar HaShomayim Talmud Torah, he published one issue of a lithographed periodical, *Di tsayt* ("Time"), the first Yiddish newspaper in Canada. Twenty years later, in 1907, Hirsh Wolofsky founded *Der keneder adler* ("The Canadian [Jewish] Eagle", often called simply the *Adler*). It became important in Jewish communal life in Canada, particularly in Montreal, and is still popular.[9]

From 1912 to 1915, the Hebrew and Yiddish writer Rueben Brainin edited the *Adler*; he used its pages (and from 1915 to 1916 those of his own Yiddish daily, *Der veg*, ["The Way"] to challenge the moneyed, assimilationist leaders of the Canadian Jewish community and to promote the concept of a large-scale, democratically elected body that would be representative of the national interests of Canadian Jewry. This popular campaign was so important in the organization of the Canadian Jewish Congress that the history of Congress cannot be studied without a close reading of the *Adler* and *Der veg*.

The *Adler* also exerted much influence on the development of Canadian Yiddish letters, especially after the noted poet J.I. Segal became the editor of its weekly literary supplement in 1941. To a certain degree, too, the success of the *Adler* can be attributed to the ability of its editor of many years, Israel Rabinovitch, a journalist, essayist, and author of a number of Yiddish- and English-language books on Jewish music.

Following Montreal's example, the Yiddish press subsequently took root in Toronto and Winnipeg.

Yiddish Theatre

Another popular Yiddish-language institution in its day was the theatre, which Eastern European immigrants enjoyed in Canada as they did throughout the world's Yiddish-speaking communities. During the heyday of the Yiddish theatre, however, Canada's Jewish communities were apparently not large enough to support permanent companies. At one point there was hope that Toronto could, and the Strand Theatre on Spadina Avenue was built as a home for a resident company. The plan did not succeed, and theatre-goers in Canadian Jewish communities had to depend on touring groups, generally from the United States.

Interestingly, a recent development at the Saidye Bronfman Center in Montreal suggests Yiddish theatre is by no means dead in Canada and its appeal is not only one of nostalgia. Under the direction of Dora Wasserman, the Yiddish Drama Theatre, a group that began as an extracurricular activity of the Jewish People's and Peretz schools, has expanded to near-professional quality and status. Its performances of Yiddish works in the original have gained the interest and loyalty of a significant number of young

Canadian Jews as well as their elders; it plays to some seven thousand people annually.

Yiddish Belles-Lettres

Canadian Yiddish poetry and prose is too varied to cover adequately in the confines of this essay, but it is possible to touch on a few high points. In general, like all Yiddish writing outside Eastern Europe, Canadian Yiddish literature is marked by tension between a desire to strike deep roots in the new land and a wish to remain loyal to the traditions of the homeland with its intense Jewish life. The Holocaust made this problem more acute; many present-day Yiddish writers display a profound need to memorialize their communities, which were destroyed by the Nazis.

Canada's foremost Yiddish poet, J.I. Segal (1896–1954), was also an essayist, critic, and an editor known for encouraging other Canadian Yiddish writers both to develop their individual talents and to establish a literary community.[10] A prolific poet, he achieved recognition beyond Canada's borders and is considered a significant voice in modern Yiddish poetry.

Segal arrived in Montreal at age fifteen and spent his entire creative life there, except for a sojourn in New York from 1923 to 1928. Nevertheless, he clearly felt torn between two worlds, a tension he attempted to sublimate in his search for beauty and purity and in his romantic view of the holiness of the Jewish past. His poetry was devoted to the ordinary experiences of daily life, to plain people, to Yiddish as a symbol of the sacred suffering and simplicity of Jewish life, as well as to Chassidic motifs from his native Podolia and Volhynia.

The way in which Segal sought solace by rejecting or fighting his own "street" and turning to the redemptive quality of art is well illustrated by "In the Book of Beauty":

> I carved the sign of my name,
> one letter at least,
> in the book of beauty.
> I fought the street

with my flesh and bone
for every breath I took.
The mockery and the abuse,
the ugly hand
that fell on my shoulders
when I had to ransom my existence somehow
and answer to the day before the next day came.
I went down under my enemies' attacks
and the acts of fate
into depths
where songs were sunken ships
and the bones of unborn generations slept.
I spoke to the believing spirit
of redeemed life — I believed
and yesterday came up from the dead,
young again, as big as life again.
I went into it
as into my father's house.
I straightened my back.
My shame fell from me.
I was a wanderer
dry, dusty, in a strange place,
like a tree
burnt by lightning and struck by the pouring rain,
and a miracle happened.
From the dry, blackened bark,
leaves — green, luminous,
branch after branch grew soft
as the blessed willow trees
planted by the shores of the rivers.[11]

It is unfortunate that the corpus of Segal's poetry is inaccessible to the English-speaking reader for he expresses so well the tensions of being an emigrant artist and a Jew in a period of tumultuous transition. In one untranslated poem he describes looking out of his window and seeing a young Jewish boy going to high school. Although the boy was called Oscar, the poet knew he was really Osher, and although he was off to study Shelley, Byron, and Keats and to gather the treasures of a universal culture while casting away those of his own, Segal believed, in an almost mystic way, that the foreign cultural treasures the boy was discovering would eventually bring him back to those treasures of his own culture that had been neglected and ignored.

Sholem Shtern (born 1907, arrived in Montreal 1927), on the other hand, has become the most Canadian of the Yiddish poets, although he, too, was steeped in Jewish tradition. In a two-volume novel in verse, *In kanade* ("In Canada", 1960, 1963), he depicted a broad range of problems of acclimatization faced by the Eastern Europen Jews in Montreal. Central to this epic was the development of Yosl, an autobiographical figure, as a young Yiddish poet of social consciousness.

In another clearly autobiographical verse-novel, *The White House* (translated into English in 1974), Shtern spotlighted the struggles of Jewish immigrants during the late 1920s through characterizations of tubercular patients — an artist, a Hebrew scholar, a young communist, a Talmudist, shopworkers, and the chief protagonist, a young working-class Yiddish radical poet — in the Mount Sinai Sanitarium in Ste-Agathe-des-Monts, Quebec. Shtern's works also portray the life of French Canadian farmers and their relationships with the Jews. As in most of his work, his settings are familiar: the landscape of the Laurentian mountains north of Montreal and the city's immigrant streets and back lanes.

A towering figure in the Canadian and world Yiddish literary community was the poet and essayist Melech Ravitch (the pseudonym of Zekharye-Khone Bergner, 1893–1976). Ravitch was more than a writer and editor. He was a dynamic, central figure in Yiddish literature who attempted to unite all creative individuals and all geographic centres and outposts for the sake of encouraging Yiddish literature on a world scale.

Having gained prominence in interbellum Poland as a member of the expressionist poets' group *Khalyastre* ("the Gang"), as an activist in the Central Yiddish School Organization *Tsisho*, as secretary of the Jewish Writers and Artists Union, and as a founder of the Yiddish section of the International PEN Club,

Ravitch became a world traveller in the 1930s. He finally settled in Montreal in 1941. Here he became a vital organizer of Yiddish literary, cultural, and educational activities and was, for many years, director of Montreal's important Jewish Public Library. Four of his twenty-one volumes of verse were compiled in Montreal. In addition, Melech Ravitch's Montreal period also saw the publication of his translation of Kafka's *The Trial*, three personalized encyclopaedic volumes on figures of the Jewish national cultural renaissance, and three autobiographical works.

Ravitch's life and voluminous writings stand as an embodiment of the humanism of the I.L. Peretz tradition of secular Jewishness. The following poem is characteristic of the pantheistic philosophic musing prevalent in his poetry.

Let us learn from the animals in the forests
to move in the path of the blazing sun,
living in the very present
now knowing that this day is now.

Let us learn from the birds —
isn't everything flight and song?
Why not live with narrow heads,
bright, multicolored, and without a thought?

Let us learn from the trees and grass
to sink roots into mud, water, and around stone.
Let us give up thinking, be as absolute
as growing things. After all, what is there
to understand in the world?

Let us learn from the omnipotent Being
who shrivels things and lets them grow,
who builds and destroys,
who is eternal because He knows the secret of secrets,
most simple of all: there is no difference between
life and death,

as it follows, no difference between death and life,
none between revelation and secret.
All that was, will be — YHWH —
and nothing comes between the sons of Adam
and God.[12]

After the Second World War Jewish immigration to Canada
strengthened the ranks of its Yiddish literary community.
Foremost among the several talented, established writers who settled here was the poet and short-story writer Rachel Korn (1898–).
A native of Galicia, she established a reputation as a writer of
stature in Poland during the late 1920s and 1930s, producing lyrics
of rural tranquility but modernist form.

In her post-Holocaust poetry, Korn has revealed and ex-
plored memories of her vanished home with great sensitivity. An
example of this synthesis is her poem rendered in English as "To
My Mother, in place of the stone that would have marked her
grave":

Now you are gone and I live
all the days that were taken from you.
You flow into me so peacefully
as if I long ago became the shore to your dream.

I am more modest and discerning, mother.
I have all of autumn in me,
and in the leaf-fall of my days
I hear the sorrow destined to me.

I know that every journey to good fortune
ends with our return to childish tears,
our doorway in the ruins,
true to us when nothing else is.

And I know the heart's withholding;
how we wait for a glimpse a word a sound
and are left at the edge of our darkness
like an empty stalk in the summer sun.

And I know the word is only the spoor
left by errors that root themselves
in the untilled ground of our being, and the word is my
bridegroom,
mated to me, binding me to the least light of day.

I know a great deal now, as if through folds
of earth you laid your hands on my head,
but even now, all I know stands poor and shamefaced
before your innocence.

Only you were fated to guide the wisdom of the heart
whole to the threshold of the lips,
so that the word would be home and daily bread
for all who were turned away by love.

Only you
trusted tears
to lead you to the very start of pain
no longer able to hide from itself.

And only you, only you were given
the encircling gaze, like a roof, like a wall,
that took into itself everything abandoned and alone,
from a sick swallow to a shamed, outstretched hand.

I have turned back from all my journeys to good fortune
to the deepest, the ultimate source of sorrow
and to the great innocence of your love:
it is stronger than death and my own loneliness.

Moscow, Elul 1944[13]

To the landscape of the old home in Eastern Europe, Korn has added a new dimension, seeing herself in the present-day world of a "supplanted reality" that has "placed her like a partition between yesterday and today". In her latest poems, she has described passing over a boundary that not everyone can cross, and "in the concealed circle" she has entered, "only saints, fools and prophets of extinct worlds feel at home". The poet belongs to the latter; her "extinct worlds" are the key to her poems as they are to much of post-Holocaust Yiddish literature.[14]

Rachel Korn's expression "extinct worlds" has a double meaning. It refers to the hopes, dreams, and expectations that have disappeared during the course of an individual, normal life and also to the world of European Jewry destroyed in the Holocaust. The unspeakable tragedy cast its shadow on all the poet's experiences and feelings and gave her a special calling to give voice to all that was lost.

Korn's reflective mood, infused with the pain of unimaginable loss, has neither weakened nor dulled the thrust of her modernist imagery:

> I fear that first line of a poem,
> the sharp slash
> that decapitates dreams
> and opens veins
> to a flood of blood.
>
> Yet that line can bring me to the fields
> moving in the wind to white, rose, and yellow
> and the house under the tall pines
> where no one waits for me any more.
>
> It can take me to that hour
> when memory is a dark knot
> and on my hair I can still feel
> the caress of hands that are no longer there.[15]

Another postwar immigrant to Canada was M. Husid. Although his first book, published in Poland in 1937, was a collection of short stories, he has since turned to poetry. His post-Holocaust work has been the product of a mature poet who tends towards intellectualism; filled with the imagery and symbolism of traditional Judaism in its Eastern European forms, his poems are veiled by the all-pervading sadness of a Jew who feels he is "a brand snatched from the fire".

I have set out to follow the day
and bring up my wagon filled with wood
      bound for sacrificial fires.
God, I will not be chased away
by all your winds.

Does one also need crematoria
now that the blazing horizons
      surround us?
Congregations of Jews follow after me
and silent ash from chimneys.

I entrust myself to the demands
      of my voice.
Prepared as I am to be the messenger
how can I stop to cast off this burden
when the cry of generations
      drives me on.[16]

In addition to the writers discussed in this section, many others have produced Yiddish-language prose and poetry in Canada, and those treated here have written many more volumes than could be mentioned in such a brief summary.[17]

Criticism, Translation, and Scholarship

Full-fledged, serious critical study of Canadian Yiddish literature has yet to be launched. H.M. Caiserman-Vital's pioneer work *Yidishe dikhter in kanade* ("Jewish Poets in Canada"), published in 1934, treated both Yiddish and Anglo-Jewish poets. In 1974, an anthology of Canadian Yiddish writing, including many more authors than mentioned here, appeared in the Masterworks of Yiddish Literature series.[18] The paucity of English translations makes it difficult to discuss Yiddish literature with the Anglophone reader. The task of translation has, however, begun, and in 1976, Montreal's Harvest House published the first English anthology of Canadian Yiddish poetry and prose.[19] One can only hope that other translators, editors, and publishers will follow suit.

Interest in Yiddish culture is growing. In 1968 McGill University's Jewish Studies Program introduced courses in Yiddish as a language and in Yiddish literature in translation; it has now expanded into a full program of Yiddish studies, which can lead to an M.A. degree. The University of Toronto and the University of Manitoba now also offer Yiddish.

Academe's recent interest in Yiddish may have gained strength from the fact that a number of Canadian Jewish scholars have used Yiddish in their work. Yiddish writers, for example, pioneered the field of Canadian Jewish historiography. B.G. Sack, the dean of Canadian Jewish historians, began his research in the field during the first decade of this century; his *Geshikhte fun yidn in kanade* ("History of the Jews in Canada") was published in 1945, in Yiddish and English editions.[20] Much historical source material also exists in Yiddish; an interesting example is M. Ussishkin's *Oksn un motorn* ("Oxen and Motors", 1945), the story of the Jewish agricultural colony of Edenbridge, Saskatchewan.

Jewish scholarship and the translation of classical Jewish texts also hold an important position in Canadian Yiddish literature. The Yiddish philologist, folklorist, and ethnologist Y. Elzet (whose real name was Rabbi Y.L. Zlotnick-Avida) lived in Canada from 1920 to 1938 and published several of his studies in this country. S. Petrushka's edition of the six orders of the Mishnah, including the Hebrew original plus his Yiddish translation of the text and commentaries, was published in Montreal from 1945 to 1949. The Jewish educator S. Dunsky has been highly praised for his annotated translation, into the traditional Yiddish used in the yeshiva, of *midrash rabbah* to the five biblical scrolls.[21] N. Shemen has published works on Chassidim and the historic Polish-Jewish community of Lublin and a series on traditional Jewish attitudes towards labour, the woman, the stranger, and the proselyte. Yekhiel Shtern was awarded the coveted Lamed Prize for his detailed study of traditional Jewish religious education in a small-town community of Poland.[22]

Yiddish Today

The 1971 census reported about 50,000 Jews in Canada who claimed Yiddish as their mother tongue — the language they first learned and still understand — but only 26,330 who regularly used it at home. The latter group is less than 10 per cent of the Canadian Jewish population and a relatively elderly group (30 per cent were 65 years old or over). By way of contrast, during the 1931 census, some 149,000 Jews, out of a much smaller population of 156,000, claimed Yiddish as their mother tongue.

In other words, during the past four decades, linguistic assimilation has caused grievous losses in the use of Yiddish among Canadian Jews. However, a small core within Canadian Jewry has preserved Eastern European tradition to the point of retaining Yiddish as the language of daily life; the group, who are mostly Chassidim, have primarily religious motives.

Today the speakers and adherents of Yiddish are conducting a determined struggle to strengthen its position on a number of fronts. In May 1969, the Canadian Jewish Congress sponsored a national conference that called for "Jewish communal responsibility for Yiddish". This gathering sparked great interest and enthusiasm within the Canadian Jewish community and led to the establishment of a National Committee on Yiddish within the CJC. This committee, mandated to organize support for the maintenance of the language and its culture, has since aided in the publication of the weekly *Der keneder adler*, encouraged the teaching of Yiddish in the Jewish day schools at the elementary and secondary level, and promoted the establishment of courses in the universities and in adult education programs. The enrolment in these classes has been encouraging, as have the large, multigenerational audiences that have turned out for events such as Yiddish cultural festivals in all the major centres of Canadian Jewry and the Yiddish Drama Theatre in Montreal.

In brief, although Yiddish in Canada continues to suffer attrition, it is making some gains among younger Jews who are just beginning to discover its cultural riches and its significance for the continuity of Jewish national life. Whether the gains will eventually compensate the losses remains to be seen. The final balance has not yet been struck.

Jewish Culture and Canadian Culture

At the request of the editors of this volume, four academics met
in March 1979 to discuss the interaction of Canadian culture
and Jewish culture. The participants were: **Ruth Wisse**,
Department of Jewish Studies, McGill University; **Mervin
Butovsky**, Department of English, Concordia University; and
Howard Roiter, Department of English, Université de
Montréal. The moderator was **Morton Weinfeld**,
Department of Sociology, McGill University.

The wide range of the ensuing discussion reflected the
interconnections of the issues involved. An informal four-way
conversation emerged as the format best suited for such a
complex, hitherto neglected topic.

The following is a somewhat abbreviated version of the tape of
the actual conversation, edited only for easier reading.
For the benefit of the general reader, we have appended
footnotes identifying the cultural references and
the Canadian Jewish writers.

Defining Jewish Culture

Weinfeld: Perhaps we can start off by asking what we mean when we use the term "Jewish culture"?

Butovsky: The problem is trying to distinguish between a normative eternal Jewish content, something that defines the Jew in age-old universalistic terms, and the East European immigrant culture that emerged as a process of acculturation. Very often, in literary criticism at least, you hear that there is a kind of universal Jewish content that has to do with ethics, morality, justice, suffering, sympathy, and so on. On the other hand, there are depictions of people who came to a new land with a foreign language and foreign literature that they had to drop to take up new ones. I think these are two separate things, and when I treat a question like yours, I'm speaking of the latter: the way in which an East European people transplanted themselves to a new world and all the attendant tensions and transformations.

Wisse: I would make distinctions slightly different from yours. To my mind, there is a great difference between the culture of Judaism and the sociology of the Jews. The former refers to the Jewish religious civilization or idea of nationalism or historical tradition, to people who are still committed to furthering those traditions in works of art or of exposition. The second refers to what Jews happen to be doing; to me, this is an interesting sociological phenomenon, but it has little to do with the essence of Jewish culture.

Roiter: I'm afraid that when you start to try to define what Jewish culture is or how Jewish a writer is, you start getting onto very thin ice. That definition is extremely hard to boil down, and you end with a catch-all that could include just about every moral, universal, humanitarian concern. I prefer to speak of the creativity of Jewish Canadian writers.

Wisse: Each of us feels the tension between universalism and particularism. But I fear a definition of Jewish culture that includes everything that Jews create. If you want to look at it one way, everyone in the world is partly Jewish. It is difficult to talk about Polish culture, Russian culture, European culture, without talking about culture that has, in some way or other, been influenced by the Jews. There's no end to it — some scholars even suggest that the Renaissance was partly the result of Marrano experience.* If you are going to focus simply on *Jews*, then we might as well drop all attempts at drawing distinctions and talk about the entire world, of which our own problem is just a very minor part. My tendency is to draw the defining line as narrowly as possible, because Jewish existence for me is dependent upon its ability to see itself as a particular cultural experience.

Butovsky: Well, could we give an example for my own clarification? Mordecai Richler's *The Incomparable Atuk* is not particularly addressed to a Jewish subject matter. But *The Apprenticeship of Duddy Kravitz* obviously is.† Now one can make out a case that *The Incomparable Atuk* also reflects Jewish satire, Jewish self-hatred, or Jewish unease in our society, though that would be, I think, a rather tenuous argument. But no one can deny that in looking at immigrant culture on St. Urban Street, Richler was addressing himself to a Jewish content. That would be defined as Jewish writing.

Roiter: I think *The Incomparable Atuk* has certain elements of Jewish humour and a traditional Jewish way of looking at things that loom very large. In a sense, it's a very Jewish book.

Weinfeld: Remember Gore Vidal's claim that Jewish authors writing in English have taken the language and twisted it to accommodate the Jewish experience — that they have used it for specifically Jewish creativity.

---

*The Marranos were the Jews of late mediaeval Spain and Portugal who "converted" to Christianity on pain of death but continued to practise Judaism in secret.

†Mordecai Richler (1931–   ), one of the best-known Canadian Jewish novelists. *The Incomparable Atuk*, one of his satiric novels, has an Eskimo as one of its focal characters. *The Apprenticeship of Duddy Kravitz* is about the social education of a young Jewish boy in an immigrant neighbourhood of Montreal.

Wisse: Well, I would also say the contrary — that the American or English or even Protestant element is tremendously powerful in the writings of these Jewish authors. It depends whether you are struck by the signs of Jewishness or by the merely residual signs of what once was Judaism or Jewish life.

Butovsky: I'm inclined not to define Jewish culture by its Judiac content, but rather as an account of what happens to Jews, an account of how Jews live to the extent that they are still self-defined as Jews. Bernard Malamud's *The Natural* strikes me as a story within the American literary tradition. But when Malamud writes another kind of story that deals more specifically with a Jewish character or a man who is identified as a Jew, it becomes part of the body of Jewish-American literary writing.

Roiter: This is where the perception of the audience is important. In my Holocaust course, I have been teaching Jerzy Kosinzki's *The Painted Bird*.* Nowhere in the work does he let on that the boy is Jewish. Kosinski himself has distanced himself from Jewish events, although I understand he appeared recently in a Holocaust commemoration service. Now here's a work that my students perceived as Jewish, but I still don't know if Kosinski is Jewish.

Wisse: Yes, he is.

Butovsky: In attempting to define the nature of Jewish culture, I put my emphasis on the consciousness of the artist, while you seem to emphasize the audience.

Wisse: Not necessarily. I think the distinction we've been making is between Jewish culture that relates to some quality of Jewishness or interpretation of Judaism and works that may be written by a Jew.

---

*Jerzy Kozinski (1933–   ). Born in Poland, he has lived in the United States since 1957 and writes in English. *The Painted Bird* is a novel about a dark-haired child trying to survive among peasants during the Second World War.

The Immigrants and Canadian Culture

Weinfeld: What was Canadian culture when the Jews entered the country in numbers significant enough to create their own — if that's what happened?

Butovsky: Until the 1940s or 1950s, there was no Canadian culture in a narrow sense. Before that, what we're talking about is an Anglo-Saxon colonial culture that Jews contacted. The comparison between our experience and the American experience is relevant here. I think that what Jews faced in Canada was a much more formidable, coercive notion of Anglo-Saxon culture. It was something that they had to join, something they had to belong to. In consequence, we don't have a Jewish literary culture until after the Second World War. When we speak of A.M. Klein and Irving Layton as prominent writers, we are speaking of the 1950s and 1960s.* They had been writing before that, but they were obscure figures.

Wisse: Yes, but that wasn't because of pressure from the Anglo-Saxon culture.

Butovsky: Well, I think that when we speak of Canadian culture at the time of large-scale Jewish settlement, we are not speaking of a situation with free cultural interplay, one in which all kinds of contributions were valid. It was not what American experience seems to have been, a culture in which every ethnic group and every religious group could participate. Our Canadian culture was much more akin to Anglo-Saxon culture. Our public schools were much narrower in their definition of what it was to be a Canadian — it usually meant British style, British speech and mannerisms, and so on.

---

*Abraham Moses Klein (1909–72), Montreal Jewish poet and author. His *Collected Poems* was published in 1974. His only published novel, *The Second Scroll*, is a symbolic account of a young Canadian Jew's quest for his uncle, a messianic figure who survived the Second World War but can never be located. Irving Layton (1912–   ), a well-known Montreal Jewish poet. He is noted both for his lusty, robust style and his impatience with social and artistic decorum.

Roiter: The problem facing the country then was that English-Canadian culture was a second- or third-rate imitative culture. Think of F.R. Scott's *The Canadian Authors Meet*, where the anxious, genteel ladies sit around with their teacups. A culture that has been following in the footsteps of a much greater culture has an inferiority complex. It's much less open to innovation and creativity, it's much harder to break into because it's restricted. Can you imagine Irving Layton at the Canadian Poetry Society of the 1930s? It would have been catastrophic!

Wisse: We've changed topics here, but the situation you're describing was certainly not different from Ludwig Lewisohn's or Lionel Trilling's experiences. Take Trilling. Now that many of his papers have been reissued — essays that had been either lost or forgotten — we see that here was a man who was a self-conscious Jew, but at a certain point in the 1920s, he decided that the culture to which he aspired demanded the sacrifice of his Jewish identity. That culture was not an imitative culture but one he very much admired. It seemed so much higher to him that he felt it was well worth the sacrifice, and he made it very consciously.

Weinfeld: Is Trilling's experience applicable to Canada?

Wisse: That's what I'm asking.

Butovsky: I want to come back to the point at which the East European immigrants and their children met Canadian culture with the notion that they might enter it. To my mind, the conditions were clearly different from those in America — I think what confronted Klein and Layton was somewhat different. The question in my mind is are we, in fact, talking here only about cultural lag? In many cases, what makes our cultural manifestations possible are precedents in American culture. I think our writers, like our institutions in general, have benefited enormously from this fact. They have been given their shape and identity by the massive American Jewish community. Without the United States next door, Canadian Jewry would be much more akin to English Jewry, which, as you know, has a paucity of cultural institutions compared to the North American situation.

Weinfeld: So you are saying that Canadian Jewish culture is not unique?

Butovsky: Yes, its shape, content, themes, and evolution conform to some degree to the preceding pattern of American Jewish culture. I think even our comedians are not Jewish comedians until they fall in the tradition of American comedians.

Wisse: I think what you said about a time lag helps to define the way in which I do perceive a great difference between American Jewish culture and Canadian Jewish culture, both popular and high. The Jewish community in Canada is much younger than the Jewish community in America. The Canadian experience is basically an immigrant or a second-generation experience, which is fresher and rawer. That's one component of the difference. There is also the Canadian proximity to the United States, as you have mentioned. The odd thing is that these two facts combine. In other words, while Canada's is the younger community, still at the point of freshness and original experience, it has right beside it the fruits of a well-entrenched Jewish community that has already developed a third and fourth generation, is already at ease with the language and general culture, and has even begun to leave its own imprint on the general culture.

A third component of the difference is that the Canadian Jewish community is much more like a European community than it is like either the British community or the American community. Canadian Jews came into a country where ethnicity is recognized. It has ethnic groups such as there were in Eastern Europe; it has already existing differences between Poles and Ukrainians and all the subgroups with their different languages. It seems to me the Jewish immigrants didn't come into an Anglo-Saxon culture but a land of ethnic distinctions.

Butovsky: May I ask you to remember the Canadian cultural situation in the 1920s and 1930s, even up to the 1940s. I don't think we can talk about an ethnic situation then. When I was growing up in Ottawa, neither my elementary nor high school had a single Jewish teacher. My high school had three Jewish students out of two thousand. It was pretty clear that all of us foreigners and immigrants' children were being Canadianized by the Miss Macdonalds, Miss Eckharts, Miss Johnsons, and so on. I think that our notion of the now familiar ethnic landscape in Canada began after the Second World War. It was not there at the time Klein or Layton was starting to write.

Roiter: You're talking from a bit of a minority position, having grown up in Ottawa. Let's face it, much of the creativity of Canadian Jewry comes from Montreal and Winnipeg. And both these communities, until recent times — and you can even make a case for the present day — have had certain similarities to a European, ghettolike existence. I don't want to push the parallel too far but there are similarities.

Wisse: I think it's true.

Roiter: Montreal really is probably one of the last collective Jewish experiences surviving in North America. My children live eight blocks from their great-grandparents. Their little cousins in the U.S. expect to live eight hundred miles from their grand-parents and great-grandparents and for us it was unthinkable. For us, that's a North American pattern that's strange and was unthinkable until the PQ election victory. If I can digress for a moment, that's why the PQ victory was such a shock. The ghetto wall has been shattered, and it's very traumatic.

Weinfeld: I think we're talking about two different things here. One is the "official" culture of the land, and I think Professor Butovsky may be correct there. In the 1920s and 1930s and 1940s, what was acceptable in Canada was a predominantly Anglo-Saxon, nonmulticultural kind of culture. It coexisted with pockets of ethnic and minority culture, but the two never met. Perhaps only in the 1950s and 1960s was there an attempt to bridge the gap.

Butovsky: That's right. The majority's accommodation of minority cultural voices was a phenomenon of the 1950s and 1960s in Canada, but in the United States, I suggest it was a phenomenon of the 1920s and 1930s. Lewisohn was a breakthrough. Ben Hecht, Henry Roth, and Daniel Fuchs all brought their

Brooklyn ghetto experience to the pages of literature in the 1930s; they came to the realization that somehow their intrinsically Jewish experiences could be appropriate for literary rendition. That didn't happen in Canada until Richler in the 1950s.

Wisse: Until that time, there simply wasn't a Canadian Jewish culture in English. During the 1920s and 1930s there were so few products of the Canadian schools that the emergence of the English-language Jewish writer was not a possibility. Such writers as there were, first-generation immigrants, were writing in Yiddish. Even in the U.S., where mass immigration of East European Jews began in the 1880s, a significant literary expression in English did not emerge until forty years later. Once again, we are talking about a time-lag in Canada — the difference between the dates of our large immigrant influx and theirs.

Varieties of Canadian Jewish Culture

Weinfeld: Maybe we might now look at Canadian Jewish culture per se. Can we talk about styles of creativity that are typical of Canadian Jewish creativity? Are there themes in which Jewish artists in Canada happen to excel or to prefer? Is there a certain sector of creativity that has a Jewish stamp in Canada?

Wisse: Well, I think we have something more typical of the Canadian reality: a community that feels itself totally at home in the European context of ethnic authenticity, that is still living as an independent community with its own linguistic culture. We have people like Klein, Layton to a lesser extent, and certainly Adele Wiseman who grew up in homes where Jewishness still permeated every aspect of daily existence, from the kitchen to the library.*

Weinfeld: With what result?

Wisse: With the result that you have a book like Wiseman's *The Sacrifice* that is based on a Jewish mythical theme; the writer self-consciously chose to write about the immigrant experience in

---

*Adele Wiseman (1928–   ), a Canadian Jewish novelist. Her book *The Sacrifice* won the Governor-General's award for fiction.

terms of an archetypical biblical experience — Abraham's readiness to sacrifice his son, Isaac. And you have a book like Klein's *The Second Scroll*, which, like much of that author's work, plays with and delights in the juxtaposition of Judaism and modernism. Here you have writers who have exploited Jewish myths and Jewish forms as the basis of their work more comfortably than they could have in the United States.

Weinfeld: So it is the themes that you stress, rather than style. Professor Roiter, you mentioned Jewish humour when we were talking about Mordecai Richler. Do you see Jewish creativity at the level of theme or in stylistic terms?

Roiter: I wouldn't say stylistic, but I'm sure that if we were given ten works without the writers' names attached to them, we could probably identify those written by Jewish authors — give or take one or perhaps two. I'm going to contradict what I said earlier — there is a certain common concern, not stylistic but thematic, that could identify them as being Jewish.

Weinfeld: I'm in the middle of *Fifth Business* by Robertson Davies. What is interesting about this book is that while it's clear that no authentic English-language Jewish writer could have written it, that in content as well as in style it is a traditional Anglo-Saxon book, I find some of his descriptions of small town life and eccentric characters recall images of Isaac Bashevis Singer.

Wisse: You see this is why I feel so much more comfortable talking about Jewishness at the level of self-consciousness. If I were compiling a list of Canadian Jewish books, it would be very short, but I would tend to take great pride in such works as *The Second Scroll*, *The Sacrifice*, certain poems of Irving Layton, and the poems of Seymour Mayne and some of the younger writers.* They seem to me to be trying to forge a Canadian Jewish tradition, and it seems that the possibility of their doing so comes out of the constraints of the historical situation in which they find themselves.

---

*Seymour Mayne (1944–   ), Canadian Jewish poet who teaches Canadian poetry at the University of Ottawa.

Weinfeld: What are the components or ingredients that are making up this Canadian Jewish tradition?

Butovsky: That's an interesting question. Could we spend a moment contrasting the kind of Jewish writer represented by A.M. Klein and the kind represented by Mordecai Richler or Irving Layton? Klein incorporates Judaism in its formidable sense — the Talmud, Hebrew, Yiddish — to literature. To the extent he treats the actualities of immigrant life, he focusses them through the forms of the two-thousand-year period that stands behind them.

I would gather though that the generation that followed Klein — Wiseman, Richler, Layton, and so on — have a lesser foundation of Judaism. Their background is much closer to that of the present-day Jew. It is precisely *Yiddishkeit* rather than Judaism. They may have gone to *cheder* and they may not; they may have spoken Yiddish in the home, and they may not; they do not know the Talmud; they never studied in a *yeshiva*; they don't know Hebrew fluently, and so on.* In other words, they're the product of an immigrant culture and the stresses, strains, and dilutions that such a culture inevitably undergoes when it meets another culture.

To my mind at least, there is a very simple distinction between a Jewish work of art by A.M. Klein and say a Jewish novel — notice I'm still calling a Jewish novel — by Richler. In Richler, I do not see the Judaistic qualities, the age-old traditional values, and so on. What I do see is the immediacy of immigrant contact with the new world. I include them both as obviously Jewish, but I think they are of a different order.

Wisse: I would make a further distinction between the works of Layton and Wiseman on the one hand and the works of Richler on the other. It seems to me that Wiseman — certainly in her earlier works — and Layton in a certain part of his work define

---

Yiddishkeit is the Yiddish term for "Jewishness"; it refers to the cultural lifestyle, religious or secular. *Cheder* is the traditional East European Jewish school for young children. A *yeshiva* is an academy or institution of higher Jewish learning; the Talmud forms the basis of the curriculum.

themselves not only as Jews for their time but as Jewish artists. Both want to use, to the greatest degree possible, those elements within their Jewish background that have somehow filtered through to them, as attenuated as they may be. Whereas in the case of writers like Richler, the Jews are socially recognizable, but they could as easily be Ukrainians or Poles.

Roiter: Very well, Klein has this "formidable Judaism", as Professor Butovsky phrased it, and Wiseman and Layton have it to an attenuated degree. But I feel that you are somewhat too severe with Richler in your reference to his lack of "Jewish depth". He may only have an environmental Judaism, a Judaism of setting (and even that is open to question — there is a certain Messianic drive behind his vision), but we have to cherish his distance from the kind of Orthodoxy that nurtured Klein and the others. That Orthodoxy was not an environment that encouraged literary creativity or any aesthetic activity outside the religious domain. You know, we don't expect literary creativity as we know it from the Bobover, the Belzer, or even the Lubavitcher Chassidim.* Klein was torn apart, in a sense destroyed, by the tension between his inherited baggage and the world he was a part of.

You know, my father is only sixty-four, but as a student, he had the bottom of one ear lobe torn off when he was found reading a philosophy text. You didn't read a Greek philosophy text in that environment, and it was not conducive to aesthetic creativity. In a sense, all of our writers since Klein have been some distance from "real" Judaism. We could debate the extent of that distance for days, but we shouldn't be too eager to denigrate it. Our secular creativity springs from it.

Butovsky: I just wanted to distinguish between two kinds of Jewish works. The point I'm making is that there will be precious few Kleins in the future.

Weinfeld: Does that mean that there are precious few encounters with authentic Judaism, and, therefore, that we are left with

---

*The Bobover, Belzer, and Lubavitcher Chassidim are ultraorthodox Jewish religious groups in Canada.

a Jewish creativity that has no Jewish content? Can't we redeem the succeeding generations in any way?

Wisse: We see here that we're faced with a problem that's not unique to Canada. Whatever Jewish culture we have grows out of the way in which Jews live, the way in which they define themselves as Jews. And though it means accepting the extreme case of an ear lobe being torn off, you cannot have a Judaism that perpetuates itself historically without individuals being willing to sacrifice aspects of their own individual quests, whether they're artistic or some other form of self-realization, to the idea of collective survival. Collective survival and collective values require that the individual Jew return some feeling of responsibility to a community and to the imperatives of Judaism. Otherwise, you cease to have a Jewish culture altogether, and, of course, you cease to have the nurturing atmosphere for the texts and for the creators of texts.

Butovsky: How would that apply to the Canadian situation? Or to any situation in which Jews are trying to create works of art out of the immediacy of their experience as Jewish Westerners? How do they promote that kind of uneasy tension between wanting to be Jews, however they wish to define that, and yet participating fully in Western secular, political, social, and economic life?

Wisse: If that full participation were all, they would have nothing particularly Jewish to draw from.

Butovsky: Perhaps we foresee that as Judaism as content is diminished in Canada, it will be replaced by historical experience within the worldwide Jewish experience. It won't necessarily be centred in Canada.

The Shaping of Modern Jewish Society

Weinfeld: If literature grows out of a social context, perhaps we should examine the present-day pressures that are shaping Jewish society in North America. Is Judaism being diminished?

Wisse: Well, I don't think that Judaism is being diminished ultimately. Jews are being assimilated in large numbers, but my image of the situation is the classical parable of the twelve original tribes of Israel, of which ten are always being lost, yet two always survive.

Weinfeld: Is it always one or the other? Is there no in-between, no dialectical synthesis, no new mode or form?

Wisse: I may have used an extreme example. There are shades in between. But there is a point at which you know what the choices are, and then your alternatives become clear. You have the choice of where to buy or rent your house, of how to bring up your child, of whether to give him or her a Jewish education and Jewish consciousness or not. You may not realize at every point that you're making these critical decisions, but it becomes very clear to you when your child tells you whom he or she is marrying and how he or she intends to live. You realize that whether you've made these choices consciously all the way along or not, you have contributed to the ten or the two.

Roiter: What we're basically talking about here is the loss or decline of faith. I feel that Professor Wisse is talking out of a particular awareness that is very, very valid, and I subscribe to it. You have seen what has happened to the world of secular Yiddish culture. You go to a Farband meeting nowadays,* and there are twelve people there. Twenty years ago there would have been two hundred people in the room.

Butovsky: The decline of Yiddish secularism is a fact. But in contrast, you can probably go to a synagogue now and find two hundred young people. In my generation they would never have been seen dead in a synagogue. Maybe we're talking about a new cultural expression or religiosity — however you define it, good or bad — as a replacement for what we used to speak of as the *folk shul* education.† Secular Jewish education may have come to a sad

---

*The Farband is a Yiddish Labour-Zionist cultural group.

†A *folk shul* is a school of the secular Yiddish tradition.

end, but in fact you find other outcroppings. Kids in university are wearing *yarmulkas*.* My generation never dreamed of wearing *yarmulkas* to university. There are other forms of self-assertion taking place, too — things are not necessarily all going in one direction.

Weinfeld: I agree. I tend to be optimistic. What are some of the forces that have developed in our time to counteract the inevitable flow of assimilation? Two come to mind: the impact of the Holocaust and of the existence of the state of Israel. It is interesting that thirty-four years after the end of the Second World War, we finally get the Holocaust series on NBC television, viewed by 125 million Americans and Canadians. This is not simply an incidental episode; in my view, it means a bit more than trying to make a buck for NBC.

Wisse: It may mean more than making a buck, but it is not at all meaningful. The Jewishness of the Jew isn't nurtured by occasional TV productions or by symbolic dress, but by daily decisions, constant reinforcement. In this country where everything is possible, including acceptance by the majority, it becomes psychologically difficult for Jews, who have longed for the precious gift of freedom more than any other people, to decide their children should put on *yarmulkas* and distinguish themselves visibly from all the other children in the group. I think this is asking something of frightened people, of people who historically have every right to be frightened. I don't like Emil Fackenheim's idea that every Jewish parent is an Abraham bringing his Isaac to the sacrificial altar.† That is his image: in the aftermath of the Holocaust, every Jewish parent who decides to raise his child visibly and politically as a Jew is an Abraham ready to offer his child as a sacrifice. I find this image overblown — especially in democratic North America — but parents who raise their children as Jews do

---

*A *yarmulka* is a skullcap worn at all times by a religiously observant Jewish male.

†Emil Fackenheim (1916–   ), a professor of philosophy at the University of Toronto and an ordained rabbi. He has written about the theological problems facing the Jew after the destruction of European Jewry in the Second World War.

give up some sense of ease. You do have to struggle here against the tide of wonderful democratic universality, of undifferentiated Canadianism or Americanism.

Weinfeld: But what I'm trying to suggest is that there may be countertrends. For example, what is the effect of Jewishness and Jews on Canadian cultural development? Isn't it possible to argue that we are in some sense seeing a Judaization of mainstream American popular culture? Take the overwhelming influence of Jews — at least New York liberal Jews — on American television. This is a new phenomenon; farmers in Idaho are watching life as viewed by New York Jewish liberals — some with greater, some with lesser degrees of Jewish backgrounds. What I'm raising as a possibility is this: if we are heading into the ghettoless society, won't there be some give and take? Are we acting on the Canadian environment, and if so how?

Butovsky: More specifically, what does the literature of Klein, Wiseman and Richler do to Canadian culture — or does it do anything?

Wisse: Well, if Canadian culture is at all different from what it was fifty years ago, if it has become a little bit more pluralistic, more cosmopolitan, some of that at least is due to the influence of Jewish writers. But on the whole, although individual Jewish writers have left their mark, they seem to have made little appreciable impact on current trends in Canadian fiction and culture. For example, Margaret Atwood's theory of Canadian literature as a mythology of survival leaves out the Jew entirely. Although she does bring in some examples from Irving Layton and Adele Wiseman, she reflects nothing of the true Jewish experience. Do you know what the term "Canada" signified in Auschwitz? "Canada" was the detail that collected the possessions of incoming prisoners; it was a synonym for "plenty". From a Jewish point of view, how can one interpret Canada as a deprived and barren country, when it is the land of all possibilities? Indeed, Jews *have* seen Canada as the land of plenty, yet clearly their image of it does not seem to have become dominant.

Roiter: Well, there is a contribution of Jewish letters to Canadian literature. Part and parcel of the Atwood argument is bleak survival in a very bleak country. And you have the neo-Atwoodians stressing this bleak aspect. But Layton's poetry doesn't describe a bleak world; it's full of vibrancy and vitality. And whatever one's position on Richler, Duddy Kravitz doesn't live in a bleak world; it too is full of vitality. So there is a contribution of Jewish writers.

Butovsky: But in all fairness, I think that one has to contrast the content of Canadian literature to these theories. A great many non-Jewish writers — Margaret Laurence, Rudy Wiebe, Robert Kroetsch — present a very vibrant, rich world. It's the theoreticians who derive these generalizations from reality.

Weinfeld: But what about the inferiority complex? Even apart from the bleakness, is there nothing to the idea that Canadians must go south to seek recognition? Don't Canadian Jews also look to New York for recognition, for their sense of self-worth?

Wisse: In this respect, the Canadian Jewish artist may enjoy unique possibilities. Potentially, they have the best of two worlds. Just south of the border, they have a marketplace that is seemingly infinite. And here there's a Canadian Jewish community — in the sense of living several blocks away from your great-grandmother — still charged with the kind of cultural specificity that nurtures great literature. Just look at the first sections of Saul Bellow's *Herzog*, which grow out of Napoleon Street, a Jewish neighbourhood of a kind that still exists here but has been declining in the United States since the Second World War.* Unfortunately, Canadian Jewish artists, by and large, do not appear to have taken full advantage of potential Jewish and non-Jewish readership in America.

Weinfeld: So you see the United States as an asset.

Wisse: Potentially, to be exploited.

---

*Saul Bellow (1915–   ). The well-known novelist and short-story writer, who won a nobel prize for literature, was born and raised in the Montreal area.

Weinfeld: To use the term of Canadian nationalists, Canadian Jewry is dependent on America for its Jewish training, for its rabbis, and so on. Is this a healthy situation?

Roiter: It's extremely unhealthy. Take the example of the 1976 election of the Parti Québécois in Quebec. Most of the province's rabbis (perhaps all, I'm not sure) were American, and they were quite unable to cope with the realities of the situation. I personally heard the rabbi of one of the largest Montreal congregations say, "What kind of culture do the Québécois have? Have they written any books, have they painted any pictures, have they written any music?" Such ignorance! I wanted to muzzle the fellow — you know, put tape across his mouth. And during the past year, two rabbis have, in private conversations, admitted that they were unable to cope with the particular problem facing Quebec Jewry, and they have gone back to the United States. The lack of our own people has definitely hurt us.

Butovsky: The question is could it be otherwise? The historical examples of Diasporas come from times in which rapid communications were not available. When we speak of the electronic age, we're talking of a kind of single community, no matter how differentiated by historical beginnings. To a large extent, there is a common community in North America, and it is probably best represented by our intellectual stimuli. Over the decades, Canadian Jews have been stimulated and nurtured by, say, magazines such as *Commentary*, *Midstream*, and *Partisan Review*. We do not have Canadian counterparts, and frankly, I don't think we ever will.

Wisse: When we need one, then we will have one.

Butovsky: Yes, but need is decided in terms of the definition of the community. If we define ourselves as a North American community, the need is probably not evident. If we define ourselves as a Canadian community somehow distinct from our southern counterpart, then our need is great. But whether the response is forthcoming is another question.

The Canadian Jew in French and English

Weinfeld: Could we shift the conversation to something I thought of when Professor Roiter described a rabbi's ignorance of the substance of French Canadian culture. What has been the image of the Jew in that culture? In other words, had the rabbi been familiar with it, what would he have found in French culture — or in English-language Canadian culture?

Roiter: French Canadian literature has shown little knowledge of real Jews. Most of its Jews are not real Jews at all but symbols of an oppressed people trying to find their way, swamped by a very large, almost alien population around them. At one point you have positive references to Israel and Judaism, but that's faded somewhat.

Butovsky: Do they use those images as a sort of typology for the future of French Canada or even for the necessity of self-assertion for the Québécois?

Roiter: They don't push it that far. They use the Jew as an exotic as well. In Claude Jasmin's novel *Ethel et le Terroriste*, Ethel is the exotic, the foreigner. The only Québécois book dealing with Jews that really touched me was Yves Thériault's *Aaron*. Thériault made an effort to study Jews, to find out about our ways of life. Of course, at times, he slipped; for instance, he said that there's a star of David hanging over every bed. But none the less, in terms of the treatment of generational conflict, *Aaron* has never been equalled.

So there's no real knowledge of the Jew in Québécois literature, which probably reflects the reality, where there is no real contact with the actual Jew. When I was teaching in a college in the Quebec countryside, a student of mine advertised a motorcycle in the campus newspaper and wrote: "Sois un bon juif, fais-moi une offre", meaning that he was ready to bargain. I said to him, "Pourquoi avez-vous utilisé l'expression 'un bon juif'?" He said, "Tout le monde l'utilise, ce n'est pas quelque chose d'extraordinaire". I asked him, "Avez-vous jamais recontré un juif?" He said: "Non."* It's lack of contact.

Wisse: But there's been a great deal of contact.

Butovsky: But in literature, it's sparse.

Weinfeld: Is it as sparse in English-language Canadian writing as well?

Butovsky: I think so. I don't see the counterparts to Hemingway's Robert Cohn or Fitzgerald's Wolfsheim. I don't think that such major figures loom.

Weinfeld: Why not?

Butovsky: I think it's probably because of the sparseness of contact, the relative smallness of the population. In the States, Thomas Wolfe came to New York in the 1930s to take up a lectureship at New York University, and immediately his impression was of Jewish kids in the class. He expresses his paranoic fear of brilliant, hard-pressed Jews pushing him against a blackboard. A fearful image! Well, in Canada until the 1940s, there were, I think, some eleven Jewish faculty members in higher education.

Weinfeld: During the past twenty years we have developed in Montreal a Francophone Jewish community. Is there any sign of a developing tradition of French-language Jewish cultural creativity in poetry, prose, or what have you? Would there possibly be any tensions between Jewish culture in the English and French languages?

Roiter: There is no evidence of a Francophone Jewish literary community. You have a few switch-hitters, such as Naim Kattan, who straddle both linguistic communities.† But we'll have to watch the next few years. Remember, when you talk about Fran-

---

*The advertisement read, "Be a good Jew, make me an offer." The following conversation ran, "Why did you use the expression 'a good Jew'?" "Everybody uses it; it's not unusual." "Have you ever met a Jew?" "No."

†Naim Kattan (1928–   ), a novelist, writer of memoirs, and editor who was born in Baghdad and arrived in Canada in 1954.

cophone Jews in Canada, you're talking about immigrants from North Africa, mostly Morocco. Right now they've been here about twenty years, and they're feeling a certain sense of confidence. They're building their own congregation, they've brought in their own chief rabbi, they're opening their own restaurants, and so on. Don't forget their old cultural milieu was, in certain respects, primitive in Western terms; life in Casablanca and Fez wasn't avant-garde. I know that sounds very condescending, but that's the way it was. But we can expect, now that this community feels a certain sense of confidence, that it will spawn creative people.

Butovsky: We're looking at a people who will probably follow the immigrant pattern of the Eastern European Jews. That is, for the first generation, even the first two generations, there will not be literary expression, but rather growing familiarity with the language and the secularization of its subjects. Remember we're speaking of a primarily religious community, and literary expression requires the secularization of the culture. It may well take another generation before we see young people with the leisure and freedom to write, rather than working to become accountants and doctors and restaurant owners, which I assume they are becoming now.

Roiter: But one variable among the North African Jews doesn't match an analogy with Eastern European Jewry. From the moment of their arrival, their intermarriage rate has been extremely high. It's estimated at 50 per cent, and that's a modest estimate.

Weinfeld: The tendency is for the out-marriages to be primarily between Jewish males and French Canadian females, but it's accompanied by an extremely high conversion rate to Judaism.

Wisse: Also, unlike the European Jews, they come with French, the host language. That may both facilitate intermarriage and make them comfortable with the culture immediately, perhaps hastening both the secularization and the development of creativity.

Roiter: In Morocco, to be Jewish meant you weren't quite as golden as the French, but you were above the Arabs. The Cremieux decree made the Jews a buffer, so in a small town in the Atlas mountains, say, the policeman was liable to be Jewish, as was the minor bureaucrat. Now they come here, and they find that in Quebec to be Jewish is a little problematic, rather than being a badge of superiority as it was back home over the Arabs. They've been trying to come to grips with that.

Jewish Culture — Past, Present, Future

Weinfeld: Moving from the idea of Jewish culture as art to Jewish culture as the way Jews live, what does the future hold?

Roiter: Ten years, fifteen years from now, I think we'll see the Jew reflected in English Canadian and French Canadian literature in a much more positive way. To take an example from social patterns, for the high holidays this year, Marianopolis College, with less than a third of its students Jewish, cancelled classes for Yom Kippur. Fifteen years ago you didn't find this kind of awareness in the McGill Faculty of Arts and Science, although its students may have been two-thirds Jewish. Nobody would have dared suggest such a thing! There is an awareness now that didn't exist before. Modern communications have helped.

Wisse: Well, let's take the example of Marianopolis College closing for a Jewish holiday. It is true that twenty years ago, when McGill had a large percentage of Jewish students, it did not cancel its classes on Rosh Hashanah and Yom Kippur; however, I dare say most of those students missed classes on the holy days, and moreover, they went with their parents to the synagogue. This year when Marianopolis let out its students on Rosh Hashanah and Yom Kippur, many, if not most, of those kids *didn't* go to synagogue. So what have we learned? The cultural acceptance is there and the possibilities of enjoying one's self-identity are greater, but the content has evaporated, as has the will to remain affiliated.

Weinfeld: You're talking about what is essentially a religious dimension. These kids are not going to synagogue, and your implication is that there is a loss.

Wisse: I only used the example of going to synagogue because what else do you do on Rosh Hashanah? But the same principle applies to nonreligious forms of Jewish identification.

Weinfeld: I know that 20 per cent of the adult Jews in Montreal *never* go to synagogue at all, except for a bar-mitzvah or a wedding. In addition, in a survey I did recently, another 30 per cent said that they go *only* on the high holidays. So that's 50 per cent that are just not *shul*-goers. The point is, what are we looking for in terms of the content of the Jewish life? Wearing a *yarmulka* implies a certain sense in which Orthodoxy is the authentic Judaism.

Wisse: You can take other indices as well, but the results will be similar.

Weinfeld: Well let me suggest one index: the large *chai* chains that people wear on their chest as a sign of Jewish identification.*

Wisse: But non-Jews wear them. They have little specific Jewish meaning today.

Butovsky: That is the problem with popular culture. The difference between reading a Sholom Aleichem story and seeing *Fiddler on the Roof* is vast. In one case, there's a kind of exchange between the history the text embodies and the reader; in the other, you might as well be seeing *The Wizard of Oz* or *Porgy and Bess*.

Weinfeld: Let me try just one last example. If a Jewish family went to the Yiddish burlesque or theatre in New York sixty or seventy years ago and had a good evening laughing, you might agree this was somehow an authentic experience of Jewish culture. However, the same family today may sit in front of the TV

---

*The word *chai*, formed by two letters of the Hebrew alphabet with the numerical equivalent of eighteen, signifies life. The number eighteen and the *chai* symbol are considered charms for good health and longevity.

and watch David Steinberg or any one of a number of Jewish comedians on "The Johnny Carson Show". Or they may see a movie in which Gene Wilder plays a Polish rabbi who comes to the Wild West. What is the difference, other than language, in those two episodes?

Wisse: Well, where is the thing going? Gene Wilder is playing off an old tradition; there are still enough signs of it around so he can use it for a couple of jokes that are now innocent and acceptable enough to become part of mass culture. But that earlier family was so steeped in traditional Jewish forms of life that the Yiddish theatre was just one tiny aspect of their new cultural situation. It didn't constitute Jewish culture. If you had asked this family how it expressed itself Jewishly, it wouldn't have said we go to the *Jewish* theatre. That action was incidental, in the line of enjoyment! Do you see what I'm saying?

Butovsky: *Cheder* or *shul* and all the rest would have been one of many aspects.

Roiter: I remember seeing a Broadway play with Menasha Skulnik.* He plays a businessman who's an atheist, a prominent free-thinker. His daughter came home with a young suitor who's not Jewish, and she said, "Dad, you'll be happy — he's an atheist like you!" and Skulnik said, "Yes, but he's not a Jewish atheist."

Wisse: Here, when I convinced my children — with difficulty — to see that French film *Rabbi Jacob,* I wanted to reinforce their Jewishness. For us, going to a Jewish movie is the Jewish deed for the day, the week, or the month. But that family that went to see the Yiddish theatre would never have defined what they were doing as something Jewish. It was something secular; it was their entertainment for the day, the week, or the month.

Weinfeld: But you know, following your Menasha Skulnik story, a few years ago, there was a film, *Pete 'n Tilly,* starring Carol Burnett and Walter Matthau. Matthau came in to a party, and the hostess introduced him to a priest. Matthau said, "Listen,

---

*Menashe Skulnick (1892–1970), a prominent Jewish comedian and Yiddish actor in the United States.

if I'd known the father was here, I would have brought my rabbi."
At which point Carol Burnett said to him, "Now just a minute,
Pete, everybody knows that you're three-quarters Lutheran and
only one-quarter Jewish. Why do you insist on calling yourself a
Jew?" And he answered, "Because I'm a social climber." Now you
wouldn't have had that kind of story thirty years ago. Many students today who look at Laura Z. Hobson's *Gentleman's Agreement* think that situation was something from the Middle Ages.

Wisse: While some may be secure in the external world, they
are less secure in their Jewishness and less comfortable in their
own communities. If we again consider some of the authors we
have mentioned, and add Leonard Cohen, Eli Mandel, Miriam
Waddington, Henry Kreisel, and so on,* we see their isolation
from Jewish life, and of Jewish life from them. The same is true
for other Canadian writers. We don't have a Canadian culture
that has grown richer over the years because there's no nurturing
society for these people on an individual basis, either within the
Jewish community or within the general community.

Butovsky: Again, looking ahead, I would expect further dimi-
nution as time goes by.

Wisse: Unless there's a different kind of community among
young Canadian Jews. It's possible that in Montreal and Toronto
in the future, there will be more of a cohesive intellectual community.

Weinfeld: What do you need a community for? To sustain the
author?

Wisse: Yes. It seems to me that unless you are talking about individual talent pure and simple, which does emerge here and
there, most great writers have come out of sometimes small but
dynamic clusters of activity.

---

*Leonard Cohen (1934–   ), a Montreal-born poet, novelist, folk singer, and
balladeer. Eli Mandel (1922–   ), a Canadian poet and critic. Miriam Waddington (1917–   ), another Canadian poet and professor of literature at
Toronto's York University. Henry Kreisel (1922–   ), a Canadian novelist
and professor of literature at the University of Alberta.

Roiter: That's a very interesting point. I've started to write a bit, myself, and I find I write about the late forties and early fifties — the Montreal that I knew. I'm unable to write about anything since then. It hasn't been a deliberate choice, it's just emerged that way. When I look at the stuff in my drawer, it's all based on that period. What was it? Did we have a community then? Did I feel a sense of cohesiveness? This is what Henry Roth said in a *New York Times* interview. "Why did you fall silent," he was asked, and he answered, "I lost the cohesiveness, the sense of community; we moved from the Lower East Side of New York to Harlem, and my world fell apart."

Butovsky: But I wonder if that doesn't coincide with our own psychological longing for a golden age.

Weinfeld: Will there be no Jewish writing without an authentically Jewish community to sustain Jewish writers?

Butovsky: I don't think I subscribe to Professor Wisse's view. I think the individual talent is everything, and my sense is it will express itself no matter what. Its content may be affected by the richness of the culture out of which it comes, but I don't think that its expressive powers are going to depend on whether there is a living culture. Anyway, I gather there's always a living culture when people are still around talking and so on. When you raise the question of authentic Judaism, we're back to square one. I'm suggesting that there will be Jewish writing so long as people defined as Jews choose to write about that area of their experience. Whether it's authentic in your terms or authentic in my terms is always going to be an open question.

Wisse: If the Jewish element is altogether casual, if it is not rooted in the dynamic power of a religious or cultural ideal, it will not yield very much. But beyond that, it seems to me that the environment is critical. I see writing very much as a sport, and if you don't have as great emphasis on hockey as you have in Canada or the Soviet Union, you don't get great hockey players. Writing is a very competitive business. I'm sure as good a writer as Saul Bellow could not have emerged from Montreal had he not gone on to major centres of cultural ferment, where he benefited from contact with Chicago and New York intellectuals.

Intellectual Life and Ideology

Weinfeld: What issues have we omitted?

Butovsky: The absence in Canadian Jewish culture of a significant body of critical commentary. Remember that what accompanied American Jewish creative expression was a body of criticism that in many ways was equal, if not superior, to the novels and poetry — critical writings of people such as Trilling, Fiedler, Howe, Isaac Rosenfeld, Harold Bloom, even Saul Bellow and more recently Philip Roth. And in many ways these have helped shape the body of literature they accompanied and provided a critical vocabulary, a kind of critical sense of how to evaluate this writing and place it within Jewish culture as a whole. In Canada, this is singularly absent. I can only think of a handful of essays — Eli Mandel recently has been writing some — but we don't have a body of critical literature.

Wisse: Unfortunately, we don't have a Jewish intellectual life in this country. And I feel the absence of that far more sharply than the absence of a Jewish seminary to train local rabbis.

Weinfeld: What do you mean by a Jewish intellectual life?

Wisse: Well, I would say that my parents' generation had a very active Jewish intellectual life in Yiddish; it still has. There were people whose regular form of entertainment, or self-expression, of pleasure was attending lectures and participating in discussion groups that argued about ideologies, the interpretation of contemporary culture, historical problems. They took pleasure in the life of ideas, in the life of the mind. In our generation, this simply does not exist. I would say you cannot be a functioning Jewish intellectual in our environment.

Weinfeld: Why not? What's missing — is it the community? Is it a way to make a living?

Butovsky: I wonder if perhaps our generation is the "end of ideology" generation. What often mobilized those Yiddish intel-

lectuals was the need to define Zionism as opposed to communism, communism as opposed to socialism, religious life as
opposed to secularism, and so on. All those ism's have very little
currency today. To the extent that there are intellectuals now,
they're intellectuals usually by being academics; in effect, they're
professionals. We're no longer dealing with a community, as you
say, whose form of entertainment and cultural expression is the
lecture. I think Howe speaks of the "Yiddish sickness", but it was
pleasure as well. And I think that to some extent this change is a
part of the secularization of culture, the absence of culture, the
absence of commitment to a cause that drew people out to hear
and listen and argue about and exchange ideas. We don't have
causes.

A Reexamination of Zionism in Canada

by Harold M. Waller

Discussing the present state of Zionism in Canada necessitates a clear distinction between "Zionism" as a specific ideological movement and "Zionism" as strong support for and indentification with Israel and the Jewish people. If the word is taken in the latter sense, then virtually all Canadian Jews are Zionists today, whether or not they belong to Zionist organizations.

This has not always been the case. At one time, participation in explicitly Zionist activities was almost essential for any Canadian Jew who wished to support the efforts to build a Jewish state, and Zionist organizations were a vital part of communal Jewish life in Canada. Because of today's changed circumstances, however, Zionist organizations have lost their monopoly on the connection between Jews and Israel. This development justifies a reexamination of the role of Zionism in Canadian Jewish life.

Zionism as Ideology and Movement

Zionism came to Canada with the wave of Eastern European immigrants at the turn of the century, but it was essentially a product of late-nineteenth-century Western Europe. As such, it reflected the experience and concerns of that society, in which many national groups had achieved or were moving towards independent statehood. If the nation-state was appropriate for the various peoples of Europe, it was surely appropriate for the Jews as well. But the fathers of modern political Zionism sought more than simply to duplicate the achievements of other nations; they also had to respond to the problems of Jewish life after emancipation and the emergence from the ghetto, to anti-Semitism, and to assimilation, phenomena that required answers unavailable in the existing tradition. In other words, Zionism was a particular political response to particular political problems, an attempt to devise an ideology for the Jews of Europe so that they might survive as a national group. Essentially, the Zionist answer was to seek the creation of a state that would be modelled on other nation states but would also provide continuity with Jewish political experience in the land of Israel before the destruction of the Temple.

Zionism was a new movement, and the need for it was not at all obvious to many Jews at the beginning of this century. Its proponents had to overcome several existing ideologies. Among them were: Bundism, a socialist view that recognized Jewish particularism but rejected the notion of a Jewish state; religious Orthodoxy, which then recognized Jewish peoplehood but rejected secular, nonmessianic routes to the restoration of Jewish national life; the Reform movement, which then rejected Jewish peoplehood outright; assimilationism, which rejected Jewish particularism; and secularism, which stressed cultural rather than national values. Despite this diversity of views, Zionism struck a responsive chord among the Jewish masses and quickly became a force to be reckoned with within European Jewry. Nevertheless, its early fight for existence against opponents within and without the Jewish community, gave it a polemical character it has never lost.

That argumentative quality was encouraged by Zionists' lack of agreement among themselves on almost everything except the overriding necessity of achieving statehood. Their controversies reflected both the religious divisions of Jewry and contemporary political and economic debates. There were three major camps: socialist, liberal, and religious (Orthodox). Both the socialists and the liberals rejected Orthodox Judaism as the basis for a Zionist society and supported the idea of a secular state. The former, however, believed that the new society should be built on socialist economic principles, while the liberals preferred free enterprise.

The religious Zionists differed among themselves on the economic question but agreed that a preeminent characteristic of a Jewish state must be its embodiment of Judaic religious values and law.

These ideological differences were so deep and pervasive that they became distinguishing features of Zionism (and eventually the basis of Israeli political parties). Lasting enmity between factions was not unknown. During the early 1930s, for example, Vladimir Jabotinsky took his Revisionists out of the World Zionist Organization because of a combination of policy and personality issues; his political heirs, Menachem Begin and the Herut Party, bitterly opposed the Labour Party that dominated Palestinian Jewry during the prestatehood period and from 1948 to 1977.

Zionist debates in Europe were intense, heated, and sometimes rancorous. To the participants, ideological differences were paramount because they represented world views. A politically neutral Zionism did not exist. An individual had to commit himself to a particular ideological position in order to become part of organized Zionism. European immigrants brought their debates across the Atlantic with them. During the first half of this century, first-generation immigrants dominated North American Zionist organizations, and they continued to see ideological differences as points of utmost importance. They fought intensely about such things as the desirability of socialism, how to bring about *aliyah* (immigration to Israel), the role of religion in the society, the proper attitude towards the British at any particular time, the proper response to the Nazi threat before the war, relations with Diaspora Jewry for political purposes, military activities within Palestine, and attitudes towards the Arabs.

Then several factors combined to make these differences less salient. In the first place, native-born Jews gradually took over both the leadership and the ranks of Zionist organizations in the United States and Canada. This generational change lowered passions and reduced factionalism because ideology was so much less important in North American society than in European.

Then the creation of the state of Israel shifted the forum for debate of most issues to the Knesset and other political institutions of that country. Previously, the Zionists had had the major responsibility for building Jewish society in Palestine; now the Israeli government took over most of it. Moreover, many of the issues that had animated the movement for decades soon appeared to be settled. The de facto coalition between Labour and the Orthodox Mizrachi became a feature of the political landscape, and Jews outside Israel accepted the country's right to make its own political decisions. Even the 1977 victory of the Likud, an amalgam of the Liberals, a free-enterprise party, and Herut, the militant nationalists, generated more skepticism about specific policies than fundamental ideological disagreements.[1]

In brief, as Ben Halpern has pointed out, the creation of Israel transformed Zionist meaning in the minds of most Jews of the West, especially those of North America. For the political goal of *aliyah*, they substituted pilgrimages, short-term service, and tourism, which all "became meritorious acts, quasi-Zionist mitzvot". In place of the cultural goal of a revived Israel as a centre of "authentic Hebrew prophetism, Israeli dance and arts and crafts became the common coin of Diaspora Jewish culture".[2]

Gerson Cohen has concurred, saying that "most Jews of the world feel no personal need for *aliyah*". Moreover, he noted, most Jews decline to subscribe to "classical Zionist formulations and their implications in terms of personal and existential decision".[3] Nevertheless, Zionist leaders have not fully met the challenge of adapting Zionist theory to the new reality; they seem to prefer extension of the old debates or jockeying for organizational status to creative theorizing. They do not even agree what issues a new Zionist ideology should address, although suggestions have included such important tasks as understanding the Jewish polity and the power relationships within it and analysing the relationship between Israel and the Diaspora.

The History of Zionism in Canada

The first stirrings of Zionism in Canada predated the intense political ideologies. As early as 1887, some thirty Canadian Jews, led by Alexander Harkavy, organized a Chovevi Zion group; its goals were primarily cultural.[4] Although the organization soon disbanded, a second was established in 1892. It was dedicated to the cause of *aliyah* and lasted until the launching of the Zionist Organization itself in 1897, at the time of the Basel Conference. At a mass meeting in Montreal in that year, some two hundred Canadian Jews affiliated themselves with world Zionism.

By the turn of the century, much of the Canadian Jewish community had accepted Zionism eagerly. It was a broadly based movement, both geographically and within the community, one that fostered not only support for a Jewish national home but also Jewish identity among the largely immigrant population.

During the next fifty years, Zionism continued to be a potent force in Canadian Jewish life. Generally, its organizational and political concepts were those of the various European Zionist groups imported by the immigrants, who continued to arrive throughout much of the period. Most Jews who wanted to support a Jewish homeland joined one of the Zionist parties, each of which operated independently on a national basis with international connections and strong local chapters. Loyalties to these organizations were very intense and long-lasting, partly, one suspects, because the groups provided strong anchors for immigrants in a strange environment.

The early part of the century was a period when there was no overarching Jewish national organization. Hence the partisan Zionist groups, with their strong local chapters in a national framework, became consequential in Jewish life. The Labour Zionists and the Orthodox Mizrachi were generally the most important, although others waxed and waned in several cities.

The first challenge to the importance of organized Zionism came in 1919 with the establishment of the Canadian Jewish Congress (CJC) as the representative body of Canadian Jewry on a national basis. Although it was designed to encompass all organizations within the Jewish community, it was not a particularly Zionist-oriented body; rather, it concentrated on domestic questions and the fate of dispersed Jewish communities overseas. Its establishment, therefore, challenged the Zionist organizations to maintain their hold on Canadian Jews.

The CJC did not prosper during the 1920s but revived in the 1930s in the face of the threat to European Jewry. During and after the Second World War, it was clearly the dominant national organization, although the Zionists continued to operate within their own sector. Here the Zionist Organization of Canada (ZOC), which supported a secular, liberal, nonsocialist approach to Zionism, became quite important, outstripping the Labour Zionists and the Mizrachi, especially because it was able to play an important role in fund-raising.

The period from 1948 to 1967 saw a centralizing trend within Canadian Jewry, characterized by the continuing preeminence of the CJC at the national level and the growth of the federations, aggregations of local health and welfare agencies, in the major urban centres. Although the goal of Zionism — support for the Jewish state — had become an integral part of the Canadian Jewish corporate consciousness, organizational Zionism was weak because its efforts were splintered among the various ideologically oriented groups. The ZOC had tried to carve out a role for itself as a Zionist organization that was really above party politics, but it never succeeded. It was left searching for a *raison d'être* after the Six Day War of 1967, when the need to increase funds for Israel (and the base of potential donors) led to the centralized local federations' taking over fund-raising.

The same year, in an effort to overcome Zionism's organizational weakness, the Jewish Agency, an international organization linking Israel to the Diaspora, influenced the various Zionist groups to form a federation, first known as the Federated Zionist Organization of Canada (FZOC) and renamed the Canadian Zionist Federation (CZF) in 1970. The new body may have added strength to Zionism as a national voice, but it ran into great difficulties, mainly because its ideologically based constituent groups wanted to retain their autonomy, initiative, and character and were never really willing to merge their separate organizational interests.[5] Politics within the FZOC were highly partisan.

Since 1970, observers within and without the Zionist movement in Canada have given it much searching criticism. Many feel that its partisan alignments based on yesterday's ideological concepts and its debates on the religious versus the secular and socialism versus the free market are irrelevant, divisive, and even dangerous because they result in a waste of organizational efforts and thus inhibit the development and maintenance of a strong and cohesive Israel-oriented community.[6]

Today's Canadian Zionist Organizations

Today Zionist organizations in Canada are grouped within the Canadian Zionist Federation (CZF), which has headquarters in Montreal and several offices in other parts of the country. Included among the constituents of the CZF are Labour Zionism, Revisionism, Mitzrachi-Hapoel Hamizrachi, Hadassah-WIZO, Friends of Pioneering Israel, Achdut Avoda-Poale Zion, La Fédération Séphardie Canadienne, Kadimah, and the Zionist Organization of Canada. All subscribe to the very general Jerusalem Program of the World Zionist Organization, but that appears to be the limit of Zionist ideological unity in Canada.[7] Almost all the CZF's 45,000 members belong to it by virtue of their membership in one of the partisan constituent groups. This traditional pattern, established long ago in Europe, impedes the development of an ideology that would attract Jews on a nonpartisan basis and enable CZF to function as an organization with its own base.

The CZF is one of Canada's three key national Jewish organizations; the other two are the Canadian Jewish Congress and B'nai B'rith. In principle, the CJC, which represents all Jewish organizations, is the dominant body in Jewish life and the spokesman for the community to the general public, to governments, and to international Jewish bodies. It does, in fact, meet in triennial plenary sessions at which all types of Jewish organizations are represented and takes the overriding responsibility for education and culture, foreign affairs, community relations, and politics. In several areas, however, one or both of the other two major organizations share power with the CJC. For example, all three jointly sponsor the Canada-Israel Committee, which handles lobbying, information projects, and other public affairs involving Israel. Congress and B'nai B'rith cooperate on the Joint Community Relations Committee and the National Committee on Soviet Jewry.

One consequence of this interlocking of national organizations is their extensive cooperation on matters of joint concern. Another is considerable jockeying for position as each tries to maintain its standing and prestige through involvement in a variety of activities. As a result, questions of organizational status are frequently as important as matters of substance, especially when it comes to initiating new activities for which organizational jurisdictions have yet to be defined.

Much of the competition between the national organizations is irrelevant, however, because the welfare federations have emerged as such powerful bodies that they tend to centralize community government at the local level. The federations have proved themselves vigorous and active, and, perhaps because they are newer than the traditional national organizations, they are more open to innovative approaches to their tasks. But the key to their position is their control over financial resources. Their fund-raising arms collect money, and the federations allocate it.

This local, centralized fund-raising is particularly important to the relative importance of the federations and organized Zionism because it includes fund-raising for Israel. The transfer of this responsibility to the federations was a watershed in Zionist organizational life in Canada. The Zionists thereby relinquished one of their major claims to power and publicity and simultaneously enhanced the status of the fund-raising bodies.

At the present time, the CZF is involved in many aspects of community activity, but its areas of sole responsibility are few. It shares political work with the Canada-Israel Committee. Education is primarily a local concern, despite the existence of a CZF education committee. What remains is encouragement of *aliyah* and some other programming, as detailed in the next section. This is not much nor is it highly visible, so the CZF is constantly forced to reassert its claim to equality in areas of shared jurisdiction.

The trend in Canada is clearly towards increasing power for the federations and increasingly centralized community decision-making. The mergers of the CJC's local operations in Toronto and Winnipeg with the cities' respective welfare federations are probably indicative of the long-range trend. (A similar merger has been considered in Montreal, and the proposal reappears periodically.) One can anticipate that the CZF will continue to find it difficult to carve out a unique niche for itself in Jewish organizational life, and that its constituent groups may have to rethink their relationships to other community bodies. In the meantime, organizational competition within the Jewish community is likely to remain intense.[8]

The Character of Present-Day Zionism

If an organization is to be seen as vital to a community and its interests, it must be perceived as performing a unique function. As circumstances and power configurations have changed over the years, Canadian Zionist organizations have watched many of their responsibilities and powers drift away to other bodies. Nevertheless the CZF argues that it still plays a vital role in Canadian Jewish life because the uniqueness of its mission lies in its approach to activities rather than in the activities themselves.

Education, for example, is a major CZF activity, although Jewish education as a whole is primarily the responsibility of local community and religious groups, with some CJC involvement. The CZF believes, however, that its educational activities, carried out by the only national department of Jewish education in Canada, have a unique content because of their Zionist ideological underpinnings. Thus, it not only sends teachers to Israel for in-service training and runs a teachers' institute in Canada but also prepares school curricula from a Zionist perspective. But it is not clear how much impact this material can have, despite recent efforts to increase its use. Most Jewish day schools exist primarily because of their religious orientation; their Zionist approach varies with the outlook of their leaders and administrators, and most are very careful to retain control over their own curricula.

Similarly, the CZF shares its role in disseminating information with several other groups, most notably the Canada-Israel Committee (CIC), but contends that its own activities have a distinctive orientation. Moreover, it insists, its efforts are directed primarily towards the Jewish community, whereas the CIC speaks more to government, media, and the non-Jewish world in general. All these activities are justified as specifically Zionistic approaches, not just Jewish ones. The implication is, of course, that one can usefully distinguish between a Jew and a Zionist today. Yet at best such a distinction is marginal, thus raising doubts about the very nature of Zionist enterprises in this area.

Another important Zionist activity is the encouragement of *aliyah*, and CZF puts a great deal of innovative effort into this program. But the results, although steady, have been unspectacular; about 1,000 persons left Canada for Israel in 1977, and that figure included former Israeli residents. Even Quebec Jews, many of whom have been driven to think of moving since the 1976 election of a separatist Parti Québécois government, are not very interested in *aliyah*. A 1978 survey of Montreal Jews showed about 45 per cent of the respondents had considered moving, but only 14 per cent of them would choose Israel; 48 per cent would prefer the United States and 26 per cent Ontario.[9]

Other activities sponsored directly by the CZF today include running a variety of programs for young people, fostering trade with Israel, and promoting tourism there.

Of course, the CZF constituent groups also carry out their own programs. Interestingly, the largest and most active Zionist organization in Canada today is Hadassah-WIZO, which deemphasizes ideology. It has about 17,000 members and runs an elaborate program that reaches into cities and towns with small Jewish populations. In addition to its traditional charitable, social, medical, and fund-raising work for Israel, it has also become active in intellectual pursuits, public affairs, and political work.

Although Hadassah-WIZO is very dynamic, some of the other Zionist organizations are not. Too many still concentrate on the interests and concerns of an earlier generation of European immigrants. Some have not seen much of a turnover in member-ship in fifteen or twenty years or rely very heavily on a small number of traditional leaders. Thus, their activities are unlikely to be innovative, and attempts to confront the ideological implica-tions of recent international developments are rare. (For example, Canadian Zionist organizations have had little serious discussion about the future of the territories Israel acquired in 1967.) When current issues are discussed at all, Zionists of a particular ideology tend to follow the lead of the corresponding Israeli political party rather than engaging in independent analysis.

Identification with Israel

In brief, although the activities and even the ideologies of the various Zionist organizations do enable some Canadian Jews to relate to Israel, they are no longer the only means for establishing such a relationship. Yet there can be no doubt that Canadian Jewry is very interested in Israel; in fact, identification with it is probably the strongest bond uniting Jews from sea to sea. It brings together individuals of all religious and political persuasions in such a general commitment that a kind of civic religion of orienta-tion to Israel seems to have supplanted both the religious and the Zionist affirmation of earlier generations.

A conclusive demonstration about the nature of Canadian Jews' commitment to Israel is difficult to achieve, but the recent survey of the Montreal Jewish community provided some perti-nent data. Nearly all the respondents were happy to be Jewish, and a similar proportion believed that Jews must do all they can to help Israel survive. Yet nearly half did not consider themselves strong Zionists. On the key question of *aliyah*, a classic indicator of Zionist commitment, about 90 per cent disagreed with the pro-position that it is necessary to move to Israel to be a good Jew.[10] (This finding is especially interesting in light of the fact that the survey was conducted in Montreal, where the political context made the question of moving in general particularly significant.)

Another indication of popular dedication to the cause of Israel is the enormous success of the federations' fund-raising drives. Some observers even feel that the glamour of the Israeli cause helps to carry the entire Jewish fund-raising effort and that less money would be raised for local needs if the local and Israel campaigns were not united. Since about 60 per cent of the money collected goes to Israel (mainly through the United Israel Appeal), the success of the campaigns is, of course, good for Israel and the essential goal of Zionism, but in some ways, it undercuts both Zionist and religious organizations. If an individual can fulfil what he sees as his responsibilities to Israel by participating in a fund-raising drive, the need for Zionist organizations is diminished. Furthermore, fund-raising and contributing do not demand a great deal of Jewish commitment, practice, knowledge, or participation. Thus, increasing emphasis on fund-raising in Jewish life is encouraging the emergence of new Jewish leaders who are very pro-Israel but not necessarily preoccupied with traditional Jewish concerns and probably not very sensitive to classical Zionist values, particularly to Israel as the centre of and political purpose to Jewish life, rather than just as a haven for persecuted Jews. Yet every fund-raiser and contributor can very easily consider his actions to be a Zionist affirmation, a way of identifying with Israel and of being a good Jew.

Israeli officials are well aware of this development. When a prominent Israeli visits Canada today, his or her public appearances are more likely to be under the auspices of a fund-raising organization than a Zionist one. Undoubtedly this enhances collection efforts, but it also serves to legitimize the implicit claim of the fund-raising organizations to be the address for Israel in Canada.

At one time only Zionist organizations could make such a claim, but their place in Canadian Jewish life is now somewhat problematic. There are simply too many other ways of expressing the commitment to Israel. Donations and working on fund-raising are perhaps the easiest and most common. Trips to Israel, prolonged study in Israel by youths, participation in Israel-oriented cultural and social activities are other pleasant, socially acceptable methods.

In other words, loosely defined Zionism has become integral to Jewish life. But in the organizational sense, it is becoming peripheral. Officially, the CZF remains an equal partner with CJC and perhaps B'nai B'rith in the national community, but it maintains that position more through the force of particular personalities than through organizational strength and vitality. Despite the present size of its membership, and its own sense of playing a unique role in Canadian Jewish life, the CZF may run into future difficulties because of the weakness of several of its constituents, some of which may eventually disintegrate.

Anti-Zionism

Combatting non-Zionist and anti-Zionist groups is a traditional Zionist activity but not a very important one for the CZF. Within the Canadian Jewish community, anti-Zionist groups are virtually nonexistent. Since the war in 1967, community attitudes have required all major organizations to become more and more involved with Israel; hence the concept of a Jewish organization being both important and non-Zionist has lost all meaning.

As for anti-Zionist groups, Canadians hear of the activities of the American Council for Judaism whose adherents assert that Jews are only a religious group and not a people. Therefore, they are very strongly opposed to Zionism as a movement and to the claims of Zionists to represent the Jewish people. Prominent Americans who are members of the ACJ frequently lend their names to anti-Zionist causes and have allowed themselves to be used by Arab opponents of Israel. But Canada has no organization comparable to the ACJ or its offshoots, although a few scattered individuals do subscribe to its point of view. (One has consorted publicly with the Libyans.)

Outside the Jewish community, some anti-Zionist activity definitely does exist. In English Canada, it comes mostly from Arab Canadians. In Quebec, labour leaders and leftists are in the vanguard; furthermore, some Québécois separatists have used attacks on Israel as responses to Montreal Jews' opposition to separation and have attempted to link the concept of independence for Quebec with that of self-determination for the Palestinian Arabs. Naturally the Jewish community has resisted efforts to make such links and has vigorously opposed anti-Zionist propaganda, such as that which appeared in the nationalistic magazine *Ici Québec* early in 1978. Here the CZF and its affiliates have taken strong stands, but so have other community organizations. Canadian Jews today see anti-Zionism as a matter of concern for the entire community, not just Zionists.[11]

The Outlook for Canadian Zionism

Canadian Zionist organizations must reassess their purpose and functions in the face of realistic considerations.

First of all, Zionism no longer provides the only — or even the main — alternative to the religious approach to Jewish identity. At one time, Zionism offered an ideology of nationhood that appealed to diverse elements in the community and supplied a sense of national purpose. More recently the welfare federations and their fund-raising agencies have developed a form of secular identification that incorporates the most popular elements of Zionist ideology in a generalized, nonpartisan framework. Therefore, it can be argued that Zionist organizations as presently constituted do not really fulfil a need.

Second, Zionist organizations have now lost many of their traditional functions to other bodies or joint committees. This sharing of power and responsibility has diminished the status of the CZF and weakened the case for its necessity. In addition, individual Jews now have multiple ways to engage in pro-Israel activity, many of which do not involve Zionist organizations. That consideration, plus the fact that virtually every Jew supports Israel morally, politically, and financially, means that most Jews probably do not believe that the Zionist organizations provide them with anything that cannot be obtained from other groups.[12]

Third, very few Canadian Jews go on *aliyah*. This fact can hardly be blamed on the CZF, which has a very active *aliyah* program; rather it reflects the well-known proclivities of North American Jews. But the low interest in *aliyah* and the unlikelihood of large increases raise questions about the program's value.

Fourth, most Canadian Zionist organizations do not now have an active and involved mass base, nor have they attracted as high a calibre of leaders as competing organizations. As a result, the Zionist presence in Canada has breadth but little depth. Consequently, it might be argued that Canadian Zionist organizations in their historical form no longer provide the best vehicle for the advancement of certain Jewish interests. If that is the case, some kind of Zionism may persist in Canada, but the Zionist organizations may prove to be vestigial.

In brief, support for the Jewish homeland is now the norm rather than something special among Canadian Jews. Zionist ideologies and party identification are not relevant to the lives of most Canadian Jews, and Zionist organizations are not offering much in the way of unique activities for which Canadian Jewry perceives a need. Hence, the outlook in Canada for the Zionist movement as we know it is somewhat cloudy. Zionism must change with the times or stand by as it continues to be incorporated into a vague Jewish ethos. To survive, Canadian Zionism must develop an ideology and an organizational structure that orient it to the tasks of the future rather than the struggles of the past.

PART V

Challenges
for the Future

No group is more concerned with its future than the Jews. In this respect, Canadian Jewry resembles Canada itself, a nation that wrestles continually with problems of survival, unity, identity, and constitutional independence. The essays in this section examine four such problems for Canadian Jewry, four items of the many on the Canadian Jewish agenda.

Threats to future survival may come from the societal context outside the group, or they may originate from within, reflecting the group's own ambiguity rather than restrictions imposed by others. Even internal pressures are, however, influenced by the external environment. Thus, for Canadian Jewry, as for many Diaspora communities, one of the greatest challenges is the internal tendency towards assimilation, which stems from an environment that seduces, rather than oppresses, Jews.

The threat of assimilation takes many forms; in a receptive host society, some of the most difficult are the quantitative and qualitative problems posed by intermarriage. As Morton Weinfeld suggests in his essay, there is little consensus on how out-marriage is affecting Canadian Jews numerically because there may be disagreement on how one should define a Jew. Should Reform conversions be seen as equally valid with Orthodox ones? What of children who are being raised "as Jews" even though one parent is not Jewish?

Neither is the Jewish community agreed on what attitude
to adopt towards intermarriage and intermarrieds. The hard-line
view would define Jews strictly and try to limit
intermarriage by strengthening identity among young Canadian
Jews and limiting their interactions with non-Jews.
The soft-line view suggests that little can be done to prevent
intermarriage and that communal resources might be
better invested in attracting intermarrieds, of whatever status,
into the Jewish community. Such an open-door policy
would view intermarriage as a possible recruitment mechanism.
Of course, it would also run the risk of diluting the quality of the
community and perhaps adding to the intermarriage rate.

Despite the obvious difficulties of these and other possible
options, Canadian Jews will have to evolve some coherent
approach to this potentially divisive problem because it will not
simply go away. After millenia of dealing with oppressive
environments, it is not surprising that Jews are still learning to
cope with one that offers near total freedom.

That freedom, of course, suggests a lack of anti-Semitism,
the classic external threat to Jews. By European standards,
anti-Semitism in Canada, as in the United States,
has been minimal. Jewish blood has not been shed on Canadian
streets in any great quantity, and organized anti-Semitism has
never mobilized large numbers of Canadians. This having been
said, it is important to understand that anti-Semitism has existed
historically in Canada, although as Arnold Ages suggests in his
essay, it has usually tended to be subtle, denying Jews entrance
to the highest reaches of society, business, or academe, rather
than condemning them to poverty or material degradation.
Today, although pockets of exclusion remain, the trend seems
one of acceptance. Attitude surveys reveal some residual
prejudice in North America against Jews, though perhaps only a
minority feel it strongly. In Canada, nonwhites and the native
peoples bear the brunt of racism, a phenomenon that ironically
diminishes the scope of expressed anti-Semitism.

Yet even in a country where "the Jews have it good", some of them note the current revival of right-wing extremist groups and fear that virulent, European-style anti-Semitism may emerge. That seems unlikely, but such groups may generate an increase in acts of violence, such as synagogue desecrations.

Classical anti-Semitism may no longer provide an analytical prism through which to study the social status of Jews in Canada. Howard Stanislawski's study of the Jewish community and the development of Canadian public policy on the Arab boycott of Israel illustrates an alternate approach. Jews can be seen as an interest group lobbying for policy preferences like other Canadian groups — labour, women, fishermen, oil companies, farmers, consumers, and so on.

In such a situation, the Jewish community must recognize that normal politics in Canada is a brokering of decisions among competing interest groups. One result is the need to form alliances and coalitions that often differ for specific issues. Another is the fact that no one interest group can win on every point. How, then, should Canadian Jews understand responses unsympathetic to their policy desires? Some analysts have termed such insensitivity a form of new anti-Semitism, and many may see prejudice lurking behind policy decisions that oppose the declared Jewish interest. What this view overlooks is the possibility that the decision-makers may have seen the situation as a competition among interest groups and given priority to one other than the Jews.

Since the latter viewpoint may be likely for many non-Jewish Canadians, it behooves the Jewish community to develop strategies for its new role. They are particularly needed for issues concerning Israel and the Middle East, a foreign-policy area in which Canada has shown itself generally supportive of Israel but opposed to some of its specific policies. Thus, a new, intensified political gamesmanship must rank as a key item on the Canadian Jewish agenda.

Few issues are more central to current Canadian politics than the place of Quebec in Confederation. For some time, the predominantly Anglophone Jewish community of Montreal has felt itself in the front lines of the ongoing battle, engaged in a continuing caucus over its future in a province that, independent or not, is bound to become increasingly French in every dimension.

Harold M. Waller and Morton Weinfeld explain that the issue facing the Jews of Montreal is not simply opposition to the use of French; as has been remarked, the centrality of English to Jewish life is not divinely preordained. Yet "francization" might limit cultural and communal interchanges within mainstream North American Jewry. Other fears are economic. Will fluency in French, rather than French ethnic origin, be sufficient to guarantee Jews equal opportunity in the work world? Latent worries centre on excessive governmental intervention in private spheres, the erosion of civil liberties, the foreign policy of an independent Quebec, and a possible resurgence of anti-Semitism should economic or political instability grow in the province.

In fact, there is little, if any, evidence of anti-Semitism on the part of the Parti Québécois or the Québécois generally. Ironically, the increasing "francization" of the Jewish community may lead, for the first time, to substantial contact between the French majority and Anglophone Jews. With good will on both sides, mutual ignorance and suspicion may yet give way to a creative synthesis in which the Jews can both remain true to their heritage and interests and participate actively in the New Quebec.

Intermarriage: Agony and Adaptation

by Morton Weinfeld

Intermarriage, long recognized as a problem in the Diaspora, is today one of the leading concerns of North American Jews. The rate has increased so dramatically over the past two decades that some Jewish leaders and scholars see intermarriage as not only a danger to the individuals involved but also as a threat to the survival of North American Jewry. Every intermarriage weakens the Jewish community, they say, and increases the likelihood of its disappearance from Canada's cultural mosaic.

The fears rest on statistical projections that show the United States' Jewish population decreasing by as much as 50 per cent by the middle of the next century, barring any large-scale immigration.[1] The Canadian pattern, scholars believe, will be similar, though the percentage of decrease may be less.

Intermarriage is generally only one of three factors cited as underlying these projections. One of the others is the low fertility rate of North American Jews. Neither in the United States nor in Canada are Jews replacing themselves.[2] Jewish fertility rates in both countries have long been well below the national averages and are now so low that some communal leaders advocate pronatalist policies, including payment from community funds to

Jewish families with more than a specified number of children. Such plans seem unlikely to succeed. Historically, fertility rates have varied in cyclical patterns. North American Jewish women are more likely to be moved by broad social changes than by appeals to duty; many, although eager to contribute to the Jewish community, refuse to be limited to doing so in the role of mother.

The second factor expected to lower the future Jewish population is the current age structure among Jews. For a number of reasons, the Jewish populations are aged compared to North American averages and can be expected to remain so for the next generation.[3] By definition, an aged population has a limited potential for growth because it includes such a small proportion of women of childbearing age. And, of course, when those women have a low fertility rate, the impact of their small number on population growth is doubly severe.

The third factor that is affecting the Jewish population of the future is intermarriage; in many ways, it is the most emotional and least understood. Today, intermarriage is seen not only as an event that has consequences for the families involved but also as a communal issue requiring a communal response. Any given intermarriage may remove a stream of descendents from the future Jewish population totals. Moreover, a high rate of intermarriage weakens the norm of Jew marrying Jew and thus makes marriage to Gentiles more acceptable in the future. And even if the Gentile partner converts or makes some form of Jewish identification, some experts argue that this family's quality of commitment to the Jewish community is invariably weaker than that of "true" Jewish families.

The intermarriage issue raises many questions. What are the dimensions of the phenomenon in Canada? Are there differences between the Canadian and the American patterns? Between patterns in different parts of Canada? What type of person intermarries and with whom? What are the patterns and consequences of conversion? Only after examining these questions can one estimate the general impact of intermarriage or consider what realistic responses to it are available to the Jewish community.

The Trend

"Intermarriage" is often used rather loosely to cover two somewhat different situations: *intermarriage*, the marriage of a Jew to someone who was not born a Jew, and *mixed marriage*, the marriage of a Jew to someone who is still not Jewish. (Mixed marriages, in other words, are intermarriages in which there is no conversion to Judaism.) For convenience, though, the terms "intermarriage" or "out-marriage" often include both types; their opposite is in-marriage, the marriage of two persons who are Jewish by birth.

Careful definitions cannot, however, change the salient fact — the rate of intermarriage is increasing and doing so rather quickly. Table 1 sets out the increase in Canada since 1961. Two points must be remembered in examining this data. First, since the civil authorities in each province usually ascertain the religion of bride and groom at the time of marriage, they theoretically do not count as an intermarriage a marriage in which a spouse has previously converted to Judaism; thus, the table's percentages approximate a mixed-marriage rate. Moreover, since 1974, this sort of data has not been available for the province of Quebec, where about 40 per cent of Canadian Jewish marriages occur.

Even when these caveats are kept in mind, the data are startling. From 1926 to 1960, the annual rate increased only 5.1 per cent. But since the mid-1960s, it has gone up roughly 1 per cent per year. It seems safe to assume that today's rate is at least that of 1978, with more than a quarter of all Jews who marry taking a mate who is not Jewish at the time of the wedding.

American data for mixed marriages show the same pattern: a slow rise until the 1960s, a sharp increase since then. In fact, the American figures are even more striking than the Canadian. The overall U.S. mixed-marriage rate for 1966 through 1972 was approximately 25 per cent, about twice the Canadian weighted average of 13 per cent for the same years.[4]

Why the sharp increase in the 1960s, and why the sizable difference between the rates in Canada and the United States?

The 1960s saw the children of the postwar baby-boom years, including many native-born young Jews, seeking marriage partners. Intermarriage is more likely for Jews with higher levels of education, particularly if their political and social persuasions are liberal.[5] The educational expansion of the time, coupled with liberal and progressive ideologies abounding on the campuses, seems to have created a climate ideally suited to promoting intermarriage. Anti-Semitism decreased after the Holocaust, and Jews and Gentiles began to mix socially more than before.

The difference between the two national rates is probably caused by the difference in the immigrant components of the two Jewish populations. Basically, Canadian Jews are one generation closer to Europe and the traditional Jewish experience than are American Jews. In 1971, the Canadian Jewish population had proportionately about twice as many foreign-born household heads as the American; nearly half the foreign-born Canadians were post-1945 immigrants.[6] If it is indeed this generational difference between the two countries that causes the difference in their intermarriage rates, the American experience suggests the future trend for Canada. As the Canadian Jewish community gains a growing proportion of third- and fourth-generation Jews, the impact of the European experience will fade, with a possible increase in intermarriage.

On the other hand, it must be noted that Jews, including native-born Jews, remain the most highly in-married of all Canadian ethnic groups. One study showed that in 1971, 90 per cent of native-born Jewish family heads had spouses of the same ethnic origin, compared with 30 per cent for Italian, 24 per cent for Polish, and 45 per cent for Ukrainian.[7]

Sexual Differences

In both Canada and the United States, intermarriage is more frequent for Jewish males than for females. As shown in Table 1, a 4 to 5 per cent difference between the sexes' intermarriage rates persisted in Canada throughout the 1960s and 1970s; in the United States, the male rate is about twice the female. Yet from

TABLE 1

Canadian Jews in Mixed Marriages

Year	Males			Females			Males and Females		
	Number Married	Number Entering Mixed Marriages	Percentage Entering Mixed Marriages	Number Married	Number Entering Mixed Marriages	Percentage Entering Mixed Marriages	Number Married	Number Entering Mixed Marriages	Percentage Entering Mixed Marriages
1926–30	......	......	......	......	......	......	......	......	2.5
1961	1562	161	10.3	1465	64	4.4	3027	225	7.4
1962	1440	174	12.1	1343	77	5.7	2783	251	9.0
1963	1485	182	12.3	1416	113	8.0	2901	295	10.2
1964	1547	185	12.0	1463	101	7.1	3010	286	9.5
1965	1655	205	12.4	1560	110	7.1	3215	315	9.8
1966	1812	201	12.0	1733	122	7.0	3545	323	9.1
1967	1999	247	12.4	1917	165	8.6	3916	412	10.5
1968	2253	312	13.8	2141	200	9.3	4397	512	11.6
1969	2353	366	15.6	2224	237	10.7	4577	603	13.2
1970	2429	394	16.2	2311	276	11.9	4740	670	14.1
1971	2462	435	17.7	2298	271	11.8	4760	706	14.8
1972	2521	456	18.1	2361	296	12.5	4882	752	15.4
1973	2316	449	19.4	2225	358	16.1	4541	807	17.8
1974*	1410	341	24.2	1329	260	19.6	2739	601	21.9
1975*	1496	377	25.2	1409	209	20.6	2905	667	23.0
1976*	1483	400	26.9	1370	307	22.4	2853	707	24.7
1977*	1329	334	25.1	1274	279	21.8	2603	613	23.5
1978*	1453	446	30.6	1357	300	22.1	2810	746	26.5

SOURCE: Data from 1926 to 1930 from Louis Rosenberg, "Intermarriage in Canada 1921-1960", in W. J. Cahnman, ed., *Intermarriage and Jewish Life: A Symposium* (New York: 1963); for 1961 to 1978, from Statistics Canada, Census Division, Vital Statistics Annual Reports.

NOTE: *Excluding province of Quebec, where about 40 per cent of Jewish marriages in Canada occur.

the point of view of Jewish religious law, intermarriage by men is even less desirable than by women. Jews claim their birthright through their mothers. If a Jewish woman marries a Gentile, the offspring of the union are recognized as Jewish, whether or not the father has converted; if the woman is the Gentile, however, the children cannot be recognized as Jewish unless she converts.

Why are Jewish men more likely to marry out than women? One reason is undoubtedly that Jewish girls, like girls in most societies, are more protected than boys and more strictly supervised in their social life. But male experimentation, including affairs with non-Jewish females, is often winked at, if not condoned. Moreover, historical precedent exists; in the late nineteenth and early twentieth centuries, it was Jewish males who intermarried in attempts to escape the prejudice and discrimination that blocked their economic success.

The table shows another puzzling male-female difference: more Jewish males than females were married each year. This fact suggests one possible "cause" of intermarriage in general: there may be a shortage of Jewish women available for marriage. The same argument can be developed from Canadian demographic data. In the age category twenty to thirty-four inclusive, the most likely time of marriage, the 1971 census counted 33,285 Jewish males but only 31,355 Jewish females.

What is the explanation for this surplus of nearly 2,000 men? First, worldwide obstetrical data shows roughly 105 males are born for every 100 females, but this early imbalance is generally counterbalanced by the substantially greater life expectancy of women. In other words, for a whole population, the sex ratio is generally nearly even, but the younger age groups tend to have higher proportions of males than females, while the middle and older age groups have more females.

Recent research suggests a second factor for Jews: they may have a higher proportion of male to female births than does the population as a whole.[8] For example, the 1971 Canadian sex ratio for children up to the age of fourteen was 104.3 boys to 100 girls, but for Jewish children, it was 107.2 to 100.

One reason for this phenomenon may be the pattern of sexual intercourse associated with Jews. The Orthodox ban on intercourse during menstruation encourages intercourse towards the time of ovulation in a woman's monthly cycle, and the closer to the actual moment of ovulation that intercourse occurs, the greater the probability of a male sperm cell successfully fertilizing the egg.[9] Many non-Orthodox Jewish couples approximate parts of this pattern of sexual behaviour through their use of rather sophisticated family planning. When they wish to have a child, they often concentrate sexual activity around the time of maximum fertility, increasing the probability of conceiving a male.

A third factor in the Jewish sex ratio may be that immigrants are more likely to be men than women. To the extent that the twenty-to-thirty-four age group includes immigrants (and there are undoubtedly many from North Africa and elsewhere), we expect a higher-than-average proportion of men.

All this may help explain not only why more Jewish men than women marry each year but also why more Jewish men than women intermarry. What else can the "surplus" of young Jewish males do? Theoretically, they could overcome the imbalance of demand and supply by marrying older Jewish women, but such marriages are rare for social reasons. Celibacy is also an infrequent choice for Jews. The main alternatives for the extra men are to postpone marriage (because the longer life expectancy of women creates more choice for the older male) or to intermarry.

In sum, then, most of the explanations offered for the high rate of intermarriage are sociological: changes in attitudes, declines in Jewish religious practice, increasing educational attainment for young Jews, the effects of an open society, and so on. But to the extent that the intermarriage of Jewish males is caused by the imbalanced sex ratio, both our understanding of and our search for solutions to the problem of intermarriage need to change. Strategies (such as Jewish singles clubs) designed to pair up young unmarried Jews cannot fully resolve the situation.

Intra-Canadian Differences

As might be expected, intermarriage rates vary widely across Canada. One researcher broke down the data for <u>1971</u> by province, and the results were revealing.[10] The <u>lowest rate of intermarriage</u> that year was 8 per cent in Quebec. Next came Ontario with a rate of 16 per cent; Manitoba, 18 per cent; Saskatchewan, 30 per cent; Alberta, 39 per cent; British Columbia, 47 per cent; and the Atlantic provinces, averaging approximately 50 per cent. The sharp differences between Quebec and Ontario and between the central provinces and those to the east and west are striking.

[margin note: More IM in West than east]

<u>How can these variations be explained</u>? Some sociologists emphasize <u>differences in lifestyles and culture.</u>[11] For example, the West has newer population centres, whose inhabitants are less rooted in local communities. And in any "frontier" areas, the <u>violation of accepted social norms is likely to go up.</u> In general, the West — especially British Columbia — has higher rates of divorce, crime, and geographically mobile residents than does the East. (These rates are also higher for Ontario than for Quebec.) Where <u>the ties of tradition and community are somewhat looser,</u> <u>we thus find more intermarriage, which is a form of breaking</u> <u>away from traditional patterns.</u>

[margin note: why?]

[margin note: (1)]

A purely cultural explanation is, however, not the only one possible for the geographical differences in intermarriage. They also correlate very highly with provincial differences in the absolute numbers of Jews, the proportion of them living in cities, and the proportion of foreign-born; the higher these three figures, the lower the rate of intermarriage. The <u>greater the Jewish population's immigrant component,</u> with its strong attachments to Jewish heritage, the less likely are Jews to intermarry. The more Jews there are to choose from in a given place, the more chance an individual Jew has of finding a compatible Jewish mate.

The argument still holds for the Ontario-Quebec difference, although the Jewish populations of the main centres, Toronto and Montreal, are roughly the same. The factor that must be added in is the difference in the Gentile populations of the two cities. Montreal's has a large number of French Catholics; Toronto's, a high proportion of Anglo-Protestants. Jews, who are predominantly Anglophone, seem more likely to intermarry with English-speaking Protestants than with French-speaking Catholics. And if French Catholics are subtracted from Montreal's Gentile population, the pool of candidates for intermarriage in that city turns out to be about half that of Toronto — and Quebec's intermarriage rate is indeed one half that of Ontario's.

The rising intermarriage rates across the country westward from Quebec are also interesting. For some time in the United States, Jews have been moving out of the Northeast and into the West and the South, where intermarriage rates are higher (rates in California are among the highest anywhere in that country). In Canada, there appears to be a clear if more modest trend of Jewish migration westward, notably to British Columbia and Alberta and from Quebec to Ontario. What will this geographic drift bring? If Western Canada retains its high intermarriage rates, then the national average will also rise. Alternatively, as the absolute and relative size of the Jewish communities in Vancouver, Edmonton, and Calgary increases, they may experience a reduction in intermarriage, particularly as these cities develop communal bases with traditions, loyalties, and settled populations of their own.

Religion and Language in Intermarriage

Two factors make the intermarriage pattern in Quebec somewhat different from that of the rest of the country. One is the fact that the province's overall population is about 80 per cent Roman Catholic and Francophone, while most of its Jews are Anglophone. (The exception to the latter is the other peculiarity of Quebec — the presence of a relatively large group of Francophone Jews who are fairly recent immigrants from North Africa. Their pattern of intermarriage is so interesting that it is examined in detail in the following subsection.)

Given the high proportion of Catholics in Quebec, it is not surprising that Jews who intermarry in that province are more likely to marry Catholics than are those who intermarry in the rest of Canada. But given the language situation, it is also not surprising to find that the percentage of Catholic intermarriage partners is much lower than 80 per cent.

Another interesting fact is that outside Quebec, Jews tend to select Catholic intermarriage partners slightly more frequently than might have been the case by chance. Catholics are about 30 per cent of the population of the other nine provinces; in 1974, 33 per cent of the Jewish men and 30 per cent of Jewish women who intermarried picked Catholic spouses.[12]

It has long been believed that Jewish-Catholic intermarriage in general is more difficult and less frequent than Jewish-Protestant intermarriage because Catholicism has a more rigid image than Protestantism and is perceived as more anti-Semitic historically. In fact, the choice of Catholic intermarriage partners is in line with provincial Catholic population proportions, except in Quebec, where language and ethnic loyalties militate against it. A comparison of this data with those of earlier years suggests that over time Jewish intermarriages have involved increasing proportions of Catholics. Possible explanations for this rise are changes in the Roman Catholic Church's attitude towards Jews and the decline in religious conservatism among its members.

The Francophone Jews of Montreal

A unique Canadian phenomenon is the intermarriage pattern of the Francophone Jewish community of Montreal. This community is composed primarily of North African Sephardic Jews who began to immigrate to Canada in sizeable numbers during the 1950s. Eager to leave persecution and minority status in Arab lands, these Francophones found Montreal attractive, even though its large and well-established Jewish community was then almost exclusively Ashkenazic and Anglophone; by the 1970s the North African group had grown to some 12,000 to 15,000 persons.

A recent study shed light on the marriage patterns of these North African Jews.[13] Their intermarriage rate was astonishingly high — 61 per cent for men during 1962 to 1972. (The rate for the comparable period for other Sephardic men was 28 per cent; for Ashkenazic men, 18 per cent.) The rate for North African women was less startling, but well above the city norm at 32 per cent (compared to 7 per cent for other Sephardic women and 4 per cent for Ashkenazic women).

In short, from 1962 to 1972, more than half of the North African men and roughly one-third of the women who married chose someone who was not originally Jewish. One must ask why. The most obvious possibility is that language separates the North Africans from the rest of Montreal's Jews but unites them with the non-Jewish Québécois. And the study showed that French Canadians were the choice of many of the North African Jews: 38 per cent of the men and 13 per cent of the women.

To the purely linguistic reason for intermarriage must be added the factor of very real prejudice towards the North Africans on the part of the majority (Askhenazic) Jewish community. It is interesting that only 14 per cent of North African men and 26 per cent of North African women married Ashkenazis. Conversely, only 2 per cent of Ashkenazic men and women married Sephardic individuals, North African or other. Marriage across the Sephardic-Ashkenazic boundary remains rare.

One can also speculate about other factors at work here. Looking at the phenomenon of so many North African men marrying French Canadian women, one wonders if there might be an element of preference as well as necessity in their choices. Sociologists have suggested that the attraction of North African Jews to the prestigious French culture originated in North Africa itself but could not develop there because of the social barriers that separated Jews, Arabs, and Christians, as well as the European and native communities. In Quebec, the immigrants encountered a more open society, no language barrier, and segregation from the Anglophone Jewish community; the possibility of integration into the French milieu, largely thwarted in North Africa, increased in the new environment.

Perhaps as significant as the large numbers of North African intermarriages is the high conversion rate to Judaism that goes with them. The informed consensus is that the majority of the non-Jewish spouses convert to Judaism, and that they manifest a sincere commitment to Jewish life — in short, that they are a net gain to the community. One reason for this high conversion rate may be the dominance of the North African male in family relationships, extending to the wife's adoption of his religious preference. Another may be the fact that the North African religious heritage is Orthodox, with no tradition of intermarriage with non-Orthodox conversion.

reasons for this conversion

Conversion and Intermarriage

Even setting the North African phenomenon aside, intermarriage may contribute to the Jewish community through conversion of the non-Jewish spouse. In general, all Orthodox and Conservative rabbis demand conversion of the non-Jewish partner before they will officiate at an intermarriage. These conversions are always based on a period of study, though the study requirement varies in rigour. Reform rabbis, by contrast, will accept less stringent conversions. (Indeed, Judaism today is facing a serious problem because of the growing number of Reform conversions, which are not accepted by the Orthodox or the Conservative rabbinate.) Reform rabbis will also perform a mixed marriage, without conversion of the non-Jew, though they ask generally for a commitment to raising the children as Jews and for membership in the temple. According to one Reform rabbi, his temple sees far more mixed marriages than marriages with a Reform conversion ceremony (about seventy-five of the former annually, compared to twenty of the latter).

1) IM may contribute to Jewish community due to conversions

Unfortunately, there have been no accurate Canadian studies on conversion among Gentiles marrying Jews. American studies have found conversion rates of 26 per cent and 21 per cent in intermarriages, with converts to Judaism tending to be less educated, of lower economic position, and less committed to their original religions than partners who do not convert. Conversely, a recent study by the American Jewish Committee found, as could be expected, that the greater the Jewish identification of the one spouse, the more likely the non-Jewish partner was to convert.[14]

The timing of the conversions, as reported in these studies, is interesting. Most took place before the marriage (some even before the future spouses met). Yet 22 per cent occurred just after the marriage, and 6 per cent more after the birth of the first child. Thus, a fair number of Gentile partners can be expected to convert *after* the marriage. This finding means the intermarriage rates presented in Table 1 (and in most statistical studies conducted in Canada) are not "final"; an individual may convert after the civil authorities record his or her religion.

Conversion rates do not, of course, tell the whole story about how an individual who was not born a Jew acts after marriage to someone who was. Discussions with several Canadian rabbis revealed sharp differences in the Orthodox, Conservative, and Reform approaches to conversion and in their perceptions of community reactions to intermarriage.

The Orthodox and Conservative rabbis reported mainly "successful" conversions. They cited cases of greater Jewish commitment on the part of the converted partner than of the birthright Jew — confirming the popular stereotype of the zealous convert. Though Jewish folklore also contains elements of distrust or suspicion of converts, the rabbis reported full acceptance of them by their congregations. Orthodox and Conservative parents, they said, also show a growing acceptance of intermarriage with conversion, although the initial reaction remains one of skepticism or rejection. Even where there is no conversion, it is now common to see parents reconciled with their intermarried children, especially after the birth of a first grandchild. The rabbis of all denominations said that those parents most difficult to reconcile are Holocaust survivors, who see in intermarriage a betrayal of their own struggle to survive.

Otherwise, the Reform picture is fundamentally different, starting with less frequent and less stringent conversion. A major factor associated with reluctance to convert to Reform Judaism is respect for the wishes and traditions of the non-Jewish parents. There is, however, little reported difference in the way Reform spouses who convert and those who do not participate in Jewish life after marriage. Many intermarried, unconverted Gentiles assume active positions in the temple and are usually admired by the Jewish members of the congregation.

Intermarriage and Marital Stability

As marriage with non-Jews gains in apparent acceptance as well as in frequency, the Jewish community must consider the stability of intermarriages themselves. Any marriage is a complex undertaking, fraught with the need for compromise and mutual understanding. Some experts argue that an intermarriage, particularly one not involving conversion, places an additional strain on the partners and increases the probability of either separation or divorce. Others suggest the reverse — persons entering intermarriage, they say, must have such a degree of love and understanding in order to overcome the obvious obstacles that the marriage may, as a result, be on an unusually sure footing.

No Canadian evidence exists on the stability and quality of intermarried relationships, but some American surveys provide useful insights.[15] In general, the divorce rate in the U.S. seems to be slightly higher for mixed marriages than for either in-marriages or intermarriages with conversion. Moreover, divorced Jews are more likely to intermarry in second marriages than in firsts. These findings suggest that as the divorce rate continues to rise among Jews, so will the remarriage rate, and by extension, so may the intermarriage rate. They do not explain, however, whether the slightly higher divorce rate among Jews in mixed marriages stems from the fact of intermarriage or from the individuals having characteristics such as a high degree of education and strong, conflicting professional commitments. The same sorts of factors are common among in-married Jews who divorce.

The U.S. surveys also gave surprising evidence of marital harmony in areas traditionally thought to be danger points for mixed marriages. Only 20 per cent of the respondents indicated any disharmony flowing from different religious backgrounds. Moreover, the spouses maintained high degrees of agreement in most decision-making, including on issues related to bringing up children. Partners in these mixed marriages also reported no significant changes in their contacts with parents, either before or after the marriage, a finding that probably reflects both the general acceptance of intermarriage and the fact that a split with parents may no longer weaken the bond of an intermarried couple. In short, the data suggested, though by no means proved, that the sources of marital strain in mixed marriages may not be linked to the religious difference.

Nevertheless, these survey responses should not disguise the fact, attested to by most intermarried couples, that intermarriage does affect daily life in both routine and serious ways. Social gatherings may become occasions for stares, puzzlement, and explanation. ("You don't look Jewish", "Johnson isn't a Jewish name, is it?", and so on). The children of intermarriages experience problems additional to those normal for growing youngsters, particularly if they have both Jewish and Gentile playmates. Jewish and Christian holidays, even if not observed by the intermarried couple, are occasions of potential discomfort. None of these situations may be significant in itself in undermining an intermarriage, but they do signal issues that must be resolved.

Finally, it must be stressed that the Canadian case is by no means a mirror of the American. Although the trend in Canada is towards increasing parental acceptance of intermarriage, the degree of acceptance is far lower in Canada than in the United States. The same factors that produce the lower rate of intermarriage in Canada (notably the larger immigrant proportion) make Canadian parents' acceptance of intermarriage far more problematic. In other words, in Canada at least, intermarriage is still likely to strain the relationship between Jewish parents and grown children.

Intermarriage and the Jewish Population

Although many other questions can be asked about the effects of intermarriage, for many people the most crucial are those that concern its effect on the survival of the community. How does intermarriage, with and without conversion, affect the next generation of Jews? How many offspring are lost to Judaism through intermarriage, and how many are recruited? Do intermarried Gentiles who declare a nominal tie with the Jewish community raise children who have a true Jewish commitment?

Since there have been no Canadian studies of the effects of intermarriage on Jewish children, one must turn again to American research.[16] This shows that the intermarried Gentiles who convert *do* have a more significant commitment to Judaism than those who do not. They manifest it not only in their attitudes about being Jewish but in their actions as parents. About 70 to 75 per cent of them provide their children with some Jewish education and join synagogues — rates equal to or higher than those for birthright Jews. Conversion does seem to make a difference.

Even some of the intermarried Gentiles who do not convert appear to make some contribution to the Jewish community. The impressions of Canadian rabbis on this point are substantiated by the sizable numbers of mixed-marriage couples who have given affirmative answers to a variety of U.S. survey questions about their own Jewish identity and the desired identity of their children. Roughly one-third of the couples in mixed marriages provided their children with some form of Jewish education, one-fifth were members of synagogues, and nearly 30 per cent expected their children to celebrate bar- or bat-mitzvahs. Given the historic pattern linking intermarriage with flight from Jewish affiliation, this sort of behaviour may seem strange, but there is no question that it exists.

Clearly, the Jewish community faces thorny problems in these areas. How is it to relate to nonconverts who express some clear form of attachment to the community? How should the children of such a marriage be treated, especially if the unconverted partner is the mother? Should one include such adults and children in any enumeration of the Jewish community? To the extent that Jews limit their count to "bona fide" Jews who meet the criteria of Orthodoxy, many "voluntary" Jews may well be excluded, leading to an underestimate of the effective Jewish population.

Conclusion

In brief, there are two ways of looking at Jewish intermarriage today. Some observers emphasize the optimistic side, noting the sizable numbers of conversions, the large numbers of voluntary affiliations, and the potential these phenomena have for adding to the Jewish population. They see intermarriage as producing additions and losses to the Jewish population in roughly equal proportions and believe the fertility rate is much more significant for future population size. The problems they note about intermarriage centre on the fact that the established Jewish community is ill-equipped to deal with the individuals involved in intermarriages and on the pressures in Orthodox and Conservative circles to hold to rigid definitions of who has membership in the Jewish community. Pessimistic observers, on the other hand, worry about both the quantitative and the qualitative impact of intermarriage and are not reassured by survey responses or periodic reports of pious converts and their valued contributions. They see intermarriage as part of a continuing process of assimilation and as a real threat to Jewish survival. A tolerant or permissive response, they fear, might eliminate the stigma from intermarriage, making it even more likely.

Both viewpoints have some value. Yet intermarriage is not likely to decrease noticeably in the near future, although increased efforts in the areas of education and raising Jewish consciousness among parents may have some preventive effect. If the Canadian Jewish community is truly concerned about losing members through intermarriage, it might be well advised to adopt a number of *post facto* strategies aimed at drawing intermarried couples closer to the community. It could promote conversion possibilities and even attempt to create bridge-building institutions for unconverted Gentile spouses. Certainly, converts must be made to feel fully welcome, and even "voluntary" Jews could be recognized as potential converts and as contributors to the growth and vitality of the community. The numbers who convert to Judaism after marriage offer support for such an approach.

In many ways, Jewish parents have forged their own response to intermarriage, generally one of grudging accommodation, while the organized community has hesitated. In times of decreasing numbers because of the declining fertility rate, an open-door policy, in which every potential Jew counts, may do justice to both the diverse nature of Canadian Jewry and the need to minimize the population loss.

Antisemitism: The Uneasy Calm

by Arnold Ages

Before exploring the nature and scope of antisemitism in Canada, it is helpful to consider the word itself. "Antisemitism" is the term traditionally used in English to denote insensate hatred of the Jewish people. It is often written "anti-Semitism". In this essay, however, I have chosen to use the lower case to avoid the inference that there is a "Semitism" to which Jew-haters are opposed. As Yehuda Bauer and others have pointed out, the word "anti-Semitism" was invented in the late nineteenth century by those who sought a scientific term to replace the rather pedestrian and incivil phrase "Jew-hatred".[1] In fact, scholarship knows no phenomenon called "Semitism". It is only acquainted with "Semitic", a linguistic family of which Hebrew and Arabic are members. The idea of some philosophical, religious, or racial aggregate called Semitism is an artifice concocted by mischievous minds.

The term "antisemitism" can have several nuances, and the differences among them must be clarified to understand the Canadian experience. Salo Baron, the historian laureate of the Jewish people, has defined antisemitism as the "dislike of the unlike".[2] Like all literary conceits, Baron's definition, however succinct, has an imprecision that requires amplification. It is possible, for example, to dislike Jews without incinerating them in concentration camps. In other words, there are different strains of what Maurice Samuels has called "the non-filterable virus".[3] In its most innocent form, antisemitism is a manifestation of the kind of ethnic prejudice that is widespread throughout the human race. In a particular individual, antipathy towards Jews can be a mild hostility resulting from an unfortunate contact with an unsympathetic Jewish merchant or simply a vague negativism imbibed from the font of anti-Jewish teachings transmitted by Christianity.

Both cases differ from diabolical antisemitism, which sees Jews not as human beings suffering from the foibles that characterize men and women in their weaknesses but as agents of an international conspiracy, as bacteriological pollutants allied with unnamed sinister forces in a campaign to dominate the world. The stock-in-trade of the purveyors of classical antisemitism everywhere in the world is to depict the Jews as a race conspiring at both ends of the political spectrum to gain control of the international markets and simultaneously to destroy existing governments. In some versions of this pathology, religious elements are important. There is stress on the "deicide" nature of the Jews, and descriptions of their current "plotting" to reverse the millenial triumph of Christianity. In other configurations, this form of antisemitism concentrates on the racial impurities of the Jews and warns against fraternization with them.[4]

All the variations of classical antisemitism make the Jew the object of fear, loathing, maniacal hatred, pathological odium — sentiments that go beyond the ordinary hostility one group of people often expresses towards another. The disease of antisemitism is irrational, and seeking its etiology is futile. In the twentieth century, Naziism took the virus, which had long caused a low-grade fever in the German consciousness, and injected it into the mainstream of political life. The result was the Holocaust.

The distinction between mild antisemitism and its more malignant expression is not a mere exercise in semantics but a differentiation that is germane to the Canadian experience. The antisemitism discernible in Canada, historically and today, belongs for the most part to the mild, incubation stage. Only for a brief time in the 1930s was there a lapse into the more virulent phase, occasioned by the spread of fascist ideology and the general economic and political turbulence of that period.

The Early Days

Until the late nineteenth century, the Jews of Canada were so few in number that they did not often come to public attention. Perhaps the best-known exception was Ezekiel Hart (1767–1843), whom the voters of Trois Rivières elected three times to the assembly of Lower Canada; Francophone members consistently prevented him from taking his seat by observing that as a Jew, he could not take the oath of office, which included the phrase "on the true faith of a Christian". Some historians explain even this apparently clear evidence of bigotry as the result of the rivalry between the contemporary English and French factions in Lower Canada rather than as antisemitism.[5]

Jewish immigration to Canada rose in the wake of the Czarist pogroms in 1881 and increased even more after the turn of the century. Jews soon established themselves in the major urban centres of Toronto, Montreal, and Winnipeg. Unlike their American counterparts, however, they never made up a very large percentage of the total Canadian population. In the late nineteenth century, they represented less than 1 per cent of the total; in the twentieth they have increased their proportion to slightly less than 1.5 per cent. The relative rarity of Jews, especially in Western Canada, permitted a congenial integration into and acceptance by the majority culture. A recent monograph depicted the history of Jewish settlement in British Columbia and the Yukon in roseate hues.[6] A similarly felicitous portrait of Jewish life in the West appeared in F.B. Maynard's *Raisins and Almonds*, an autobiographical account of a Jewish girl growing to maturity on the prairies.[7] Historical studies of Jewish farming communities in Saskatchewan indicate that, although the settlers had to suffer the rigours of prairie temperatures and the lack of amenities, they did not encounter the antisemitism that many had fled in Eastern Europe.

Most of the immigrants, however, settled in Ontario and Quebec, where the commercial and economic life of the country was centred. Beginning as peddlers and small entrepreuners, Jews in both provinces quickly moved up the economic ladder to become members of the bourgeoisie. Their rise was not without

intermittent difficulties, especially in Quebec, where they were
wedged between the numerically superior French Canadians and
the economically dominant English Canadians. For reasons of
commerce and culture, the Jews of Quebec tended, then as now,
to become Anglophones and hence to be identified with the
English faction. Some of the hostility the Québécois directed
against the Jewish community may, therefore, have come less
from traditional antisemitism than from resentment against Jews
as representatives of English society. (The phenomenon of Jews
being caught between two ethnic rivals is not unknown in Jewish
history.)

The 1930s and 1940s

Neither Quebec nor Ontario Jews, however, had to face organized
antisemitism of the malignant strain until the 1930s when Adrien
Arcand's populist political cadres began to whip up anti-Jewish
sentiments among the French Canadians. In her survey, *The
Swastika and the Maple Leaf*, Lita-Rose Betcherman has shown
how Arcand orchestrated a campaign of antisemitism through
public pronouncements and through the press.[8] He edited three
weekly newspapers, *Le Goglu*, *Le Miroir*, and *Le Chameau*, all of
which promoted French Canadian chauvinism and at the same
time indulged in anti-Jewish propaganda.

At first, Arcand translated his antipathy towards Jews into
an attempt to deny them minority status, arguing that Canada
had only two *bona fide* minorities: the English in Quebec and the
French in the other provinces. As his group gained popularity,
Arcand's antisemitism quickly passed from the primary to the secondary stage. His speeches became little more than harangues on
the Jewish problem. From both the speaker's platform and the
editorial page, he claimed that Jews had isolated themselves, were
materialistic, controlled the film and media empires, regarded
themselves as the chosen people, and promoted such perverse
notions as internationalism and liberalism. He also alleged that
they were the cause of the Bolshevik Revolution. Arcand filled his
three papers with vicious antisemitic articles culled from Nazi
sources and distributed by the Imperial Fascist League. One article

was a reprint of one of Alfred Rosenberg's libels, illustrated with ugly caricatures. In a scandalous essay entitled "The Drinkers of Blood", readers were asked to believe the "Israelites had butchered 40,000 Christians in less than five years in Russia".[9]

At one point Arcand effected a rapprochement with Nazi-minded groups in Ontario and other parts of Canada, although they never achieved the cohesiveness of the Quebec-based organization. This did not stop the demagogic imitator of der Führer from trying to spread his venom across Canada. In 1938, for example, he addressed a crowd at Toronto's Massey Hall on the evils of international Jewry.

In general, however, Ontario was spared the excesses of an Arcand-type movement, though the province did not offer its Jewish citizens as many possibilities for enjoying life as might have been expected in a democratic society. From the 1930s through the Second World War, Jews found it difficult to enter certain professions and to live where they wished. Summer resorts in the Muskoka region barred Jewish guests. Some hotels posted signs with the legend "Jews and Dogs Not Wanted". Jews could study law, medicine, and dentistry only on a *numerus clausus* basis, and many a worthy Jewish student had to seek his livelihood in other pursuits. At the University of Toronto School of Dentistry, a dexterity requirement was a favourite ploy for keeping Jewish students out; the small number who made it into the program often found themselves subjected to open abuse by anti-semitic professors. Graduates of the University of Toronto Medical School found that their prestigious diplomas could not obtain internships for them so an entire generation of Jewish medical students emigrated to the United States seeking hospital posts to hone their craft. Canada did not want them.[10]

This mild antisemitism may have disrupted families, but it did not destroy them. The same cannot be said, however, for the antisemitism that disposed Canadian government officials to prevent European Jewish refugees from coming to Canada.[11] In this regard, of course, Canada was not unique; the democracies in general turned a blind eye to Jewish requests for asylum from Hitler's territorial prison. Archival materials have now revealed the Canadian government's secret policy at that time; Mackenzie King's diaries show he entertained caricatured ideas about the Jewish people — ideas that were undoubtedly translated into policy. In a recent book, Emil Fackenheim, one of the few lucky German Jews to be admitted into Canada said, "Another democracy — my own Canada — pursued a stingy immigration policy, and while the policy itself was secret, it was no secret that antisemitism contributed to its stinginess." Fackenheim also reported that during the war itself, Jews serving in the Dutch Legion training in Canada requested that their families be offered asylum here until the war was over. He quoted a communication to the Dutch government from its minister in Ottawa:

> The chief criterion for admission to Canada is race. . . . It is a fact that Jews, having once obtained permission for their families to join them, if only temporarily, are exceedingly difficult to get rid of again.[12]

Although antisemitic impulses undoubtedly helped to determine Canada's policy towards Jewish refugees, no political party ever formally adopted such an animus. Even during the turbulent 1930s when Arcand was riding high in Quebec, the major parties maintained a distance from anti-Jewish machinations. Various political figures did, however, indulge from time to time in anti-semitic activities. Maurice Duplessis, the leader of the Union Nationale in Quebec, exploited the Jewish immigration issue in his drive towards political power, warning the Québécois that a large influx of Jews would upset the province's ethnic balance.

The closest that Canada ever came to a mainstream political movement with overtones of antisemitism was the early incarnation of the Social Credit party. In 1935, this evangelical and fundamentalist religious-political party gained power in Alberta. Fringe elements within it adopted a plank from the international antisemitic fraternity accusing Jews of being part of a worldwide conspiracy to manipulate and control the money markets. Norman Jacques, MP from Wetaskiwin, and John Blackmore, MP from Lethbridge, occasionally uttered anti-Jewish sentiments in public, expressing some of the extremist views of the Major Douglas school of Social Credit — a faction that fortunately never gained ascendancy in the movement. In the postwar years, too, party leader Solon Low was injudicious enough to link political Zionism and international finance in the manner of classical anti-semites. Towards the end of his career, however, Low reversed his position and became a warm supporter of Israel. The party has always been extremely sensitive to the charge that it harbours antisemitism within its philosophy and has gone out of its way to assuage the apprehensions of Jewish residents in those provinces where it has held power.[13]

After the Second World War

Attitudes towards immigration aside, the outbreak of the Second World War quickly put an end to the antisemitic rabble-rousing of the 1930s. Arcand was interned in Quebec, and pro-German and Nazi organizations were disbanded across the country.

During the first decade and a half after the war, the Jewish community of Canada enjoyed a period of economic prosperity, demographic growth, and general acceptance in the country's political and social infrastructures. Restrictive real estate covenants were quietly relaxed. Admission to professional schools came to take merit into account, and many Jewish students flocked to the institutions of higher learning. In politics and finance, Jews found increasingly congenial receptions; Toronto elected two Jewish mayors, and Ontario appointed a Jewish justice to its high court. The executive suite was slower to give Jews access to positions of responsibility, but during the 1970s, even this barrier began to be lifted. During the same decade, Bora Laskin, a Jew, was named chief justice of the Supreme Court of Canada.

Widespread knowledge of the horrors of the Holocaust made antisemitism unpopular, even in its milder forms, during the years immediately after the Second World War. This period of quiescence was not restricted to Canada; it was a universal reaction to a people's tragedy. By the 1960s, however, the quarantine appeared to have been lifted. A recrudescence of antisemitic activity appeared among certain fringe groups. Purveyors of classical antisemitic literature centred in Ontario, where the small town of Flesherton achieved the distinction of having a newspaper that dispensed crude anti-Jewish libels. Much of the slanderous printed material originated with Ron Gostick, who retailed the infamous "Protocols of Zion", probably the most scurrilous piece of literature ever directed against Jews. For a time Gostick attempted to gain a constituency among the right-wing political elements of Ontario, but he never succeeded in gaining more than marginal support for his views.[14]

The eruption of a neo-Nazi movement in Ontario in the early 1960s was more serious. Led by two youthful propagandists, David Stanley and John Beattie, the small group shocked the Toronto public by holding open-air meetings in a park in the centre of the city. Their Nazi regalia and inflammatory speeches were provocative in the extreme. The group, which was allied with similar organizations in the United States, attracted a great deal of attention, and its meetings were soon punctuated by scuffles and occasional fist fights. Jewish organizations, hamstrung by statutes guaranteeing free speech, were in a difficult situation. Finally a coalition of Holocaust survivors created the N3 Group (named after Newton's third law of motion, which states that every action produces an equal and opposite reaction). The members of this unofficial organization carried out a systematic campaign of harassment and physical confrontation during the neo-Nazi meetings. Their willingness to engage speakers and their supporters in combat eventually led the Toronto police department to ban the meetings. When David Stanley, one of the youthful leaders, recanted his position and joined the mainstream of Canadian life, this group disbanded; however, others, such as the Western Guard, have since become active in anti-Jewish expression.[15]

Meanwhile, the Canadian Jewish Congress had been urging the federal government to enact legislation against the spreading of hate directed at racial or religious groups. In response to this call, the Ministry of Justice decided in 1965 to appoint a seven-man committee to examine the hate-propaganda question. Debate on the resulting proposed legislation was extremely vigorous. Civil libertarians, including not a few Jews, spoke out against the bill on the grounds that it was an infringement of freedom of speech. After contentious discussion, Parliament passed the act in 1970, but not until 1978 was anyone prosecuted under it. Even then, the charge was against a person who had attempted to stir up hatred against French Canadians living in southwestern Ontario.

Any discussion of postwar antisemitism in Canada must explore the role traditional antisemitism has played in determining views of the state of Israel. It is, of course, absurd to suggest that all criticism of Israel should be equated with antisemitism, virulent or mild. Numerous political factors can be involved in forming an individual's or a government's stance on a political issue. For example, Lester Pearson, who was deeply involved in the United Nations' creation of Israel in 1948 and continued to play an active role in Middle Eastern affairs for many years, criticized Israel on a number of occasions when he felt that the policies of its government were short sighted. No one, however, ever suggested that Pearson was antisemitic.

It is equally absurd, however, to believe that purely political instincts have motivated all criticism of Israel. There is a point at which opposition to the Jewish state goes beyond simple political disapprobation and becomes identical to traditional antisemitism. In recent years, it has become fashionable for mischievous men to mask their hostility towards Jews with the guise of anti-Zionism. Drawing a distinction between the "bad" Zionists and the "good" Jews, they make all criticism of Israel and Zionism legitimate. This sort of anti-Zionism is merely recycled antisemitism and a particularly subtle form of attack upon the integrity of the Jewish people. In the hands of the unscrupulous, such anti-Zionism is a marvellous weapon with which to attack Jews with near impunity. Anyone who is challenged has merely to say, "You see, if you attack Israel, they call you antisemitic." However, many purveyors of anti-Zionist views are probably not even aware of the antisemitic resonances of their utterances. They may truly believe they are engaging in a purely political exchange.

An understanding of the phenomenon of the anti-Zionist facade is important to understanding the tensions that emerged between the Canadian Jewish community and certain critics of Israel in the wake of the June 1967 war. For several years, *The United Church Observer*, a semiofficial publication of the denomination, carried out a systematic campaign of vilification against Israel. Editorials and articles in the periodical represented the Jewish state not merely as a human institution, with all the weaknesses and deficiencies of that species, but as a cosmological principle of sin. Claiming to present the untold Arab version of the Middle East conflict, the journal apportioned all guilt for war and tragedy to Israel without the slightest consideration of any possible Arab culpability. The editor of the publication denied categorically that he was engaging in antisemitic stereotypes in his reporting, but many Jewish readers thought differently and called upon church officials to repudiate him.[16] At one point the B'nai B'rith in Toronto was sued for libel over its allegation that the *Observer* was printing antisemitic materials, but the case never reached the courts. Tensions ran high and were not lessened when a former moderator of the United Church of Canada wrote in the *Toronto Star* that Jews could cause antisemitism if they continued to attack those who spoke out against Israel, thereby inhibiting even Jewish protest against alleged antisemitism. During the height of the controversy, a Toronto rabbi wrote *Family Quarrel* in which he analyzed the confrontation between the United Church and the Jewish community and concluded that one might label the church's attitude as insensitivity but not as antisemitism.[17] But the book merely demonstrated that one Jewish observer felt it necessary to question the antisemitism that the majority of Jewish people perceived in the *Observer* and in various statements issued by the church's leaders.

Recent Incidents

In recent years, "insensitivity" has become a popular term for describing an animus directed against Jews; it is used especially in connection with Quebec, where the 1976 election of a Parti Québécois government signalled a progressive deterioration in the position of the Jews. The problem in Quebec seems to originate not in a specific antisemitism but in the traditional identification of the province's Jews with its English minority. On several occasions, however, prominent Québécois have engaged in a classic form of scapegoatism by attributing problems in the economic sector to specific Jewish individuals. Even more disquieting was the appearance of crude antisemitism, linking Zionism and racism as typical Jewish manifestations, in a political publication linked to the Parti Québécois. Government spokesmen, however, repudiated the articles when they were brought to their attention.[18]

The government has no control over the position taken by some of Quebec's radical labour chieftains, who have been the source of some of the most blatant antisemitic utterances heard in the province since the days of Arcand's fulminations. In particular, Michel Chartrand, former head of the Montreal section of the Confederation of National Trade Unions, has combined advocacy of the extremist PLO position with the secondary stage of antisemitism that construes Jews as agents of a sinister international conspiracy. The spectacle of Chartrand haranguing union colleagues about the iniquities of Jews is cause for concern.[19]

The Canadian Jewish community has also been concerned about the reluctance of the federal government to enact legislation forbidding compliance with the clearly antisemitic parts of Arab boycott practices. Such a statute is already operative in the United States, and the province of Ontario has passed similar legislation. But the Ottawa government, despite the energetic prodding of Herb Gray, MP for Windsor, and representatives of the Canadian Jewish Congress, has not acted on this matter.[20]

The refusal to enact such laws has had the effect of preventing Canadian Jews from participating in major industrial projects and represents a retrogressive step towards the primary antisemitism endemic in Ontario and Quebec in the 1930s. Informed Jewish spokesmen have lamented the government's lack of resolve on this question, pointing out the anomaly of permitting the Arabs to dictate not only the terms of their own boycott against Israel but the employment practices of Canadian firms doing business with the Middle East. The *Globe and Mail*, commenting on a speech by Sheikh Yamani of Saudi Arabia in the fall of 1978, called the boycott practices simple blackmail. Yet some Canadian companies, anxious to obtain lucrative contracts with Arab countries, have complied with them to the point of assuring their Arab interlocutors that no Jews occupy executive positions within the Canadian firms. Other Canadian companies have sought to evade the boycott restrictions by urging Jewish employees to list themselves as Protestants. For a short period in 1977, the Canadian high commissioner to Great Britain began issuing affidavits to Canadian businessmen validating their statements of religious persuasion (in other words, their non-Jewishness) so they could obtain visas for Saudi Arabia. Pressure from concerned Canadians forced the high commissioner to discontinue the practice.[21]

Conclusion

Despite such incidents, the experience of Canadian Jews, viewed from the broad perspective, has been a largely salutary one. The antisemitism with which the community has had to cope has been mostly of the less noxious variety, directed primarily against Jews in the social sector and in professional training. During the last two decades, even this form of bigotry has declined steadily.

Antisemitism of the more serious strain has, except for a period in the 1930s and 1940s, been peripheral to Canadian society. The swastika daubings of Jewish institutions in the early 1960s, the noisy demagoguery of Toronto neo-Nazis during the same period, the ugly sloganeering of members of the Western Guard in the same city, the willingness of the Canadian high commissioner to provide government authentication of statements of religious affiliation — all have given Canadian Jews cause for concern, but all have turned out to be transitory phenomena.

From the vantage point of Jewish history, the experience of Canadian Jews as they enter the 1980s is a happy one. Canada's multiethnic nature, its abundant natural resources, its relative economic and political stability, and its lack of external enemies are characteristics of nations generally tolerant of minorities. Jewish history, however, has seen such societies in the past and has also unfortunately seen them plunge into decline and chaos. One hopes fervently that this will not be so in the case of Canada.

Canadian Jewry and Foreign Policy in the Middle East

by Howard Stanislawski

The political awareness of the Canadian Jewish community has increased significantly in recent years. The causes include the increased participation by Jews at all levels of the political process, the growing effectiveness of the communication of Jewish concerns to the general public and the press, and the diversification of political choices through the rise of viable third parties. The greatest credit, however, must go to the increased willingness of the Jewish community to act forcefully in urging its policy requests through behind-the-scenes involvement, through aggressive public positions, and, above all, through organized lobbying.

Historically, the Jewish community has taken an active role in the functioning of the Canadian political system since Confederation. During the twentieth century, and even the late nineteenth, Jews served as mayors, members of provincial legislatures, and members of the federal parliament. In the major centres of Jewry — Montreal, Toronto, and Winnipeg — the concentration of Jews in particular neighbourhoods and many immigrants' tradition of progressive ideological fervour combined to create strong electoral bases for candidates, Jew or Gentile, who would ensure accommodation of Jewish needs and aspirations.

The highly organized infrastructure of the Jewish community also helped assure the presentation of its members' concerns to all levels of government. The Canadian Jewish Congress has had numerous contacts with and made representations to government since its inception in 1919. From the 1930s onwards, the issues in question were not only domestic but included foreign policy concerns, such as the federal government's immigration policies, its response to the Holocaust, and its policy on Middle East issues. Despite all this political activity, the Jewish community, like other ethnic groups in Canada, did not really make its presence felt in the corridors of power until the 1970s. The reasons were threefold, if interlocking, and are all connected with perceptions of interest-group activity — or lobbying, to use the common American term — in the Canadian political process.

First, although lobbying has long been going on in Canada, Canadian politics does not readily acknowledge its validity, especially in overt forms.[1] Activities specifically designed to influence decision-makers' policies are frowned upon; the very word "lobbying" is often perceived as pejorative, and a lobbyist is often seen as an individual trying to exercise less-than-legitimate influence on officials who embody Canada's true national interest. Of course, lobbyists for domestic and foreign groups are present in Ottawa, but there is no overt acknowledgement of their status.

Second, Canadian ethnic groups have rarely employed professional lobbyists. Rather, they work through two different levels of representatives. On one level, official delegates attempt to secure meetings with ministers of the Crown at which to make representations concerning a particular problem; such meetings normally include departmental officials as participants. The other customary level is unofficial; any available emissaries are sent to speak privately with the appropriate minister. Official representations are basically petitions addressed to the government, and influencing policy through them is often difficult indeed. Unofficial, quiet diplomacy sometimes works, but its very nature means that lack of success usually does not result in any overt expression of community disapproval.[2]

Canadian Jews' third problem with marshalling support also arose because they are an ethnic group. In Ottawa, the general representational function is most successfully fulfilled through various old-boy networks that cross government, business, and special-interest lines. But Canadian politics and business do not reflect the radical transformation of Canada from a basically English society with a major French-speaking component to a highly variegated, multicultural ethnic mosaic.[3] Therefore, many people continue to see the ethnic component in politics as a less-than-legitimate force intruding itself into the national interest.

For decades, the Canadian Jewish community accepted these three elements — the lack of legitimacy ascribed to overt lobbying, the absence of professional representation by ethnic groups, and the lack of legitimacy ascribed to ethnic interests — and the consequent circumscribing of overt Jewish political activity. The year 1967 was a watershed. As Canada joyously celebrated its centennial, Israel's very survival was placed in precarious balance. The events of May and the Six Day War of June galvanized Jewish communities around the world. Large numbers of Jews, even those who had felt assimilated into their general societies, lost their sense of security. Many of them expressed their profound concern not only through philanthropy but also by seeking political support for Israel from the countries in which they lived.

The Canadian Jewish community already had organizations that gave expression to community concerns, including support for the Jewish state. In particular, the Canadian Jewish Congress and the Zionist Organization of Canada expressed the political consensus of the Jewish community. Service organizations, such as B'nai Brith, representing scores of thousands of Canadian Jews, had also often sought direct channels to government before. Now current events gave impetus to collective concern about Israel. Demands for the creation of an infrastructure of sufficient institutional depth to reflect concerns became much stronger.

An effective organization was not created without difficulty, but by 1972, the Canada-Israel Committee (CIC), a joint creation of the Canadian Jewish Congress and the Zionist Organization of Canada, was operating. By 1973 it represented B'nai Brith as well. The birth of the CIC, based in Montreal under the directorship of Myer Bick, marked the beginning of a new phase in Canadian

Jewish institutional life. For the first time, the Jewish community had created a professional organization to present its interests, specifically those related to Canada-Israel public affairs, to the Canadian government. Economic and political concerns were now to be set forth by professional lobbyists. In undertaking an initiative in professional issue-advocacy in Ottawa, the representative organizations of the Jewish community were embarking on a new, uncharted, and somewhat perilous course. But in doing so, they were acknowledging what labour unions, banks, the business community, and native-rights groups had already acknowledged: the important role interest groups can play in Canadian politics.

A detailed examination of one foreign policy issue — the Canadian government's response to the Arab economic boycott of Israel — illustrates the relation between the activities of the organized Jewish community and the making of Canadian foreign policy.

The Quest for Antiboycott Legislation

Since the Yom Kippur War, the Arab boycott question has been one of the most prominent issues involving interaction between the Jewish community and the Canadian government. Moreover, it is a good example of that community's new, activist approach to politics. It also illustrates recent emphasis on public-information activities, since the problem's relative complexity required the continuing involvement of a major Jewish institution to educate government leaders, the Jewish community, and the public at large.

The Boycott: History and System

The Arab boycott originated in Palestine during the British Mandate; Arabs resident there attempted to damage the economic viability of the developing Jewish community by refusing to buy or deal with goods manufactured by Jews or to sell land to them. After the establishment of the state of Israel in 1948, the boycotting groups, which by now included all members of the Arab

League, refused to buy or deal with any goods or services emanating from Israel, notwithstanding their source therein. Within a few years, the Arabs elaborated a complex set of rules, regulations, and blacklists geared to expanding their direct boycott into one that enlisted foreign parties in economic warfare.

The boycott system became a significant policy concern in Canada after 1973. The Arab oil embargo of 1973/74 dramatically illustrated the dependence of a number of Western states on Middle East oil supplies. Moreover, the quintupling of oil prices provided many Arab states with great financial resources, opening up that area of the world to Western-produced, technologically advanced goods and services. The demand for oil and the quest for new markets for the West enabled the Arab states to intensify their attempt to destroy Israel economically. In the post-1973 period, forced compliance with the discriminatory restrictions of the boycott became an important mechanism for intensified political warfare launched against Israel.

The mechanisms of the Arab boycott are complex. What is important to understand here is that it operates on several levels:

1. The *primary boycott* is a direct boycott of Israel by Arab states; the latter refuse to do business with the Jewish state or its inhabitants. Canada is not involved in this boycott and has no role to play in it.

2. The *secondary boycott* is an attempt by Arab states, firms, and individuals to pressure firms of other countries (including Canada) to refrain from dealing with Israel. Doing so is a condition of trade with Arab states, firms, or individuals. Thus, the Arabs attempt to compel the creation of a Canadian boycott against a country with which Canada has friendly relations.

3. The *tertiary boycott* is an attempt to prevent firms of other countries (including Canada) from dealing with firms (of their own or other noninvolved countries) that have trade relationships with Israel. Ending such dealings is a condition of doing business with Arab states, firms, or individuals.

The secondary and tertiary boycotts constitute extraterritorial application of Arab laws and regulations and a direct interference in the economic affairs of Canada. They require Canadians to sign clauses in contracts that are overtly discriminatory against Jews (whom the boycotters refer to euphemistically as "Zionists") or that require Canadians to commit themselves to refrain from engaging in any significant commercial activities with Israel.

U.S. and Canadian Positions on Boycotts

In 1973, the North American Jewish community became seriously concerned about the implementation of secondary and tertiary clauses. By 1974, the CIC began to include analyses of the boycott in its briefs to the secretary of state for external affairs.

The Canadian situation was quite different from that of the United States, where general antiboycott policies had already been developed. The Export Administration Act of 1969 had declared American compliance with secondary and tertiary aspects of any international boycott to be against government policy and established a mechanism through which U.S. firms were supposed to report their experiences with boycott clauses. These provisions were haphazardly applied, but they did exist in 1975 when American Jewish organizations began to pressure federal and state representatives to enact effective antiboycott legislation. That year New York state adopted the first new U.S. antiboycott statute, while several federal congressional committees began investigations into the boycott's national applications.

Meanwhile, President Ford ordered the federal reporting provisions tightened. One year later the now-stringent reporting mechanism revealed that from 1 October 1975 to 1 October 1976, 3,477 U.S. exporters, banks, freight forwarders, insurers, and carriers had received 169,710 boycott-related requests in connection with 97,491 transactions with a total value of $7.7 billion. Comprehensive antiboycott legislation did not yet exist, and the firms involved indicated they had complied with the requests in over 90 per cent of the cases reported.[4] The release of these startling statistics fanned federal and state legislative investigations and led, by mid-1977, to the passage of thirteen state antiboycott statutes and two major federal laws, the Tax Reform Act of 1976 and the Export Administration Act of 1977.[5] Jewish organizations played a major role in the investigative and legislative process.

In stark contrast to this U.S. activity was the lack of any official investigation of the question by the Canadian government and the seeming reluctance of its politicians and bureaucrats to undertake any actions that might affect Canadian trade with the Middle East.[6] The achievements of the Canadian Jewish community's representatives, therefore, though they sometimes appeared to be modest, were actually accomplished in the face of very serious governmental and bureaucratic resistance.[7]

Pressure and Research Begins

The first public political mention of the boycott question in Canada took place in April 1975, when Minister of Consumer and Corporate Affairs Herb Gray revealed that the federal government's Export Development Corporation had been providing export insurance financing for a number of Canadian firms' transactions with Arab countries, although it knew that the contracts involved included terms in compliance with the Arab boycott. In response to Gray's revelations, Prime Minister Trudeau told the House of Commons on 8 May 1975, "I think it is sufficient to say that this type of practice is alien to everything the government stands for and indeed to what in general, Canadian ethics stand for." Gray's revelation and Trudeau's statement of federal principle were not translated into any concrete legislative action. They did, however, increase public awareness of the issue and heighten concern in the Jewish community.

In the autumn of 1975, the CIC expanded its operations by opening an Ottawa office; it was the first time any national Jewish organization had had professional lobbyists in the nation's capital. About the same time, a number of incidents occurred, most notably in Ontario, in which government leaders acknowledged that Arab financial interests had brought anti-Jewish pressures to bear on them. Ontario Treasurer Darcy

McKeough disclosed in November 1975 that his government had been asked to exclude Jewish underwriters from bond issues for both Ontario Hydro and the province. At an October meeting with Allan MacEachen, the secretary of state for external affairs, the CIC made representations regarding the Arab boycott and the need to deal with its discriminatory impact in Canada.

In early 1976, the CIC decided the boycott merited both detailed research and a high profile. It compiled extensive information on the question, then prepared a special publication entitled "The Arab Boycott: Implications for Canada" for distribution at a special symposium on the boycott during the CIC's annual conference in Ottawa in late April. At a CIC meeting with MacEachen in May, the issue was a major topic for discussion.

The results of public education became apparent throughout the spring and summer. Newspaper reports featured boycott stories more prominently than before; political leaders became more aware of the question. The opposition parties began to use the information now available; they assailed the Liberal federal government for its inaction, called for comprehensive antiboycott legislation, and suggested that the civil service was eager to avoid any action on the issue. In the summer of 1976, the Cotler Commission, a blue-ribbon citizen's panel chaired by Irwin Cotler of McGill University's Faculty of Law, began an investigation into the boycott under the auspices of the Centre for Law and Public Policy. While Professor Cotler's investigation was under way, the CIC continued its own research and information distribution.

In early August, the *Globe and Mail* revealed that the Canadian high commission in London had been authenticating signatures on the certificates of religious affiliation required by Saudi Arabia of Canadians for entry visas to that state. Both Jews and non-Jews, including the editorial writers of major Canadian newspapers, protested the Canadian government's willingness to help prove that certain Canadians were not Jewish. The Department of External Affairs first argued that it was only authenticating signatures and not the documents upon which these signatures were located, but it finally agreed to provide no more authentications.[8] Such discriminatory activity could not be defended; nonetheless, External Affairs did not issue administrative guidelines implementing this change until 11 May, 1977.

Meanwhile, in late September 1976, newly appointed External Affairs Minister Don Jamieson referred to the Arab boycott as "repugnant" and "unacceptable" during a formal visit to Ottawa by Israeli Foreign Minister Yigal Allon. After this indication that significant federal action might soon be undertaken, the CIC met with Jamieson in early October. One full hour of the two-hour discussion was devoted to an examination of the boycott in great detail, and the minister indicated his determination to deal with the question quickly and effectively.

The Promise of a Policy

On 21 October 1976, Jamieson presented the House of Commons with the government's first policy statement on the Arab boycott. The two-part program avoided antiboycott legislation but included denial of government support or facilities, including the services of trade commissions abroad, financing, and market information, to Canadian firms for transactions in which they had accepted certain types of boycott clauses. A compulsory, comprehensive reporting mechanism was also to be established. According to Jamieson, all Canadian firms were to be required to report on their contacts with the boycott and boycott clauses; the government would then make these reports of compliance public.

Although this policy fell significantly short of the hoped-for antiboycott legislation, the CIC responded with a statement welcoming the move as an important first step along the road to dealing effectively with the problem. MPs Claude Wagner and T.C. Douglas, speaking for the Conservatives and the New Democrats respectively, welcomed the federal policy but pointed out its limited coverage and the fact that they felt it long overdue. Herb Gray also welcomed its introduction but noted its restricted application and the absence of any date for its implementation.

The lack of an effective date was unusual in instituting policy in a new area, and it proved to be a problem. Although the minister for external affairs had announced the program, it was left to the Department of Industry, Trade and Commerce for implementation. And that department did not act quickly.

On 13 January 1977, before the new policy was implemented, the Cotler Commission released its report at a press conference in Ottawa. Filled with new documentation of the incidence of the boycott in Canada, the report revealed a pattern of widespread Canadian compliance and complicity with the Arabs in both the private and public sectors. The ninety-two page document detailed the ways in which private firms, banks, boards of trade, and government corporations and agencies had been participating in both the restrictive trade and religious discrimination aspects of the boycott. It called for strong federal legislation and administrative directives to prevent the continued application of the boycott in Canada. The media gave the Cotler Commission report heavy coverage and favourable treatment. National radio and TV newscasts led with the story of public and private bodies' scandalous behaviour. Newspapers were unanimous in calling for comprehensive federal antiboycott legislation.[9]

On 21 January 1977, however, the Department of Industry, Trade, and Commerce finally issued its guidelines implementing the October policy statement and substantially reduced the latter's potential effectiveness. The reporting mechanism was scrapped, and certain boycott-related contract provisions were listed as acceptable and, therefore, not leading to any loss of government support.[10] The CIC and other groups and individuals protested vigorously, then awaited the department's semiannual reports that would detail the government's experience with implementation of the policy. (Meanwhile, in May 1977, Minister of Industry, Trade, and Commerce Jean Chrétien confirmed the very limited nature of the government's policy in a speech to the CIC's annual conference in Ottawa.)

It was the timing and content of these reports that gave the most substantial impetus to protests against the government's policy. The first report, due in July 1977, did not appear until February 1978; the second, due in January 1978, was released in May 1978. Each successive report showed that the government had eroded more and more of its limited policy, revised the terms and definitions of that policy, and even permitted the acceptance of some extreme tertiary clauses in contracts that received government support. Each time department officials had discovered that a company had signed a clause contravening the policy, they had either changed the policy to eliminate the contravention or ignored it. Each time a company should have been named in the report as having contravened the policy, they had found an excuse not to include the name and thereby release it to the public.[11]

Opposition party spokesmen and Jewish community leaders became increasingly frustrated by and angry with this clear policy erosion. Editorials criticized the government for having a scandalously weak antiboycott policy. With the release of the second report in May 1978, Jewish community frustration gave way to rage.[12] During the first week of June, a CIC press conference detailed the many problems with the government's policy and announced a national educational campaign on the boycott issue. The opposition parties criticized the government vigorously. Various non-Jewish organizations, from the Canadian Labour Congress to the Canadian Association of Statutory Human Rights Agencies (which represents all eleven Canadian human rights commissions), enunciated public positions supporting comprehensive antiboycott legislation.

The Ontario Legislature Acts

Meanwhile, other levels of government had begun to act on the question. In the Ontario legislature, MPP Larry Grossman, then parliamentary assistant to Attorney-General Roy McMurtry, had introduced a private member's bill to outlaw Arab boycott practices in May 1977. An election campaign followed almost immediately, and all three party leaders — Conservative William Davis, Liberal Stuart Smith, and New Democrat Stephen Lewis — took strong antiboycott positions, promising to introduce strong preventive legislation into the provincial parliament.

The electorate returned a Tory minority government, and in December 1977, Premier Davis tabled "An Act to Prohibit Discrimination in Business Relationships" for first reading. After some revisions to clarify the bill's intent, the government reintroduced it in early 1978 and gave it second reading in June. The legislature's Standing Committee on the Administration of Justice held two weeks of detailed hearings on the proposal in September, and on 9 November 1978, Bill 112 received royal assent and became law. A milestone in the history of the boycott question in Canada, the statute prohibited the acceptance of secondary or tertiary boycott clauses by any company in Ontario.

Complete cooperation within and between all Jewish organizations marked the entire process of passing Bill 112. Many Jewish organizations, including the Canada-Israel Committee, Canadian Jewish Congress, B'nai Brith, and the Jewish War Veterans of Canada, presented briefs to and testified before the Justice Committee hearings on it. In the process, the province's Jewish community made its views known to all the political parties, and the bill received the support from all parties at all stages of its parliamentary progress. With its passage, the Davis government fulfilled its campaign pledges, and on this issue the Tories received the warmest possible approval of the Jewish community.

In the Manitoba legislature, in the spring of 1978, Liberal MLA Lloyd Axworthy introduced a private member's bill aimed at outlawing boycott compliance in that province. The bill was never considered fully.

The Federal Government Starts to Move

The success of the PC government's move in Ontario and the support for antiboycott legislation in labour and human rights circles no doubt contributed to the federal government's perception that its floundering boycott policy required alterations quickly. During the summer of 1978, federal Liberals consulted extensively with each other and contacted Jewish leaders familiar with the boycott question. Although bureaucratic pressure to avoid extensive tightening of the policy continued, and although Minister of

Industry, Trade, and Commerce Jack Horner demonstrated his fundamental opposition to any significant antiboycott action, the cabinet decided to revise its position on the question.[13]

On 21 August, Minister of National Defence Barney Danson and Secretary of State John Roberts held a press conference in Toronto at which they announced two significant changes to the government's program. The first involved the tightening of existing guidelines, effective 1 October, by denying government assistance to contracts that included two types of boycott clauses previously regarded as acceptable. The other was a commitment to pass legislation establishing a compulsory, comprehensive reporting system — in other words, to implement part of what the government had stated as policy nearly two years earlier.

The CIC responded with a statement welcoming the changes as significant additions to the existing policy. (This statement reflected Jewish organizations' consensus approach to a complex problem that the government had clearly begun to perceive as one that could significantly affect a federal election, then thought to be only months away.) The opposition parties, however, responded critically, pointing out that what the government had proposed was not antiboycott legislation but merely reporting legislation. Even if it were passed, they argued, companies would still be free to sign whatever boycott clauses they chose to accept.

As the boycott question became more and more politically partisan, the Jewish community prepared to see the Liberal government meet its essentially simple commitment to legislate a reporting mechanism. But although the House of Commons reconvened in October, Bill C-32 was not tabled for first reading until mid-December 1978, shortly before the Christmas recess. It was not called for second reading or referred to any committee for study, although the opposition parties periodically took the floor to ask the government about its plans.

In response to repeated CIC representations, the government finally indicated in February 1979 that it would bring Bill C-32 back if all other parties agreed to a one-day debate for passage of the bill through all stages. The CIC communicated with the PC and NDP house leaders, who agreed to this procedure and indicated that they would so inform House Leader Allan MacEachen, if he asked them. For several weeks, he did not raise the issue.

Finally, Horner reopened the entire boycott controversy by demonstrating his opposition to his own government's policy in repeated public references to alleged losses of trade occasioned by Ontario's antiboycott law.[14] Stung by the controversy, the government finally requested and received agreement to a one-day debate from the opposition leaders. On 22 March, from the floor of the House of Commons, MacEachen sought to hold that debate immediately. He could not, however, achieve the required unanimous consent of the members despite the party leaders' agreement; independent Leonard Jones (of Moncton, New Brunswick) and dissident Tory William Skoreyko (of Alberta) cast negative votes. The Conservatives suggested a one-day debate for 27 March. Without indicating express agreement but apparently accepting the notion, MacEachen moved on to other business.

On the evening of 26 March, however, Prime Minister Trudeau requested the dissolution of the Commons, calling an election for 22 May. Bill C-32, the cornerstone of the Liberal government's revised antiboycott policy, died on the order paper on the eve of its expected passage.

Campaign Promises

During the election campaign of April and May 1979, the Arab boycott issue received frequent mention, especially in Metropolitan Toronto. Horner's statements of mid-March received considerable censure and opposition. All three major parties forcefully restated their positions: the Liberals promised to reintroduce Bill C-32, while the Progressive Conservatives and New Democrats repeated their commitments to enact comprehensive antiboycott legislation along the lines of the Ontario and U.S. statutes. The Tories won the election, and analyses of voting patterns suggested the boycott issue may have played a role in the defeat of Liberal candidates by Conservative opponents in some central Metro Toronto constituencies with substantial numbers of Jewish voters.

Throughout the PC government's brief reign — it was to be defeated by a nonconfidence vote in the Commons in December 1979 — it was continually assailed for another campaign commitment: to move Canada's embassy in Israel from Tel Aviv to Jerusalem. Arab states, many Canadian corporations, and the opposition parties fought to prevent implementation of this promise, arguing that such a move would have dire economic consequences for Canada and would, in addition, damage the process of searching for peace in the Middle East. Phantom threats of grossly exaggerated consequences and fears about losing lucrative Arab markets built into a campaign against the embassy move.[15]

In the wake of this controversy, the government did nothing to implement its other promise of enacting comprehensive antiboycott legislation. Seeking to defuse the Jerusalem issue, Prime Minister Joe Clark appointed Robert Stanfield, the former Progressive Conservative Party leader, as a special representative of the government to examine the whole range of Canada–Middle East relations. His interim report, filed in October 1979, called for abandoning the commitment to move the embassy, and his final report, in February 1980, advised against antiboycott legislation.

Meanwhile, the government fell, and during the ensuing campaign, Liberal spokesmen asserted that their party, if elected, would reintroduce and enact Bill C-32. But soon after the Liberal victory of February 1980, it became clear that antiboycott legislation was not a policy priority for the Trudeau government. Herb Gray, the Liberals' foremost antiboycott activist, was made minister of industry, trade, and commerce and thus responsible for the government's antiboycott policy and program. Yet more pressing economic and constitutional issues preoccupied the new government. During its first year in power, it did nothing with respect to the boycott question.

An Evaluation

The Arab boycott issue provides a clear context within which to evaluate the relationship of the Jewish community and the federal government. Since antiboycott legislation still does not exist in

Canada at the national level, the Jewish community's organized attempt to obtain it might be regarded as a failure. It is more instructive, however, to what it did accomplish and to consider what this accomplishment means for future attempts by Jews (and perhaps other minority groups) to influence federal policies, especially those with international implications.

In making this evaluation, it is important to remember that the professional foreign policy elite of Canada has had very few points of contact with the general public. Unlike other government departments, which have long seen themselves as both representing and directly responsible to the public, the foreign service officers of the Department of External Affairs have tended to see their own policy views as embodying Canada's national interest; they have not developed an apparatus for seeking public opinion.[16] In large measure, the overwhelming apathy of Canadians in foreign affairs has sustained this exclusivist perspective.

To begin with, then, Canadian Jews' determined and educated interest in the Middle East distinguished that community from most other segments of Canadian society. Moreover, in the eyes of the foreign policy elite, the Jewish community's development of coordinated policy perspectives and a professional operation to promote them elevated Jewish activism from an uninformed, bothersome, and less-than-legitimate ethnic interest to a highly informed, bothersome, and somewhat less-than-legitimate ethnic interest. That simple transformation forced department officials to reappraise the manner in which they responded to the Jewish community and its interest in Middle East policy-making.

As the bureaucracy began to receive Jewish community interventions with greater respect, the political activities and involvements of Canadian Jews and Canadian Jewish leaders made certain that it regarded those interventions as often supported by considerable political authority. And as Jewish access to political leadership expanded as a result of developing political activism, the responsiveness of the foreign policy elite had to increase. The Department of External Affairs recognized that informed, sophisticated, and politically active Canadian Jews would monitor its actions regularly and would not hesitate to have recourse to political leaders if they perceived problems in Middle East policy as originating in the bureaucracy.

The expertise developed by Jewish organizations, the articulate nature of their representations, the existence of a sound Jewish electoral base, the intensive involvement of Jews at all levels of the political process, and the willingness of Jewish leaders to voice their policy interests to both the bureaucracy and the political leadership all worked to increase both Jewish awareness of foreign policy and the impact of the Jewish community on its formulation. In responding to the increased level of interest and activity of the Jewish community, the Canadian political system affirmed its versatility, its democracy, and its inherent sense of responsibility to its constituents. And the democratization of the Canadian foreign policy process is both a process and a goal that can only make that crucial sector more effective, more honest, and more reflective of the concerns of all Canadians.

The Jews of Quebec and "Le Fait Français"

*by Harold M. Waller and
Morton Weinfeld*

"The Jewish Question" is an overriding concern today for
Quebec's approximately 115,000 Jews. Essentially, the question is
how the Jewish community should respond, collectively and individually, to *le fait français*, to the new "French fact". What is the
Jews' best reaction to the new reality in Quebec, to the resurgence
of Québécois power that was dramatically accelerated by the 1976
election of a Parti Québécois (PQ) provincial government and its
reelection in 1981?

From the outside, the question may appear to be one of
language — and perhaps a bit of politics. And both language and
politics are important factors in the situation and will continue to
be vital components of whatever resolution evolves. What is less
easy to see is that the Jews of Montreal are now having to face
fundamental questions of personal and communal reactions to a
larger society that has changed radically in the last twenty years.

Even the chief players in this drama are difficult to identify
from newspaper headlines or catch phrases. Speaking of "the Jews
of Quebec" blurs an important distinction. Almost all (98 per cent)
of Quebec's Jews live in or near Montreal, and their loyalties,

---

Sections of this essay were adapted from Harold M. Waller, "Montreal Jews
Face the Challenge of Quebec Nationalism", *Analysis*, no. 65 (September
1978), published by the Institute for Policy Planning and Research of the Synagogue Council of America.

which are strong, are to that city, rather than to the province. Yet because of its cosmopolitan nature and heterogeneous population, Montreal has long been the least typical area in Quebec.

It is nearly as confusing to speak of "the problem of the PQ" or "the separatist threat". The present situation did not spring up on the evening of the first PQ victory or even arise only as that party gained strength in the preceding years. Although Jewish fears have undoubtedly been magnified by some of the PQ government's actions, as well as by its pursuit of sovereignty for Quebec, unease over Québécois nationalism dates from the 1960s and the Quiet Revolution of the province's Francophone majority.

Historical Background

It is impossible to understand today's question without understanding its historical background. The roots of the Jews in Montreal run deep. Their first congregation, that of the Spanish and Portuguese Jews, established a synagogue (Shearith Israel) over two centuries ago, in 1768. Gradually, German Jews joined them, although the community grew slowly; according to Canadian census records, an estimated fifty Jews lived in Montreal by 1831 and 1,000 by 1881. Rapid growth began at the end of the last century with the influx of Eastern European immigrants fleeing anti-Semitism. By 1901, the Jewish population had jumped to almost 7,000; by 1921, continued immigration and a high fertility rate had brought the number to 46,000, an almost sevenfold increase. Since then, the rate of growth has been more modest, but sizable; according to the 1971 census, 109,480 Montrealers defined themselves as Jews-by-religion — about 4 per cent of the metropolitan population. In terms of ethnic origin, Jews accounted for roughly 11 per cent of the city's non-French population and nearly 18 per cent of those whose background was neither English nor French.

The character of Jewish life in Montreal has been shaped by its waves of immigration. The present community absorbed a relatively large number of survivors of the Holocaust, European Ashkenazim like most of the receiving group. The most recent arrivals have been Sephardim from North Africa, who have created a large Francophone minority within the Jewish community. These two components of Montreal Jewry make the city's Jewish community unique in North America, and the Francophone presence has produced internal strains not unlike the tensions at the turn of the century in the United States between the established German Jews and the immigrants from Eastern Europe.[1]

The language of the recent North African immigrants is important in context. Historically, all the other Jews who have settled in Montreal have oriented themselves towards the Anglophone community for several reasons. First, Jews, like many other immigrants, perceived Quebec as part of North America, a continent whose language was English. Their friends and relatives in other cities were learning English, and it seemed natural to follow suit, even in a city whose host majority was Francophone. Furthermore, although the Anglophones were a minority in Montreal by the time of the large-scale immigrations, they were economically dominant. Newly arrived Jews quickly realized that, in Quebec as in the rest of North America, English was essential for advancement in business and the professions.

The main reason, however, for the Montreal Jews' identification with the Anglophone community was the Quebec school system. All the province's public school boards were (and still are) established on a religious basis; Catholic children attended Catholic schools, non-Catholic children — Protestant or not — attended Protestant schools. Because of the province's historical association between language and religion, the language of instruction in most of the Catholic schools was French and in nearly all the Protestant schools, English. Hence, until very recently, Jewish children were schooled in English.

All these factors encouraged the Jewish community to adopt English. In the 1971 census, 77 per cent of Montreal Jews listed English as the language most often spoken at home (10 per cent listed French, 7 percent Yiddish, and 6 per cent "other"). Among Canadian-born Jews, 93 per cent said they spoke English at home. Their language of work was also generally English.

This English-speaking Jewish community never integrated with the majority Québécois. Language and culture were the main barriers; religion and ethnicity were important, too. Although Jews became active in various aspects of the city's political, legal, cultural, educational, social, and economic life, they always participated as Jews or Anglophones — as outsiders.

In fact, one can speak of a "Jewish solitude" in Montreal, for its Jewry has never really integrated with the English community either. The city's Jews, like its Protestants and Catholics, have developed their own organizational infrastructure of social, cultural, and welfare services. Even more significant is the high degree of social segregation common for Jews in their private lives. In a recent survey of Montreal Jewish heads of households, over 87 per cent indicated that all or most of their friends were Jewish, 53 per cent that all or most of their neighbours were Jewish, 35 per cent that all or most of their business associates were Jewish.[2]

Such a high degree of communal segregation has resulted from many factors. Actual and perceived anti-Semitism of both French and English has played a role. During the 1930s Jews were inviting targets for French prejudices because they were connected with the English community in language, schooling, and commerce. Strong anti-Semitic elements could be detected in such French Canadian movements as Achat Chez Nous, Jeune-Canada, and L'Action Nationale. In their publications and speeches, these nationalistic groups frequently mentioned themes such as the international conspiracy of Jews, the Jews' usurpation of the legitimate birthright of young Québécois, and economic pressure resulting from unethical competition.[3] At the same time, Jews were as likely to encounter anti-Semitism from the province's Anglo-Saxon elite as from French Canadians. Jews were often excluded from senior positions in dominant corporations, prevented from attaining prominence in social institutions, and denied access to elitist private clubs.

Most, if not all, of this discrimination has disappeared today, yet the memories linger, playing a part in encouraging Jews to keep to themselves. Moreover, the role of voluntary preference, in the past and in the present, cannot be ruled out, especially in a Jewish community as heavily immigrant as Montreal's. Neither can the bonds of Yiddish language and culture. Moreover, the role of the Jewish religion should not be overlooked. Particularly among the Orthodox, religious requirements, such as the dietary laws, the avoidance of travel and work on the Sabbath, and the proscription of intermarriage, have reinforced Jewish isolation.

It would not, however, be fair to characterize Montreal Jews as living in a complete ghetto. To some degree, they have inter-acted for many decades with the English and other Anglophones, with whom they share language, public education, and professional, commercial, and cultural interests. At times they have joined with other minority ethnic groups on matters of common concern, such as civil liberties. They have also interacted with the French, whom they have viewed in past decades as fellow sufferers from snobbish Anglo-Saxon discrimination. Another bond is the empathy many Montreal Jews have felt with the French struggle for survival as a cultural minority in Canada. The concern for language, cultural renewal, and identity strikes a responsive chord in many Jews committed to their own collective survival. Perhaps reflecting this sympathy as well as the economic realities of a Francophone market, significant numbers of Montreal Jews have learned French as well as English. A decade ago, the 1971 census showed a bilingual rate of 44 per cent, a rate topped by no other ethnic group classified and equalled only by the Italians. (In comparison, members of the French ethnic group displayed only 38 per cent bilingualism and the English 32 per cent.)

Before the PQ Victory of 1976

By the mid-1970s, Montreal Jews found themselves in a peculiar but not alarming situation. Over decades — and in many cases, generations — they had built themselves a good life. They were members of Canada's oldest, most populous, and perhaps most organized Jewish community. They lived in what many people considered North America's most cosmopolitan and exciting city, one that tends to evoke passionate attachments from its residents.

In many ways, the Quiet Revolution — the modernization of French social, political, cultural and economic life in Quebec beginning in the 1960s — had added to the quality of life in Montreal. Still, many Jews realized that a result of these trends was the inevitable dominance of French in most areas of commercial and public life. The high bilingual rates shown by the 1971 census may have reflected this understanding of reality, as may the relative lack of Jewish protest to such mid-1970s innovations as requiring proficiency in French for obtaining various professional licences. They did not even react as strongly as most other non-Francophones to the 1974 passage of Bill 22, a measure designed to limit access to English-language public schools.

Thus, Jews were relatively happy with their lot in Quebec in the mid-1970s and saw no reason to increase their traditionally low visibility in the political realm. Some were active — one, Dr. Victor Goldbloom, was a member of Robert Bourassa's Liberal cabinet — but most were content to ignore provincial politics.

In their own eyes and everyone else's, however, they were identified with the Liberal party, both provincially and federally (though it had been a Union Nationale government with which they had negotiated the first agreement for public funding of Jewish day schools during the late 1960s). Thus, although few Jews expected the PQ victory of 1976, many did see the preceding election as something of a puzzle. On the one hand, most Jews were used to voting Liberal; their leaders had reasonably good channels of communication with the provincial Liberal party; as staunch federalists, they were unalterably opposed to the separatist stand of the PQ. Moreover, the PQ's platform included abolishing grants to all private schools. On the other hand, Jews were by no means satisfied with all the policies or the performance of the outgoing Liberal government of Premier Bourassa.

Consequently, although neither of the other provincial parties made the kind of appeal that would normally attract Jews, some individuals began discussing the protest option of voting for the Union Nationale, which had promised to repeal Bill 22. The leaders of Montreal Jewry did not agree, for they feared a split in the federalist vote. Clearly, they thought that too many votes for the other "federalist" party might enable the Parti Québécois to win a majority of seats without a majority of the vote. Thus, while some in the organized Italian, Greek, and other immigrant communities openly attacked the Liberals and praised the Union Nationale position, no public political expression ever emerged from the organized Jewish community.

Soon after preelection polls revealed the PQ lead, however, an advertisement appeared in Montreal newspapers on behalf of Goldbloom, who was running in the heavily Jewish district of D'Arcy McGee. The ad was a private statement, but it was signed by fifty prominent English and French Quebecers, including Charles Bronfman, lay leader and philanthropic patron of the Montreal Jewish community, and other well-known Jewish professional and lay leaders. Though the names appeared without affiliations, the ad gave many informed Montreal Jews the impression that it was a direct plea from the Jewish community leadership to support the Liberal party.

It is not known if any pressures or inducements prompted the ad. Neither is it known if similar forces kept Jewish communal leaders relatively silent on the issue of Bill 22. Certainly, the thought of jeopardizing the Jewish day schools' substantial provincial subsidies may have inhibited any serious criticism of the Liberals' language-of-education policies.

What is certain is that on the eve of the election, at a meeting of some 400 Montreal Jews held in the Allied Jewish Community Services (AJCS) building, industrialist Bronfman predicted dire consequences in the wake of a PQ victory. He went so far as to threaten to leave the province and remove his corporate holdings from it if the Parti Québécois should win. To the chagrin of many Jews, Bronfman's remarks were much publicized in the local and national media. The day after the PQ victory, Bronfman issued a public retraction, claiming that the result could not be construed as a mandate for independence. In spite of his effort to minimize the damage, Bronfman's remarks at the meeting were broadly interpreted as symbolic of coordinated Jewish opposition to Quebec independence and even Quebec nationalism.

The results of election night are history. Although the PQ received just over 41 per cent of the vote, it swept to a commanding majority in the National Assembly. The stunning electoral victory came as a surprise to most Jews, who woke up the next morning to find that the threatening but previously distant idea of an independent Quebec was now the policy of their provincial government. Although the PQ had played down the independence issue during the campaign, presumably for tactical reasons, it was evident that the party's *raison d'être* was to achieve autonomy for Quebec. Moreover, since Jews had never had ties to the separatists, they now found themselves completely out of touch with their government. Without proper channels of communication, they felt they were standing outside Quebec's political and even social life.

Fears and Dilemmas since 1976

Although the referendum initiative in support of Quebec's negotiating sovereignty association was defeated in May 1980 by a 60:40 margin, many Montreal Jews remain unnerved today. Most fear the possibility of an independent Quebec. Moreover, they feel marginal to their society. Although they are residents of Quebec and many have deep roots in Montreal, they feel they cannot be true Québécois. Minorities are uncomfortable, at best, during the triumph of a nationalist movement.

Hence even after five years, the Jews of Montreal view the success of the PQ with a sense of foreboding. Some of their reasons for apprehension are shared by other Anglophones. Others are unique to the Jewish community.

Anti-Semitism: Actual and Perceived

A very real effect of the PQ success has been increased psychological pressure on minority group members, both individually and collectively. This phenomenon has been observed widely in the Jewish community, which, with its sense of history, is wary about the way in which nationalist movements can accentuate minority status. Particularly sensitive to such developments are those Jews who came to Montreal to escape the horrors of persecution in Europe. Since between one-fifth and one-fourth of the adult Jews of Montreal are Holocaust survivors, the community includes a large number of people for whom such fears are rooted in personal memories. For many other older members of the community, Quebec's own history heightens fears that they may suffer in an increasingly nationalistic French Canadian environment. The fact that the province saw open displays of anti-Semitism during the 1930s contributes to the belief that it could surface again.

Perhaps more unsettling have been instances of a generalized prejudice against Anglophones that may or may not focus on Jews. Because the English have so long controlled the banks and large corporations, the Québécois often hold them responsible for the sorry state of the province's economy. But they often do not direct opprobrium only at the English ethnic group. For example, according to a newspaper account of an economic meeting conducted by the government, Yvon Charbonneau, president of the radical separatist teachers' union, "lashed out at terrorists in the business community and named only two — Sam Steinberg, owner of the supermarket chain, and Bernard Finestone, president of the Montreal Board of Trade".[4]

A few incidents of public anti-Semitism have fanned these fears. The most blatant appeared in a small-circulation pro-separatist magazine, *Ici Québec*. During the first few months of 1978, it carried several virulent articles; one, for example, described Zionism as "the cancer of humanity". Government spokesmen, however, have denied any connection with the magazine and have repudiated the sentiments expressed in it. Such incidents, whether directed at the ethnic English, Jews, or anyone else, evoke uneasiness among those with a memory of history.

Let it be said clearly that the Parti Québécois has given no evidence whatsoever of overt anti-Semitic tendencies or influences. On the contrary, many PQ leaders have distinguished records as civil libertarians for whom anti-Semitism is as revolting a concept as it is to fair-minded individuals anywhere in the world. Moreover, most Jews appreciate full well the personal honesty and respect for democracy that have characterized Premier René Lévesque's public career and have earned him the grudging admiration of even the bitterest foes of independence. When the Montreal Jews consider Lévesque, the European analogue they fear is never Hitler or Stalin but Kerensky. They see Lévesque as threatened by factions of the left and the right, elements both within and without his party that are eager to assume control and to shape Quebec's destiny according to their own visions. That the party has systematically purged many radical elements from its ranks and from leadership positions or that Lévesque himself enjoys overwhelming support from the caucus, the party structure, and PQ supporters in general does not mitigate the fears. Lévesque himself has tried to reassure Jews about their future in an independent Quebec. He has not been altogether successful in this attempt, partly because of skepticism about his own orientation. Although few Jews doubt his personal lack of anti-Semitism, many find his public statements on Middle East questions unnerving and some of his cohorts' frightening.

Clearly, the reality of anti-Semitism in Quebec today compares favourably with that in Europe and is no worse than in other Canadian provinces or the American states, which have all had their share of anti-Semitic movements and still see occasional manifestations of it in mild forms. It is even easy to overstate the fabled paranoia of Montreal Jews. In the 1978 survey of Jewish household heads, only 12 per cent perceived "a great deal" of prejudice against Jews in Quebec. And although 10 per cent thought there was "much more" anti-Semitism in Quebec than elsewhere in Canada, 5 per cent felt there was "much less". Most respondents (57 per cent) felt it was "about the same". Still, 35 per cent felt that anti-Semitism had "increased" in the province in the previous five years.[5]

Who Are the Québécois?

Marginality is another problem for Montreal's Jews. Although Premier Lévesque has argued that any resident of Quebec is a Québécois, most minority group members perceive that the concept is generally used more restrictively. Even the ability to speak

French well is not enough; the true Québécois must also be part of the correct ethnic group, with all that entails in terms of culture, religion, society, history and language.

This attitude creates difficult problems for the Jews of Montreal. Despite the fact that Canadian Jews, like other minorities, have always seen themselves as somewhat apart or distinct, they have also seen themselves as full citizens, with equal rights and opportunities — with a chance to share in some of the decision-making that shapes the political system. But in the new Quebec, many Jews see themselves as threatened with decidedly inferior status and little opportunity to participate meaningfully in the political process. The result is they feel alienated from the mainstream of the society, marginal and rootless in a city where some of their families have lived for almost a century. They believe that things are out of control politically and that policy contrary to Jewish interests will evolve.

Economic Insecurity

Quebec's Jews, like most members of its business and professional communities, are also worried about the province's economic future. Since the first PQ victory, the Canadian dollar has declined against the American and even more markedly against the world's most stable currencies. Many factors have been at work here, but the Anglophones of Montreal perceive them as including the PQ's nationalist and economic policies. Private capital has been leaving Quebec, and businessmen attest to a slowdown in activity in the province, particularly in new investment and expansion, though by 1980/81 things had somewhat improved.

The social and economic policies of the PQ are essentially no more "socialist" than those of Canada's New Democratic Party, as Premier Lévesque and his economic advisors have attempted to reassure the private sector. But they have also reiterated a long-term commitment to reform along the lines of Swedish socialism and to bringing basic financial institutions as well as Quebec's cultural industries — publishing, radio and television, film-making, and recording — under government control. Since the occupational history of the party's MNAs reveals little experience in the private sector (most members come from the ranks of the teaching profession, government, the labour movement, journalism, and the arts), concurrent reassurances of PQ support for private investment have been confusing.

Many economic analysts agree that Quebec's inherited budget deficits and capital needs are too high to encourage new government initiatives that might jeopardize foreign investment. (The effort to take over the American-owned General Dynamics Corporation in the asbestos industry is an exception.) At the same time, left-wing PQ supporters undoubtedly favour a larger measure of government intervention in the Quebec economy and have strong commitments to the many needed but costly social welfare proposals in the party's early platforms. The PQ economic planners have shown themselves capable, but they still face the difficult task of balancing goals of fiscal moderation and economic confidence against the raised expectations of Quebec labour and the left-wing reformers — all in a period of high inflation and recession. Many people question whether they (or anyone) can accomplish such a feat.

These fears of a general economic decline are grafted on to personal worries of Jews, especially younger Jews, whose French is less than perfect. The PQ's most spectacular legislation is Bill 101, the Charter of the French Language, which is designed to assure the primacy of French in all aspects of Quebec life. Some of its provisions attempt to make French the province's language of work in all situations except certain educational institutions and small businesses. The policy is summed up in the word *francization*. In general, firms with more than fifty employees must set up *francization* committees to work out detailed plans for converting to a French working environment and must eventually obtain certificates of compliance. Other provisions require almost all professionals not only to show competence in French but to take their licencing examinations in that language.

The Montreal Jews' concern about *francization* is not solely about their linguistic ability. Most can learn French. Even some who are already bilingual are concerned about a perceived premium on being not just French-speaking but Québécois. An implicit purpose of the legislation is to provide better employment opportunities for Francophones, who in times past often had to be able to speak English in order to work. Consequently, as firms increasingly stress French competence as a criterion for hiring and promotion, many non-Québécois are concluding that bilingual or not, they will soon face a range of economic opportunities that is narrower than that available to Francophones of the same age and education. Surveys have found that economic worries among Jews are three to four times more likely to lead to emigration from Quebec than fears of anti-Semitism.

The Language of Education

Bill 101 is having a great enough effect in the workplace. The provisions that most concern the Jewish community directly, however, are those that govern the language of education and severely restrict admission to the English-language schools. These regulations present immediate educational problems for both the Anglophone public schools and the Jewish day schools and funding problems for the latter. They also appear to offer long-range threats to the community's size, make-up, and religious life.

The Bill 101 regulations are complex and may be amended; parts restrict general access to the English schools to children who have at least one parent educated in English in Quebec. This means that families that moved to Quebec after August 1977, including those that come from other parts of Canada and from English-speaking foreign countries, are forced to send their children to French-language schools. Obviously, an American who moved to Paris would not expect to be able to send his or her child to an English-language public school. And Jews know that the Montreal-area school boards had long been troubled by the tendency of immigrants who spoke neither French nor English to choose the English-language schools for their children. (The Liberals' earlier Bill 22 had been designed to combat this problem.) In a province where the majority is Francophone, many Jews can sympathize with the desire to channel immigrants who speak neither of Canada's official languages into French-language schools. However, the English school systems of Montreal have long-standing legitimacy under both federal and provincial law, a legitimacy many believe to be guaranteed by the British North America Act. In addition, the minority these schools serve numbers over one million, more than 30 per cent of metropolitan Montreal's population.

From the point of view of the government, Bill 101 preserves these schools for the existing Anglophone community, but not for newcomers. But some people who already reside in Quebec, including a number of Jews, are finding that their children are forced to attend French schools even though they speak only English. In addition, Francophone children, including North African Jews, are barred from publicly funded English schools, a category that includes most Jewish day schools.

Perhaps nowhere is the issue of *francization* of more concern to the organized Jewish community than in the problem of the day schools — and their funding. The government has insisted that they be regarded as English-language schools and that the Bill 101 admissions requirements apply to them. In return the PQ, despite its platform commitment to ending public grants to private schools, is prepared to continue substantial grants to those Jewish day schools that adhere to the Bill 101 admissions restrictions and move towards using French as almost the exclusive language of instruction in their secular curricula.

The problem is a knotty one because the number of children involved is so large (almost half the Jewish community's youngsters) and the amounts involved so substantial as to be the envy of the Jews of most other provinces and the United States, where no public funding for Jewish schools is available. The subsidies are given on a per-student basis to all private schools in the province that "serve the public interest" (by providing education that meets government guidelines). For the Jewish day schools, the funding has generally covered a major part of the secular studies programs.

When the grants were first awarded, the language of instruction was not an issue. Aside from two French schools (primarily for North African children) and one French immersion school (primarily for Anglophones), Montreal's Jewish day schools ran in a manner similar to that of their Toronto or American counterparts: half a day of Judaic studies conducted in Hebrew or perhaps Yiddish, and half a day of secular studies conducted in English. During the early 1970s, however, the Department of Education began to attach linguistic strings to the subsidies; it required increased instruction in French, necessitating a corresponding reduction in the amount of time devoted to studies in English and/or Hebrew. (It should be noted that such stringent requirements were not placed on the Protestant public schools, which had long been notorious for their inability to produce graduates who could communicate effectively in French.)

During the early 1970s, the Jewish day schools were not hostile to the idea of increased instruction in French because they recognized that the times were changing and their pupils would need to be able to speak French if they continued to live in Quebec. By the 1976/77 school year, for example, the number of hours of French per week had reached eight, which educators considered a manageable amount for schools that operated on thirty-two-hour weeks. Typically, the rest of the time was divided into about twelve hours each of Judaic instruction and of English studies (including mathematics), reducing the Judaic program below 50 per cent of the total. English was still regarded as the secular program's primary language of instruction.

The 1976 PQ victory came after this pattern had been established. But in negotiations for the 1977/78 school year, the new government demanded that the day schools virtually eliminate studies in English in order to maintain the grants. These demands posed a dilemma, but popular opinion in the Jewish community was clear. Most Jews valued the provincial subsidies *and* the Judaic programs. Only 5 per cent of the respondents in the 1978 survey supported the extreme course of rejecting all provincial funding (and thus being able to limit the amount of French used).

Neither did many think the hours of Judaic instruction should be cut. Most preferred the option of lengthening the school day or of using more French in the secular or even in the Jewish studies.

The leaders of the organized community seemed to agree. During the negotiations with the government, the AJCS publicly announced, on two occasions, that if the funding were lost, it would somehow find a way to support the schools, but it never explained how this would be done. Behind the scenes, the leaders were clearly eager for a settlement that would keep the money flowing, even if it meant increasing the amount of French beyond the point that some experts believed educationally desirable.

Eventually, the government modified its extreme position. The settlement involved increasing the number of hours of French instruction to eleven for 1977/78 and scheduling a further increase of one hour per week in each succeeding year. A corresponding reduction in the hours of English was assumed. The Jewish day schools now offer trilingual (and in some cases quad-rilingual — English, French, Hebrew, and Yiddish) programs. By 1980/81, the schools were required to offer fourteen hours in French per week. Even a longer school day allows only about twelve hours per week for the Judaic program and eight or ten hours per week for English-language studies.

Barring an unanticipated change in government policy, which even a Liberal government might not bring down, it is evident that the Jewish day schools will have to continue increasing the proportion of French in their curricula until they reach the point at which there are only a few hours of English left at best. This prospect raises very serious questions for a community so committed to day schools. Jewish parents in North America are notably sensitive about their children's education and frequently willing to go to great lengths to ensure its meeting their standards. Fears that competence in English may suffer may not be quieted by assurances of a high-quality French-language education.

At present, the schools can continue to receive government support while preserving their primary mission in the Judaic area so long as they are willing to continue to move towards a French-language secular program. Nevertheless, this approach does not guarantee success because *francization* may encourage parents to insist on other educational options. Moreover, the PQ government ultimately may withdraw grants to all private schools as a matter of principle. In the event that the grants are lost, either as the result of general government policy or because the schools find that they can no longer meet the requirements for continued funding, the parents and the community will have to make up the shortfall. Since the amount involved is likely to reach $10 million by the early 1980s, it would be a significant drain on the community's resources. On the other hand, if the resolution of the question results in a significant drop in the Judaic content of the curricula or a significant loss in the number of children attending Jewish day schools, the effects on the quality of the community's religious life would be deleterious.

Another problem is the effect of Bill 101's admissions restrictions. Since new members of the community may find their children barred from the day schools and the English-language public schools, families considering moving to Montreal may decide not to do so. This would inhibit the ability of the community to recruit professionals, such as rabbis, cantors, teachers, educational administrators, social workers, and community executives, from other parts of Canada or the United States. The long-range impact could be very serious for a community that has long depended on outsiders to staff many key positions. Moreover, if the general policy of *francization* in education and in employment causes large numbers of Jews to move away from Montreal, the synagogues and religious institutions — not to mention the schools — will no longer have sufficient members to support themselves.

Demographic Change in the Community

Fears of *francization*, of educational and professional problems, and of discrimination in employment have already driven large numbers of Anglophones from Quebec, a movement that started with the growing climate of Québécois nationalism in the 1960s and increased sharply with the first PQ victory. Despite government statements to the contrary, many Anglophones simply decided that there was no more place for them in Quebec society.

Jews have been among these emigrants, and if this number should increase dramatically, Montreal Jewry could face grave difficulties. The problem is not only one of absolute losses but also involves demographic spread. At the time of the 1971 census, before the wave of out-migration began, the Montreal Jewish community already had disproportionately more older people and fewer younger people than Quebec society as a whole and thus faced a serious situation in which increasing numbers of aged Jews looked for support (including financial support) from a narrowing base of young and middle-aged adults. Now, it is generally agreed that younger people are more likely to leave the province than older people and that those most likely to leave are recent university graduates and professionals under thirty-five or forty years of age. This tendency can only exacerbate the demographic spread, and if the out-migration increases much beyond present levels (say, because a future referendum supports an independent Quebec), the community may well find itself unable to maintain solid organizations and programs. Furthermore, since the individuals most likely to leave are or have the potential to be some of the more affluent members of the community, their departure would shrink the base for effective fund-raising.

The figures from the 1978 survey of Jewish householders offered some estimates of both current emigration trends and those likely to occur if a referendum were to show "clear support for independence". Given a continuation of the status quo, 20 per cent of the respondents under age forty said they would definitely or probably leave Quebec within the next five years. This percentage increased to 70 per cent under a scenario of the passage of a referendum that supported independence in some form.

The survey provided another interesting gauge of emigration trends among young Jews by asking respondents questions about their children over age eighteen. Thirty-four per cent of the younger generation were not living in Montreal; of this group, parents thought 87 per cent would either definitely or probably not return to the city within the next five years. Of the 66 per cent of grown children who did live in Montreal, 25 per cent were estimated as definitely or probably not remaining there at the end of five years. Thus, parents expect 46 per cent of the next biological generation not to be in Montreal by 1983. Such a generational loss is bound to pose severe problems for community organization.

Since a substantial wave of Jewish immigration to Quebec seems unlikely in the near future and since Jewish fertility, in Quebec as elsewhere, is declining, the future Jewish population of Montreal depends primarily on the volume of emigration. Of course, the actual emigration rate will depend on unfolding events. Any lessening of the likelihood of independence for Quebec may well have a salutary effect on out-migration.

Indeed, simply maintaining the status quo may have happier results than were suggested by the 1978 survey. At least one observer, writing in December 1980, suggested that a certain stability has set among Montreal Jews. Those eager to leave have already done so; those who remain have made their peace with the new Quebec.[6] Indeed, one hears of reports of Jews, usually professionals, who have returned to Montreal after emigration to the United States or western Canada. As a qualitative Jewish community, Montreal still compares favorably with any city on the continent.

From Nationalism to Quebec Sovereignty

The issues described in the previous section are ones actually facing the Jewish community in Quebec within the current federal system. It goes without saying that in a sovereign Quebec (or in a Quebec with vastly increased powers) these fears and problems would be exacerbated. It may be for this reason that Montreal Jews have an overwhelming commitment to federalism. The 1978 survey found 98 per cent of those who advocated the community's taking a public position on the issue of the status of Quebec (about two-thirds of the respondents) supported federalism (35 per cent) or revised federalism (63 per cent). Only 2 per cent favoured sovereignty-association or outright independence.

Should the province achieve sovereignty, the Montreal Jewish community might face three additional problems: an emphasis on collective rights at the expense of the individual, economic difficulties, and a distasteful foreign policy.

Possible Erosion of Civil Liberties

The philosophy of the Parti Québécois is such that it places collective rights and the needs of the collectivity on a higher plane than individual rights and needs. In other words, it may limit individual rights in order to protect or further the perceived needs of the society as a whole. Most Jews, on the other hand, remain firmly committed to the Anglo-American emphasis on individual liberties and find talk about collective rights alien and disquieting.

The talk is not merely theoretical. The Jew of Montreal have already seen how Bill 101 subordinates individual rights to the collective interest in the educational sphere, and many consider the clauses of the same act that limit the language of commercial signs to French are a form of restricting the freedom of speech or expression. Another area of concern is the possibility of preferential hiring of Québécois, even over bilingual Anglophones.

The Economic Perils of Sovereignty

Other problems that Jews foresee if Quebec becomes independent are in the economic sphere. Their concerns are both general and personal. Of course, only the most naive militants ignore economic concerns, no matter what their position on the question of separation. The PQ believes it could handle the inevitable economic problems of independence, but its vision of achieving it assumes the Quebec government's negotiating an orderly arrangement with the federal government and eventual economic cooperation in many spheres between the two entities. But many Montreal Jews — and others — question this assumption — and others. What if the reaction of the federal government were one of anger or resentment manifested in forms of economic warfare? Would the anticipated inflow of American (or Arab) capital be sufficient to compensate for the economic dislocation?

Again, during the initial period after independence, what if unemployment were to rise well up beyond its present level? What sorts of measures, economic and political, might the Quebec government have to take in an effort to restore order? Might assets be frozen? Confiscated? Amid this turmoil, who would suffer? Quebec Jews, who are overrepresented in business and the professions and by far the most affluent of the province's ethnic groups, are sensitive to the consequences of economic down-turns and nervous about possible government reactions to them.

Foreign Policy of a Sovereign Quebec

The probable foreign policy of an independent Quebec also worries Jews. The intellectual and political elites among the Québécois are partial to aspects of Third World ideology and already generally favour the Arab cause. Hence, an independent Quebec could be expected to pursue at least a relatively pro-Arab policy in the Middle East. Montreal's Jews might then find themselves not only politically impotent, unable to influence their new country's foreign policy, but even impaired in their ability to provide financial and other aid to Jews in Israel. Such a situation might have serious repercussions for the local community as well as for Israel. At present, in Montreal, as across the continent, support for Israel is a major mechanism for the expression of Jewish identity and constitutes a focus for Jewish organizational activity. If such activity were inhibited by an anti-Israel foreign policy, would it be possible to maintain the kind of community life that now exists?

These foreign policy concerns in no way imply that a sovereign Quebec might become a "northern Cuba" or a Soviet satellite, as one occasionally hears. Such a transformation seems highly unlikely. The Québécois are becoming increasingly North American in their economic and leisure patterns and would be very unlikely to allow any government to adopt a too leftist stance. What they might do, however, is tilt slightly towards neutral positions (à la France) with less binding commitments to the Western alliance. Jews find even this prospect upsetting, however, because most of the mainstream Jewish community tends to support a geopolitical position of reflexive anti-Sovietism and strong defence of liberal democracy and Western (including U.S.) interests.

Towards the Future

As the Jews of Montreal look to the future, they combine ambiguous attitudes of apprehension and willingness to adapt. Four years of PQ government have proved some of their most extreme postelection fears false, but they have also suggested other, more subtle problems.

The referendum of May 1980 removed the immediate threat of Quebec independence but not the possibility of such a movement in the future. The Jews of Montreal sense that support for the Parti Québécois and/or for sovereignty in some form is strongest among young Québécois, and experts confirm this perception.[7] Thus they know that even if the Liberals win a future provincial election, the possibility of subsequent reverses and a renewed mandate for the PQ cannot be discounted. (It is partly for this reason that many Jews, like most minority group members in Quebec, hope for some sort of constitutional arrangement that will give the province greater powers within a federal system and thus induce the Québécois to remain part of Canada.)

The Jewish dilemma goes well beyond the current regulations of the PQ. It also goes beyond strictly linguistic difficulties. In a general sense, a French-speaking society is not a threat for Jews or any other minority group. Jews live quite well speaking French in Paris, Lyons, Nice, Geneva, Brussels, Rabat, and many other places. The North African Sephardim who have immigrated to Quebec have maintained their identity in two quite different Francophone environments. At present, most Anglophone Jews of Montreal, like most of the province's other Anglophones, have come to terms with the imposition of French by force of law. Some find this too threatening — or just too complicated — and are leaving if they possibly can. Others are able to adjust, and their children, who are more likely to receive a good grounding in French, will probably find language even less of a difficulty.

The more basic question is: do the Jews of Montreal want to adjust? Do they want to adapt themselves and their community to a larger society whose ground rules are changing rapidly? One factor here is subtly linguistic. If the community becomes predominantly Francophone it might in the long run be somewhat cut off from the rest of North America's Jewish communities. At present, most of the Montreal Jews' religious and cultural organizations are closely tied to counterparts in Toronto or the United States. At least one observer believes the community might be

> committing cultural and religious suicide by cutting itself off from the mainstream of Jewish life and organizations on this continent and in those non-English-speaking countries, including Israel, in which English is the major second language.[8]

A related concern is the effect of *francization* on Anglophone culture, general and Jewish, in Quebec. Montreal Jews have long taken great pride in this aspect of their community. Yet an obvious target for a nationalist-oriented government would be to increase the scope of *francization* in the world of English-language universities, theatres, films, newspapers, and publishing. Bill 101 and other PQ regulations have only begun to touch these institutions. Others might go much further.

Beyond these points are the facts that some fundamental aspects of Quebec society are changing and that many developments are now largely out of the hands of Jews but will structure the choices available to them. This raises the question of identifying the community's basic interests. These have never been well-defined, but their articulation can no longer be deferred. In general, the Jewish community requires a society that permits the free exercise of religion, recognizes and respects cultural pluralism, protects individual rights and liberties, recognizes individuals as equal before the law, and provides a reasonably stable economic system that permits individual advancement economically and professionally. These conditions obtain in Quebec, and so long as they do, the Jewish community can persist in a manner comparable to that achieved in other parts of North America.

Beyond this lies the question of whether the Jewish community ever *can* integrate fully with Québécois society. The answer would appear to be that complete integration would be difficult, but individuals and the community could achieve greater integration than they have heretofore. Whether they want to make the effort is yet another question, but it is the one whose answer indicates the appropriate course of action. Or, to use the words of two astute observers analyzing the situation:

> Does the uniqueness of the Montreal Jewish community justify a special effort at adaptation to the new situation, in order to protect and nurture the community's many institutions and cultural achievements? Or is the Montreal experience now being revealed as just another piece of evidence corroborating the old Zionist contention that the Diaspora can never provide a wholly comfortable home for Jews?[9]

At the present time most Montreal Jews probably endorse efforts at adaptation, if only because they are not ready to emigrate en masse. Most want to preserve their community and its institutions, and they are apparently willing to make significant adjustments in order to do so. Thus one can anticipate efforts to increase linguistic, cultural, and social integration.

One suggestion that has been made in this connection is that the time is ripe for Montreal Jews to involve themselves in the political and social life of Quebec at all levels. Such involvement, its proponents suggest, would enable the Jewish community to put forth its concerns and interests in a more effective way. Thus, Jewish participation in the school boards, political parties, and voluntary organizations of the general Francophone community could be a strategy of

> multiplying the political influence and contacts of any one of the participants and educating elements of the English, French and ethnic communities about some of the characteristics of our own community.[10]

Overall, however, the Montreal Jews' greatest resource in this time of dilemma is probably their capacity for self-government and self-financing. If it does nothing else, the present crisis should stimulate communal activity as the importance of Jewish community life becomes more evident. The response may well be circular in a positive fashion: as individual Jews see the *community's* ability to maintain its viability and vitality in the midst of change, they may well be influenced to make adaptive responses to the changes that are taking place in *their own* lives.

Certainly, the dramatic changes in Quebec society since 1960 have already tested the adaptive powers of the Jewish community. Today the Jews of Montreal find themselves subjected to a kind of uncertainty that they share with no other Jewish community in North America. But many have cast their lot with Quebec and have begun to accept *francization* as a new reality. This adaptive, evolutionary process is still incomplete. Its final outcome will be determined by events largely outside the control of Montreal Jewry.

List of Contributors

Irving Abella is a professor of history at Glendon College, York University. He is the author of *Nationalism, Communism and Canadian Labour, On Strike,* and *The Canadian Worker in the Twentieth Century* and the coauthor, with Harold Troper, of a forthcoming study of Canada and Jewish refugees. He also chairs the editorial board of *Labour/Le Travailleur: The Journal of Canadian Labour History* and the Archives Committee of the Canadian Jewish Congress.

Arnold Ages is a professor of French language and literature at the University of Waterloo and has written articles and monographs on the literature of the French Enlightenment. He is currently involved in a research project on Jews and Judaism in the *Prélude aux lumières.* He also serves as a consultant in adult education at Toronto's Beth Tzedec Synagogue.

Abraham J. Arnold is the executive director of Manitoba's Association for Rights and Liberties and a former director of the Western Region of the Canadian Jewish Congress. A journalist and historian, he is the coauthor, with William Kurelek, of *Jewish Life in Canada* and the founding director of the Jewish Historical Society of Western Canada.

Mervin Butovsky is a professor of English at Concordia University and has lectured widely in modern Jewish literature. At present, he is engaged in a series of interviews with Canadian Jewish writers. He serves as vice-president of the Jewish Public Library in Montreal.

Irwin Cotler is a professor of law at McGill University and an international human rights lawyer. His areas of specialization include poverty law, constitutional law, and civil liberties. He was elected president of the Canadian Jewish Congress in 1980.

Leo Davids is an associate professor of sociology at Atkinson College, York University. He has researched and written on topics involving the family, delinquency, and Canadian Jewish demography and has worked with Toronto's Jewish Family and Child Service and York's Counselling and Development Centre.

Gerald E. Dirks is an associate professor in the Department of Politics, Brock University and the author of *Canadian Refugee Policy: Indifference or Opportunism?.* He is currently undertaking an evaluation of the 1978 Canadian Immigration Act and Regulations.

Yaacov Glickman received his Ph.D. from the University of Toronto, where he is a research associate at the Centre for Urban and Community Studies. His current research interests include a study of religious conversion to Judaism and an analysis of the treatment of the Holocaust in Canadian history and social science textbooks.

Norma Baumel Joseph teaches religion at Concordia University and is presently also teaching at the State University of New York at Albany. She has lectured extensively on women in Judaism in Montreal and the United States.

Joseph Kage is the national executive vice-president of the Jewish Immigrant Aid Services of Canada and a frequent consultant to the country's federal and provincial governments on matters of immigration. He received his doctorate from the Université de Montréal.

Jean-Claude Lasry is a research associate at the Institute of Community and Family Psychiatry of the Sir Mortimer B. Davis Jewish General Hospital of Montreal and a professor of psychology at the Université de Montréal. He was a founder of Ecole Maimonide in 1969 and has held several leadership positions in the Sephardic and general Jewish communities of Montreal. He is founder and president of the Family Therapists Association of Quebec.

Morty M. Lazar is an assistant professor of sociology at Mount Saint Vincent University in Halifax. He has written on the role of women in synagogue ritual and is currently engaged in research on ethnic identity among Jews in Atlantic Canada.

Sheva Medjuck is an assistant professor and chairperson of the Sociology and Anthropology Department of Mount Saint Vincent University in Halifax. She has written on the relationship of the nineteenth-century household to economic development in New Brunswick. Currently, she is researching ethnic identity among the Jews of Atlantic Canada.

Eugene Orenstein is an associate professor in the Jewish Studies Program of McGill University. His research includes the history of the Jewish labour movement, modern Jewish national ideologies, and problems of Yiddish culture. Professor Orenstein is also chairman of the National Committee on Yiddish of the Canadian Jewish Congress.

Howard Roiter is an associate professor of English literature at the Université de Montréal. He taught Canada's first university course on the Holocaust, and has written extensively on Holocaust literature, including *Voices from the Holocaust, Echoes de l'Holocaust*, and, as coauthor, *A Voice from the Forest*. He is on the executive of the Canadian Jewish Congress (Quebec Region).

Albert Rose is a professor and former dean of the Faculty of Social Work at the University of Toronto and has conducted research on matters of social welfare policy, housing, and urban development. He is the author of five books, the latest of which is *Canadian Housing Policies*. In 1959, he edited *A People and Its Faith: Essays on Jews and Reform Judaism in a Changing Canada*.

Stuart Schoenfeld is an assistant professor of sociology at Glendon College, York University. He has taught and written in the areas of Jewish community studies, urban studies, and formal organizations. He is a founding member of the board of the Downtown Jewish Community School in Toronto and secretary of the Narayaver Congregation.

William Shaffir is an associate professor in the Department of Sociology at McMaster University. He has written several books and articles on medical-student professionalization, field research, and Chassidic communities. He is currently investigating the nature of the Chassidic family.

Howard Stanislawski is now a policy analyst for the Commission on International Affairs, American Jewish Congress, in New York. From 1975 to 1980, he served as associate national director of the Canada-Israel Committee and director of its Ottawa bureau. He received his doctorate from Brandeis University in Waltham, Massachusetts.

Jim Torczyner is an associate professor of community organization in the School of Social Work at McGill University. He is the founder and first president of Project Genesis, a multiethnic, activist citizens' organization in Montreal. He is currently researching and writing in the areas of Jewish poverty, community organization, and strategies of social change.

Harold Troper is an associate professor of the history of education at the Ontario Institute for Studies in Education. He has written widely on the history of immigration and ethnicity and was coauthor of *Immigrant: A Portrait of the Urban Experience*. Currently he is coauthoring a study on Canada and the Jewish refugee crisis.

Harold M. Waller is an associate professor of political science at McGill University. He has directed several studies of Canadian Jewish communities, is the author of *The Governance of the Jewish Community of Montreal*, and the coeditor of *The Politics and Organization of Canadian Jewry* (forthcoming). In addition, Professor Waller is director of the Canadian Centre for Jewish Community Studies.

Morton Weinfeld is an assistant professor of sociology at McGill University. He has taught, researched, and written in the area of Jewish sociology. His current research interests include Jewish economic behaviour, the second-generation effects of the Holocaust, and issues of cultural pluralism and public policy in Canada.

Ruth Wisse is a professor of Yiddish Literature at McGill University. She is the author of *The Schlemiel as Modern Hero*, editor of *A Shletl and Other Yiddish Novellas*, and coeditor of *The Best of Sholem Aleichem*. She writes frequently for *Commentary*.

Notes

Introduction

Shaffir and Weinfeld

1. Royal Commission on Bilingualism and Biculturalism, *Book IV: The Contribution of the Other Ethnic Groups* (Ottawa: Information Canada, 1969), p. 180.

2. Oscar Handlin, *The Uprooted* (Boston: Little Brown, 1951), pp. 155-6.

3. Isaac Metzker, *A Bintel Brief* (New York: Ballantine Books, 1971).

4. For an authoritative description of present-day American Jewish life, see Marshall Sklare, ed., *The Jew in American Society* (New York: Behrman House, 1974) and *The Jewish Community in American Society* (New York: Behrman House, 1974).

5. For a discussion of this role of religion, rather than ethnicity, in American society, see Will Herberg, *Protestant, Catholic, Jew* (New York: Doubleday, 1960).

6. For the 1971 census, Canadian officials tried to correct the situation by deciding to accord to all those who said they were Jews-by-religion the status of Jews-by-ethnic-origin; unfortunately, this procedure mistakenly ascribed a Jewish ethnic origin to converts to Judaism.

7. See John Porter, "Melting Pot or Mosaic: Revolution or Reversion", *The Measure of Canadian Society* (Toronto: Gage, 1979).

8. For a general review of past and present racism in Canada, see David Hughes and Evelyn Kallen, *The Anatomy of Racism: Canadian Dimensions* (Montreal: Harvest House, 1974).

9. "Institutional completeness" means the degree to which a minority group can meet the various needs of its members through its own institutions, rather than those of the general society. (See Raymond Breton, "Institutional Completeness of Ethnic Communities and the Personal Relations of Immigrants", *American Journal of Sociology* 70, no. 2: 193-205.)

10. Morton Weinfeld and William Eaton, "The Jewish Community of Montreal: Survey Report", photocopied (Montreal: Jewish Community Research Institute, 1979).

Early Encounters

Kage

1. For more information on the early Jewish settlers in Atlantic Canada, see Sheva Medjuck and Morty M. Lazar, "Existence on the Fringe: The Jews of Atlantic Canada", in this volume.

2. For more information on frontier Jewish settlement, see Abraham J. Arnold, "The Mystique of Western Jewry", in this volume.

3. *Free Press* (Winnipeg), 27 May 1882.

4. Ibid., 2 June 1882.

5. I. Medres, *Montreal Fun Nechten* (Montreal, 1947), my translation. The author was a reporter for *Der keneder adler*, the first Yiddish newspaper in Canada. The book, which is written in Yiddish, is in the form of reportage memoirs.

6. L. Rosenberg, *A Gazetteer of Jewish Communities in Canada*, (Montreal: Canadian Jewish Congress, 1957).

7. See, for example, Eugene Orenstein, "Yiddish Culture in Canada Yesterday and Today", in this volume.

8. E.M. Kulisher, "Displaced Persons in the Modern World", *Annals of the American Academy of Political and Social Science*, March 1979.

9. For more information on North African Jewry in Quebec, see Jean-Claude Lasry, "A Francophone Diaspora in Quebec", in this volume.

10. B.R. Blishen, "The Construction and Use of an Occupational Class Scale", *Canadian Journal of Economic and Political Science* no. 4 (1958). For a current description of the economic profile of Canadian Jewry, see Harold M. Waller, "Power in The Canadian Jewish Community", in this volume.

Abella and Troper

1. Wrong et al to King, 7 June 1939, King Papers, 238579, Public Archives of Canada [PAC], Ottawa.

2. King Diary, 8 June 1939, PAC; King to Skelton, 8 June 1939, King Papers, 237087.

3. Skelton to King, 9 June 1939, King Papers, 237095-6.

4. Blair to Skelton, 8 and 16 June 1939, Department of Immigration Records, file 64452, PAC (our italics).

5. See, for example, *Canada Year Book*, 1939, p. 158.

6. Blair to Mrs. I. Grenovsky, 5 December 1938, Immigration Records, file 644452; Blair to R.A. Bell, private secretary to Manion, 29 February 1938, Manion Papers, PAC.

7. Interview with James Gibson, Vineland, Ontario, 26 June 1978.

8. See Gerald Dirks, *Canada's Refugee Policy: Indifference or Opportunism?* (Montreal: McGill-Queens University Press, 1977), pp. 44–97.

9. Blair to Crerar, 12 October 1938, Immigration Records, file 54782/5.

10. Blair to F.N. Scandlers, commissioner of Saint John Board of Trade, 13 September 1938, Immigration Records, file 54782/5.

11. Blair to Crerar, 28 March 1938, Immigration Records, file 54782/5.

12. Blair to H.R.I. Henry, 30 January 1939, Immigration Records, file 644452.

13. Blair to W. Baird, 4 May 1938, Immigration Records, file 54782/5.

14. Blair to W.A. Little, 24 October 1939, Immigration Records, file 54782/6.

15. Blair to Sclanders, 13 September 1938, Immigration Records, file 54782/5.

16. See Simon Belkin, *Through Narrow Gates: A Review of Jewish Immigration, Colonization and Immigrant Aid in Canada* (Montreal: Canadian Jewish Congress and Jewish Colonization Association, 1966), pp. 169–170, and Joseph Kage, *With Faith and Thanksgiving* (Montreal: Eagle Publishing Company, 1962), pp. 66–69.

17. Blair, memo for file, 20 January 1936, Immigration Records, file 54782/4.

18. Report of Jewish Immigration Aid Society [JIAS], Montreal, 18 February 1937, files of Hebrew Immigrant Aid Society, Jewish Historical Collection, YIVO Institute, New York; interview, Saul Hayes, Montreal, 20 June 1978. See also Leo Heaps, *The Rebel in the House: The Life and Times of A.A. Heaps, M.P.* (London: Niccolo, 1970), p. 155.

19. Blair, memo for file, 19 April 1938, Immigration Records, file 54782/5.

20. Canadian Pacific Railways to H. Heinemann, 8 May 1938, Canadian Jewish Congress files. Heinemann sent a copy of this telegram to the Congress with a plea for help to save his family from the Nazis.

21. Memo from the United States Delegation, 25 March 1938, in John Munro, ed., *Documents on Canadian External Relations*, vol. 6 *1936–39* (Ottawa, 1972), pp. 790–1.

22. King Diary, 29 March 1938.

23. Skelton to King, 25 March 1938, King Papers, C122621.

24. King Diary, 29 March 1938.

25. Quoted in David Rome, "A History of Anti-Semitism in Canada", Montreal, 1978, unpaginated.

26. For a review of anti-Semitism in Quebec in the 1930s, see Lita Rose Betcherman, *The Swastika and the Maple Leaf* (Toronto: Fitzhenry and Whiteside, 1975).

27. H. Blair Neatby, *William Lyon MacKenzie King* (Toronto: University of Tronto Press, 1976), vol. 3, *The Prism of Unity*, p. 268. Canadian Jewish leaders were not unaware of the position of cabinet ministers from Quebec. Following the provincial Liberal party's defeat in Quebec, the president of JIAS in Montreal reported to his board "that he had it on good authority that the French Canadian element in the Federal Cabinet is strongly opposed to the admission of Jews to Canada". (Minutes of the Board of Directors, 9 December 1936, JIAS Eastern Region [Montreal]).

28. King Diary, 6 July 1938.

29. Blair draft, 19 April 1938, Immigration Records, file 644452.

30. Blair to Skelton, King Papers, 14 April 1938, C122627.

31. Blair, memo for file, 19 April 1938, Immigration Records, file 644452.

32. Ibid.

33. Skelton to King, 21 April 1938, King Papers, C122124.

34. King to Simmons, 26 April 1938, Munro, *Documents* 6: 793–4.

35. Caiserman to M.A. Averbach, 15 April 1938, Western Canadian Jewish Historical Society Papers, 101, PAC.

36. Caiserman to D.B. Roger, 25 April 1938, Canadian Jewish Congress files.

37. Heaps to N.A. Gray, 25 May 1938, Canadian Jewish Congress files.

38. Cabinet Memorandum, 18 May 1938, King Papers, 214192.

39. Pickering to King, 2 June 1938, King Papers, 214193; Heaps to Caiserman, 23 May 1938, Canadian Jewish Congress files.

40. King to Wrong, 11 June 1938, Munro, *Documents* 6: 801–5.

41. Blair to Little, 4 and 6 June 1938, Immigration Records, file 644452.

42. Blair to Jollife, 13 June 1938, Immigration Records, file 644452.

43. Wrong to Skelton, 21 June 1938, Munro, *Documents* 6: 860–7.

44. King to Wrong, 30 June 1938, King Papers, 223086.

45. King to Simmons, 28 June 1938, Munro, *Documents* 6: 807–10.

46. Blair to Skelton, Blair memorandum, 13 June 1938, and Blair to Crerar, 14 June 1938, Immigration Records, file 644452.

47. Wrong's speech to Evian Conference, External Affairs Records, box 187, file 327-1, PAC.

48. M.A. Salkin to Hebrew Immigrant Aid Society, 23 June 1938, Canadian Jewish Congress files.

49. Robinson to Oscar Cohen, 14 July 1938, Canadian Jewish Congress files.

50. Blair memo on meeting with Crerar, 20 August 1938, Immigration Records, file 54782/5.

51. Blair to W.W. Judd, October 1938, Immigration Records, file 54782/5.

52. Heaps to King, 9 September 1938, King Papers, 214195.

53. H.R.L. Henry to Heaps, 15 September 1938, King Papers, 214197.

54. King Diary, 12 November 1938.

55. Ibid., 13 November 1938.

56. Ibid., 17 and 20 November 1938.

57. Memo from H. Caiserman, 15 November 1938, Canadian Jewish Congress files.

58. Regional reports on 20 November meetings: Canadian Jewish Congress clipping file November 1938, with excerpts from 35 newspapers and weeklies; *Globe and Mail* (Toronto), 22 November 1938.

59. King Diary, 22 November 1938; *Toronto Star*, 23 November 1938.

60. *Hebrew Journal*, 23 November 1938.

61. King Diary, 23 November 1938; A.J. Freiman, president of the Zionist Organization in Canada, to King, 23 November 1938, King Papers, 213348.

62. King Diary, 24 November 1938.

63. Ibid., 1 December 1938.

64. "Draft Statement . . . regarding Refugees", 12 December 1938, Immigration Records; Pickersgill to King, 13 December 1938, King Papers, 644452.

65. King Diary, 21 December 1938.

66. Ibid. For details, see Immigration Records, file 916207.

67. Interview with James Gibson. See also, Vincent Massey, *What's Past Is Prologue* (Toronto: Macmillan, 1963), pp. 114–5.

68. J.L. Granatstein and R. Bothwell, "A Self-Evident National Duty: Canadian Foreign Policy 1935–9", *Journal of Imperial and Commonwealth History* 3 (1975): 214; King Diary, 5 October 1935; and Lester B. Pearson, *Mike: The Memoirs of the Right Honourable Lester B. Pearson* (Toronto: University of Toronto Press, 1972), vol. 1 *1897–1948*, pp. 105–6.

69. Massey to King, 29 November 1938, and Massey to Skelton, 1 December 1938, Munro, *Documents* 6: 837, 844–5.

70. Massey to King, 2 December 1938, External Affairs Records, box 1870, file 327-II.

71. Neatby, *King* 3: 304–5.

72. See Arnold Ages, "Antisemitism: The Uneasy Calm", in this volume. See also files on anti-Semitism in Canada 1939–40, Canadian Jewish Congress. The latter contains reports to the Congress from Jews throughout Canada on anti-Jewish attitudes and behaviour in their localities.

73. Report of interview with T.A. Crerar and F.C. Blair, 24 February 1939, Canadian Jewish Congress files.

74. *Toronto Star*, 10 March 1939.

75. King to Wrong, 25 February 1939, King Papers, 238576-8.

76. Caiserman to Sheps, 13 March 1939, Canadian Jewish Congress files. During the war years, Hayes was to prove such an effective advocate for Jewish refugees on the government's refugee board that Blair complained, "To prevent the more generous scale of assistance to Jewish cases . . . I think the best way to do this would be to get rid of Sol [sic] Hayes." (Blair to Byers, 20 September 1941, Immigration Records, file 694687.)

77. *Hebrew Journal*, 2 May 1939.

78. Blair to Skelton, 6 November 1939, Immigration Records, file 644452.

Dirks

1. Heaps to King, 9 September 1938, King Papers, Public Archives of Canada [PAC], Ottawa.

2. Ibid.

3. Cairine Wilson, speech, Wilson Papers, PAC.

4. Canadian National Committee on Refugees and Victims of Persecution [CNCR], minutes of the first general meeting, Ottawa, 6 and 7 December 1938, appendix 4.

5. Ibid.

6. Ibid.

7. CNCR, *Should Canada Admit Refugees?* [Toronto, 1939].

8. Resolution passed by a public meeting, Vancouver, 20 November 1938, Manion Papers, PAC.

9. Interview with Constance Hayward, 25 June 1969.

10. CNCR, minutes of the second general meeting, Toronto, 20 March 1939.

11. Blair to Manion, 28 February 1939, Manion Papers.

12. Blair to H.R.I. Henry, 30 January 1939, King Papers.

13. E.M. Howse, "Refugees, a Policy for Canada" [sermon, Winnipeg, 1939].

14. *Globe and Mail* (Toronto), 19 June 1939.

15. C. Godfrey to Manion, 5 March 1939, Manion Papers.

16. Wilson to M. McGeachy, March 1940, Wilson Papers.

17. For elaboration, see Gerald Dirks, *Canada's Refugee Policy: Indifference or Opportunism?* (Montreal: McGill-Queen's University Press, 1977), pp. 89–98.

18. Department of External Affairs, internal memorandum, 6 February 1945, file 5127, EA-40.

Social and Political Institutions

Davids

1. See Leo Davids, "Family Change in Canada, 1971–1976", *Journal of Marriage and The Family* 42, no. 1 (February 1980): 177–83.

2. Jewish women ages forty-five to sixty-four (now past their child-bearing years) at the time of the 1971 census had given birth to an average of 2.08 children. This is below replacement level, precisely as revealed by earlier analyses of Jewish fertility. See Calvin Goldscheider, "Fertility of the Jews", *Demography* 4, no. 1 (1967): 196–209. A major book in this area is Paul Ritterband, ed., *Modern Jewish Fertility* (Leiden: Brill, 1979).

3. See Jacques Henripin, *Trends and Factors of Fertility in Canada* (Ottawa: Statistics Canada, 1972), pp. 178–9, 195–203.

4. See Arthur Ruppin, *The Jews in the Modern World* (London: Macmillan & Co., 1934), chap. 5, and the relevant discussion about parental attitudes and socio-economic achievement by Gerald S. Berman, "The Adaptable American Jewish Family", *Jewish Journal of Sociology* 18, no. 1 (June 1976): 5–16.

5. See John Kralt, *Ethnic Origins of Canadians* (Ottawa: Statistics Canada, 99–709), p. 53.

6. Jerome Diamond, "Annual Report: Jewish Family and Child Service, 1978–79", (Toronto, 1979). See also Jacob Freid, ed., *Jews and Divorce* (New York: Commission on Synagogue Relations of the Federation of Jewish Philanthropies of New York, 1968), and National Jewish Welfare Board, *Proceedings: Consultation on Single-Parent Families* (New York, 1974).

7. See Robert Gordis, *Love and Sex: A Modern Jewish Perspective* (New York: Farrar, Straus and Giroux, 1978), and Chaim I. Waxman, "The Threadbare Canopy", *American Behavioral Scientist* 23, no. 4 (March 1980): 467–86.

8. Some years ago, Jewish illegitimacy rates were the *lowest* of all Canadian ethnic groups. See Henripin, *Trends and Factors of Fertility*, p. 333, table 11.9.

9. See Norman Linzer, *The Jewish Family* (New York: Commission on Synagogue Relations, Federation of Jewish Philanthropies, 1972), pp. 40-46, and Peter Elman, ed., *Jewish Marriage* (London: Jewish Marriage Education Council/Soncino Press, 1967), chap. 5, 9.

10. See Gordis, *Love and Sex*, chap. 10.

11. Statistics Canada, *Vital Statistics: Marriages and Divorces*, 2 vol. (Ottawa, 1978) 2: 29, table 11. (These 1977 data show that a small increase in total Canadian divorce rates had occurred (1976/77), but with a decrease in that year for divorces in the provinces of Quebec, Alberta, and British Columbia.) Other evidence on the rising occurrence of divorce among Jews is found in the reports of family service agencies, such as the Jewish Family and Child Service in Toronto.

12. See Ann-Marie Ambert, *Divorce in Canada* (Don Mills, Ont.: Academic Press Canada, 1980), especially chap. 3.

13. See Allen S. Maller, "A Religious Perspective on Divorce", *Journal of Jewish Communal Service* 55, no. 2 (December 1978): 192–4, and Linzer, *The Jewish Family*, pp. 62–9.

14. See Jim Torczyner, "To Be Poor and Jewish in Canada", in this volume.

15. See National Jewish Welfare Board, *Single-Parent Families*, and American Jewish Committee, *Sustaining the Jewish Family*, (New York: American Jewish Congress, Jewish Communal Affairs Department, 1979).

16. Special tabulations prepared for the author by Statistics Canada, April 1979. Only the 1971 data included Quebec marriages; information from 1977 was not available from that province.

17. These generational changes have been abundantly documented in many community studies and historical works, such as Judith R. Kramer and Seymour Leventman, *Children of the Gilded Ghetto* (New Haven: Yale University Press, 1971), and Evelyn Kallen, *Spanning the Generations: A Study in Jewish Identity* (Don Mills, Ont.: Longman Canada, 1977).

18. See Chaim I. Waxman, "The Centrality of the Family in Defining Jewish Identity and Identification", *Journal of Jewish Communal Service* 55, no. 4 (summer 1979): 353–9, and Gladys Rosen, "The Jewish Family: An Endangered Species?", *Journal of Jewish Communal Service* 55, no. 4 (summer 1979): 345–52.

19. See Gerald Cromer, "A Comparison of Intergenerational Relations in the Jewish and Non-Jewish Family", *Adolescence* 13 (summer 1978): 297–309.

20. See Fred Massarik, "Affiliation and Non-Affiliation in the U.S. Jewish Community: A Reconceptualization", *American Jewish Year Book* 78 (1978): 262–74, and Bernard Olshansky, "Jewish Education in a Time of Change", *Journal of Jewish Communal Service* 54, no. 4 (summer 1979): 323–8.

21. See Yaacov Glickman, "Jewish Education: Success or Failure?", in this volume.

Glickman

1. In Montreal and the city of Quebec, separate Catholic and Protestant school systems had already been established through an act passed in 1846. For a detailed account of these and subsequent historical developments in relation to the position of the Jews in Quebec's educational system, see Stuart E. Rosenberg, *The Jewish Community in Canada*, 2 vols. (Toronto: McClelland and Stewart, 1970-71), 1: 210–17; Harold M. Waller, *The Governance of the Jewish Community of Montreal*, Canadian Jewish Community Reports, no. 5 (Philadelphia: Center for Jewish Community Studies, Temple University, 1974), pp. 27–31, and Joseph Kage, "The Education of a Minority: Jewish Children in Great Montreal", in Paul M. Migus, ed., *Sounds Canadian* (Toronto: Peter Martin, 1975), pp. 93–104.

2. See Harold M. Waller and Morton Weinfeld, "The Jews of Quebec and 'Le Fait Français'", in this volume.

3. See Yaacov Glickman, "Organizational Indicators and Social Correlates of Collective Jewish Identity" (Ph.D. diss., University of Toronto, 1976), pp. 78–98, 415–38.

4. Ibid., pp. 228–70, 541–73.

5. Toronto Board of Jewish Education, Study on Jewish Education (Toronto: United Jewish Welfare Fund, 1975).

6. Joseph Gedalia Klausner, "Education, Canada", in Encyclopedia Judaica 1971 ed., vol. 6: 452–5.

7. Toronto Board of Jewish Education, Jewish Education. On the other hand, a family with at least one child attending a Jewish school may well differ radically from a family with not even one child attending a Jewish school. Thus, the sampling procedure may be more valid than would appear at first glance.

8. Herbert Zvi Berger et al., Jewish Education in Greater Montreal (Montreal: Allied Jewish Community Services and Canadian Jewish Congress, Eastern Region, 1972).

9. Figures in this section, unless otherwise stated, are from Klausner, "Education, Canada".

10. For a general discussion of the increasing prominence of the day school, see Alvin I. Schiff, "The Jewish Day School", Tradition 13 (summer 1972): 118–24, and David Singer, "The Growth of the Day-School Movement", Commentary 56 (August 1973): 53–7.

11. Walter I. Ackerman, "The Present Moment in Jewish Education", Midstream 18 (December 1972): 16.

12. Berger, Jewish Education in Montreal, p. 95. On the ambiguous effects of Jewish schooling on Jewish identity in the United States, see, for example, Daniel J. Elazar, "Jewish Education and the American Jewish Community: What the Community Studies Tell Us", The Pedagogic Reporter, March 1970, pp. 3–9; Charles Liebman, "American Jewry: Identity and Affliction", in David Sidorsky, ed., The Future of the Jewish Community in America (New York: Basic Books, 1973), pp. 127–52; Joshua A. Fishman, "Childhood Indoctrination for Minority-Group Membership", Daedalus 90 (spring 1961): 329–49; Arnold Dashefsky and Howard M. Shapiro, Ethnic Identification Among American Jews (Toronto/London: Lexington Books, 1974); and "The Future of the Jewish Community in America: A Task Force Report" (New York: The American Jewish Committee, 1972).

Schoenfeld

1. This paper deals with *Canadian* Judaism and *Canadian* society. In using this focus, no slighting of the pronounced regionalism of Canada is intended. Other essays could be written on regional differences in Canadian Judaism. Much excellent work from the regional perspective has been inaugurated by regional and local Jewish historical societies and by Jewish historians who have taken local and regional communities as their focus of research.

2. Data about the affiliation of American Jews with the various branches of Judaism are from Fred Massarik and Alvin Chenkin, "United States National Jewish Population Study: A First Report", *American Jewish Yearbook* 74 (1973): 282. The percentages given for affiliation patterns of Canadian Jews are estimates based on a series of studies of specific cities. For more detailed figures, see Stuart Schoenfeld, "The Jewish Religion in North America: Canadian and American Comparison", *Canadian Journal of Sociology* 3 (1978): 213, table 2.

3. Louis Rosenberg, *Canada's Jews: A Social and Economic Study of the Jews in Canada* (Montreal: Bureau of Social and Economic Research, Canadian Jewish Congress, 1939), p. 197.

4. Margaret Goldstein, ed., *American Jewish Organizations Directors*, 9th ed. (New York: Frenkel Mailing Service, 1974), lists forty-nine Canadian congregations that identify themselves as Conservative.

5. For more information on the synagogue-centre, see Marshall Sklare, *Conservative Judaism* (New York: Schocken Books, 1972), pp. 135–8, and Joseph L. Blau, *Judaism in America: From Curiosity to Third Faith* (Chicago: University of Chicago Press, 1976), pp. 107–10. Specific information about Beth Tzedec was provided by Jack Orenstein, executive vice-president.

6. Louis Rosenberg, *Canada's Jews*, p. 198.

7. The honour of being the first *secular* (nonreligious) Jewish day school in Canada goes to the Yiddish-language Peretz School in Winnipeg, which graduated its kindergarten into first grade in 1919.

8. Benjamin G. Sack, *Canadian Jews — Early in this Century*, trans. Anne Glass (Montreal: Canadian Jewish Congress, National Archives, 1975), p. 54.

9. Ibid, p. 49.

10. See Stephen Speisman, *The Jews of Toronto: A History to 1937* (Toronto: McClelland and Stewart, 1979), chap. 11, 17.

11. The others are the Rabbinical Council of America, which is the largest and made up mainly of graduates of Yeshiva University, and the Rabbinical Alliance of America, which is mainly composed of graduates of Eastern-European-style *yeshivot* founded in North America since the end of the Second World War. (See Charles Liebman, "Orthodoxy in American Jewish Life", *American Jewish Yearbook* 66 (1966): 21–97.

12. Evelyn Kallen, *Spanning the Generations: A Study in Jewish Identity* (Don Mills, Ont.: Longman Canada, 1977).

13. For a rationale for those ritual observances that are retained, see Marshall Sklare, *America's Jews* (New York: Random House, 1971), pp. 114–7.

14. Charles Liebman, *The Ambivalent American Jews* (Philadelphia: Jewish Publication Society, 1973), p. 67.

15. Blau, *Judaism in America*, pp. 69–72.

16. Nineteenth-century Reform Judaism consciously contrasted ethics and ritual. In twentieth-century Reform, they are more often considered compatible. Several articles in Albert Rose, ed., *A People and Its Faith: Essays on Jews and Reform Judaism in a Changing Canada* (Toronto: University of Toronto Press, 1956), which was published as part of the centennial celebration of the Holy Blossom Temple, combine respect for the traditional customs of the Jewish community with commitment to the prophetic mission.

17. Jewish morality entered Western society largely through Christianity. The latter modified and transformed much that it received from Judaism; moreover, there are varying approaches to moral issues in both Judaism and Christianity. Nevertheless, the sharing of sacred texts is often seen as a source of similar orientations. For a derivation of nontheistic radical humanism from Jewish sources, see Erich Fromm, *You Shall Be As Gods* (New York: Holt, Rinehart and Winston, 1966).

18. John R. Seeley, R. Alexander Sim, and Elizabeth W. Loosley, *Crestwood Heights: A Study of the Culture of Suburban Life* (Toronto: University of Toronto Press, 1956), pp. 239–43, 212–6, 401.

19. See Daniel Yankelovich, *The New Morality: A Profile of American Youth in the Seventies* (New York: McGraw-Hill, 1974), and Michael Maccoby, *The Gamesman: The New Corporate Leader* (New York: Simon and Schuster, 1976), pp. 189–209.

20. Thomas Luckmann, *The Invisible Religion* (New York: Macmillan, 1967).

21. Martin Buber, *The Eclipse of God* (New York: Harper and Brothers, 1952), pp. 166–7.

22. See Christopher Lasch, *The Culture of Narcissism* (New York: Norton, 1978).

23. Quoted in William Abrams, "Toward an Organic Jewish Community", *Viewpoints* 10, no. 1 (spring, 1979): 22.

Waller

"Power in the Jewish Community"

1. Daniel J. Elazar, "Some Preliminary Observations on the Jewish Political Tradition", Workshop in the Covenant Idea and the Jewish Political Tradition, working paper no. 10 (Ramat Gan: Department of Political Studies, Bar-Ilan University, 1978), p. 11.

2. See Bernard Susser and Eliezar Don Yehiya, "Prolegomena to the Study of Jewish Political Theory", Workshop in the Covenant Idea and the Jewish Political Tradition, working paper no. 8 (Ramat Gan: Department of Political Studies, Bar-Ilan University, 1978), p. 16.

3. Daniel D. Elazar, "The Kehillah", Workshop in the Covenant Idea and the Jewish Political Tradition, working paper no. 6 (Ramat Gan: Department of Political Studies, Bar-Ilan University, 1977), p. 19.

4. See Charles S. Liebman, "Dimensions of Authority in the Contemporary Jewish Community", *Jewish Journal of Sociology* 12 (1970): 35–6.

5. See Ernest Stock, "In the Absence of Hierarchy: Notes on the Organization of the American Jewish Community", Study of Jewish Community Organization, working paper no. 3 (Philadelphia: Center for the Study of Federalism, Temple University, n.d.), p. 4.

6. Daniel J. Elazar, *Community and Polity: The Organizational Dynamics of American Jewry* (Philadelphia: Jewish Publication Society of America, 1976), p. 336.

7. For further details on the relationship of Congress and the welfare federation in Montreal, see Harold M. Waller, *The Governance of the Jewish Community in Montreal*, Canadian Jewish Community Reports no. 5 (Philadelphia: Center for Jewish Community Studies, Temple University, 1974), and *The Canadian Jewish Community: A National Perspective* (Philadelphia: Center for Jewish Community Studies, Temple University, 1977).

8. See John Porter, *The Vertical Mosaic: An Analysis of Social Class and Power in Canada* (Toronto: University of Toronto Press, 1965), and Wallace Clement, *The Canadian Corporate Elite: An Analysis of Economic Power* (Toronto: McClelland and Stewart, 1975). For personality

details, see Peter C. Newman, *The Canadian Establishment* 1 (Toronto: McClelland and Stewart, 1975).

9. Clement, *The Canadian Corporate Elite*, p. 238. In all, Clement found that Jews constituted 4.1 per cent of the elite at a time when they were only 1.4 per cent of the population (p. 237). Yet their activities were not really central to the economic life of the country.

10. Morton Weinfeld and William Eaton, "The Jewish Community of Montreal: Survey Report", photocopied (Montreal: Jewish Community Research Institute, 1979).

11. Toronto has had some exceptions in the last category; Rabbis Gunther Plaut and Jordan Pearlson have achieved major community leadership positions.

12. The increasing status of the professionals and the relative scarcity of able ones have resulted in very adequate remuneration for the top people. For example, the national executive director of one Canadian Jewish organization received a salary of $60,000 when he was less than forty years old.

13. See Yaacov Glickman, "The Organization and Governance of the Toronto Jewish Community", mimeographed (Toronto, 1974), pp. 77, 82; and Waller, *Governance*, p. 85.

14. Glickman, "Organization and Governance", pp. 98, 100.

15. Myra Piasetzki, "Decision-Making in the Jewish Community" (M.S.W. research report, School of Social Work, McGill University, 1977), p. 150.

16. Waller, *Governance*, and Glickman, "Organization and Governance".

17. Zachariah Kay, *The Governance of the Jewish Community of Ottawa*, Canadian Jewish Community Reports no. 6 (Philadelphia: Center for Jewish Community Studies, Temple University, 1974), p. 22.

18. Anna Gordon, *The Governance of the Jewish Community of Winnipeg*, Canadian Jewish Community Reports no. 10 (Philadelphia: Center for Jewish Community Studies, Temple University, 1974), p. 39.

19. Harvey Rich, *The Governance of the Jewish Community of Calgary*, Canadian Jewish Community Reports no. 1 (Philadelphia: Center for Jewish Community Studies, Temple University, 1974), p. 26.

Beyond the Mainstream

Torczyner

1. Naomi Levine and Martin Hochbaum, *Poor Jews: An American Awakening* (New Brunswick, N.J.: Transaction Books, 1974). For two of the major studies, see Anna Silberman, *Who Are the Jewish Poor?* (Chicago: The Ark, 1971), and *New York's Jewish Poor and Jewish Working Class: Economic Status and Social Needs* (New York: Federation of Jewish Philanthropies of New York, 1973).

2. J. Torczyner, "The Poor Among Us: Project Genesis", photocopied (Montreal: Graduate Research Council, McGill University, 1976). The statistical data on poor Montreal Jews used in this essay are based upon this earlier study.

3. These levels were determined according to the Canadian Senate Committee on Poverty's definition. Many people consider the Senate's definition of poverty a conservative one. See, for example, Adams et al., *The Real Poverty Report* (Edmonton: M.G. Hurtig, 1971).

4. The projection assumed poor Jews would be the same percentage of the population in 1976 as in 1971. If inflationary pressures, the increased number of pensioners, the tendency of the young and above-poverty families to leave the province, and the influx of newly arrived low-income immigrants are considered, one can conservatively estimate the number of poor as 10 to 15 per cent higher in 1976 than in 1971.

5. Louis Rosenberg, *Population Characteristics of the Jewish Community of Montreal* (Montreal: Canadian Jewish Congress, 1956).

6. Unfortunately the census' occupational categories do not distinguish between levels of responsibility and position within each profession. Moreover, of the Jewish working poor in the study, 14 per cent of the men and 17 per cent of the women were listed in "other" occupations, a category that includes many diverse jobs. The high percentages in this category suggest that future researchers would find it worthwhile to subdivide it.

7. Ann G. Wolfe, "The Invisible Jewish Poor", *Journal of Jewish Communal Services* 48, no. 3 (1972): 259–65.

8. See *Your Community News* [bulletin of the Allied Jewish Community Services of Montreal] 30, no. 4, and *Facts 77* (Montreal: Combined Jewish Appeal and Israel Emergency Fund, n.d.).

9. Harold Waller, *The Governance of the Jewish Community of Montreal*, Canadian Jewish Community Reports, no. 5 (Philadelphia: Center for Jewish Community Studies, Temple University, 1974), and his "Power in the Jewish Community", in this volume.

10. Alfred J. Kahn, *Studies in Social Policy and Planning* (New York: Russel Sage Foundation, 1969), p. 246.

11. Penni Reichson-Kolb, "Access to Social Services in the Jewish Community: Issues and Responses", (M.S.W. thesis, School of Social Work, McGill University, 1978).

12. Ibid.

Rose

1. Figures for the mid-1970s and 2001 are from Statistics Canada, *Population Projections for Canada and the Provinces 1972–2001*, catalogue 91-514 (Ottawa: Information Canada, June 1974), pp. 119-33, projection B. Those for 2031 are from Community Health Directorate, "The Final Report of a Working Group of the Federal-Provincial Advisory Committee on Community Health", mimeographed (Ottawa: Health and Welfare Canada, August 1976), appendix B, p. 8.

2. Figures for Winnipeg from Statistics Canada, *Population, Ethnic Groups by Age Groups*, Catalogue 92-731, vol. 1, part 4 (Ottawa: Information Canada, January 1974); for Vancouver, from Jewish Community Fund and Council of Greater Vancouver, Gerontology Committee, "Gerontology Report", mimeographed (Vancouver, 1972), p. 3; for Toronto, from personal interview with Michael Scheinert, executive director, Coordinated Services for the Jewish Elderly, 23 November 1978, and personal letter from Jerome D. Diamond, executive director, Jewish Family and Child Service of Metropolitan Toronto, 8 November 1978.

3. Josephine Chaisson and Albert Rose, "Report of the Survey on the Needs of the Aged of the Jewish Community of Toronto", mimeographed (United Jewish Welfare Fund of Toronto, Committee on Health and Welfare, January 1958), p. 30, table 21. There may have been earlier studies in Toronto, as well as in Montreal, because Dr. Louis Rosenberg, of the Canadian Jewish Congress (CJC), published many analyses of the demographic characteristics of the Jewish communities in the major urban centres. Concerned about the numbers of the Canadian Jewish community as revealed in the decennial census, Dr. Rosenberg and his small staff worked with great dedication in the Research Department of CJC and established a relationship with the Dominion Bureau of Statistics (later Statistics Canada). On occasion, the CJC paid for special tabulations of ethnic origin and/or religious preference by census tracts.

4. Jewish Community Fund and Council of Greater Vancouver, "Community Survey Report", mimeographed (Vancouver, 1972).

5. Because the study combined information on the distribution of the population by age groups with information on distribution by location, it revealed a great deal of planning information to persons particularly interested in the education of children as well as those primarily concerned with the elderly.

6. A 1977 report of the Jewish Family Service Agency of Vancouver, based on a sample survey of 125 clients, confirmed the earlier study's general findings about significant needs. Elderly persons made up less than 12 per cent of the active cases in the agency at that time, but cases recently closed included 31 per cent of retired persons and aging families. (Jewish Family Service Agency of Vancouver, *Report 1977*, [Vancouver, 1977], pp. 5–8).

7. Jewish Community Council of Winnipeg, "Needs of the Jewish Elderly: Interim Report", mimeographed (Winnipeg, 1978), p. 12.

8. Damos and Smith, Ltd., consultant planners, "An Analysis of Selected Census Variables (1971) on the Population of Jewish Ethnic Origin, 60 Years and Over, in Winnipeg, Manitoba" (Winnipeg: The Commission on the Aged, Jewish Community Council of Winnipeg, August 1976), p. 31.

9. Jewish Community Council of Winnipeg, "Needs", p. 5.

10. Ibid., p. 6.

11. Diamond, personal letter. His estimates on camp survivors and persons at risk may have included ages sixty to sixty-four.

12. See Albert Rose, ed., *A People and Its Faith: Essays on Jews and Reform Judaism in a Changing Canada* (Toronto: University of Toronto Press, 1959), pp. 14–29.

13 David D. Mansur, remarks at the inauguration of an extension course in housing and urban development (School of Social Work, University of Toronto, January 1954).

Joseph

1. See Paul Berman, "The Status of Women in Halakhic Judaism", in *The Jewish Woman: New Perspectives*, ed. Elizabeth Koltun (New York: Schocken Books, 1976).

2. Paula E. Hyman, "The Other Half: Women in the Jewish Tradition", *Response* 7 (summer 1973): 72.

3. Hebrew Union College ordained its first female rabbi in 1972. It seems possible, however, that there were female rabbis in the past. See Harry M. Rabinowicz, *The World of Hasidism* (London: Hartford House, 1970), pp. 202–10, and Greta Fink, *Great Jewish Women* (New York: Bloch, 1978), pp. 67–71.

4. For an interesting rebuttal of that idea, see A. Silver, "May Women be Taught Bible, Mishna and Talmud?", *Tradition* 17 (summer 1978): 74–83.

5. See Judith Hauptman, "Images of Women in the Talmud", in *Religion and Sexism*, ed. Rosemary Reuther (New York: Simon and Schuster, 1974), pp. 189–90.

6. Cynthia Ozick, "Continuing to Examine the Matter", *Face to Face* 5 (spring 1978): 13.

7. Rachel Adler, "Full Participation in Jewish Life", *Face to Face* 5 (spring 1978): 15.

8. Sanhedrin 37a; Yevamot 63a. See Phyllis Bird, "Images of Women in the Old Testament", in *Religion and Sexism*, pp. 71–7.

9. See Isidor Epstein, "The Jewish Woman in the Responsa", in *The Jewish Library: Woman*, ed. Leo Jung (New York: Soncino Press, 1970), and Hauptman, "Images of Women", pp. 194–6.

10. For an example of pioneering work in this area of linguistic analysis and worldview, see Benjamin Lee Whorf, *Language, Thought, and Reality: Selected Writings*, ed. John Caroll (Cambridge: Technology Press of Massachusetts Institute of Technology, 1956).

11. Ann Lapidus-Lerner, *Who Hast Not Made Me A Man* (New York: The American Jewish Committee, 1977), p. 22.

12. For example, Rabbi David Feldman at the Shaar Hashomayim Congregation, Montreal, 2–3 May 1975, and Rabbi Steve Riskin, at the Tiffereth Beth David Jacob Synagogue, Montreal, spring 1978.

13. See Deborah Weissman, "Bais Yaakov: A Historical Model for Jewish Feminists", in Koltun, ed., *The Jewish Woman*.

14. See Nina Cardin, "The J.T.S. Women's Hakafa, Symbolic Event", *Sh'ma* 6 (15 October 1976): 145. The Talmudic ruling on women being able to handle a Torah is in Ber 22a. For an interesting discussion of menstrual taboos, see Rachel Adler, "Tumah and Taharah; Ends and Beginnings", *Response* 7 (summer 1973): 117–24.

15. Megillah 23a.

16. See, for example, Daniel Leifer and Myra Leifer, "On the Birth of a Daughter", in Koltun, ed., *The Jewish Woman*, pp. 21–30.

17. Kid 16b; Maim. Yad Ishut 2: 9–10.

18. Yoseph Chaim, *Ben Ish Hai* (Baghdad, n.d. [19th century]).

19. Some examples from Montreal congregations: Shaar Hashomayim publicly celebrates a group confirmation at the end of a year of study, though individual ceremonies only began in 1980; Tiffereth Beth David Jacob allows girls to celebrate after Sabbath afternoon services; the Spanish and Portuguese Synagogue allows girls to express their commitment publicly during Sabbath morning services in the sanctuary, although it does not permit them an accompanying *aliyah*; at Beth El a girl may have an *aliyah* only on her bat-mitzvah; at the Reconstructionist Synagogue, there are frequent female *aliyot*.

20. See Charlotte Baum, "What Made Yetta Work? The Economic Role of Eastern European Jewish Women in the Family", *Response* 7 (summer 1973): 32–9.

21. Carol Kur, "Hadassahway", *Moment* 19–28.

22. Ibid., p. 19.

23. Ozick, "Continuing to Examine", p. 13.

24. Koltun, ed., *The Jewish Woman*, p. 125.

25. Weissman, "Bais Yaakov", p. 148.

Lasry

1. The term "Sephardim" originally referred to Jews who settled around the Mediterranean Sea, in England, the Netherlands, Curacao, and the Americas after having been expelled from Spain (1492) and Portugal (1496) following the Inquisition. "Sephardim" is also used today to refer to Jews who lived in Arabic countries (Iraq, Yemen, Iran, and so on). It is preferred to geographic labels such as "Orientals" and "from Asia-Africa", since they negate the cultural and religious heritage conveyed by the term "Sephardim". (See William W. Eaton, Jean-Claude Lasry, and John J. Sigal, "Ethnic Relations and Community Mental Health in Israel", *Israel Annals of Psychiatry and Related Disciplines* 17 (1979): 166–74.

2. In Morocco, the *Toshavim* ("inhabitants") finally reconciled themselves with the *Megorashim* ("refugees") only after many years of bickering. The enmity was carried to the absurd in Tunisia, where the local Jews made representation to the Dey "to expel the false Jews". (See André N.

Chouraqui, *Between East and West: A History of the Jews of North Africa* [Philadelphia: Jewish Publication Society of America, 1968]]. The two communities were officially united by two decrees of the French government, one in 1899 and a second in 1944 a few years before the final dispersal of the Tunisian Jewish community.

3. Chouraqui, *Between East and West*. See also André N. Chouraqui, *La Saga des Juifs en Afrique du Nord* [Paris: Hachette, 1972].

4. For example, two weeks after the Protectorate of Morocco was signed, on 12 March 1912, sixty Jews were massacred and the *mellah* of Fes sacked in retaliation for the alliance of the native Jews with the French invaders. [See Chouraqui, *Between East and West*, 1968.]

5. In 1941, King Mohammed V opposed the application of occupied France's Vichy Laws and refused to sign a decree requiring his Jewish subjects to declare all their possessions, to return to their traditional garb [black *djellaba* [a flowing robe] and *babouches* [leather slippers]] and to return to the *mellah*. The king and his son, today King Hassan II, recalled these protective acts on several occasions, especially during a message they delivered personally on Yom Kippur in the main synagogue of the community. [Personal communication from Salomon Benbaruk, a community leader in Morocco and Montreal.]

6. World Jewish Congress, "Proceedings of the Seminar on the Muslim-Jewish Relations in North Africa", photocopied [New York: World Jewish Congress, 1975], p. 28.

7. See Gerard Nahon, "Le Judaïsme algérien de l'antiquité au décret Crémieux", *Les Nouveaux Cahiers* 29 [1972]: 1–19.

8. J. Taieb and C. Tapia, "Le Destin des Israëlites de Tunisie", *Les Nouveaux Cahiers* 42 [1975]: 3–34.

9. The high degree of literacy in the Jewish communities all over the world can be attributed to the *shema*: "And thou shalt teach these words unto thy children . . ." [Deut. 6: 7]. The daily repetition of this prayer has conditioned the Jewish mind to learning for more than four millenia. When Western culture forced its way into the ghetto or *mellah*, study of religious matters was simply transferred to study of secular subjects.

    The Alliance Israëlite Universelle [AIU] set up its first school in Tetuan [Spanish Morocco] in 1862. The network spread to Tunisia, Algeria, Turkey, Palestine, Iran, and so on. Morocco offers a good example of the rapidity with which the AIU schools spread and rooted themselves in the Arabic soil. By 1913, there were twenty-five schools with more than 5,000 pupils, and by 1950, sixty-eight schools and close to 25,000 pupils. [See Alliance Israëlite Universelle, "L'Alliance Israëlite Universelle", *Les Cahiers de l'A.I.U.* 184, numéro spécial [avril 1973].]

10. Doris Bensimon-Donath, *Immigrants d'Afrique du Nord en Israël: évolution et adaptation* (Paris: Anthropos, 1970) and *L'Intégration des Juifs nord-africains en France* (Paris: Mouton, 1971).

11. The Statistical Abstract of Israel (1975, table 2/24) also shows that 80 per cent of the North African Jews living in Israel were born in Morocco or Tangiers, 20 per cent in Algeria or Tunisia.

12. Statistics from the Federal Department of Manpower and Immigration (1971, table 15) permit this estimate. From 1946 to 1971, 16,093 persons born in Morocco, Algeria, and Tunisia settled in Canada; 75 per cent of the immigrants whose last country of residence was in North Africa settled in Quebec. Research has shown that more than 92 per cent of the Moroccan citizens admitted to Canada were Jewish. (Gerald Berman, M. Daphne Nahmiash, and H. Carol Osmer, "A Profile of Moroccan Jewish Immigration in Montreal, 1957–1967 [master's thesis, School of Social Work, McGill University, 1970], table 3.) Hence, of the 12,000 North-African-born immigrants who settled in Quebec, we can estimate 11,000 were Jewish.

13. See Jean-Claude Lasry and John J. Sigal, "Durée de séjour au pays et santé mentale d'un groupe d'immigrants", *Canadian Journal of Behavioural Science* 7, no. 4 (October 1975): 339–48; Jean-Claude Lasry and John J. Sigal, "L'Influence sur la santé mentale de la durée de séjour, de l'instruction, du revenu personnel et de l'âge chez un groupe d'immigrants", *Revue Internationale de Psychologie Appliquée* 25, no. 3 (décembre 1976): 215–22; Jean-Claude Lasry and John J. Sigal, "Mental and Physical Health Correlates in an Immigrant Population", *Canadian Journal of Psychiatry* 25 (1980); Jean-Claude Lasry, "Cross-Cultural Perspective on Mental Health and Immigrant Adaptation", *Social Psychiatry* 12, no. 2 (1977): 49–55; Jean-Claude Lasry, "Mobilité occupationnelle chez les immigrants d'Afrique du Nord", *International Review of Applied Psychology* 1, no. 29 (1980); William W. Eaton and Jean-Claude Lasry, "Mental Health and Occupational Mobility in a Group of Immigrants", *Social Science and Medicine* 12 (1978): 53–8.

14. See Canada Manpower and Immigration, "Three Years in Canada", first report of the longitudinal survey on the economic and social adaptation of immigrants (Ottawa: Information Canada, 1974).

15. Only 9 per cent said they had economic motives, compared to 64 per cent who emigrated for a political motive. The North African Jews who have settled in France gave almost identical reasons for emigration. (See Bensimon-Donath, *L'Intégration*.)

16. One weekly quoted the executive director of the Jewish Immigrant Aid Services as saying: "They want to keep at any cost their religious tradi-

tions, and this is one of the problems faced by the Jewish community of Montreal." (*Dimanche-Matin*, 29 November 1964.)

17. Centre Communautaire Juif du YM-YWHA, undated.

18. Bensimon-Donath, *Immigrants d'Afrique.*

19. In Canada, the traditional North African family roles have evolved to resemble those of the more egalitarian North American society. The tendency is for more diffusion and less sex-specificity, with, for example, men and women sharing family tasks and responsibilities. (See Phyllis Amber and Irene Lipper, "Towards an Understanding of Moroccan Jewish Family Life" [M.S.W. thesis, School of Social Work, McGill University, 1968].)

20. The following table presents the survey's findings for the 258 male respondents.

Years of Education Completed	Before Immigration	At Time of Interview
5 to 6 years	23.3%	22.5%
7 to 11 years	44.6	36.4
12 to 15 years	26.0	20.9
16 years or more	6.2	20.2

21. According to the 1971 census information for Montreal, 2.5 per cent of the Greek-born hold a university degree, 1.3 per cent of the Italian-born, and 5.6 per cent of the French Canadians. The percentage is 7.7 among the European-born Ashkenazim, compared to 12.8 for the Jewish North Africans (who immigrated much later than the European Jews and hence in better social times).

22. The following table presents the survey's results on income-producing occupations held at the time of interviewing, according to sex:

Occupation	Men (N=226)	Women (N=88)
Owner, manager	10.6%	0.0%
Small business owner	5.3	7.9
Professional, technical	21.7	19.3
Clerical	20.8	39.8
Sales	19.9	9.1
Services, transport	9.3	10.2
Craftsman, worker	11.9	11.4
Labourer, other	0.4	2.4

23. See Naomi Moldofsky, "The Economic Adjustment of North African Jewish Immigrants in Montreal" (Ph.D. diss., McGill University, 1968); Anthony H. Richmond, "Social Mobility of Immigrants in Canada", in B.R. Blishen et al., eds., *Canadian Society: Sociological Perspectives* 3rd ed. (Toronto: Macmillan, 1968), pp. 724–40; Canada Manpower and Immigration, "Three Years"; Lasry, "Mobilité".

24. See Le Groupe de Recherches Sociales, "La situation des immigrants à Montréal, Etudes sur l'adaptation occupationnelle, les conditions résidentielle et les relations sociales, mimeographed (Montréal: Conseil des Oeuvres de Montréal, 1957).

    In our sample only 8 per cent of the eligible women had acquired Canadian citizenship; about 20 per cent stated they will not acquire it, compared to 6 per cent of the men. This difference could be caused by the more traditional attitude of the women; they may be more reluctant to repudiate their home country through the acquisition of a new citizenship. They also intermarry less. (See Jean-Claude Lasry and Evelyn Bloomfield-Schachter, "Jewish Intermarriage in Montreal, 1962–1972" *Jewish Social Studies* 27 [1975]: 267–8.)

25. Only 6 per cent reported having no friends.

26. Some even quit their jobs for that reason and confided that their later French Canadian Catholic employers had more respect for Jewish religious practices than their former Jewish bosses.

27. For more details, see Lasry and Bloomfield-Schachter, "Jewish Intermarriage".

28. For the study, intermarriage was defined as a marriage in which one of the partners was not of the Jewish religion at the time of courtship. Religious conversion was still mandatory if the marriage was performed in either of the two Orthodox synagogues.

29. Arnold Schwartz found the American intermarriage rates to be around 15 per cent. (See "Intermarriage in the United States", *American Jewish Year Book* 71 (1970): 101–21.

30. The survey used an "Attraction Score" that was the difference between the percentage of "Likes" and "Dislikes". For the North Africans, the Attraction Score (82 per cent) reflected a very positive self-esteem, which was also evident in the way the concept "Myself" rated much more positively than did the main four ethnic group concepts. The Attraction Score was 48 per cent for French Canadians, 38 per cent for Canadian Jews, 24 per cent for French, and 13 per cent for Ashkenazim. For the Israeli studies, see Judith T. Shuval, "Emerging Patterns of Ethnic Strain in Israel", *Social Forces* 40 (1962): 328, and "Self-Rejection among North African Immigrants to Israel", *The Israel Annals of Psychiatry and Related Disciplines*, 4, no. 1 (1966): 102.

31. *Washington Post*, 9 December 1979.

32. For example, a senior member of the Association of Jewish Day Schools, who negotiated those hours as well as consequent subsidies with the Quebec government, openly declared at an AJDS meeting (which the author attended) that the very difficult situation the Jewish day schools faced was caused by the existence of L'Ecole Maimonide.

33. When all the Jewish day schools of Montreal were invited to take part in a parade for the thirtieth anniversary of the state of Israel, L'Ecole Maimonide was "forgotten".

34. Unfortunately, a recent power struggle within the CSQ threatens its unique character. If the rabbinate succeeds in playing a political role by directly controlling the CSQ board, the organization will likely explode. This would segregate community from religious affairs in the pattern set decades ago by the other Jewish organizations of America.

35. An AJCS senior staff confessed to the author the fantasy he held about the ASF leaders: he pictured them in heated discussion, in a smoke-filled room, arguing over ways to overthrow the Jewish leadership of Montreal.

36. As the Anglophone Jews of Montreal developed relationships with the leaders of the Association Sépharade Francophone, they came to use the term "Francophone" to refer to North African Jews. This label is a definite step in mastering the threatening difference: "You are Francophones which we are not." Implied in the use of this term is also the desire to show respect for the identity of the North African Jews, by referring to them as they define themselves.

37. The Centre Hillel, the Université de Montréal's branch of the B'nai B'rith Hillel Foundation, has led the opposition on a few occasions.

38. See note 34.

39. According to its charter, the school has three aims: 1) the teaching of Jewish and Sephardic values and traditions; 2) the teaching of French as the main language of communication; and 3) the teaching of a working knowledge of English.

40. The author recalls the minister summing up the meeting with the wish that Sephardim should live as they had to this day: "*Continuez d'être. Votre simple présence démontre que, au Québec, il est possible de vivre pleinement en tant que Juif, et en français.*" ["Continue to be. Your very presence shows that in Quebec it is possible to live fully as a Jew, and in French."]

Medjuck and Lazar

1. Nathan Glazer and Daniel P. Moynihan, "Introduction", in Nathan Glazer and Daniel P. Moynihan, eds., *Ethnicity: Theory and Experience* (Cambridge, Mass.: Harvard University Press, 1975), p. 4.

2. The role played by religious and communal facilities in the maintenance of ethnic identity is well known to sociologists. For example, Lenski and Sklare and Greenblum have pointed out that ethnic life has two major components: one that revolves around the group's religious institutions, another around its communal, nonreligious life. Sklare and Greenblum further observe that Jewish organizational life provides a secular alternative for Jews who have little religious involvement. (See Gerhard Lenski, *The Religious Factor* [Garden City, N.Y.: Anchor Books, 1961] and Marshall Sklare and Joseph Greenblum, *Jewish Identity on the Suburban Frontier* [New York: Basic Books, 1967], p. 263.)

3. Leo Driedger, "Introduction: Ethnic Identity in the Canadian Mosaic", in Leo Driedger, ed., *The Canadian Ethnic Mosaic: A Quest for Identity* (Toronto: McClelland and Stewart, 1978), p. 12.

4. Land Grant Papers, Nova Scotia Public Archives.

5. Stuart Rosenberg, *The Jewish Community in Canada*, 2 vol. (Toronto: McClelland and Stewart, 1970–71) 1:111.

6. B.G. Sack, *History of the Jews in Canada*, trans. Ralph Novek, 2 vol. (Montreal: Canadian Jewish Congress, 1945), 1:229.

7. Michael Baig, "The Folklore of Moncton Jewry", unpublished, n.d.

8. Ibid.

9. *Shalom* 4, no. 2 (November 1978): 21–23.

10. Rosenberg, *The Jewish Community*, p. 110.

11. Jan Goeb, "The Maritime Jewish Community", mimeographed (Halifax: Jewish Historical Society, n.d.), p. 11.

12. C. Bruce Fergusson, "Jewish Communities in Nova Scotia", *Journal of Education* 2, no. 1 (October 1961): 46.

13. Aaron Horowitz, *Striking Roots*, (Oakville, Ont.: Mosaic Press, 1980), p. 7.

14. Public Record Office, Board of Trade, Nova Scotia, vol. 7, E29.

15. Sack, *History of the Jews*, pp. 47–9.

16. Goeb, "The Maritime Jewish Community", p. 31.

17. For more on these points, see M.M. Lazar, *Sociology and Ethnic Research In Atlantic Canada*, International Education Centre, Occasional Paper no. 2 (Halifax, 1979), p. 3, and Sheva Medjuck, "Wooden Ships and Iron People: The Lives of the People of Moncton, New Brunswick 1851 to 1871" (Ph.D. diss., York University, Toronto, 1978), p. 208.

Arnold

1. Many of the pioneers did not come just to receive accolades; they also contributed personal memoirs that became a basis of the archives and oral-history programs then being launched by the newly established Jewish Historical Society of Western Canada.

2. See "Trials and Tribulations of Victoria Synagogue Builders in 1863", *Jewish Western Bulletin*, 25 September 1957, pp. 4, 6, 80, 82.

3. See *Jewish Western Bulletins*, 30 June 1958, p. 5ff, and A.J. Arnold, "Was Amor de Cosmos the Louis Riel of British Columbia", *Transactions, Historical and Scientific Society of Manitoba, 1971–72*, series 3, no. 28, p. 50.

4. *Jewish Western Bulletin*, 30 June 1958, p. 9.

5. See Max Bookman, "Jewish Canada by Numbers", in Max Bookman, ed., *Canadian Jewish Reference Book and Directory* (Ottawa: E. Gottesman, 1963).

6. Stephen Speisman, *The Jews of Toronto* (Toronto: McClelland and Stewart, 1979), p. 58.

7. A.J. Arnold, "The Earliest Jews in Winnipeg 1874–82", *The Beaver Magazine*, autumn 1974.

8. A.J. Arnold, "The Contribution of the Jews to the Opening and Development of the West", *Historical and Scientific Society of Manitoba 1968–69*, series 3, no. 25, pictorial supplement, and "Jewish Pioneer Settlements", *The Beaver*, autumn 1975, and "Jewish Immigration to Western Canada in the 1880s", *Journal of the Canadian Jewish Historical Society* 1, no. 2 (October 1977).

    The high point for Jews in agriculture in all of Canada came in 1921, when there were 631 Jewish-owned farms accounting for a total population of 2,568; well over half of them were in Saskatchewan. Even in 1931, when the drought and locust years arrived, Saskatchewan still maintained its lead position, with a total of 196 Jewish farms out of 348 in the West and 477 in all of Canada. See Louis Rosenberg, *Canada's Jews: A Social and Economic Study of the Jews in Canada* (Montreal: Bureau of Social and Economic Research, Canadian Jewish Congress, 1939).

9. Arthur Chiel, *The Jews in Manitoba* (Toronto: University of Toronto Press, 1961), pp. 54–5, and Abraham Arnold, *Jewish Life in Canada* (Edmonton: Hurtig Publishers, 1976), p. 51. See also note 8 above.

10. Abraham J. Arnold, "The Jewish Farm Settlements of Saskatchewan", *Canadian Jewish Historical Society Journal* (spring 1980): 330–9.

11. Rosenberg, *Canada's Jews*, p. 26.

12. From 1901 to 1911, the number of Jews in Winnipeg increased more than eightfold (1,164 to 9,408), while Toronto Jews grew close to sixfold (3,103 to 18,294) and Montreal's just over fourfold (6,924 to 28,838).

13. Mrs. Alcin was not the first Jewish woman elected to public office in Canada. That distinction appears to belong to Mrs. Hannah Director, elected to the school board in Prince George, British Columbia in 1917. See Cyril Leonoff, *Pioneers, Pedlars and Prayer Shawls: The Jewish Communities in British Columbia and the Yukon* (Vancouver: Jewish Historical Society of British Columbia, 1978).

14. See Rosenberg, *Canada's Jews*, p. 303; Chiel, *Jews in Manitoba*, p. 180; Lloyd Stinson, *Political Warriors* (Winnipeg: Queenston House, 1975), p. 87–8; Arnold Ages, "Antisemitism: The Uneasy Calm", in this volume.

15. See Percy Barsky, "How Numerus Clausus Was Ended in the Manitoba Medical School", *Canadian Jewish Historical Society Journal* 1, no. 2 (October 1977).

16. See Speisman, *The Jews of Toronto*, pp. 320–35, and Irving Abella and Harold E. Troper, " 'The Line Must Be Drawn Somewhere': Canada and Jewish Refugees, 1933–39", in this volume.

17. According to the 1971 census, Manitoba then had 500 Jews living outside Winnipeg, down from 600 in 1961; Saskatchewan had 500 living outside Regina and Saskatoon, down from 1,100, and Alberta had 500 outside Calgary and Edmonton, down from 600. During the same years, British Columbia's small-town Jewish population went from 300 to 500.

Shaffir

1. For several relevant citations relating to writing on Chassidic Jews, see A. Lavender, *A Coat of Many Colors: Jewish Subcommunities in the United States* (Westport, Conn.: Greenwood Press, 1977).

2. For a description of the Tasher community's efforts and their result, see "A Strange Bid for Autonomy", *Maclean's*, November 1979.

3. Although newspaper reports and magazine articles have sometimes featured the Chassidim of Montreal, there has been little research on the city's Chassidic communities. Its Lubavitcher community has been described in a few works: Jacques Gutwirth, "The Structure of a Hassidic Community in Montreal", *The Jewish Journal of Sociology* 14 (June 1972): 43–62; "Hassidism et Judaicité à Montréal", *Recherches Sociographiques* 14 (septembre/decembre, 1973): 291–325; "Fieldwork Method and the Sociology of the Jews: Case Studies of Hassidic Communities", *The Jewish Journal of Sociology* 20 (June 1978): 49–58; and William Shaffir, *Life in a Religious Community: The Lubavitcher Chassidim in Montreal* (Toronto: Holt, Rinehart and Winston, 1974). In contrast, however, the Chassidic communities of New York have been the subject of several research projects. See G. Kranzler, *Williamsburg: A Jewish Community in Transition* (New York: Philip Feldheim, 1961); J. Mintz, *Legends of the Hasidim* (Chicago: University of Chicago Press, 1968); S. Poll, *The Hasidic Community of Williamsburg* (New York: The Free Press of Glencoe, 1962); and I. Rubin, *Satmar: An Island in the City* (Chicago: Quadrangle Books, 1972).

4. For a more detailed description of how some of the data were collected, see my *Life in a Religious Community*.

5. Louis I. Newman, ed., *The Hasidic Anthology: Tales and Teachings of the Hasidim* (New York: Schocken Books, 1963), p. xiii.

6. It is truly difficult for outsiders to appreciate the magnetic role of the *rebbe* in a Chassidic community. Some fascinating accounts of his power and influence have been documented and can be found in the works on the Chassidim that are cited throughout this essay.

7. Gutwirth, "Fieldwork Method", p. 51.

8. Mintz, *Legends*, p. 154.

9. Though such contacts may be viewed as contrary to the community's efforts at insulation, exposing Lubavitcher to the assimilative influences of the wider society, I have argued elsewhere that they, in fact, serve to strengthen the community's boundaries, rather than erode them. (William Shaffir, "Witnessing as Identity Consolidation: The Case of the Lubavitcher Chassidim", in Hans Mol, ed., *Identity and Religion: International, Cross-Cultural Approaches* [Beverly Hills, Calif.: Sage Publications, 1978].)

10. Toronto has a Lubavitch community numbering approximately forty to fifty families, as well as a few followers of other Chassidic dynasties (notably, Bobov). The presence of one or two Lubavitch families in a few other Canadian cities is a relatively recent phenomenon, reflecting this group's social and religious work among minimally observant Jews.

11. In addition to the institutions of the seven groups mentioned, Montreal has a handful of quasi-Chassidic *shteeblech* that attract Orthodox Jews whose family backgrounds were once Chassidic.

12. Population figures are difficult to calculate exactly. No Chassidic community maintains membership lists, and, as one Tasher asked me, "What do you mean by member? There are no membership rules." Adherents of the same group often provided varying estimates of its size. The estimate of 4.5 children per family, however, is in line with approximations provided by Chassidim in different communities.

    The figure of 540 families does not include out-of-town students studying at the communities' yeshivos and living in dormitories. (For example, Tash has roughly one hundred such students, Lubavitch somewhat fewer.)

13. The Chassidic yeshivos directly involved in this body include Belz, The First Mesiphta, Maor Hagolah, and the Satmar. The Bobover and Vishnitzer Chassidim send their male students to these yeshivos and are thus also involved. Lubavitch does not belong. The planned curriculum pertains both to male and female students, who attend separate schools. A number of female students from families of various Chassidic groups, notably Bobov, Vishnitz and Klausenburg, attend the Beth Jacob Girls School — a non-Chassidic institution, founded in the late 1940s, that caters to students from Orthodox families.

14. This area is bordered by Mount Royal Boulevard to the south, Van Horne Avenue to the north, and by St. Urbain Street and De Vimy Street to the east and west respectively. The Klausenburger and Tasher communities retain prayer houses in the neighbourhood.

15. The *rebbe* believed a rural setting to be more conducive to Torah study than the city. The community has thrived; in addition to a yeshiva complex, it now maintains a boys' and girls' school, a ritual bath, matzeh-baking facilities, and a slaughterhouse.

16. In any particular Chassidic school, the community's perception of the nature and degree of disruptiveness of secular education determines the nature and degree of manipulation of the secular curriculum. Although this protective manipulation occurs with both boys' and girls' curricula, the norms governing attendance and class content differ considerably for the sexes because boys and girls are assigned such different amounts of religious obligations. Inevitably, girls are exposed to a broader range of secular subjects, and their secular programs are coordinated differently.

17. Although the communities' schools experience some difficulty in recruiting staff for their religious studies departments, they have generally been able to produce enough of their own teachers.

18. Poll, *The Hasidic Community of Williamsburg*, p. 173.

19. Rubin, *Satmar*, p. 150.

20. See Gutwirth, "Fieldwork Method", and Shaffir, *Life in a Religious Community.*

Culture and Ideology

Orenstein

1. Around 1000 A.C.E., Jews from northern Italy and northern France, who spoke Laaz, a Judaeo-Romance language, began to settle in Lotharingia (the Lorraine area of modern France plus the Mainz-Speyer area of Germany). They were exposed to several varieties of early German and developed Proto-Yiddish (1000-1250); the vocabulary and phonetic elements of Laaz remained prevalent in their speech for many generations although few vestiges are left today. In accord with the well-established Diaspora tradition, they obtained additional vocabulary from the holy tongue, Hebrew-Aramaic, which made their speech diverge to an even greater degree from that of their Gentile, Germanic neighbours. As Jews usually do to their languages, they applied the Hebrew alphabet to the new tongue.

   Another decisive factor in the development of this new language was the migration of many Ashkenazic Jews, now Yiddish-speaking, from German to Slavic territories, particularly during the period between the First Crusade and the Black Death (1096–1348). The Slavic influence remoulded many aspects of the grammatical system and weakened the connections between Yiddish and German.

2. See Shloyme Vaysman [Shlomo Wiseman], "Yidishe togshuln in Montreal", in *Shul-pinkes*, ed. Shloime Bercovich et al. (Chicago: Sholem Aleichem Folk Institute, 1948), pp. 433–56.

3. See Rudolph Glanz, *The German Jew in America: An Annotated Bibliography* (Cincinnati: Hebrew Union College, 1969), and Bertram W. Korn, "Jewish 48'ers in America", *American Jewish Archives* 2, no. 1 (June 1949).

4. See Elias Tscherikower, *The Early Jewish Labor Movement in the United States*, trans. and rev. Aaron Antonovsky (New York: YIVO Institute for Jewish Research, 1961).

5. These parties included the Bund, a social democratic Marxist party founded in Russia in 1897, which, after a certain ideological development, included in its platform autonomism, devotion to the Yiddish

language, and a moderate form of Diaspora Jewish nationalism; Poalei Zion (Labour-Zion), a movement devoted to a synthesis of Zionism and Socialism; Socialist Territorialism, a party that hoped to concentrate the Jewish masses in "a free territory" other than Palestine and eventually create a Jewish socialist state; and the Sejmists, a group that called for special legal status for Russian Jews, to be embodied in extraterritorial "national personal autonomy" (i.e., the basis for Jewish autonomy should be a Jewish national parliament or *sejm*).

6. See Vaysman, "Yidishe togshuln", and Zevi Scharfstein, "Jewish Education in the British Commonwealth", *The Jewish People Past and Present*, vol. 2 (New York: Jewish Encyclopedic Handbooks, 1955), p. 184.

7. The few short-lived experiments prove the rule. A Sholem Aleichem day school in the Bronx, New York, existed for a very short time in the mid-1920s. A Yiddish-language boarding school in the Jewish socialist colony of Harmony, New Jersey lasted from the 1920s until the Depression; however, it served a tiny elitist group and was not based in the heart of a Jewish community. The two labour-Zionist day schools in New York City rapidly became Hebrew-language schools, and even after this change in linguistic and cultural orientation, their influence and success in the community were minimal.

8. Vaysman, "Yidishe togshuln", pp. 434–9.

9. *Der adler* appeared as a daily until 1963; for the next four years it was published three times a week. Since 1967, it has appeared as a weekly, with interruptions.

10. After Segal's death, the J.I. Segal Fund was established to award Canadians for achievement in Yiddish literature and other fields of Jewish cultural endeavour.

11. J.I. Segal, "In the Book of Beauty", trans. Seymour Levitan, in *Canadian Yiddish Writings*, ed. Abraham Boyarsky and Lazar Sarna (Montreal: Harvest House, 1976), pp. 105–6.

12. Melech Ravitch, "Let Us Learn", trans. Seymour Mayne with Rivka Augenfeld, *Canadian Yiddish Writings*, pp. 126–6.

13. Rachel Korn, "To My Mother, in place of the stone that would have marked her grave", translated for this volume by Seymour Levitan. An earlier version by the same translator appeared in *Canadian Yiddish Writings*, pp. 93–4.

14. The phrases in quotation marks here are all translations of images that appear in a collection of her verse, *Farbitene vor* (Tel Aviv: Israel Book Publishing House, 1977). The title of the volume itself means "supplanted reality".

15. Rachel Korn, "The First Line of a Poem", trans. Seymour Mayne with Rivka Augenfeld, *Canadian Yiddish Writings*, p. 97.

16. M. Husid, "The Cry of Generation", trans. Seymour Mayne with Rivka Augenfeld, *Jewish Dialogue*, Hanukah 1974, p. 23, my emendation.

17. For a more detailed overview of Yiddish literature in Canada, see my article in *University of Toronto Quarterly* (summer 1977), pp. 500–6.

18. Sh. Rozhansky [S. Rollansky], ed., *Kanadish, Musterverk fun der yidisher literatur* vol. 62 (Buenos Aires: Literaturgezelshaft baym yivo, 1974).

19. *Canadian Yiddish Writings*, see note 11.

20. Canadian Jewish historiography is also represented in the following works: Abraham Rhinewine, *Der yid in kanade* ["The Jew in Canada"], 2 vols. (1925–7); S. Belkin, *Di poyle-tsienbavegung in kanade, 1904–1920* ["The Poalei Zionist Movement in Canada, 1904–1920"], 1956; and Dr. Joseph Kage, *Tsvey hundert yor fun yidisher imigratsye in kanade* ["Two Hundred Years of Jewish Immigration to Canada"], 1960.

21. "Lamentations Rabbah" (1956), "Esther Rabbah" and "Ruth Rabbah" (in one volume, 1962), "Ecclesiastes Rabbah" (1967), and "Song of Songs Rabbah" (1973).

22. *Kheyder un bes-medresh* ["Heder and House of Study"], 1950.

Waller

"A Reexamination of Zionism in Canada"

1. Some observers expected that Zionist theoretical thinking might experience a revival with the election of Menachem Begin, who seemed the archetype of the traditional Eastern European Zionist ideologue, a man who would use the premiership to attempt to influence world Jewry closer to the principles espoused by his mentor, Vladimir Jabotinsky. However, Begin in office proved to be relatively pragmatic on diplomatic and security questions, while his economic policies, though a sharp break from the past, were hardly successful enough to persuade any ideological fence-sitters. Therefore, in general, North American Jewry did not respond to Begin and his government in ideological terms but preferred to evaluate individual issues on their own merits. North American Jewry was never overwhelmingly Labour and is not likely to be pulled into the Likud camp by Begin. Rather it appears to be committed to Israel as a nation.

2. Ben Halpern, "The United States" in *Zionism in Transition*, ed. Moshe Davis (New York: Arno Press, 1980), p. 55.

3. Gerson D. Cohen, "From 'Altneuland' to 'Altneuvolk' — Toward an Agenda for Interaction between Israel and American Jewry", in *World Jewry and the State of Israel*, ed. Moshe Davis (New York: Arno Press, 1977), pp. 240, 243.

4. The accounts of the history of Canadian Zionism prior to 1900 are based on B.G. Sack, *History of the Jews in Canada*, trans. Ralph Novek, rev. ed. (Montreal: Harvest House, 1965), pp. 220–59. Chovevi Zion ("Lovers of Zion") originated in Eastern Europe before Herzl's political Zionism. Despite its lack of central organization, it had representation in a number of European and North American cities.

5. See Yaacov Glickman, "The Organization and Governance of the Toronto Jewish Community", mimeographed (Toronto, 1974), p. 121.

6. Ibid., p. 122.

7. The Jerusalem Program was adopted by the World Zionist Organization in 1969, some two years after the reunification of Jerusalem. It was designed to define the content of Zionism for both Israeli and Diaspora Jews and thus unite both elements of world Jewry in common purpose. Subscription to the Jerusalem Program is a minimum ideological requirement of membership in any Zionist organization. The program consists of the following points: 1) the unity of the Jewish people and the centrality of Israel in Jewish life; 2) the ingathering of the Jewish people in its historic homeland, *Eretz Israel*, through *aliyah* from all countries; 3) the strengthening of the state of Israel, which is based on the prophetic vision of justice and peace; 4) the preservation of the identity of the Jewish people through the fostering of Jewish and Hebrew education and of Jewish spiritual and cultural values; 5) the protection of Jewish rights everywhere.

8. For a more complete discussion of the dynamics of Jewish communal organizations, see Harold M. Waller, "Power in the Jewish Community", in this volume.

9. Morton Weinfeld and William Eaton, "The Jewish Community of Montreal: Survey Report", photocopied (Montreal: Jewish Community Research Institute, 1979). The survey, conducted in 1978, comprised 657 completed interviews (from an original sample of 1000). The writer is grateful to the principal investigators for making their data available.

10. Ibid.

11. A longer-range matter of concern for the Jews of Montreal is the effect that Quebec independence would have on Zionist interests. There is a

distinct possibility that an independent Quebec would pursue a pro-Arab foreign policy; major elements of its intellectual and political elites are partial to aspects of Third World ideology and already favour the Arab cause. If Quebec should separate, Montreal's Jews would probably find themselves with little hope of influencing their country's foreign policy. Furthermore, it is not inconceivable that their ability to provide financial and other forms of aid to their Israel brethren would be seriously impaired. Of course, another effect of Quebec independence would be the weakening of all national Jewish organizations, which might lose one-third of their members. See Harold M. Waller and Morton Weinfeld, "The Jews of Quebec and 'Le Fait Français'", in this volume.

12. Similar questions concerning American Zionist groups were raised by Daniel J. Elazar, *Community and Polity: The Organizational Dynamics of American Jewry* (Philadelphia: Jewish Publication Society of America, 1976), p. 168.

Challenges for the Future

Weinfeld

1. For the most pessimistic demographic projections, see Elihu Bergman, "The American Jewish Population Erosion", *Midstream*, October 1977. A change in immigration patterns could, of course, change any projection based on current evidence. Yet it is difficult to make any assumptions about future trends in this area. In recent years, tens of thousands of Jewish immigrants from Israel and the Soviet Union have arrived in North America. One cannot rule out possibilities of large-scale movements from Latin America or South Africa.

2. See Samuel Lieberman and Morton Weinfeld, "Demographic Trends and Jewish Survival", *Midstream* 24, no. 9 (November 1978): 9–19. According to the 1971 Canadian census, Jewish fertility (the number of children born per 1,000 women) for females aged fifteen to forty-four stood at 1,869 compared with a Canadian average of 2,307 for the same age group. Replacement fertility (zero population growth) is roughly 2,100.

3. Such reasons include a longer life expectancy for Jews, the arrival of a large number of Holocaust survivors in the 1940s, and the historically lower Jewish fertility rates. For example, according to the 1971 census, the overall Canadian population had 8.1 per cent of persons over sixty-five years of age, but the similar figure for Canadian Jews was 11.8 per cent.

4. See Morton Weinfeld, "A Note on Comparing Canadian and American Jewry", *Journal of Ethnic Studies*, spring 1977, pp. 95–103.

5. See Albert Gordon, *Intermarriage: Interfaith, Interracial, Interethnic* (Boston: Beacon Press, 1964).

6. Weinfeld, "A Note".

7. See Warren G. Kalbach, "Propensities for Intermarriage in Canada as Reflected in the Ethnic Origins of Native-born Husbands and Their Wives: 1961 and 1971", paper presented to the Canadian Sociology and Anthropology Association, Toronto, 1974.

   Even more impressive are the same study's calculations estimating the "propensity for intermarriage" (the ratio of actual ethnic group inter-married to the expected number based on the relative size of the group in a given population). Not only do the native-born Jewish family heads have the lowest propensity for intermarriage, but that propensity actually decreased slightly between 1961 and 1971. Jews still remain highly resist-ant to intermarriage, at least in comparison to all other groups in Canada.

8. Alan F. Guttmacher, *Pregnancy, Birth and Family Planning* (New York: Signet, 1973), p. 89.

9. The male sperm cells are faster moving than the female, so if intercourse occurs close to the period of ovulation, they have a greater chance of reaching the ovum first. On the other hand, the female sperm cells are hardier and longer lived; therefore, they have a greater chance of surviv-ing to fertilize an ovum released sometime after intercourse. (See Linda Ferrill Annis, *The Child Before Birth* [Ithaca: Cornell University Press, 1978], pp. 165–6, and David M. Rorvik and Landrum Shettles, *Choose Your Baby's Sex* [New York: Dodd, 1977].)

10. Werner Cohn, "Jewish Outmarriage and Anomie", *Canadian Review of Sociology and Anthropology*, February 1976, pp. 90–105.

11. Ibid.

12. Kalbach, "Propensities for Intermarriage".

13. Jean-Claude Lasry and Evelyn Bloomfield-Schachter, "Jewish Intermar-riage in Montreal: 1962–1972", *Jewish Social Studies* 37 (summer-fall, 1975): 267–78.

14. For a summary of recent American surveys of intermarried couples, see Yehuda Roseman, "The Effects of Inter-marriage on Jewish Identity and the Jewish Community", paper presented at the International Conference of Jewish Communal Service, Jerusalem, 1978.

15. Ibid.

16. Ibid.

Ages

1. Yehuda Bauer, *The Holocaust in Historical Perspective* (Seattle: University of Washington Press, 1978), p. 8.

2. Salo Baron, "Changing Patterns of Antisemitism: A Survey", *Jewish Social Studies* 38, no. 1 (winter 1976): 5–38.

3. Maurice Samuels, "The Great Hatred" in *The Worlds of Maurice Samuels*, ed. Milton Hindus (Philadelphia: Jewish Publication Society, 1977), pp. 137–56.

4. For a discussion of the insidious nature of antisemitism, see Norman L. Cohn, *Warrant for Genocide* (London: Eyre and Spottiswood, 1967); Joshua Trachtenberg, *The Devil and the Jews* (New York: Harper and Row, 1945); and Jules Isaac, *The Teaching of Contempt* (New York: Holt, Rhinehart, and Winston, 1968).

5. The best treatment of the history of the early days of the Jews of Canada is found in B.G. Sack, *History of the Jews in Canada*, trans. Ralph Novek, rev. ed. (Montreal: Harvest House, 1965).

6. Cyril Edel Leonoff, *Pioneers, Pedlars and Prayer Shawls: The Jewish Communities in British Columbia and the Yukon* (Vancouver: Jewish Historical Society of Western Canada, 1978).

7. Fredella Bruser Maynard, *Raisins and Almonds* (Toronto: McClelland and Stewart, 1965).

8. See Lita-Rose Betcherman, *The Swastika and the Maple Leaf: Fascist Movements in Canada in the Thirties* (Toronto: Fitzhenry and Whiteside, 1975), pp. 20–31.

9. Ibid., p. 12

10. See B.G. Kayfetz, "Only Yesterday: From Discrimination to Acceptance", *The Chronicle Review*, September 1972, pp. 25–34.

11. See Irving Abella and Harold Troper, " 'The Line Must Be Drawn Somewhere': Canada and Jewish Refugees, 1933-39", in this volume.

12. Emil Fackenheim, *The Jewish Return Into History* (New York: Schocken Books, 1978), p. 157, 159.

13. B.G. Kayfetz, "Canada" in *Encyclopedia Judaica* 1971 ed., vol. 5, pp. 110-11.

14. Ibid., p. 112

15. Ibid.

16. See Arnold Ages, *The United Church Observer and the State of Israel* (Toronto: ADL Basic Documents, 1971).

17. See Reuben Slonim, *Family Quarrel* (Toronto: McGraw Hill-Ryerson, 1976).

18. See Harold M. Waller and Morton Weinfeld, "The Jews of Quebec and 'Le Fait Français'", in this volume.

19. See *Canadian Jewish News*, 4 and 11 January 1979.

20. See Howard Stanislawski, "Canadian Jewry and Foreign Policy in the Middle East", in this volume.

21. Ibid.

Stanislawski

1. For an examination of the role of public opinion in external affairs and the perspectives of foreign service officers on this question, see Dennis Stairs, "Public Opinion and External Affairs: Reflections on the Domestication of Canadian Foreign Policy", *International Journal* 32 (1977): 128–49.

2. Information from interviews with officials of the Canada-Israel Committee, the Canadian Zionist Federation, the Canadian Jewish Congress, and B'nai B'rith, 1977 and 1978.

3. See Dennis Olsen, "The State Elites" in Leo Panitch, ed., *The Canadian State: Political Economy and Political Power* (Toronto: University of Toronto Press, 1977).

4. For further details, see U.S., Congress, House of Representatives, Committee on Interstate and Foreign Commerce, Subcommittee on Oversight and Intelligence, 94th Cong., 2d sess., *The Arab Boycott* (Washington, D.C.: U.S. Government Printing Office, September 1976).

5. For in-depth reports on and assessments of these various U.S. statutes, see the 1976 to 1978 issues of *Boycott Report*, a nine-times-a-year newsletter published by the American Jewish Congress, New York.

6. For an assessment of the Canadian government's attitude of the period, see *Report of the Commission on Economic Coercion and Discrimination* (Montreal: Centre for Law and Public Policy, January 1977).

7. See *Globe and Mail* (Toronto), 6 August 1976, for a detailed report on a leaked Cabinet document that clearly indicated the perspectives of the Department of External Affairs on proposed policies for dealing with the Arab boycott.

8. *Globe and Mail*, 7-13 August, 1976.

9. For example, see the *Globe and Mail, Ottawa Journal, Montreal Star,* and *Gazette* (Montreal), 14-25 January 1977.

10. Department of Industry, Trade, and Commerce, *Guidelines on International Economic Boycotts*, 21 January 1977.

11. For example, Westinghouse Canada should have been named in the second semiannual report but was not. (*Globe and Mail*, 31 May 1978.)

12. See, for example, the statement by Canada-Israel Committee, 31 May 1978. It was reported in an interview with Gadi Homer by Standard Broadcast News, 2 June 1978.

13. *Globe and Mail*, 22 August 1978.

14. *Globe and Mail*, 21 March 1979.

15. For an account of the concerted opposition to the move, see the *Toronto Star*, 6–29 June 1979.

16. See Dennis Stairs, "Publics and Policy-Makers: The Domestic Environment of Canada's Foreign-Policy Community", *International Journal* 26 (1970): 221–48.

Waller and Weinfeld

1. For more details, see Jean-Claude Lasry, "A Francophone Diaspora in Quebec", in this volume.

2. Morton Weinfeld and William W. Eaton, "The Jewish Community of Montreal: Survey Report", photocopied (Montreal: Canadian Community Research Institute, 1979). All the statistical evidence presented in this paper is drawn from this report unless otherwise indicated.

3. For more details, see Arnold Ages, "Antisemitism: The Uneasy Calm", in this volume.

4. Irwin Block, "Charbonneau Hits Business 'Terrorists'", *Montreal Star*, 26 May 1977.

5. For a discussion and analysis of perceived anti-Semitism and emigration from Quebec, see Morton Weinfeld, "The Jews of Quebec: Perceived Anti-Semitism, Segregation, and Emigration", *Jewish Journal of Sociology* 22 (June 1980): 5–19.

6. Robert Kanigel, "Les Juifs du Québec", *Moment* 6, no. 1 (decembre 1980): 39–48.

7. For a readable, sympathetic account of past and present political developments in Quebec, see Dale Postgate and Kenneth McRoberts, *Quebec: Social Change and Political Crisis* (Toronto: McClelland and Stewart, 1980).

8. Stanley M. Cohen, "Jewish Concerns in Quebec", *Canadian Zionist*, January-February 1977, pp. 11–12.

9. Ruth R. Wisse and Irwin Cotler, "Quebec's Jews: Caught in the Middle", *Commentary* 64, no. 3 (September 1977): 55–56. For another review, see Morton Weinfeld, "La Question Juive au Québec", *Midstream* 23 no. 7 (October 1977): 20–29.

10. Jack Kantrowitz, "Jews in the New Quebec", *Viewpoints* 10, no. 1 (spring, 1979): 10.

Bibliography

The following bibliography consists of sources specifically on Jews in Canada and does not include any of the excellent works available on Jewry in general or in the United States or on the full range of ethnic and religious groups in Canada. Items were included to assist the general and the professional reader.

Abella, Irving. "Portrait of a Jewish Professional Revolutionary". *Labour/ Le Travailleur* 2, no. 2 (1977).

Ages, Arnold. *The United Church Observer and the State of Israel.* Toronto: ADL Basic Documents, 1971.

Allied Jewish Community Services. "Study on Immigration". Mimeographed. Montreal: Research Department, Allied Jewish Community Services, 1972.

Amber, Phyllis, and **Lipper, Irene.** *Toward an Understanding of Moroccan Jewish Family Life.* M.S.W. thesis, School of Social Work, McGill University, 1968.

Arnold, Abraham J. "Trial and Tribulations of Victoria Synagogue Builders in 1863". *Jewish Western Bulletin,* 25 September 1957.

_____. "The Contribution of the Jews to the Opening and Development of the West". *Transactions, Historical and Scientific Society of Manitoba,* series 3 no. 25 (1968-9), pp. 23–39.

_____. "Was Amor de Cosmos the Louis Riel of British Columbia?". *Transactions, Historical and Scientific Society of Manitoba,* series 3, no. 28 (1971-2), pp. 45–59.

_____. "The Earliest Jews in Winnipeg, 1874–82". *The Beaver Magazine,* autumn 1974, pp. 4–12.

_____. "Jewish Pioneers' Settlements". *The Beaver Magazine,* autumn 1975, pp. 20–26.

_____. "Jewish Immigration to Western Canada in the 1880s". *The Journal of the Canadian Jewish Historical Society* 1, no. 2 (October 1977): 82–96.

Arnold, Abraham J. and **Kurelek, W.** *Jewish Life in Canada.* Edmonton: Hurtig Publisher, 1976.

Barsky, Percy. "How Numerus Clausus Was Ended in the Manitoba Medical School". *Canadian Jewish Historical Society Journal* 1, no. 2 (October 1977): 75–81.

Belkin, Sh. *Di poyle-tsien bavegung in Kanada 1904–1920.* Montreal: Aktsions komitet fun der tsienistisher arbeter bavegung in Kanada, 1956.

Belkin, Simon. *Through Narrow Gates: A Review of Jewish Immigration, Colonization and Immigrant Aid in Canada.* Montreal: Canadian Jewish Congress and Jewish Colonization Association, 1966.

Benaim, Esther. "Francophone Jews and the French Fact". *Viewpoints* 10, no. 1 (spring 1979): 11–17.

Berger, Herbert Zvi, et al. *Jewish Education in Greater Montreal.* Montreal: Allied Jewish Community Services and Canadian Jewish Congress, Eastern Region, 1972.

Berman, Gerald; Nahmiash, M. Daphe; and Osmer, H. Carol. "A Profile of Moroccan Jewish Immigration in Montreal, 1957-1967". Master's thesis, School of Social Work, McGill University, 1970.

Betcherman, Lita-Rose. *The Swastika and the Maple Leaf: Fascist Movements in Canada in the Thirties.* Toronto: Fitzhenry and Whiteside, 1975.

Bloomfield-Schachter, Evelyn, and **Lasry, Jean-Claude.** "Jewish Intermarriage in Montreal". *Jewish Social Studies* 37, no. 3–4, (summer-fall, 1975): 267–8.

Bowerman, Jennifer K. *The Governance of the Jewish Council of Edmonton.* Canadian Jewish Community Reports, no. 2. Philadelphia: Center for Jewish Community Studies, Temple University, 1974.

Boyarsky, Abraham, and **Sarna, Lazar,** eds. *Canadian Yiddish Writings.* Montreal: Harvest House, 1976.

Breton, Raymond. "Institutional Completeness of Ethnic Communities and the Personal Relations of Immigrants". *The American Journal of Sociology* 70 (September 1964): 193–205.

Chiel, Arthur. *The Jews in Manitoba: A Social History.* Toronto: University of Toronto Press, 1961.

Clement, Wallace. *The Canadian Corporate Elite: An Analysis of Economic Power.* Toronto: McClelland and Stewart, 1975.

Cohen, Alan M. *The Governance of the Jewish Community of London.* Canadian Jewish Community Reports, no. 4. Philadelphia: Center for Jewish Community Studies, Temple University, 1974.

Cohn, Werner. "Jewish Outmarriage and Anomie". *Canadian Review of Sociology and Anthropology*, February 1976, pp. 90–105.

_____. "English and French Canadian Opinion on Jews and Israel: Some Poll Data". *Canadian Ethnic Studies* 11, no. 2 (1977): 31–48.

Creighton, D.C., et al. *Minorities, Schools and Politics.* Toronto: University of Toronto Press, 1969.

Cukier, Golda. *Canadian Jewish Periodicals, A Revised Listing.* Montreal: The Collection of Jewish Canadiana, Jewish Public Library, 1978.

Dirks, Gerald E. *Canada's Refugee Policy: Indifference or Opportunism?* Montreal: McGill-Queens University Press, 1977.

Driedger, Leo. "In Search of Cultural Identity Factors: A Comparison of Ethnic Students". *The Canadian Review of Sociology and Anthropology* 12 (May 1975): 150–62.

Driedger, Leo, and **Church, Glenn.** "Residential Segregation and Institutional Completeness: A Comparison of Ethnic Groups". *The Canadian Review of Sociology and Anthropology* 2 (February 1974): 31–52.

Eaton, William W., and **Lasry, Jean-Claude.** "Mental Health and Occupational Mobility in a Group of Immigrants". *Social Science and Medicine* 12 (1978): 53–8.

Etre Nous-Mêmes. Montréal: Centre Communautaire Juif du YM-YWHA, no date.

Figler, Bernard M. *Biography of Louis Fitch, Q.C.* Montreal, 1968.

_____. *S.W. Jacobs: Member of Parliament.* Ottawa: Harpell's Press, 1970.

Gillis, A.R., and **Whitehead, Paul.** "Halifax Jews: A Community within a Community". In *Immigrant Groups*, edited by Jean Leonard Elliott. Scarborough, Ont.: Prentice Hall, 1971.

Glickman, Yaacov. "The Organization and Governance of the Toronto Jewish Community". Mimeographed. Toronto, 1974.

_____. "Organizational Indicators and Social Correlates of Collective Jewish Identity". Ph.D. dissertation, University of Toronto, 1976.

_____. "Ethnic Boundaries and the Jewish Parochial School in Toronto: The Inevitability of False Expectations". In *Emerging Ethnic Boundaries*, edited by Danielle J. Lee. Ottawa: University of Ottawa Press, 1979.

Gordon, Anna. *The Governance of the Jewish Community of Winnipeg.* Canadian Jewish Community Reports, no. 10. Philadelphia: Center for Jewish Community Studies, Temple University, 1974.

Gottesman, E. *Canadian Jewish Reference Book and Directory.* Montreal: Jewish Institute of Higher Research, Central Rabbinical Seminary of Canada, 1963.

Groupe de Recherches Sociales. "La Situation des immigrants à Montréal. Etudes sur l'adaptation occupationnelle, les conditions résidentielles et les relations sociales. Miméographié. Montréal: Conseil des Oeuvres de Montréal, 1959.

Greenspan, Louis. *The Governance of the Jewish Community of Hamilton.* Canadian Jewish Community Reports, no. 3. Philadelphia: Center for Jewish Community Studies, Temple University, 1974.

Gutkin, Harry. *Journey into Our Heritage: The Story of the Jewish People in the Canadian West.* Toronto: Lester and Orpen Dennys, 1980.

Gutwirth, Jacques. "The Structure of a Hassidic Community in Montreal". *The Jewish Journal of Sociology* 14 (June 1972): 43–63.

_____. "Hassidism et Judaicité à Montréal". *Recherches Socio-graphiques* 14 (septembre-décembre 1973): 291–325.

_____. "Fieldwork Method and the Sociology of Jews: Case Studies of Hassidic Communities". *The Jewish Journal of Sociology* 20 (June 1978): 49–58.

Hart, Arthur Daniel, ed. *The Jew in Canada.* Toronto: Jewish Publications, 1926.

Heaps, Leo. *The Rebel in the House: The Life and Times of A.A. Heaps, M.P.* London: Niccolo, 1970.

Henripin, Jacques. *Trends and Factors of Fertility in Canada.* Ottawa: Statistics Canada, 1972.

Hoffer, Clara, and **Kahan, F.H.** *Land of Hope.* Saskatoon: Modern Press, 1960.

Horowitz, Aaron. *Striking Roots.* Toronto: Mosaic Press, 1980.

Kage, Joseph. *With Faith and Thanksgiving.* Montreal: Eagle Publishing Co., 1962.

_____. "The Education of a Minority: Jewish Children in Greater Montreal". In *Sounds Canadian: Languages and Cultures in Multi-Ethnic Society,* edited by Paul M. Migus. Toronto: Peter Martin Associates, 1975.

Kalbach, Warren G. "Propensities for Intermarriage in Canada as Reflected in the Ethnic Origins of Nativeborn Husbands and Their Wives: 1961 and 1971". Paper presented at the annual meeting of the Canadian Sociology and Anthropology Association, Toronto, 1974.

Kallen, Evelyn. *Spanning the Generations: A Study in Jewish Identity.* Don Mills, Ont.: Longman Canada, 1977.

Kanigel, Robert. "Les Juifs du Québec". *Moment* 6, no. 1 (décembre 1980): 39–40.

Kantrowitz, Jack. "Jews in the New Quebec". *Viewpoints* 10, no. 1 (spring 1979).

Kay, Zachariah. *The Governance of the Jewish Community of Ottawa.* Canadian Jewish Community Reports, no. 6. Philadelphia: Center for Jewish Community Studies, Temple University, 1974.

_____. *Canada and Palestine: The Politics of Non-Commitment.* Jerusalem: Israel Universities Press, 1978.

Kayfetz, Ben. "The Evolution of the Jewish Community of Toronto". In *A People and Its Faith,* edited by Albert Rose. Toronto: University of Toronto Press, 1959.

_____. "Toronto Jewry: An Historical Sketch". 1957. Reprint. Toronto: Canadian Jewish Congress, 1969.

_____. "Canada". In *Encyclopedia Judaica,* 1971 ed., vol 5, pp. 102–13. Jerusalem: Keter and Macmillan.

_____. "The Development of the Toronto Jewish Community". *Tradition* 13 (summer 1972): 5–17.

_____. "Only Yesterday: From Discrimination to Acceptance". *The Chronicle Review,* September 1972, pp. 25–34.

Klausner, Joseph Gedaliah. "Education, Canada". In *Encyclopedia Judaica,* 1971 ed., vol. 6, pp. 452–5. Jerusalem: Keter and Macmillan.

Lasry, Jean-Claude. "Cross-Cultural Perspective on Mental Health and Immigrant Adaptation". *Social Psychiatry* 12, no. 2 (1977): 49–55.

_____. "Mobilité occupationnelle chez les immigrants d'Afrique du Nord". *International Review of Applied Psychology* 29 (1980):1.

Lasry, Jean-Claude, and **Bloomfield-Shachter, Evelyn.** "Jewish Intermarriage in Montreal, 1962-1972". *Jewish Social Studies* 37 (summer/fall 1975): 267–78.

Lasry, Jean-Claude, and **Sigal, John J.** "Durée de séjour au pays et santé mentale d'un groupe d'immigrants". *Canadian Journal of Behavioural Science* 7, no. 4 (October 1975): 339–48.

_____. "L'influence sur la santé mentale de la durée de séjour, l'instruction, du revenu personnel et de l'âge chez un groupe d'immigrants". *Revue Internationale de Psychologie Appliquée* 25, no. 3 (décembre 1976): 215–22.

_____. "Mental and Physical Health Correlates in an Immigrant Population". *Canadian Journal of Psychiatry* 25 (1980).

Latowsky [Kallen], Evelyn. "Three Toronto Synagogues: A Comparative Study of Religious Systems in Toronto". Ph.D. dissertation, University of Toronto, 1969.

Leonoff, Cyril Edel. *Wapella Farm Settlement: A Pictorial History.* Winnipeg: Jewish Historical Society of Western Canada, 1974.

_____. *Architecture of Jewish Settlements in the Prairies: A Pictorial History.* Winnipeg: Jewish Historical Society of Western Canada, 1975.

_____. *Pioneers, Pedlars and Prayer Shawls: The Jewish Communities in British Columbia and the Yukon.* Vancouver: Jewish Historical Society of British Columbia, 1978.

Lieberman, Samuel, and **Weinfeld, Morton.** "Demographic Trends and Jewish Survival". *Midstream* 24 no. 9 (November 1978): 9–19.

Magnusson, Roger. *A Brief History of Quebec Education.* Montreal: Harvest House, 1980.

Mandel, Stephen, and **Wagenberg, R.H.** *The Governance of the Jewish Community of Windsor.* Canadian Jewish Community Reports, no. 9. Philadelphia: Center for Jewish Community Studies, Temple University, 1974.

Maynard, Fredelle Bruser. *Raisins and Almonds.* Toronto: McClelland and Stewart, 1965.

Moldofsky, Naomi. "The Economic Adjustment of North African Jewish Immigrants in Montreal". Ph.D. dissertation, McGill University, 1968.

Newman, Peter C. *The Canadian Establishment.* 2 vol. Toronto: McClelland and Stewart, 1975.

_____. *The Bronfman Dynasty.* Toronto: McClelland and Stewart, 1979.

Norland, Joseph A. "Canada's Jewish Population". Canadian Jewish Population Studies, vol. 3, no. 3. Montreal: Canadian Jewish Congress, 1974.

_____. "Canada's Jewish Population, 1971: Composition by Sex, Age, Marital Status and Language". Canadian Jewish Population Studies, vol. 3, no. 4. Montreal: Canadian Jewish Congress, 1974.

Oberman, Edna. *The Governance of the Jewish Community of Vancouver.* Canadian Jewish Community Reports, no. 8. Philadelphia: Center for Jewish Community Studies, Temple University, 1974.

Orenstein, Eugene. "Yiddish Literature in Canada". *University of Toronto Quarterly,* summer 1977, pp. 500–506.

Paris, Erna. *Jews: An Account of Their Experience in Canada.* Toronto: Macmillan, 1980.

Piasetzki, Myra. "Decision-Making in the Jewish Community". M.S.W. research report, School of Social Work, McGill University, 1977.

Plaut, Gunther W. "Canadian Experience: The Dynamics of Jewish Life since 1945". In *Movements and Issues in American Judaism,* edited by Bernard Martin. Westport, Connecticut and London, England: Greenwood Press, 1978.

Porter, John. *The Vertical Mosaic: An Analysis of Social Class and Power in Canada.* Toronto: University of Toronto Press, 1965.

Presthus, Robert. *Elite Accommodation in Canadian Politics.* Toronto: Macmillan, 1973.

Pross, Paul, A., ed. *Pressure Group Behaviour in Canadian Politics.* Toronto: McGraw-Hill Ryerson, 1975.

Ravitch, Melech. "Yiddish Culture in Canada". In *Canadian Jewish Reference Book and Directory,* compiled by Dr. E. Gottesman. Montreal: Jewish Institute of Higher Research, Central Rabbinical Seminary of Canada, 1963.

Reichson-Kolb, Penni. "Access to Social Service in the Jewish Community: Issues and Responses". M.S.W. thesis, School of Social Work, McGill University, 1978.

Rhinewine, A. *Looking Back a Century.* Toronto: Kraft Press, 1932.

Rich, Harvey. *The Governance of the Jewish Community of Calgary.* Canadian Jewish Community Reports, no. 1. Philadelphia: Center for Jewish Studies, Temple University, 1974.

Richmond, Anthony H. *Ethnic Residential Segregation in Metropolitan Toronto.* Toronto: York University Institute for Behavioural Research, 1972.

Rome, David. *The First Two Years, A Record of Jewish Pioneers on Canada's Pacific Coast 1858–60.* Montreal: H.M. Caiserman, 1942.

_____. "A History of Anti-Semitism in Canada". Photocopied. Montreal, 1978.

Rose, Albert, ed. *A People and Its Faith: Essays on Jews and Reform Judaism in a Changing Canada.* Toronto: University of Toronto Press, 1956.

Rosenberg, Louis. *Canada's Jews: A Social and Economic Study of the Jews in Canada.* Montreal: Bureau of Social and Economic Research, Canadian Jewish Congress, 1939.

_____. *The Jewish Community of Canada.* Montreal: Canadian Jewish Congress, 1954.

_____. *Population Characteristics of the Jewish Community of Montreal.* Montreal: Canadian Jewish Congress, 1956.

_____. *Chronology of Canadian Jewish History.* Montreal: Canadian Jewish Congress, 1959.

_____. "Jewish Children in the Protestant Schools of Greater Montreal in the Period from 1878–1958: A Statistical Study". Canadian Jewish Congress Research Papers, series E. no. 1. Montreal: Canadian Jewish Congress, 1959.

_____. "Two Centuries of Jewish Life in Canada". *American Jewish Year Book* 62 (1961): 28–49.

_____. "A Statistical Study of the Number and Percentage of Jewish Children in the Protestant Schools of Greater Montreal and the Suburb of Chomedy as at April 30, 1964". Canadian Jewish Congress Research Papers, series E, no. 3. Montreal: Canadian Jewish Congress, 1965.

Rosenberg, Stuart E. *The Jewish Community in Canada.* 2 vols. Toronto: McClelland and Stewart, 1970–71.

_____. "Canada's Jews". *Judaism* 20 (fall 1971): 476–89.

Sack, B.G. *History of the Jews in Canada.* Translated by Ralph Novek. 1945. Rev. ed., Montreal: Harvest House, 1965.

_____. *Canadian Jews—Early in This Century.* Translated by Anne Glass. Montreal: Canadian Jewish Congress National Archives, 1975.

Sarna, Jonathan D. "Jewish Immigration to North America: The Canadian Experience". *Jewish Journal of Sociology* 18, no. 1 (1976): 32–43.

Schlesinger, Benjamin. *The Jewish Family.* Toronto: University of Toronto Press, 1971.

Schoenfeld, Stuart. "The Jewish Religion in North America: Canadian and American Comparisons". *Canadian Journal of Sociology* 3 (1978): 209–33.

Seeley, John R.; Sim, R. Alexander; and **Loosley, Elizabeth W.** *Crestwood Heights.* Toronto: University of Toronto Press, 1956.

Shaffir, William. *Life in a Religious Community: The Lubavitcher Chassidim in Montreal.* Toronto: Holt, Rhinehart and Winston of Canada, 1974.

Slonim, Reuben. *Family Quarrel.* Toronto: McGraw Hill-Ryerson, 1976.

Speisman, Stephen. *The Jews of Toronto: A History to 1937.* Toronto: McClelland and Stewart, 1979.

Stanislawski, Howard. *The Arab Boycott: Policies and Perspectives.* Montreal: Canada Israel Committee, 1977.

Stinson, Lloyd. *Political Warriors.* Winnipeg: Queenston House, 1975.

Teboul, Victor. *Mythes et images du Juif au Québec.* Montréal: Editions de Lagrave, 1977.

Torczyner, J. "The Poor Among Us: Project Genesis", Photocopied. Montreal: Graduate Research Council, McGill University, 1976.

Torgov, Morley. *A Good Place to Come From.* Toronto: Totem Books, 1976.

Toronto Board of Jewish Education. *Study on Jewish Education.* Toronto: United Jewish Welfare Fund, 1975.

United Jewish Welfare Fund of Toronto. *A Demographic Report.* Toronto: Social Planning Committee, United Jewish Welfare Fund, 1969.

Waller, Harold M. *The Governance of the Jewish Community of Montreal.* Canadian Jewish Community Reports, no. 5. Philadelphia: Center for Jewish Community Studies, Temple University, 1974.

_____. *The Canadian Jewish Community: A National Perspective.* Philadelphia: Center for Jewish Community Studies, Temple University, 1977.

_____. "Canadian Politics and the Jewish Community". Washington, D.C.: Institute for Jewish Policy Planning and Research of the Synagogue Council of America, 1978.

_____. "Montreal Jews Face the Challenge of Quebec Nationalism". *Analysis* no. 65 (September 1978), p. 9.

Warschauer, Heinz. *The Story of Holy Blossom Temple.* Toronto: Holy Blossom Publication, 1969.

Weinfeld, Morton. "A Note on Comparing Canadian and American Jewry". *Journal of Ethnic Studies,* spring 1977, pp. 95–103.

_____. "La question Juive au Québec". *Midstream* 23, no. 8 (October 1977): 20–29.

_____. "The Jews of Quebec: Perceived Anti-Semitism, Segregation, and Emigration". *Jewish Journal of Sociology* 22 (1 June 1980): 5–15.

Weinfeld, Morton and **Eaton, William.** "The Jewish Community of Montreal: Survey Report". Photocopied. Montreal: Jewish Community Research Institute, 1979.

Yam, Joseph. "Selected Data on the Canadian Population Whose Mother Tongue is Yiddish". Canadian Jewish Population Studies, vol. 3, no. 2. Montreal: Canadian Jewish Congress, 1973.

Index